Nuevomexicano Cultural Legacy

Pasó Por Aquí

Series on the
Neuvomexicano Literary Heritage

EDITED BY

GENARO M. PADILLA,

ERLINDA GONZALES-BERRY,

AND A. GABRIEL MELÉNDEZ

Nuevomexicano Cultural Legacy
Forms, Agencies, and Discourse

Edited by
Francisco A. Lomelí,
Víctor A. Sorell,
and
Genaro M. Padilla

University of New Mexico Press
Albuquerque

Library of Congress Cataloging-in-Publication Data

Nuevomexicano cultural legacy : forms, agencies, and discourse / edited by
Francisco A. Lomelí, Víctor A. Sorell, and Genaro M. Padilla.—1st ed.
     p. cm.
Includes bibliographical references and index.
ISBN 0-8263-2224-7 (cloth : alk. paper)
   1. New Mexico—Civilization.   2. New Mexico—History.   3. Pluralism
(Social sciences)—New Mexico.   4. Ethnicity—New Mexico.   5. Regionalism—
New Mexico.   6. Social change—New Mexico.   I. Lomelí, Francisco A.
II. Sorell, V. A. (Víctor A.)   III. Padilla, Genaro M.,
1949–
  F796.5 .N84 2002
  978.9—dc21
                       2001006524

Contents

Contents

Note from the Series Editors

The original, and continuing, intention of the Pasó Por Aquí series is to recover and present the Hispanic literary and cultural production of New Mexico. When the series opened with Villagrá's 1610 epic *Historia de la Nuevo México*, we dedicated ourselves to producing a bookshelf that would bespeak a cultural heritage that can be traced to the Spanish colonial mid-sixteenth century.

Along with recovering this rich heritage, it is our goal to provide a field of scholarship that illuminates the origins, intercultural hybridization, social and aesthetic foundations of this cultural production as it developed over some four centuries. This collection of essays by the leading scholars in literary history, anthropology, history, art practice, folklore, philosophy, and social theory provides interdisciplinary commentary on New Mexico's Hispanic cultural legacy. These scholars provide a history and analysis of Nuevomexicano musical-dramatic ballads and captivity narratives, wool weaving practices that have roots in the centuries-old relations between Hispanos and native peoples; they also consider the reclamation of tradition in fiestas; the formation of mutualistas, or mutual aid societies, that provided a network of social interaction that nurtures culture; the work of influential journalists who during the late nineteenth century sustained the Spanish language and native literary discourse in newspapers; and, crucial to understanding the between Nuevomexicanos and Americans after 1848, they examine the ways in which literary, visual, and cultural practice continue to be shaped by intercultural relations.

As editors of Pasó Por Aquí, we look forward to building a series that marries the recovery of our cultural legacy with the very best scholarship on Nuevomexicano culture.

Erlinda Gonzales-Berry
A. Gabriel Meléndez
Genaro M. Padilla

General Editors
Pasó Por Aquí Series

Acknowledgments

A WORK OF THE magnitude of *Nuevomexicano Cultural Legacy* implies a high degree of collaboration at many levels. With that in mind, we extend our sincerest appreciation to a number of individuals, academic units, and institutions for their assistance and timely help.

First of all, the Rockefeller Foundation provided a major fellowship grant to the Southwest Hispanic Research Institute (SHRI) at the University of New Mexico, which, in turn, provided the impetus for our gathering together as scholars of Nuevomexicano cultural studies. SHRI organized the strong residential research environment as well as the necessary infrastructure that allowed us to carry out our respective studies from 1986 to 1993. Professor José Rivera, then the director of SHRI, played a key role in promoting the sharing of research and in designing the Rockefeller Seminar Conference, "Hispanic Expressive Culture and Contemporary Public Discourse," convened in Summer 1994 in the Continuing Education facility on the UNM campus in Albuquerque. His successor, Professor Felipe Gonzales, showed determination and perseverance in ensuring that the project would continue into its final stages.

In ways that are too numerous to list but which will never be forgotten, the entire University of New Mexico Chicano Studies leadership steadfastly supported the project and our residential fellowships. Professor Tobías Durán from the Chicano Studies Program was instrumental in contributing a subsidy to ensure that our manuscript would be visually representative of the subjects it covered. SHRI's Rosemarie Romero provided much-needed clerical assistance at critical stages of the project. At the University of California at Santa Barbara, the Affirmative Action Office, the Dean's Office of Social Sciences, and the Center for Chicano Studies contributed significant financial assistance toward the completion of the manuscript. We also express our gratitude to the Chicago State University Foundation for its support.

Finally, we would like to extend our thanks to Beth Hadas, our original editor at the University of New Mexico Press, for believing in this project, and to Wendell Ricketts for the editorial insights he provided.

Francisco A. Lomelí, Víctor A. Sorell, and *Genaro M. Padilla*

Preface

José A. Rivera

THE ESSAYS THAT appear in this volume resulted from two blocks of humanities fellowship grants provided by the Rockefeller Foundation to the Southwest Hispanic Research Institute (SHRI) at the University of New Mexico. The SHRI guidelines announcing the first fellowship program invited humanities scholars from around the country to propose research residency topics that would inquire into the transformation of Nuevomexicano regional culture of the Southwest in terms of continuance, conflict, cooperation, transition, and change. During the first grant period, six humanities scholars participated: Olivia Arrieta, Francisco A. Lomelí, Mónica Espinosa, Genaro Padilla, Helen Lucero, and Gabriel Meléndez.

The applicants for the second fellowship program were asked to focus on the initial theme of Nuevomexicano regional culture and transformation—in particular, they were challenged to exemplify how expressive culture scholarship can better inform public discourse about the contemporary issue of diversity and how humanities scholars can apply historic, cultural, and humanistic perspectives to the solution of emergent problems associated with the multicultural regional society and its institutions. A total of four outside scholars were selected to participate in this second project joined by counterpart faculty from the host institution: Ana Perches, Michael Candelaria, Víctor Sorell, and Ramón Gutiérrez. The four University of New Mexico scholars were: Miguel Gandert, Sylvia Rodríguez, Enrique Lamadrid, and Tey Diana Rebolledo.

The Rockefeller Project lasted for five years and culminated with a seminar presentation of the scholars' work. An additional twenty-five researchers and community artists and writers working in similar or related humanities topics served as discussants. Consistent with the broad theme of the fellowship program, the cross-disciplinary seminar was titled: "Hispanic Expressive Culture and Contemporary Public Discourse." The scholars presented their papers with time provided to elicit discussion, comments, and alternative interpretations. At the concluding session, all participants freely engaged in a conclusions-and-reflections session highlighting cross-current themes, key issues, and projections of emerging and future scholarship.

As noted earlier, the collective goal of the Rockefeller Project was to examine how humanities scholarship of the region could better inform public discourse about the contemporary issues of cultural diversity and social change. Most often, debates in the public-policy arena are defined and driven by work emanating from social-science paradigms and policy-research investigations. The SHRI fellowship program, on the other hand, which produced the essays in this volume, set out to provide a space and a forum that allowed a new generation of humanities scholars to explore the link between expressive culture scholarship originating in the territorial period of the New Mexico region and the increased complexities of a pluralistic society within the greater Southwest.

A theme common to all the scholarly work was the research requirement to recuperate textual materials beginning with the crucible period after 1848 and extending into the statehood years for both New Mexico and Arizona. In every instance, the tools, techniques, and methods of the humanities were employed to reconstruct events and to chart the great wave of change in the region brought about by transformations in every sphere of human activity: language, politics, history, economics, government agencies, and cultural practices. The scholars located and brought to light sources of information not previously included in the canons of scholarship: community newspapers in Spanish or bilingual format; autobiographical narratives and unpublished memoirs; family oral histories; forgotten diaries; documentary photos and assorted documents; old ballads depicting Indo-Hispanic life dramas and other sources of popular literature and village folklore; visual images embedded in wood and other crafted materials; and organizational records of mutual-aid societies and other Nuevomexicano groups.

With the aid of scholarly analysis and interpretation, these neglected texts resonated as new voices from the past to recapture the cultural history of the region and to help interpret and redirect contemporary discourse on ethnic identity, resistance, citizenship, hybridization, Indo-Hispanic relations and customs, cultural politics, and maintenance of community boundaries. The body of this work made clear that "old" issues in human and cultural relations continue to be revisited by each succeeding generation of scholars and that the pluralization and cultural *mestizaje* of societies across regions and borders forebodes a nation and hemisphere with more transcultural complexity than purity. This observation makes clear the central and strategic role of humanistic scholarship—cultural studies in particular—at the front end of the policy-making process at once initiating, activating, and elevating the character of the discourse.

The interdisciplinary essays that appear in this volume would not have been possible without the painstaking editing of Francisco A. Lomelí, Víctor A. Sorell, and Genaro Padilla. We owe them our most sincere and deeply felt gratitude for bringing the work of the Rockefeller Project to the attention of a broader public audience. We should also acknowledge Elizabeth Hadas of the University of New

Mexico Press for her early and continuing interest in publishing the results of the project. Many thanks also to the SHRI staff at the University of New Mexico who provided the administrative support to facilitate the hosting of the Rockefeller fellows and who organized the concluding seminar: Frances Rico, Rosemarie Romero, Cynthia Ramírez, and Rose Díaz. Last and most certainly not least, we gratefully acknowledge the generous financial support of the Rockefeller Foundation, especially the two officials who reviewed and approved our year-to-year activities: Alberta Arthurs and Tomás Ybarra-Frausto of the Division for the Arts & Humanities.

Introduction
Beyond the Land of Enchantment

Francisco A. Lomelí
Víctor A. Sorell
Genaro M. Padilla

THE STARK BEAUTY of the New Mexican landscape is stunning; the spare lines of its high desert evoke a sense of wonder and awe. The ascetic geography of this landscape is distinctive; so, too, is the rich cultural legacy produced by its Indo-Hispanic and Anglo inhabitants. The past thrives here and speaks through collective memory, popular lore, legend, and myth. But if this land is sacred, its spiritual qualities have been simplified and commodified by outsiders who have mythified its "enchanting" qualities, at the same time ignoring its paradoxes and contradictions. While souvenirs celebrate the "land of enchantment," a rich reservoir of stories that have remained unacknowledged as if subterranean or invisible provide us with a more complicated picture of this region. The essays in this book make visible the presence of these stories, stories that reference New Mexico's mixed origins and testify to its capacity to accommodate outside influences without losing its native character.

This collection provides sustained examinations of Nuevomexicano culture that identify its distinct character: its treatment of the sacred, its discourses on identity and difference, its historical legacy from colonial times to the social infrastructures of the present. While the state's literary and historical records are extensive, helping us to document its current artistic prominence, its chronicles appear increasingly remote. Memories fade as people age, cultural artifacts succumb to the elements, and the past appears even more fragile at the beginning of a new millennium. Time pressures make the effort to document and decode the cultural legacy of the state increasingly important. With this idea in mind, we have assembled a diverse group of scholars whose interdisciplinary expertise is well suited to articulating complex, intersecting world views of Nuevomexicano culture. The essays in this collection grew out of the Southwest Hispanic Research Institute (SHRI) at the University of New Mexico, which, in the 1980s and 1990s, furthered research into Nuevomexicano culture by sponsoring a cluster of professional and intellectual activists through its Rockefeller fellowships and lecture series. The research that has evolved out of SHRI has prompted new and revisionist perspectives on the region.

The essays in this volume focus upon the key cultural resources of this area that together have produced what the contributors argue is the region's distinct matrix for storytelling: its geography, best emblematized through its *llanos,* and its demographic *mestizaje* (mixture). Combined, their investigations create a new metatext about New Mexican culture, derived through a cross-disciplinary inquiry into histories, memories (individual and collective), rituals, and traditions previously elided. The process of reclamation, recovery, and reconstruction that these essays put into practice depends upon a notion of agency that has too frequently been ignored in representations of the state's cultural practices.

The collection provides a revisionary appraisal of New Mexico's legacy because it charts relationships between the geographic and cultural parameters that have informed the state's history. Rather than reduce the region to rigidly defined cartographic borders, this interdisciplinary perspective provides a more expansive cultural map of the state. The groundbreaking combination of empirical, philosophical, and scholarly materials in this volume speaks in dialogue with other regional cultural studies. We hope that the diverse and complex arguments articulated in this book will make the volume useful for both the general and the scholarly reader.

While each writer speaks in her or his own voice, the book collectively expresses a *mutualista* (self-help) vision as defined in Olivia Arrieta's essay, "*La Alianza Hispano-Americana,* 1894–1965: An Analysis of Collective Action and Cultural Adaptation." As Arrieta demonstrates, *La Alianza Hispano Americana* (The Spanish American Alliance) was an important mutual-aid society that served as a tool not only of survival but of cultural affirmation. As she explains, "people engage in collective behavior when attempting to repair and reconstitute a ruptured social structure." In "Contesting Social and Historical Erasure: Membership in *La Prensa Asociada Hispano-Americana,*" A. Gabriel Meléndez underscores how this kind of collaboration among Nuevomexicanos "[contests] social and historical erasure." Ultimately, this book is about the culture of empowerment and the empowerment of culture. These essays work together to articulate the parameters and underpinnings of a Nuevomexicano identity indigenous to the region.

I: Background and Gestation: New Mexico Reinvented

The links among the essays in this volume establish a framework through which to better understand Nuevomexicano cultural practices. Some of these links go back to Spain—see, for instance, Michael Candelaria's "Images in Penitente Ritual and Santo Art: A Philosophical Inquiry into the Problem of Meaning." Most, however, hinge on identifying Mexican social phenomena as they have taken root within New Mexico. While cultural identification is complicated by the relationship between U.S. Hispano and Mexican practices (as Ana Perches argues in "*Ni de Aquí ni de Allá:* The Emergence of the *Mexicano*/Chicano Conflict"), the central thrust of these essays is to describe the region as characterized by an Indo-Hispanic *mestizaje*. Rather than perpetuate the "fantasy heritage" Carey McWilliams defined in *North from Mexico,* the objective of this volume is to elucidate a *cultura nuevomexicana.* This scholarly stance is not defensive; instead, it confronts intellectual topics through a wide-ranging series of cultural, philosophical, historical, and anthropological analyses. The first section of this volume, "Background and Gestation," offers three pivotal studies that further Nuevomexicano self-definition through historical analysis of self-referential literary allusions.

The first essay, by historian Ramón Gutiérrez, unveils an eloquently subversive narrative. Tracing a fascinating lineage of outsiders' perceptions of New Mexico, especially those evident in Charles Fletcher Lummis's prolific writings, Gutiérrez concludes his essay by arguing in activist fashion, for he interrogates some of the basic premises by which Nuevomexicano culture has been judged. Invoking Lummis's portrait of New Mexico as a place immune from "the troubles of civilization," Gutiérrez deconstructs this trope of "civilization" itself by identifying it as the locus from which

> Charles Lummis and his Anglo American compatriots spun their elaborate mythologies of racial supremacy. . . . The Southwest belonged to Anglo Americans. The forces of evolution had been unleashed in the region. Anglo-Saxon vigor, when combined with the healthfulness of the sun, was producing that paragon of civilization, the new American—manly, violent, imperialistic.

Gutiérrez problematizes the "civilizer's" edifice, removing a superimposed "Orientalist" mantle and uncovering New Mexico's cultural landscape from a nativist vantage.

In an illuminated discussion of *periódicos* (newspapers) and *periodiqueros* (newspaper people), A. Gabriel Meléndez notes the reciprocal activities of newspapers, literary production, and *mutualistas.* His more specific concern, however, is to detail the story behind *La Prensa Asociada Hispano-Americana.* This preeminent group, according to Meléndez, brought together a diverse cadre of journalists, editors, poets, and other writers. United by a common language and culture, their literary agency was keyed to the social, educational, and cultural progress of the Spanish-speaking people of the Southwest. This is not to imply that the organization was ideologically or politically homogenous; it was not. Nonetheless, Meléndez asserts, the emergence of a culture of print in Mexican-origin communities remained an expression of resistance and opposition to Anglo American political, social, and cultural hegemony in the Southwest after 1848. The Padilla-Martínez resolutions of 1891 committed *La Prensa Asociada* to public advocacy, an objective that made it, according to Meléndez, the first professional group among

Spanish-speaking peoples of the Southwest to embrace a civil rights platform. The author points out the proliferation of Spanish-language weeklies that enjoyed a high circulation, suggesting that they reached a majority of New Mexico's citizens, most of whom were *nativos* (natives) who read exclusively in Spanish. Newspapers such as *La Voz del Pueblo, El Boletín, El Tiempo, La Opinión Pública, La Flor del Valle, El Sol de Mayo, El Mosquito, La Bandera Americana, El Combate,* and *El Nuevo Mexicano* flourished in the landscape of the region, easily debunking the myth of Nuevomexicanos' illiteracy.

In the third introductory essay, literary critic Francisco A. Lomelí documents the evolution of a Nuevomexicano literary consciousness, including benchmarks that signal an early but oftentimes ignored literary production. Noting New Mexico's Indo-Hispanic character, Lomelí describes a cultural dynamic distinct from any other region in the United States. The region's sensibility and world vision are bound by a colonial experience that eventually develops into an ethnic framework. Lomelí claims that a cultural identity, "even a regional ethos," emerges and has been shaped by the string of communities along the Río Grande, much as Mexico City was influenced and fashioned by Tenochtitlan and Lago Texcoco. He asserts that the literary production of Nuevomexicanos is superior among Hispanic print sources in terms of longevity, variety, and abundance. Like other authors in the collection, he also notes the distinctive place of *sociedades mutualistas* that contributed toward sponsoring full-fledged literary societies throughout urban and rural New Mexico in an effort to improve literacy in the region. He provocatively claims that, unlike subsequent minority artistic productions such as the Harlem Renaissance of the 1920s, which was largely underwritten by white patrons, the New Mexican literary societies were literally a popular mass movement that intersected Indo-Hispanic society at all levels, promoting published writings by both popular and élite authors. Lomelí concludes by establishing literary connections with other scholars in the collection (Lamadrid and Rebolledo) when he comments on a captivity story cited in an 1898 newspaper.

II: Construction of Identities: A Regional Ethos

The second section expands the notion of a Nuevomexicano identity through specific social inquiries, thus grounding, with material illustrations, what the first set of essays posits. An accomplished, seasoned documentary photographer, Miguel Gandert has long been invested in the visual examination of the Indo-Hispanic traditions of the Río Grande Valley or Corridor, as he refers to the region. Cultural identity and *herencia* (heritage) are vitally significant markers that he holds before the camera, an instrument Gandert admits is fully controlled and directed by the user's subjective perspective and criteria. By examining Comanches, Apaches, and Matachines, he helps to explain the blurring lines between Native American culture and what has traditionally been described as Hispanic culture in the Southwest. Gandert's innovative artistic approach is consistent with his subject matter: "The theatrical quality of my shooting is not problematic in relation to the ritualistic pageantry, for my images and the goals of those presenting that pageantry are similar." His photos restore what has been read as lost in New Mexico: land, language, oral history, spiritual traditions—in short, culture. His photographic illustrations affirm nuances by providing us with a face and a gesture.

On the other hand, Ana Perches discusses the oscillating and sometimes conflicted relationship between Mexicans and Chicanos/Hispanos as a set of mirror images not always viewed as reciprocal. Although her thesis is framed with respect to the Southwest generally, its implications are particularly important for New Mexico. That is, Mexicans who misunderstand, misrepresent, or mistrust the Chicano and *pocho*[1] in different degrees live throughout the United States. Perches focuses her essay on three early twentieth-century writers who wrote in California but helped define aspects of cultural politics that reverberated in New Mexico, while revitalizing a bilingual activist press: Benjamín Padilla (pen-named Kaskabel), Julio Arce (whose pseudonym is Jorge Ulica), and Daniel Venegas. These writers, Perches argues, perceived themselves as exiles, not immigrants, a conservative and class-conscious distinction. Each is paternalistic, if not blatantly contemptuous, when assessing the "other," but each also manages to bring to the forefront topics of identity and language at a time when such subjects generally remained in intracultural circles.

The last essay in this section, by Olivia Arrieta, introduces another important topic generally omitted in representations of Nuevomexicano history and culture: the role of *sociedades mutualistas* as agencies of collective action, cultural adaptation, and survival. By focusing on the *Alianza Hispano-Americana,* a mutual-aid society that was organized in 1894 and which became the first national organization for people of Mexican descent in the United States, Arrieta meticulously outlines the group's agenda and effectiveness. Registered first in Arizona in 1896 as a fraternal insurance society, by 1942 it had thirty-five lodges in that state and forty-five in New Mexico, cementing a sense of kinship and a distinct social conscience that provided both camaraderie and assistance. While the society afforded some economic security to its members and their families, largely through life insurance, the reach of the organization embraced religious, educational, legal, political, cultural, and social areas as well as something generally unheard of at the time for peoples of Indo-Hispanic background whose marginalization in society was becoming an issue of acute concern. The society's motto was revealing: "*Protección, Moralidad, e Instrucción*" (Protection, Morality, and Instruction). These words translated into unity, solidarity, and integrity of the community, a strong support for the integrity of the family, and an acquisition of knowledge, not merely for its own sake, but as a means of social advancement and self-improvement. Instruction also safeguarded the Spanish language, viewed as a cultural symbol of continuity and pride. The mutual-aid societies provided a unique space for affiliation and identification, allowing people to challenge existing power structures at the same time as they afforded protection from them.

III: Cultural Forms, Agencies, and Discourse: New Mexico's Coming of Age

The final section presents studies of specific cultural representations from the religious-philosophical (Michael Candelaria) and anthropological-folkloric (Sylvia Rodríguez) to the visual (Víctor Sorell) and literary (Tey Diana Rebolledo, Enrique Lamadrid, and Luis Leal). The essayists in this section expand and supplement the previous sections by analyzing thematic concerns through groundbreaking theoretical frameworks. The section documents and analyzes material seldom studied, offering theoretical justifications for a Nuevomexicano cultural studies.

Literary scholar Tey Diana Rebolledo considers captivity narratives between the seventeenth and nineteenth centuries. These narratives, Rebolledo contends, constitute a subset of the colonizing literary tradition within the larger arena of Anglo American literature. Of particular concern is the alleged barbarity of Native American groups represented in these stories. Such captivity narratives constitute a special genre of "horror stories," including, as they do, "infanticide, rape, violence, and barbarism." The essay masterfully deconstructs narrative structures in order to shed light on Indo-Hispanic relations. This deromanticization offers a critical foundation for reassessing New Mexican literary forms.

Luis Leal examines magical realism in Nuevomexicano narrative. He establishes pivotal distinctions between magical realism and *lo real maravillo* (the marvelous real) as the latter was defined by Cuban writer Alejo Carpentier. Leal asserts: "Magical realism offers an alternative theory helpful in analyzing Chicana/o literature." Without resorting to the mythification of a Land of Enchantment, Leal points out that the real and imaginary coexist and come together in distinctive modes in Nuevomexicano letters. The essay's definitive discussion contributes a "methodology born from the American soil, just like the texts to which it is applied."

In a dense and provocative piece, folklorist Enrique Lamadrid uses an interdisciplinary methodology, focused upon ethnomusicology and popular literary studies, to address traditional cultural expressions within "the complex profile of New Mexican *mestizaje* or cultural synthesis" in order to reveal lyrics and melodies that are both Hispanic and Native American. He adopts the "dynamic concept of alterity (in the) construction and negotiation of cultural otherness and its dialectical relation to cultural identity." The principal objective of his study is a thorough critical analysis of two Nuevomexicano *inditas* or captivity ballads: *"Plácida Romero"* and *"San Luis Gonzaga."* The former is a captivity ballad dating to the Apache wars of the 1880s and the latter represents a miracle ballad from the 1898 Spanish-American War. Lamadrid uncovers much new material surrounding these musical-dramatic forms, which have remained limited to a fairly small group of Nuevomexicanos and reserved for special ritualistic performances. He explains the content and salient qualities of the form, including variants, which shed light on their social function and popular poetic resonance. He argues that these ballads have a religious function, indicating captivity as the symbolic equivalent of a journey into hell or purgatory, in which survival is a sign of God's favor.

Anthropologist Sylvia Rodríguez examines the Taos Fiesta in order to scrutinize the tension between its commercialization and its function as a reclamation of tradition. Rodríguez documents the Fiesta's context and its creation. The result is a close examination of how cultural groups with different interests and agendas come together to produce a Fiesta whose symbolic value varies depending upon who is viewing it. Rodríguez argues that the Fiesta instills a "fictional tradition" while also affirming a tricultural fabric. She observes, "As a genuine artifact of tourism, the fiesta embodies, enacts, and symbolizes an impulse of local resistance as well as capitulation to the relentless advance of capitalism." Public space, then, is multivalent, serving a number of cultural functions simultaneously.

Critic and historian of visual culture Víctor Sorell skillfully demonstrates, in his examination of representations of *la Virgen de Guadalupe* in New Mexican popular art, that the goddess is as powerful an icon in New Mexico as she is in Mexico, affirming a cultural-religious link of profound importance between both places. While her particular forms vary, her iconography endures in both the U.S. and Mexico. What Sorell has chosen to examine with unprecedented attention is this sacred image's inscription on cloth and the human body. His approach to New Mexican visual culture critiques as it expands traditional notions of artistic form, viable media, and aesthetic value. Is cloth, he asks, a so-called "second skin," in some ways encoded with divine meaning? Is human skin, as a "first skin," similarly consecrated? Beyond his careful examination of regionally representative artists, their innovative uses of varied media, and the aesthetic value they ascribe to their respective works, Sorell is also mindful of the extensive cross-cultural appeal of *la Guadalupana. La Virgen* transcends the Indo-Hispanic world, embracing Anglo and African American "lived realities" as well. This Marian icon can be said to bridge differences among disparate communities and constituencies in New Mexico.

Museum curator and visual- and textile-arts scholar Helen Lucero underscores, in her essay, the significant artistic and extra-artistic roles assigned to textiles in New Mexico. An ongoing Hispano tradition in Chimayó—a Spanish-land-grant community established in 1696—the art and craft of weaving have had a profound cultural and economic impact in the area since at least the nineteenth century. Selecting three distinguished families for whom weaving is a major calling—the Martínez, Ortega, and Trujillo clans—Lucero examines Chimayó weaving as an art form unto itself, invested with collective ethnic pride and individual creative virtuosity. She is particularly attentive concerning the interaction among merchants and consumers, and among the weavers themselves, affording her readers a rare glimpse into the familial "fabric" that is so much a part of the warp and weft of weaving when it is truly a labor of the heart.

The last essay, by philosopher and theologian Michael Candelaria, discusses the Penitentes of New Mexico as "a pious confraternity, (itself) a mutual-aid society," which emerged to deal with frontier life among a people whose institutional insularity produced a sense of solidarity and a common bond. He claims that *bultos* and *retablos* (sculptural and two-dimensional artistic representations of religious imagery) project images of "any man and any woman." Candelaria also argues that images of Christ reflect self-understanding and that *santos* (saints) reveal a liberating ethic. Selecting images of the Crucified Christ and Doña Sebastiana (Death), he asks two profound questions: 1) Do the Penitentes and *santeros* (carvers of images of the saints) preserve the spiritual core of Nuevomexicano culture through ritual and art? and 2) Can we find in these cultural expressions a resource for an authentic Nuevomexicano philosophy? It is through the concept of the Trinity that the Penitentes allow us to gain some insight into ostensibly inaccessible ontological and theological matters. They entertain two Trinities: the Holy Trinity of God the Father, the Son, and the Holy Spirit of traditional Catholic theology, and the Trinity of the Holy Family that reflects the sacredness of the human family in Hispanic culture. In other words, Nuevomexicano culture makes sacred the earthly, elevating the human to divine status while at the same time humanizing the divine.

The essays speak to one another within and across disciplines, collectively invoking a kind of Nuevomexicano aesthetic that unfolds unlike any that has previously been explained or documented. There is a real possibility that such a body of cultural studies will render a new portrait of New Mexico, one that was sensed at the popular level among Nuevomexicanos but, for a variety of reasons, had not until now been fully appreciated.

Notes

1. "*Pocho*," in its literal sense, means "small," but it is also a pejorative term used by Mexicans for Chicanos, particularly with respect to the latter's assumed inability to speak standard Spanish (as compared to a conflation of Spanish and English, or "Spanglish").

Background and Gestation:
New Mexico Reinvented

Charles Fletcher Lummis and the Orientalization of New Mexico

Ramón A. Gutiérrez

STANDING BEFORE THE members of the American Historical Association gathered in Chicago for their annual meeting on July 12, 1893, Frederick Jackson Turner emphatically declared that the American frontier was no more: "[F]our centuries from the discovery of America, at the end of a hundred years of life under the Constitution, the frontier has gone, and with its going has closed the first period of American history" (Turner 1993, 88). In the rest of Turner's speech on "The Significance of the Frontier in American History," he described the stages of frontier advance, the movement first to the Eastern Seaboard to escape English tyranny, then across the Plains and Rockies to the Pacific shore. Led by traders and followed by merchants, ranchers, farmers, soldiers, and industrialists, these men had destroyed barbarism and brought civilization to all the peoples and lands in their paths. Turner explained that American nationalism and American identity had been created through the process of westward expansion. "In the crucible of the frontier the immigrants were Americanized, liberated and fused into a mixed race" (Turner 1993, 76). What characterized the American was:

> That coarseness and strength combined with acuteness and inquisitiveness, that practical, inventive turn of mind, quick to find expedients, that masterful grasp of material things, lacking in the artistic but powerful to effect great ends, that restless, nervous energy, that dominant individualism, working for good and for evil, and withal that buoyancy and exuberance which comes with freedom—these are traits of the frontier, or traits called out elsewhere because of the existence of the frontier. [Turner 1993, 88]

Frederick Jackson Turner's essay made clear that the closing of the frontier and the elaboration of an American national identity had been made possible by significant material changes. An integrated national market criss-crossed by roads, rivers, and railways existed by 1893, interpolated by print journalism in the form of dailies, weeklies, and assorted printed works. By 1893 the United States reached from coast to coast. Finally one could imagine the nation on a continental scale, travel across it rapidly, and learn of events quickly whatever the locale.

With the closing of the frontier the nation's gaze turned inward. In the closing decades of the nineteenth century the rediscovery of the Southwest began anew, charting the strange and remote corners of the republic and the odd customs of its exotics. This hunger to know and to map the nation fed both the production and consumption of travel literature and led to the touristic marketing of the Southwest—still then a territory. Before such territories could be incorporated into the United States as states, they needed a numerically dominant white Anglo population. Immigrants and tourists would guarantee this, and it was in this way that New Mexico, as the "Land of Enchantment," entered the consciousness of residents of the Eastern United States.

The story Turner's essay tells, then, is the story of New Mexico's touristic discovery and exploration, which at the end of the nineteenth century was constructed through an Orientalist discourse drawn largely from biblical lore.[1] In New Mexico's late nineteenth-century history, several men were responsible for introducing the terrain and its people to the larger republic. Beginning in the 1860s, John Wesley Powell cognitively mapped the geology and ethnology of New Mexico and Arizona through his own writings and those he eventually commissioned as the director of the U.S. Geological Survey and the Bureau of American Ethnology (Goetzmann 1966, 1–88). William R. Ritch, Secretary of the Territory of New Mexico and president of the New Mexico Bureau of Immigration, broadly publicized the history, resources, and attractions of New Mexico in the 1880s, hoping thereby to attract Anglo American immigrants (Gutiérrez 1989). Adolph F. Bandelier, as the chief archaeologist of the Archaeological Institute of America, directed the Institute's excavations of Pueblo Indian sites and from that scientific pulpit shaped what was then known of the area's prehistoric past (Keen 1971). As for the touristic marketing of New Mexico, no name is more important than that of Charles Fletcher Lummis.

Charles Fletcher Lummis is our central protagonist here for he was the Pied Piper for a whole class of financiers, philanthropists, journalists, writers, and artists who came to see in New Mexico a romantic refuge from the machine age and modernity. In the minds of these women and men, modernity was producing faceless drones, obliterating cultural differences, and standardizing mass-marketed commodities. In the quaint villages of New Mexico and in its prehistoric sites was a preindustrial America, a vestige from the past that offered mystical and romantic repose. Here was an America uncontaminated by the values of Europe, with aesthetic sensibilities quite independent of historic centers of fashion, and with cultures of creative genius that had constructed splendid edifices while Europe was still in the dark ages.

Charles F. Lummis, one of the early advocates of the "See America First" movement, through his photos, his publications, and his pranks, created some of the most enduring representations of New Mexico as the "Land of Enchantment," and of the greater Southwest. Anglo literary images of the Pueblo Indians, the Hispanos, the Navajo, the Apache, and especially of the terrain were largely forged by Lummis's writings. If, in the late nineteenth century, American tourists were fascinated by and eager to behold the Snake Dance of the Hopi Indians, the Crucifixion rite of the *Penitentes*, or the Egyptian quality of the terrain, it was because Lummis created these desires in his readers.

Charles F. Lummis: Man and Mission

Charles Fletcher Lummis was born in Lynn, Massachusetts in 1859. Son of a Methodist minister, raised and educated at the Bristol female seminary at which his father taught, Lummis received a classical education at Harvard in preparation for the ministry. If as a child Lummis had been smart, sickly, and surrounded by women, at Harvard he pursued a vigorous, manly life. He took up boxing, wrestling, baseball, running, cycling, and mountain climbing and excelled at each. At Harvard, too, he befriended Theodore Roosevelt, a life-long friend and role model of racial vigor. But days before his 1881 commencement, Charles suffered a debilitating "brain fever" (Bingham 1955, *passim;* Fiske and Lummis 1975, *passim*). To recuperate, Lummis moved to a farm near Chillicothe, Ohio, eventually becoming the editor of *The Scioto Gazette*. In 1884, however, he contracted malaria. Fashioning himself an avid athlete and outdoorsman, and hoping through physical exercise to regain his health, he contacted Colonel Harrison Gray Otis, the owner of the *Los Angeles Times*, with a proposition. Following in the steps of thousands of health-seekers in the Southwest, Lummis traveled by foot to Los Angeles, regularly reporting on his activities for the *Times* as he crossed the continent. Otis accepted, even promised Lummis the city editorship of the newspaper when he arrived. On September 12, 1884, Lummis left Cincinnati, Ohio, beginning a 3,507-mile, 143-day trek that would take him through St. Louis, Denver, Santa Fe, and Albuquerque, finally ending with Lummis's arrival in Los Angeles on February 1, 1885. Lummis's dispatches to the *Times* were later collected and published in book form under the title, *A Tramp Across the Continent* (1892).

As the city editor of the *Los Angeles Times*, Lummis exuded the authority of a true renaissance man. He was part poet, explorer, adventurer, folklorist, archaeologist, and historian. Immoderate in his use of alcohol and tobacco, addicted to his work, and known for his wanton womanizing, in less than three years at his post he suffered a stroke. The left side of his body was paralyzed. In February 1888, Lummis returned to New Mexico to recuperate at the hacienda of Amado Chaves, a man he had first met in 1884. There, despite a physical regimen to regain his health, he suffered two more strokes. Finally, by 1890, his health restored, Lummis emerged as one of the most prolific and popular writers on the Southwest. Late in 1893 Charles Lummis returned to Los Angeles, where he spent the rest of his life as a promoter of Indian causes, working tirelessly to restore the deteriorating California missions, building the Southwest Museum, editing *Land of Sunshine/ Out West,* and thereby establishing the parameters of taste and authenticity in Indian crafts and Hispanic arts. Long after Charles Lummis's 1928 death, his legacy is still strongly felt in New Mexico.

The exact nature of the "brain fever" Charles Fletcher Lummis suffered in the spring of 1881, which ultimately propelled him westward, will never really be known. Histories of Victorian middle-class manhood in New England on the eve of the millennium have long asserted that Lummis's "brain fever" was hardly unique or limited to his person. Scores of men suffered the same affliction. In the popular science of the time he was allegedly suffering from neurasthenia, a disease marked by fatigue, headaches, dizziness, restlessness, and depression. The best medical knowledge of the day maintained that the body was a closed and limited energy field. Any particularly grueling activity might dissipate the body's energy. Nothing was perhaps more lethal than the excessive "brain work" a young male raised in a female seminary might experience at Harvard.

We now think of neurasthenia and of the neurasthenic condition that was so widely suffered by men in the late nineteenth century as an imaginary disease that produced acute psychosomatic manifestations. Frederick Jackson Turner alluded to the condition in his essay on the closing of the frontier when he noted that what characterized American national identity in 1893 was a "restless, nervous energy." Historians Gail Bederman (1995), Tom Lutz (1991), and F. G. Gosling (1987) have all located the material foundations of this widespread American nervousness in social relations. In the 1870s and 1880s, middle-class men were intensely preoccupied over how best to recuperate their place in society and often spoke of the "crisis of masculinity" and of a need to pursue a "strenuous life" and to experience what the Progressives called the "virility impulse." Earlier in the nineteenth century, white middle-class manhood had been defined by one's character and by one's ability simultaneously to control one's manly passions while exerting control over subordinates: women, children, and the lower classes. But by the 1890s, manhood seemed to falter. Severe economic depressions—in 1873 and again in 1896—destroyed the dreams of many self-made men to reach middle-class power and status. The proportion of self-employed middle-class men dropped from 67 percent to 37 percent between 1870 and 1910. The number of males in sales and clerical positions, typically defined as "women's" work, expanded simultaneously. Working-class labor uprisings and unrest, the entry of immigrants into local politics, and women militating for greater freedoms and the right to vote were all seen as contests over manhood, as indeed they were (Bederman 1995, 12–15).

If white, middle-class men were again to gain mastery over society and their subordinates, they had to recoup their manliness and construct what became validated as masculinity. It was widely held that men suffered from too much femininity. Men had become "sissies" and "pussy-footed"; they had gotten "cold feet" and become "stuffed shirts"—epithets all coined in the 1890s to describe passive, effeminate men. Even Basil Ransom, Henry James's fictional character in *The Bostonians* (1886) complained: "The whole generation is womanized; the masculine tone is passing out of the world; it's a feminine, nervous, hysterical, chattering canting age. . . . The masculine character, the ability to dare and endure, to know and yet not to fear reality, to look the world in the face and take it for what it is[,] this is what I want to preserve, or rather . . . recover" (quoted in Bederman 1995, 16). This was indeed the problem, as many men saw it. Where would salvation be found?

Historian E. Anthony Rotundo has recently argued that many middle-class men in the 1870s developed an ideology of primitive masculinity inspired by the lives of "primitives," "savages," and Indians to recuperate their manhood. Many flocked to fraternal organizations such as the Freemasons, the Oddfellows, and The Improved Order of Red Men (Rotundo 1993, 220–247). In this latter group, men enacted their fantasies of what Indian rituals were all about. Prizefighting, body building, and college football all became popular activities. They glorified the muscular male body as a symbol of a rehabilitated manhood (Gorn 1986, *passim.*). Others tried to make boys into men through the Boy Scouts and the Young Men's Christian Association (YMCA), taking them on excursions into the "wild" and having them read Western novels and heroic adventure tales (Macleod 1983, *passim*). Boston minister Thomas Wentworth Higginson urged men in his parish to tramp through the countryside in search of game, camping in the wilderness, and by so doing, "you are as essentially an Indian on the Blue Hills as among the Rocky Mountains" (Rotundo 1993, 227).

Charles F. Lummis's initial publications tapped deeply into this national preoccupation over virility. His were adventure stories of primitive Indian masculinity that appeared in magazines meant for young boys, such as *Youth's Companion, St. Nicolas,* and *Century.* His very first book, *A New Mexico David And Other Stories and Sketches of the Southwest,* appeared in 1891 (Lummis [1891] 1969). Containing stories of adventure and heroism, the very first episode in the book told of a New Mexican match that resembled the biblical battle between David and Goliath, thus the story's title, "A New Mexican David." Lucario Montoya was a young New Mexican boy who in 1840 triumphantly slew a large and particularly vicious Ute Indian brave, who had killed several of his relatives. The rest of the stories in the tome told of how New Mexican boys were taught practical self-reliance in the wild. "The out-door life, the hardships and the responsibilities to which they are trained, make them sturdy and self-reliant," wrote Lummis ([1891] 1969, 29–30).

In the year that followed, the articles Lummis penned as he trekked across the Southwest appeared as *A Tramp Across the Continent* (1892). Hailed in the book's dust jacket as a work "Full of life and spirit—just such stories as every healthy-minded boy delights to read," it was, said Lummis, "a truthful record of some of the experiences and impressions of a walk across the continent—the diary of a man who got outside the fences of civilization and was glad of it" (1892, vii). The journey was sometimes "fatiguing, but never dull; full of hardship and spiced with frequent danger in its latter half, but always instructive, keenly interesting, and keenly enjoyed, even at its hardest, and it had some very hard sides" (1892, 3). The trip liberated him from the "fences of society" so that his athletic and well trained body could experience life "with a perfect body and a wakened mind, a life where brain and brawn and leg and lung all rejoice and grow alert together" (1892, 2).

Given the success of his initial works, Lummis quickly published *Pueblo Indian Folk Tales* (later editions bore the title *The Man Who Married the Moon*), *Some Strange Corners of Our Country* (1892), *The Land of Poco Tiempo* (1893), *The Spanish Pioneers* (1893), *The Gold Fish of Gran Chimu* (1896), *The Enchanted Burro* (1897), and *The King of the Broncos* (1897). These were all extremely popular books of adventure in the U.S. Southwest, writes literary historian Martin Padget (n.d.), which cognitively mapped and narrated for his American reading public "Our Wonderland of the Southwest—Its Marvels of Nature—Its Pageant of the Earth Building—Its Strange People—Its Centuried Romance."[2] Lummis added: "I am an American and felt ashamed to know so little of my own country as I did, and as most Americans do" (1892, 2). This was the reason he had explored the Southwest and written about it.

New Mexico: The Land of Poco Tiempo

Charles Fletcher Lummis's writing about New Mexico and its history was prolific, and his published corpus is immense. Here we will focus on *The Land of Poco Tiempo* primarily because it was in this tome that Lummis most fully employed Orientalist tropes, describing the Río Grande as the Nile and New Mexico as Egypt. Published in 1893, the very year Frederick Jackson Turner declared the frontier closed and aptly described the restless manhood the frontier had unleashed, the book's first chapter is entitled "The Land of Poco Tiempo." In that chapter, Lummis asked his readers to leave the Eastern United States and its industrial pace behind, to relax, and to imagine an escape to a very different place.

> Here is the land of poco tiempo—the home of "Pretty Soon." Why hurry with the hurrying world. The "Pretty Soon" of New Spain is better than the "Now! Now!" of the haggard States. The opiate sun soothes to rest, the adobe is made to lean against, the hush of day-

long noon would not be broken. Let us not hasten—mañana will
do. Better still, pasado mañana." [1893, 3]

Once the majesty of the landscape had been drawn, Lummis introduced his
readers to the Pueblo Indians, whom he claimed were the most striking ethno-
logic figures in America. Though certainly not of the "superior race," the Pueblo
Indians were physically, mentally, morally, socially, and politically sophisticated,
and thus "not poor from any point of view" (1893, 29).

Once the Pueblo Indians were inscribed as a permanent and unchanging feature of the landscape, the remaining chapters of *The Land of Poco Tiempo* were
rapid linear tours to the remote corners of New Mexico. Writing as if the reader
were gazing from the windows of a railroad car or an automobile, Lummis
allowed strange customs and exotic peoples to pass rapidly by, appearing and then
quickly disappearing—a conventional technique in travel literature. Standing
atop Acoma Pueblo, "The City In The Sky," Lummis attests in Chapter 3 that here

one feels as in a strange, sweet, unearthly dream—as among scenes
and beings more than human . . . [as in] a shadowy world of crags
so unearthly beautiful, so weird, so unique, that it is hard for the
onlooker to believe himself in America. [1893, 58]

If one wanted to visit Acoma, it was quite easy to reach, Lummis informed his
readers—only a few miles south of the Atlantic & Pacific Railroad stations at
Laguna and McCarty, New Mexico. Readers, by accepting Lummis's invitation,
learned about Acoma's history under Spanish rule, the town's physical organization, its people, its church, its waterworks, its architecture, and its landscape. The
tour ended "as the rumbling farm-wagon jolts you back from your enchanted
dream to the prosy wide-awake civilization" (1893, 76). Visitors undoubtedly were
haunted forever by "that unearthly cliff, that weird city, and their unguessed
dwellers" (1893, 76).

Having described New Mexico's sedentary population in the first three chapters of *The Land of Poco Tiempo*, Lummis organized the remainder as adventure
and action-packed episodes. The chapter on "The Penitent Brothers" recounted a
processional Way of the Cross; "The Chase of the Chongo" (*chongo* means pony-
tail) described a foot race at Isleta Pueblo; "The Wanderings of Cochití" turned
to the historic migrations of that people; "The Apache Warrior" focused on the
peripatetic lifeways of this group. And finally, nomadic Indian raiders were hotly
pursued in "On the Trail of the Renegades." These were all chapters in which the
subjects of the narrative were in rapid movement over a linear (progressive) space
(Hinsley 1990). Many years later, John Ford, the famous movie director of Western
films, commented that the formula for his movies was the presentation of exotic

characters moving rapidly westward across space. In *The Land of Poco Tiempo,* Lummis began with the landscape and with the static, motionless Pueblo Indians who were picturesque relics of another America. The Mexicans and Navajo followed: they were deficient peoples, but nonetheless caught in the flux of history moving forward because of Anglo American territorial conquest. Before Anglos arrived, Mexicans were "in-bred and isolation-shrunken . . . ignorant as slaves, and more courteous than kings" (Lummis 1893, 5–6). The Navajo likewise were "sullen, nomad, horse-loving, horse-stealing, horse-living vagrants of the saddle; pagans, first, last, and all the time . . ." (1893, 5). Curiously, the unmarked ethnic category was Anglo American, the position of power from which humans are aestheticized and objectified for consumption by readers. This was also the position of power through which Lummis and his readers were joined as active subjects gazing at the "others" they constructed.

Egypt, Orientalism, and New Mexico

By taking Anglo American readers to New Mexico, to *The Land of Poco Tiempo,* Charles Lummis took them on an Orientalist adventure to fantasies and hallucinations of Egypt, Babylon, Assyria, and to deepest, darkest Africa:

> The brown or gray adobe hamlets [of New Mexico] . . . the strange terraced towns . . . the abrupt mountains, the echoing, rock-walled cañons, the sunburnt mesas, the streams bankrupt by their own shylock sands, the gaunt, brown, treeless plains, the ardent sky, all harmonize with unearthly unanimity. "Picturesque" is a tame word for it. It is a picture, a romance, a dream, all in one. It is our one corner that is the sun's very own. Here he has had his way, and no discrepancy mars his work. It is a land of quaint, swart faces, of Oriental dress and unspelled speech; a land where distance is lost, and eye is a liar; a land of ineffable lights and sudden shadows; of polytheism and superstition, where the rattlesnake is a demigod, and the cigarette a means of grace, and where Christians mangle and crucify themselves—the heart of Africa beating against the ribs of the Rockies. [1893, 4–5]

In chapter after chapter and description after description, New Mexico was made knowable through comparisons to exotic places in the Orient and Egypt. Describing New Mexico's unique light, Lummis wrote: "Under that ineffable alchemy of the sky, mud turns ethereal, and the desert is a revelation. It is Egypt, with every rock a sphinx, every peak a pyramid" (1893, 9). The residents of Acoma Pueblo were "plain, industrious farmers, strongly Egyptian in their methods . . ." (1893, 69). At Taos, Zuñi, and Acoma Pueblos, Lummis saw houses shaped into "pyramid" blocks (1893, 51–52). Pueblo girls cloaked themselves in "modest, artistic Oriental dress . . ." (1893, 53). The Indian *chongo* was "the Egyptian queue in which both sexes dress their hair" (1893, 111). In the wind-eroded sand sculpture of the desert, Lummis saw "suggestion of Assyrian sculpture in its rocks. One might fancy it a giant Babylon . . ." (1893, 61). For Lummis the Apache were the "Bedouin of the New World," and the land they inhabited a "Sahara, thirsty as death on the battlefield. . . ." (1893, 175–176) And like "the ancient Egyptians [who] flogged themselves in honor of Isis," so too did New Mexico's Penitent Brothers "whip themselves every Good Friday in memory of their redeemer" (1893, 80).

When Lummis described New Mexico as Egypt and the Orient, he was harking back to an older trope that had long been employed in European travel writing. Drawing on memories of eight centuries of occupation of the Iberian Peninsula by the Moors, when Hernán Cortés first described the ceremonial centers of the Aztecs in his *Cartas de relación,* he called them *mezquitas* or Arab mosques. In the middle of the sixteenth century the Spanish chronicler, Francisco López de Gómara, proclaimed that the pyramids the Aztecs and Incas had constructed surpassed those of ancient Egypt. And even the early Spanish settlers of New Mexico saw Moors when they stared into Indian faces. The Pueblo Indians were said to carry "Moorish bows," or bows and arrows, to worship in "mosques," or kivas, and to attack as clandestinely as Moors (Gutiérrez, 1991, 194–195).

In Anglo American travel writing of the eighteenth century forward, similar Orientalist tropes were standard fare. They were employed to give readers unfamiliar with particular places some readily identifiable comparisons drawn from their own culture and textual tradition. The Holy Bible was then the most widely read book. Naturally its legends and places conjured up familiar scenes. Accounts of trips to the Holy Land by compatriots further underscored comparisons.

Historian William B. Taylor (1991) has argued that what ignited Orientalist images of Mexico as Egypt in Anglo-American travel narratives written from the 1750s on was the presence of extensive archaeological zones and pyramids akin in size to those in Egypt. In the early 1840s Frances Calderón de la Barca, of Boston Scottish ancestry, likened Mexico City's dry season to "a perfect Egyptian desert." Sullivan McCollester, a native of New Hampshire, in 1897 marveled that in Mexico "the surface of the land and the works of man wore the aspect of Syria and Mesopotamia. It struck us with amazement to find how the orient had fixed its seal upon this land" (Taylor 1991, 6). Such comparisons were heightened by the fact that some of the travelers to Mexico had previously written about their treks across Egypt. John Lloyd Stephens, for example, wrote *Incidents of Travel in Egypt, Arabia, Petraera, and the Holy Land* in 1838, before publishing *Incidents of Travel in Central America, Chiapas, and Yucatán* in 1841. The Mexico-Egypt link was made even more explicit in Channing Arnold and Frederick Frost's 1909 book, *The American Egypt: A Record of Travel in Yucatan.*

Early anthropological studies of New Mexico's population were similarly filled with orientalist analogues. "How strangely parallel have been the lines of development in this curious civilization of an American desert, with those of Eastern nations and deserts," wrote anthropologist Frank Hamilton Cushing in 1879, concerning what he had observed at Zuñi (quoted in Babcock 1990, 406). Writing in 1890, John G. Owens was reminded "of the pictures of Palestine" when he observed Zuñi Pueblo women porting water in large jars called *ollas* (quoted in Babcock 1990, 404). From anthropology to popular journalism, visions of New Mexico as the Orient spread. During the 1880s, in a series of articles later reprinted as *The Land of the Pueblos,* Susan Wallace was reminded "of Bible pictures" when she observed Hispanic villages. Mexican women carried water-jars on their heads or shoulders, Wallace remarked: "like maidens of Palestine. Now and then an old black shawl, melancholy remnant of the gay rebosa [*sic*], shrouding an olive forehead, suggested the veiled face of gentle Rebecca" (Wallace 1891, 43–52).

New Mexican tourist boosters continued employing Orientalist themes well into the twentieth century. Harriet Monroe proclaimed in 1920 that Pueblo Indian dances resembled Homeric rites and Egyptian ceremonies (Weigle and Fiore 1982, 17). "Motorists crossing the southwestern states are nearer to the primitive than anywhere else on the continent," vaunted Erna Fergusson, writing promotional literature for the Santa Fe Railroad's "Indian Detours" to the exotic Southwest. Regarding the experience one would have on seeing New Mexico, Fergusson continued: "They are crossing a land in which a foreign people, with foreign speech and foreign ways, offer them spectacles which can be equaled in few Oriental lands" (quoted in Thomas 1978, 196).

Some forty years ago, writing about the tourist literature that opened up the Western United States to Eastern residents at the end of the nineteenth century, historian Earl Pomery drew attention to the escapist fantasies in much of this literature. Travelers passing through the villages of New Mexico were explicitly asked to recall "the villages of ancient Egypt and Nubia, Ninevah and Babylon, rather than to study the remains of American aboriginal life . . ." (Pomeroy 1959, 39). Pomeroy's point, forcefully underscored in Mary Louise Pratt's book, *Imperial Eyes* (1992), was that by imagining the residents of New Mexico as frozen in the past, as echoing a remote and primitive place, writers and observers could ignore the present in which they lived. Egypt offered "one powerful model for the archeological rediscovery of America," writes Mary Louise Pratt. "There, too, Europeans were reconstructing a lost history through, and as, 'rediscovered' monuments and ruins." By reviving indigenous history and culture as archaeology they were being revived as dead and insignificant to the progress of history (Pratt 1992, 134). In her analysis of Orientalism in the Americas, literary critic Julia A. Kushigian argues that many of the modernist writers of the late nineteenth century were drawn to Orientalist themes not only because of the exoticism and escapism they offered, but also because

> the Orient stood as a symptom of the loss of faith in reason and Western values. The eccentricities of Oriental life, with its exotic spatial configurations and perverse morality, opposed European notions of morality, time, space, and personal identity. Orientalism of the . . . turn of the century, was a presentiment of the end of things. [1991, 7–8]

The various ideological strands in Charles Lummis's Orientalism were clearly of complicated genealogy. What evoked the sights, sounds, and smells of Egypt in New Mexico for Lummis were the women who carried clay water jars on their heads, the cool mud (adobe) houses that dotted the landscape, the donkey beasts of burden, the two-wheeled *carretas* or transport carts, the desert sun, light, and heat, and the presence of sedentary and nomadic "primitives" amid the ruins and abandoned architectural vestiges of former grandeur.

The political reactions that these picturesque Egyptian scenes were meant to evoke among Lummis's readers were critiques of New Mexican despotism and of religious fanaticism that had no place in a republic governed by Anglo Protestants. Like the Israelites who were led out of the darkness and idolatry of their Egyptian captivity, so too the peoples of New Mexico had to be freed from their "paganism" (read Roman Catholicism) and brought into the modern era. How this should be done differed for the three peoples Lummis recognized as inhabiting New Mexico—the Pueblo Indians, the Navajo, and the Mexicans. The sooner the latter two disappeared, the better, for only the Pueblo Indians were a true romance. Only they were picturesque. They were the true America that had to be preserved for citizens of the Eastern United States to consume.

If for the Pueblos Lummis had only praise, for the Mexicans he had disdain, primarily because of the despotism they had created while under autonomous rule. Communitarian democracy had been nurtured and sustained by the Pueblos. Peonage was the legacy Mexicans had bequeathed to the zone. Lummis charged that the sheep-herding economy was to blame:

> [Sheep] rendered the Territory possible for three centuries, in the face of the most savage and interminable Indian wars that any part of our country ever knew. He fed and clothed New Spain, and made its customs, if not its laws. He reorganized society, led the fashions, caused the only machinery that was in New Mexico in three hundred years, made of a race of nomad savages the foremost of

blanket-weavers, and invented a slavery which is unto this day in despite of the Emancipation Proclamation.... Society gradually fell apart into two classes—sheep-owners and sheep-tenders. One man at the beginning of this century had two million head of sheep, and kept twenty-seven hundred peons always in the field with them, besides the thousands more who were directly dependent.... The social effects of such a system, wherein four-fifths of the Caucasian male population were servants to five to eight dollars a month to a handful of mighty amos [bosses or masters], are not far to trace. The most conscientious of these frontier czars had perforce a power beside which the government was a nonentity; and the unscrupulous swelled their authority to an unparalleled extent. It was easy to get a few hundred poor shepherds into one's debt; and once in, the amo, with the aid of complaisant laws, took care that they should never get out. He was thenceforth entitled to the labor of their bodies—even to the labor of their children. They were his peons—slaves without the expense of purchase. And peonage in disguise is still effective in New Mexico. [1893, 19–20]

New Mexico was "a land of ineffable lights and sudden shadows" (1893, 5), thought Lummis, a place of "violent antitheses of light and shade" (1893, 9). And like the ancient Israelites who had been led out of the darkness of paganism and into the light, so too New Mexico's Mexicans had to be rescued from their "horrendous" religious rites. Chief among these were the rituals of the Penitent Brothers, members of the Confraternity of Our Lord Jesus Nazarene, also known as the *Hermanos Penitentes,* or derisively as *Penitentes.* "[S]o late as 1891 a procession of flagellants took place within the limits of the United States," Lummis complained. He continued:

> A procession in which voters of this Republic shredded their naked backs with savage whips, staggered beneath huge crosses, and hugged the maddening needles of the cactus; a procession which culminated in the flesh-and-blood crucifixion of an unworthy representative of the Redeemer. Nor was this an isolated horror. Every Good Friday, for many generations, it has been a staple custom to hold these barbarous rites in parts of New Mexico. [1893, 79]

Mortification of the flesh, long outlawed in Europe, was still common both among Indians and Mexicans in the Southwest. The crucial difference was that Indians engaged almost exclusively in fasts for communal spiritual ends. But Mexicans were individualistic. "These fanatics do penance for themselves only, and in Lent achieve their sin-washing for the year," wrote Lummis (1893, 24). The evidence Lummis cited for his argument that the Penitent Brothers were thieves was the New Mexican *dicho* or folk saying:

Penitente pecador,	Penitente sinner,
Porqué te andas azotando?	Why do you go whipping yourself?
Por una vaca que robé	For a cow that I stole,
Y aquí la ando disquitando.	And here I go paying for her (1893, 108).

Lummis maintained that while some of the Brothers were "good but deluded men," the majority were "petty larcenists, horse-thieves, and assassins" (1893, 106). The brotherhood was widely feared because it controlled political power in Northern New Mexico. "No one likes—and few dare—to offend them; and there have been men of liberal education who have joined them to gain political influence. In fact it is unquestionable that the outlawed order is kept alive ... by the connivance of wealthy men, who find it convenient to maintain these secret bands for their own ends" (1893, 106).

The discourse Charles Lummis deployed to describe the Confraternity of Our Lord Jesus Nazarene and its members, the *Hermanos Penitentes*—calling them "Penitent Brothers" and the negative term *Penitentes*—has been the primary frame of reference used by almost every Anglo American writer on the brotherhood ever since. Lummis began his discussion by likening the floggings that the boys of Sparta received at the altar of Artemis Orthia, the whippings the Egyptians gave themselves in honor of Isis, and the thongs of the Luperci that Roman citizens received during Lupercalia, to those of New Mexico's "*Penitentes*." Lummis also advanced what is now the well-worn theory of the Confraternity's genealogy—that it was a corruption of Third Order Franciscanism first performed by Don Juan de Oñate when he entered New Mexico in 1598; Lummis mistakenly claims it was 1594 (1893, 80). The observer's gaze on the flagellation, on the blood letting, on the use of cacti for mortification, on the shrill of the *pito,* and on the nature and extent of crucifixion deviated little in the textual descriptions that followed Lumis. Lummis's eye-witness report of a Good Friday procession and crucifixion has been the starting point for every author who has subsequently written on the topic.

Charles Lummis profoundly shaped what generation after generation has been able to perceive in the brotherhood. Part of the reason for this is that Lummis photographed a Good Friday procession and crucifixion he observed in San Mateo, New Mexico, in 1888. In Lummis's mind the process by which he was able to photograph this penitential rite was quite similar to the cunning and adventure one experienced when out on a safari hunting large game animals. "Woe to him if in seeing he shall be seen. ... But let him stalk his game, and with safety to his own hide he may see havoc to the hides of others" (1893, 85). Lummis reported how he waited feverishly for Holy Week to arrive, hoping to photograph the impossible—the Penitent Brothers: "No photographer has ever caught the *Penitentes* with his sun-lasso, and I was assured of death in various unattractive forms at the first hint of an attempt" (1893, 87). But as soon as he heard the shrill of the *pito,* his prudence gave way to his enthusiasm. He set up his camera and waited for what he called a "shot." Though the Brothers vehemently protested the presence of his camera, "well-armed friends . . . held back the evil-faced mob, while the instantaneous plates were being snapped at the strange scene below" (1893, 91). Photographs of this "barbaric" rite were necessary, said Lummis, because Mexicans were "fast losing their pictorial possibilities . . ." (1893, 9).

The depravities of modernity were quickly demoralizing America, and it was necessary to return to an older time, to a pre-industrial America. In New Mexico, in the land of no rush, one could find "the National Rip Van Winkle . . . the United States which was not United States." Lummis implicitly did plenty of preaching about the decadence of industrial capitalism in the East by elaborating on the healthy values of New Mexico's peoples. They worked hard to sustain themselves, but not with "unseemly haste, no self-tripping race for wealth" (1893, 10). Lummis loved New Mexico because it was not troubled "with the unrest of civilization." In New Mexico, "The old ways are still the best ways." Society was still patriarchal, children were still obedient, well-mannered, and never quarrelsome. Age was respected, a father here was still the master of his brood, and hospitality was greatly valued and extremely generous (1893, 16–17).

The gospel Lummis preached was undoubtedly of great appeal to a class of alienated Anglo American intellectuals, writers, artists, and financiers who packed their belonging and headed to northern New Mexico at the end of the nineteenth century and in increasing numbers after World War I. They came rejecting the tastes, aspirations, and pretensions of the "Blue Bloods" who mimicked European aristocracy. They imagined a national culture rooted, not in Europe, but on this continent in the cultures of New Mexico. As Molly Mullin (1992), Warren Susman (1973), and others have argued, the discovery of cultures, both by academics and the larger public, was an attempt to deflect attention from the class conflict that plagued the Eastern centers of industrial capital and to create a new metaphor for American nationalism.

The preservation of the simple authentic cultures these Easterners found in New Mexico, and their critique of the industrial age, was localized in Pueblo and Hispano "colonial" art. In these products created largely for touristic consumption, Anglos imagined the possibility and romance of non-alienating labor. Such artistic production was hand-crafted and appeared to stand in isolation, defying the principles of global capitalism (Mullin 1992, 395). The accelerated rate of circulation in global capital, David Harvey explains in *The Condition of Postmodernity* (1989), created by necessity a strong nostalgia for place-specific identity. Mabel Dodge Luhan captured this flight from modernity and to the cultural pluralism of New Mexico well when she instructed her son, "Remember, it is ugly in America . . . we have left everything worthwhile behind us. America is all machinery and money-making and factories . . . ugly, ugly, ugly . . ." (quoted in Mullin 1992, 412).

Charles Fletcher Lummis lured a whole generation of Anglo Americans to New Mexico, hoping there to resist industrial capital, to preserve the quaint picturesque cultures they found, and to market Pueblo and Hispano handicrafts as an authentic American art that offered a solution to national alienation.

Finally, one cannot fully understand the larger ideological forces that shaped Charles Lummis and his vision of the Southwest without understanding how important Theodore Roosevelt's influence was on his thinking (Bederman 1995, 170–216). The two met as students at Harvard. The two had been smart if sickly children. The two turned to muscularity, the outdoors, and the salubrity of the West both for personal salvation and as a site for national redemption. "I owe everything to the West!" Roosevelt once vaunted to Charles Lummis. "It made me! I found myself there" (Starr 1985, 262). Roosevelt imagined the West as that site where the white American race first emerged as a masculine world force through Darwinian racial conflicts with weaker and effeminate savage races. A millennial evolutionary struggle between barbarism and civilization was unfolding, he thought. American men, by virtue of the superior manhood of their white race, had to take up the "strenuous life," as Roosevelt called it, and through racial violence and imperialistic wars implant civilization where once only savagery and barbarism had ruled. The moral mission of the race and the nation was to advance civilization. Civilization was white racial supremacy and the eradication of inferiors.

In his tramp across the continent, Charles Lummis proclaimed that he had embarked on a journey "outside the fences of civilization" (1893, vii), and in New Mexico he found a land of inferior types, a place untroubled by "the troubles of civilization" (1893, 16). It was in this trope of "civilization" that Charles Lummis and his Anglo American compatriots spun their elaborate mythologies of racial supremacy. If New Mexico could be conceived as an oriental place, as an Egypt locked in a time warp in the past, New Mexicans could be romantically depicted as specimens of degenerate races destined to collection in museums and extinction on the earth. The antiquity of the cultures studied and collected in the Southwest were the source of sensual delight in the American imagination, but belonged not to the very people who had produced them. The Southwest belonged to Anglo Americans. The forces of evolution had been unleashed in the region. Anglo Saxon vigor, when combined with the healthfulness of the sun, was producing that paragon of civilization, the new American—manly, violent, imperialistic (Starr 1985, 262).

Notes

1. Orientalism is a term that has been largely theorized by Edward Said in his book *Orientalism* (New York: Vintage Books, 1979). Orientalism to him "is knowledge of the Orient that places things Oriental in class, court, prison, or manual for scrutiny, study, judgment, discipline, or governing.... Orientalism reinforced, and was reinforced by, the certain knowledge that Europe or the West literally commanded the vastly greater part of the world's surface" (41).
2. This quotation is the subtitle of Lummis's book, *Mesa, Cañon, Pueblo* (New York: The Century Company, 1925).

Literature Cited

Arnold, Channing and Frederick J. Tabor Frost. 1909. *The American Egypt: A Record of Travel in Yucatan*. London: Hutchinson & Co.

Babcock, Barbara A. 1990. A New Mexican Rebecca: Imaging Pueblo Women. *Journal of the Southwest* 32(4) (winter): 398–413.

Bederman, Gail. 1995. *Manliness and Civilization: A Cultural History of Gender and Race in the United States, 1880–1917*. Chicago: University of Chicago Press.

Bingham, Edwin R. 1955. *Charles F. Lummis: Editor of the Southwest* (San Marino, Calif.: Huntington Library.

Fiske, Turbese and Keith Lummis. 1975. *Charles F. Lummis: The Man and His West*. Norman: University of Oklahoma Press.

Goetzmann, William H. 1966. *Exploration and Empire: The Explorer and the Scientist in the Winning of the American West*. New York: Alfred A. Knopf.

Gorn, Elliott J. 1986. *The Manly Art: Bare-Knuckle Prizefighting in America*. Ithaca, N.Y.: Cornell University Press.

Gosling, F. G. 1987. *Before Freud: Neurasthenia and the American Medical Community, 1870–1910*. Urbana: University of Illinois Press.

Gutiérrez, Ramón A. 1989. Aztlán, Montezuma, and New Mexico: The Political Uses of American Indian Mythology. In *Aztlán: Essays on the Chicano Homeland*, eds. Rudolfo A. Anaya and Francisco Lomelí, 172–190. Albuquerque: University of New Mexico Press.

———. 1991. *When Jesus Came, the Corn Mothers Went Away: Marriage, Sexuality, and Power in New Mexico, 1500–1846*. Stanford: Stanford University Press.

Harvey, David. 1989. *The Condition of Postmodernity: An Enquiry into the Origins of Cultural Change*. Cambridge, Mass.: Blackwell.

Hinsley, Curtis M. 1990. The World as Marketplace: Commodification of the Exotic at the World's Columbian Exposition, Chicago, 1893. In *Exhibiting Cultures: The Poetics and Politics of Museum Display*, eds. Ivan Karp and Steven D. Lavine, 344–365. Washington, D.C.: Smithsonian Institution Press.

Keen, Benjamin. 1971. *The Aztec Image in Western Thought*. New Brunswick, N.J.: Rutgers University Press.

Kushigian, Julia A. 1991. *Orientalism in the Hispanic Literary Tradition*. Albuquerque: University of New Mexico Press.

Lummis, Charles F. 1893. *The Land of Poco Tiempo*. New York: Charles Scribner's Sons.

———. [1891] 1969. *A New Mexico David And Other Stories and Sketches of the Southwest*. Freeport, N.Y.: Books for Libraries Press.

————. 1892. *A Tramp Across the Continent*. New York: Charles Scribner's Sons.

Lutz, Tom. 1991. *American Nervousness, 1903: An Anecdotal History*. Ithaca, N.Y.: Cornell University Press.

Macleod, David I. 1983. *Building Character in the American Boy: The Boy Scouts, YMCA, and Their Forerunners, 1870–1920*. Madison: University of Wisconsin Press.

Mullin, Molly H. 1992. The Patronage of Difference: Making Indian Art "Art," Not Ethnology. *Cultural Anthropology* 7(4) (November): 395–424.

Padget, Martin. n.d. Travel, Exoticism, and the Writing of Region: Charles Fletcher Lummis and the "Creation" of the Southwest. Unpublished paper.

Pomeroy, Earl. 1959. *In Search of the Golden West: The Tourist in Western America*. New York: Alfred A. Knopf.

Pratt, Mary Louise. 1992. *Imperial Eyes: Travel Writing and Transculturation*. New York: Routledge.

Rotundo, E. Anthony. 1993. *American Manhood: Transformations in Masculinity from the Revolution to the Modern Era*. New York: Basic Books.

Starr, Kevin. 1985. *Inventing the Dream: California Through the Progressive Era*. New York: Oxford University Press.

Stephens, John Lloyd. 1838. *Incidents of Travel in Egypt, Arabia, Petraera, and the Holy Land*. New York: Harper & Brothers.

————. 1841. *Incidents of Travel in Central America, Chiapas, and Yucatan*. New York: Harper & Brothers.

Susman, Warren. 1973. *Culture and Commitment, 1929–1945*. New York: George Braziller.

Taylor, William B. 1991. Mexico as Oriental: Early Thoughts on a History of American and British Representations since 1821. Unpublished paper.

Thomas, D. H. 1978. *The Southwestern Indian Detours: The Story of the Fred Harvey/Santa Fe Railway Experiment in "Detourism."* Phoenix: Hunter Publishing.

Turner, Frederick Jackson. 1993. The Significance of the Frontier in American History. In *History, Frontier, and Section: Three Essays by Frederick Jackson Turner*, ed. Martin Ridge, 59–91. Albuquerque: University of New Mexico Press.

Wallace, Susan. 1891. *The Land of the Pueblos*. New York: Columbian Publishing Co.

Weigle, Marta and Kyle Fiore. 1982. *Santa Fe and Taos: The Writer's Era, 1916–1941*. Santa Fe: Ancient City Press.

Contesting Social and Historical Erasure
Membership in La Prensa Asociada Hispano-Americana

A. Gabriel Meléndez

El Periodista:	The Journalist:
Quien se mete a periodista,	He who becomes a journalist
¡Dios le valga! ¡Dios le asista!	God stand by him! God help him!
El ha de ser director,	He will have to be the director,
Redactor y corrector,	He will be redactor and proofreader
Regente; editor y cajista,	Manager, editor and cashier,
Censor, colaborador,	Censor, contributor
Repartidor, cobrador,	Paper boy and bill collector,
Corresponsal, maquinista,	Correspondent, press operator,
Ha de suplir al prensista	He shall fill in for the printer
Y a veces ... hasta al lector.	And, at times ... even for the reader.

La Flecha, *Wagon Mound, New Mexico, January 7, 1887*

Ꮟ IN DECEMBER OF 1891 a group of Nuevomexicano journalists met in Las Vegas, New Mexico and held the first organizational meeting of *La Prensa Asociada Hispano-Americana*—the Spanish-American Associated Press. The major Spanish weekly in the region, *La Voz del Pueblo,* underscored the importance of such developments when it reported, in February 1892, "No longer a mere possibility but a sure thing" (*Ya no es simplemente una posibilidad sino un hecho asegurado*) (*La Asociación* 1892, 1). Now, as on prior occasions, New Mexico's Spanish-language journalists were reiterating the promise that a vigorous and well-organized regional press "has the potential to bring us innumerable improvements" (*tiene posibilidades de hacernos mejoras incalculables*) (*La Asociación* 1892, 1). Hispano *periodiqueros,* or newspapermen as they had come to refer to themselves, were a pragmatic and forward-thinking group. Their immediate goal was to inform and educate the masses of Spanish-speaking *nativos,* but their vision of change rested on the conviction that collectively their presses would contest the tendencies of Anglo Americans to dismiss and dehistoricize the *mexicano* presence in the Southwest.

La Voz del Pueblo's report suggests that the moment for concerted action was at hand when it added,

The Hispano press will organize as it should and, when this has been done, certainly, it will benefit, first, the Latin race in general, and second, it will facilitate great advantage for the journalists who represent that group. (*[S]e) asociará como debe la prensa Hispano-Americana; y cuando esto se haya verificado será por cierto una inauguración que beneficiará primeramente a la raza latina en lo general, y segundo, facilitará grandes ventajas á los periodistas que representan la misma.)*[1] [*La Asociación de La Prensa Asociada Hispano-Americana* 1892]

These expectations were not ill-founded; Spanish-language weeklies in the 1890s had large circulations that reached the majority of New Mexico's citizens, most of whom were *nativos* who read Spanish exclusively. By early in the decade Spanish weeklies had outpaced and eclipsed newspapers published in English.

Such enthusiasm had already increased the quality and professionalism of member papers, a trend noted by José Escobar of Denver's *Las Dos Repúblicas:*

This very press has improved noticeably over the last few years, and, in its editorials and bulletins, one observes something beyond the embryonic style of a press in its infancy; [this can be seen] in its logical and well conceived commentary. It struggles, not for the party line, rather, for something greater yet, for the betterment of the masses irrespective of political or religious belief. (*Esa misma prensa, en los últimos años ha mejorado de una manera bien notable, y en sus editoriales y boletines, se observa a algo más que ese estilo embrionario de la prensa que nace; la argumentación lógica y justa que combate, ya no por una idea de partido; sino por algo mucho más grande todavía; por el mejoramiento de las masas sin diferencias de creencias religiosas y políticas.* [Escobar 1896b, 1]

In the months following the Las Vegas meetings, *La Prensa Asociada* scheduled region-wide meetings in Las Vegas, Santa Fe, Las Cruces, and El Paso,[2] and throughout the decade the association met in earnest and with great regularity. José Segura of Santa Fe's *El Boletín Popular* reported that several of the most prominent Spanish-language journalists attended a meeting of *La Prensa Asociada* in Santa Fe in early December 1893. Present at the meeting were José Escobar of *El Progreso* (Trinidad, Colorado), Teófilo Ocaña Caballero of *La Lucha* (El Paso, Texas), Marcial Valdez of *El Tiempo* (Las Cruces), Pedro G. de la Lama of *La Opinión Pública* (Albuquerque), and Marcelino Lerma of *La Flor del Valle* (Las Cruces). Other important Spanish-language publications from across the territory were also represented at the meeting. *La Prensa Asociada* continued to grow throughout the decade and boasted of being the first professional organization of its kind among the Spanish-speaking in the Southwest. *La Prensa Asociada* formalized relationships among member editors and brought recognition to the idea that Spanish-language journalists maintained a standing in both Anglo and *mexicano* societies as members of a respected profession, not a minor accomplishment in light of the paucity of such opportunities for Nuevomexicanos since the colonial period.

La Prensa Asociada was by no means an ideologically or politically homogeneous group. Even as the association espoused a defense of the interests of the community, its membership often held varying positions on how to solve societal problems. Member newspapers were drawn from the Democrat and Republican ranks, and the political credos of individual editors were often a source of friction and political infighting. Nonetheless, the organization gave formal recognition to the idea that the Spanish-language press should act in concert to oppose injury to the community it represented. Its charter from the outset was

> to reach consensus on the measure and means best suited and needed for the progress and betterment of the community it [the association] represents. (. . . *convenir en los medios y medidas que sean mas propios y necesarios adoptar para el adelanto y mejoramiento del pueblo a quien ella representa.*) [*La Prensa Asociada Hispano-Americana* 1892b]

Member editors created a space in the context of their publications for the use of the terms "Nuevomexicano," "Neo-Mexicano," and "Novo Mexicano." The neologisms "Neo-" and "Novo Mexicano" became particularly useful in describing their movement. In consciously adopting these terms, editors made it clear that they saw themselves as the active agents of an emerging social force—on the one hand, heirs to the *mexicano* culture of their forebears and, on the other, active participants in the technological and societal transformations of their time. Such moves to define and organize the group were tantamount to the calls for unity that were periodically invoked by the leadership of *La Prensa Asociada*. Overcoming factionalism so as to extend the benefits of a "culture of print" to outlying communities throughout the region was dear to the hearts of member editors. In José Escobar's view, the betterment of the masses was "the true mission of the honest press" (Escobar 1896b, 1).

It must be kept in mind that the emergence of a culture of print in Mexican-origin communities across the region remained an expression of resistance and opposition to Anglo American political, social, and cultural hegemony in the Southwest after 1848. The discourse activated by the Nuevomexicano press—rebellious and oppositional—remained subject to the maceration of the "cultural other" by the dominant group. Contained and never totally free, the discourse of *Prensa Asociada* member editors sounded angry and defensive to Anglos, but it was essential to preserving Nuevomexicano cultural integrity.

Writing in March 1892, Manuel C. de Baca of *El Sol de Mayo* (Las Vegas) saw in the existence of *La Prensa Asociada* an antidote to social and cultural erasure:

> Our people will come to see that the New Mexican [*Neo-Mexicano*] Press Association will take up the shield so as to do its duty, and this without causing harm or injury to anyone. The time is right for Hispanos to bring to an end the repeated injuries that all too frequently are directed against them. (*Nuestra raza lo verá que La Prensa Asociada neo-mexicana tomará el escudo en sus manos para hacer su deber sin necesidad de maltratar ni injuriar a nadie, pero si aseguramos que el tiempo está muy oportuno cuando los hispano-americanos pondrán fin á las repetidas injurias que muy comunmente se le cometen.*) [de Baca 1892, 1]

Grounded in these concerns, *La Prensa Asociada Hispano-Americana* assumed the role of guarantor for the community it served:

> [T]he Spanish-speaking press, by nature and by consequence, should be the trustee and defender of the race it represents. . . . (*[L]a prensa hispano-americana es naturalmente y por consecuencia debe ser el fideicomisano y defensor del linaje que representa. . . .*) [de Baca 1892, 1]

In the decade prior to the formation of *La Prensa Asociada*, Spanish-language editors often took and reprinted items from one another. They also spent much time citing the works of fellow journalists, which they praised or derided as occasions dictated. *La Prensa Asociada* had the immediate effect of enhancing the exchange of information among its membership. The network of syndication created by the association improved dialogical exchange among member editors and provided Nuevomexicano editors with a steady and inexhaustible source of texts from member newspapers in northern Mexico which, in turn, reprinted items from Latin American sources. This work had the effect of reinvigorating Nuevomexicano cultural identity and discourse. The organization also pressed railroad, telegraph, and postal officials to provide association members and the communities they represented with improved service. The full extent of the work of *La Prensa Asociada* attains greatest acuity in the activity of individual editors and is best represented in the impact wrought by the enterprises they established along the Río Grande.

I. Discursive Agency and *La Prensa Asociada*

José Segura, the editor of *El Boletín Popular* in Santa Fe, was a founding member of *La Prensa Asociada.* During his lifetime Segura held no prominent political posts and exercised no other profession apart from that of a journalist. Mention of Segura in newsprint always appears in connection with his work as an editor, a fact that makes it possible to conclude that José Segura emerges as the first full-time professional Nuevomexicano journalist.

Throughout its years in publication, *El Boletín Popular* was the most constant and long-standing voice in Nuevomexicano journalism. Its impact and presence in Santa Fe was felt by all segments of the community. On the matter of *El Boletín's* following among Nuevomexicanos, F. Stanley remarked:

> *El Boletín Popular* commenced publication in 1885 and continued to 1910. This gave lie to the theory that New Mexicans did not want Spanish reading or that they couldn't read Spanish. This latter may be true of the post-war generations of the two World Wars, but up to 1912 many Santa Feans read and wrote in Spanish. [1965, 171]

As a response to *El Boletín's* growing importance among the Spanish-speaking, W. H. Manderfield, owner-editor of the *Santa Fe New Mexican,* found it necessary to publish a Spanish-language counterpart to his paper. In competing with *El Boletín Popular,* Manderfield employed several Nuevomexicanos to edit *El Nuevo Mexicano,* which began publication in 1890.

El Boletín Popular, which described itself as "*Periódico político, literario y de anuncios*" (A Literary, Political Newspaper with Advertisements), provided readers with local, regional, national, and international news. In addition, *El Boletín Popular* published a wide array of literary works, devoting a segment of every issue to literature. Literary offerings ranged from submissions by local Nuevomexicano poets, to works by Mexican writers in the Southwest, to international works of literature. The work of renowned authors from Latin America and Spain was especially evident in the paper. The careful editing and attention to detail that José Segura brought to the paper is evidence of the improved quality of Spanish-language publications in the 1890s.

El Boletín Popular soon came to reflect the concerns and aspirations of Nuevomexicanos of distinct classes and walks of life. Many of the most prominent voices in the Nuevomexicano community spoke through *El Boletín Popular.* The paper featured the works of J. M. H. Alarid, Eleuterio Baca, Benjamín M. Read, Camilo Padilla, and many others. Through editorials and commentaries, José Segura contributed some of the most important distillations of Nuevomexicano thought during the period. Segura embodied the aspirations of a generation intent on leaving a cultural legacy to its descendants. He was a member of *La Sociedad Literaria y de Debates de la Ciudad de Santa Fe* (The Literary and Debate Society of the City of Santa Fe), a literary arts group made up of Nuevomexicanos that met regularly to discuss literary topics, engage in debate, and promote the general cultural welfare of the capital city.

Segura's Jesuit education accounted in part for his knowledge of world literature, particularly that of Latin America, and his extensive experience and travel in Mexico and the eastern United States made him particularly adept at recognizing consequential and important literary and cultural trends, which he then imparted to his readership. As part of *El Boletín*'s efforts in this regard, the paper often noted the arrival of significant and important publications from the eastern United States, Mexico, and other Latin American countries. In May 1894, Segura shared with his readership news of the arrival of the Mexican modernist journal, *La Revista Azul.* Summarizing the importance of the journal, Segura suggests:

> The weekly needs no recommendation other than to say that it is edited by the Mexican writers Señores Gutiérrez Nájera, Carlos Díaz Dufoo, Luis G. Urbina and others. (*No necesita más recomendación que decir que está redactada por los literatos mexicanos Sres. Gutiérrez Nájera, Carlos Díaz Dufoo, Luis G. Urbina y otros.*) [Segura 1894]

Segura, like a number of other *periodiqueros,* served as a conduit and custodian of a cultural epistemology that tied New Mexico to other parts of the Spanish-speaking world, and in spite of the fact that cultural or literary events were few and far between in New Mexico, *El Boletín Popular* made every effort to call serious attention to them. For example, Segura noted the visit of the Mexican writer and diplomat, Vicente Riva Palacio, to Santa Fe in July 1886.[3] Riva Palacio, an adherent of romantic dicta in literature, was well-known and well-published in Mexico. Segura worked to keep alive the memory of the Mexican writer's chance visit to Santa Fe in follow-up reports and in the frequent publication of Riva Palacio's poetry in the columns of *El Boletín Popular.* José Segura not only drew from a Mexican literary foundation, but frequently utilized the presses of *El Boletín Popular* to disseminate the work of local authors. For example, Eusebio Chacón's novellas *El hijo de la tempestad* and *Tras la tormenta la calma* were issued in a slim volume by *La Imprenta Tipográfica de El Boletín* (The *El Boletín* Popular Press] in 1892.[4] As a publisher, Segura sought to display *nativo* achievement and increase the cultural potential of Spanish-speaking communities in the region.

Language, culture, and ethnicity provided a foundation for the unity of action that drove *La Prensa Asociada*'s cultural agenda. The resulting dialogue and exchange fostered mutual support, thus encouraging the work and writing of association members. In its early years *La Prensa Asociada* encouraged professional fraternalism among member editors. A communiqué from Washington, D.C. forwarded by Camilo Padilla to Enrique H. Salazar, the editor of *El Independiente* of Las Vegas, demonstrates the high degree of solidarity among members of *La Prensa Asociada*. Expressing pleasure at having a source to inform him in Washington of happenings in his native New Mexico, Padilla encourages the work of his colleague:

> Let nothing divert you from the path you have taken—neither politics, nor self-interest—and if by misfortune you should find the need to return to private life, you can do so with the sweet satisfaction that you have done your duty as a patriot—as does the man whose heart beats in consonance with the sentiments of a people. (*No dejes que nada te desvié de la senda que has tomado— ni la política, ni ningún interés particular—y si por mala suerte algún día te ves obligado a retirarte a la vida privada lo harás al menos con la dulce satisfacción de que has hecho tu deber como patriota—como lo hace el hombre cuyo corazón palpita en consonancia con los sentimientos de un pueblo.*) [Padilla 1894]

Padilla's words acknowledge the high regard New Mexicans had for Enrique H. Salazar (1858–1915), an important and long-standing voice among *Prensa Asociada* members. Salazar, along with an associate, Nestor Montoya, had founded *La Voz del Pueblo* in Santa Fe in 1889. In 1890 Salazar moved the paper to Las Vegas, New Mexico, sixty miles from the capital, and later sold his interest in *La Voz* to rising businessman, Félix Martínez. Salazar remained in journalism, launching *El Independiente* in Las Vegas in 1894. Salazar's front-page editorial essays consistently offered a critical assessment of the social decline he believed resulted from Anglo American economic and political domination. In his many editorials, Salazar urged Nuevomexicanos: "Let us end that fiction of racial inferiority which our enemies use to label us" (*Acabemos con la ficción de inferioridad de raza con que nos motejan nuestros amigos*) (Salazar 1895b). Salazar often opined that ethnic defacement was a root cause of the political and economic marginalization of the Spanish-speaking people. Salazar's editorial opinions are among the clearest articulations of *La Prensa Asociada*'s socio-cultural concerns:

> Many are the discerning observers who note and comment on the anomalous position currently occupied by the Hispano population of this Territory, [and] with just reason are surprised by what is happening. This awe stems from the fact that the Hispanos are a majority, constituting four-fifths of the population of New Mexico, yet their social and political importance in most cases does not match

[their] numerical superiority—it is necessary to confess that [its importance] diminishes daily. (*Muchas son las personas observadoras que notan y comentan de la anómala posición que actualmente guarda la población hispano-americana de este Territorio, y con sobrada razón se admiran de las cosas que están pasando. Esta admiración proviene de hecho que aunque los hispanoamericanos forman la mayoría e incluyen las cuatro quintas partes de la población de Nuevo México, sin embargo, su importancia social y política en la mayoría de los casos no es en nada equivalente a su superioridad numérica, y preciso es confesar que cada día va disminuyendo.*) [Salazar 1895a]

Active at the outset of the *periodiquero* movement, Camilo Padilla would devote his life's energy to the work of educating the populace of New Mexico by means of the press. As one of the last remaining Spanish-language publishers in New Mexico, Padilla struggled on with the work begun by *La Prensa Asociada* as the organization's last president. Padilla, owner-editor of *El Mosquito*, a paper he issued at Mora, New Mexico, and Félix Martínez, then owner of *La Voz del Pueblo*, were selected from the floor of *La Prensa Asociada*'s first organizational meeting in 1891 to draft a set of resolutions to guide the work of the association. The Padilla-Martínez resolutions speak to the failure of society to insure the rights guaranteed to Nuevomexicanos under the Constitution:

[I]nasmuch as the credo of society and of prevalent affairs in the United States of America have not proved satisfactory at this present time at keeping the standing which the rights of the American constitution guarantees us, it is incumbent upon us to form associations so that our capacities increase in equal measure to those of the rest of our fellow citizens with the goal that the dignity of our forebears and descendants be justly respected. . . . (*Por cuanto el dogma de la sociedad y negocios prevalente en los Estados Unidos de América, en la presente época, no ha satisfecho que á fin de guarder el rango que los derechos de la constitución americana nos garantiza se nos hace incumbente formar asociaciones para que nuestras fuerzas medren á la par de los demas de nuestros conciudadanos y con el objeto de que la dignidad de nuestra antecedencia y descendencia sea debidamente respetada. . . .*) [La Prensa Asociada 1892]

In addressing the matter of equal representation for Mexican Americans under the U. S. Constitution, the Padilla-Martínez resolutions committed *La Prensa Asociada* to public advocacy, thus making *La Prensa Asociada* the first professional organization among the Spanish-speaking peoples of the Southwest to embrace a civil rights platform.

Camilo Padilla was among the best read and most seasoned travelers of his generation. His many trips to the U.S. east coast came to represent some of the earliest visits by Nuevomexicanos to the nation's seat of government. In 1890, Padilla traveled to Washington, D.C. in the capacity of private secretary to Antonio Joseph, New Mexico's territorial delegate to the U.S. Congress. In the early years of the decade, Padilla had interspersed his visits to Washington as Joseph's secretary with the time he spent working on newspapers in Mora County when Congress was not in session. From 1898 to 1901 Padilla resided continuously in the nation's capital.

In the early 1890s Padilla began to lay the foundation for his own work in journalism. From July to September 1890, he edited *La Gaceta de Mora*. In December 1891, he began publication of his own paper with the feisty name *El Mosquito* and added its voice to the growing number of Prensa Asociada newspapers. Padilla moved to El Paso, Texas, in 1907, where he began the publication of *Revista Ilustrada*, which became the most important and best developed contemporary publication issued by any Nuevomexicano editor and publisher. The complete record of Padilla's work as a publisher has yet to emerge, and information regarding the issuance of his magazine is sketchy and incomplete. Few issues of his magazine made their way to libraries or archival repositories. The publishing history of *Revista Ilustrada*, which was issued at both Santa Fe and El Paso, is further complicated by the fact that the magazine also appeared under the title *Sancho Panza*. Padilla reverted to using the name *Revista Ilustrada* and continued to publish under that title in Santa Fe through the first decade of the twentieth century. Sometime in the 1920s, Padilla once again returned to El Paso and began to reissue *Revista Ilustrada*. Remaining there until the summer of 1925, Padilla moved the magazine for the last time to Santa Fe. There, *Revista Ilustrada* remained in publication until Padilla's death in 1933.

Padilla's collaborations with Nuevomexicano periodicals began early in his life. His first submissions to Spanish-language newspapers are important on a number of levels. Among these is a letter to the editor of *La Voz del Pueblo* in Las Vegas in May of 1889. Printed with the title "Crónica nacional," the communiqué was meant to provide *La Voz del Pueblo* and its readership with news and information from Washington, D.C., where Padilla resided. During the early part of the decade, Padilla contributed many such items to Santa Fe's most established newspaper, *El Boletín Popular*. Through such communiqués—including editorial opinions, travel narratives and cross-cultural observations—Padilla came to be regarded as the paper's official correspondent in Washington.

Nuevomexicanos had little information and few means to make sense of the enormity of the socioeconomic disparity that existed between New Mexico and the rest of the United States. This lack of understanding was exacerbated by the air of haughtiness and superiority that conditioned Anglo American interactions with the native populations of the territory. Padilla obviously sensed the importance of issuing his communiqués from Washington, where the experience of travel and fellowship with other Nuevomexicanos living in Washington continually returned him to a deeper reverence for New Mexico as cultural homeland:

> [W]hen, finding ourselves far away from our beloved homeland, we thought often about this land which today, like an old plow is on the auction block; when, in company of the young patriot, Maximiliano Luna, we contemplated the future of our peaceful and righteous people, and contemplated that which has arrived here like the plague—the discord of our fellow citizens. (*[C]uando lejos de nuestra patria adorada nos encontrábamos y pensábamos sobre este suelo que está hoy, como un arado viejo, en el mercado; cuando en compañía del joven patriota Maximiliano Luna, contemplábamos lo que aguardaba á nuestro pacífico y buen pueblo, lo que ha llegado como una plaga aquí, la discordia entre nuestros compatriotas.*) [Padilla 1892]

Padilla distilled his reflections of the cross-cultural interactions between "Americanos" and Nuevomexicanos in literary form in short stories like "*Camilo en Virginia*" (1889) and "*Historia original neo-mexicana: Pobre Emilio*" (1890). These items, published in the local press, began to delineate the social and cultural boundaries that conditioned interpersonal relationships between Nuevomexicanos and Anglo Americans.

II. A Voice for the People:
La Compañía Publicista de La Voz

Félix Martínez, the owner and proprietor of *La Voz del Pueblo* during most years of its publication, commanded great presence as a speaker in the nineteenth-century vein of political oratory in New Mexico. As far as can be determined, however, he authored few literary or editorial texts. His contribution to Nuevomexicano journalism was nonetheless an extremely important one from the standpoint of his work as proprietor and entrepreneur. Martínez was present at the founding of *La Prensa Asociada* and helped draft the organization's resolutions, becoming the organization's first vice-president in 1891.

After purchasing *La Voz del Pueblo* from Enrique H. Salazar, Martínez became proprietor and editor-in-chief of the first successful Nuevomexicano printing company to emerge from Spanish-language newspaper activity of the 1890s. Martínez

fig 1   Offices of *La Voz del Pueblo,* Las Vegas, New Mexico, ca. 1900. Used by permission of the Citizens' Committee for Historical Preservation, Las Vegas, New Mexico.

ran the business end of the paper until his death in 1916. A shrewd businessman and investor, he employed Ezequiel C. de Baca and Antonio Lucero as associate editors, bringing to the staff of *La Voz del Pueblo* the finest and best-prepared journalists in the territory, providing them with a modern, well-staffed printing room. Housed in one of the largest and most impressive buildings in (Anglo) East Las Vegas, *La Voz del Pueblo* remained a profitable business. Published for some thirty-seven years, the venture marked new possibilities for Nuevomexicano success in the field of printing and publishing. For example, the La Voz Publishing Company published several early works of Mexican American literature including Manuel C. de Baca's 1896 novelette, *Historia de Vicente Silva: Sus crímenes y retribuciones.* In many respects, Félix Martínez personified the potential and possibility of a new era in which a Nuevomexicano sense of cultural integrity might emerge intact and be compatible with the institutions and technological advances of the age. Given Martínez's singular accomplishments amid the great inequities that continued to be experienced by the bulk of Nuevomexicanos, his death in 1916 represented a void that was not to be soon filled (Necrology 1916, 286).

A populist, Martínez openly supported *Las Gorras Blancas* ("white caps") and *El Partido del Pueblo Unido*. These popular movements had their base of support in the poorest sectors of Nuevomexicano society and among those groups directly impacted by Anglo American encroachment on the communal land grants, by biases (toward *mexicanos*) in the legal system, by a dual wage system in employment for Anglos and *mexicanos*, and by unequal living standards between an Anglo East Las Vegas and *mexicano* West Las Vegas. These causes found strong advocacy in *La Voz del Pueblo*, a paper that was outspoken in its demand for change and reform. By focusing on these highly charged issues, *La Voz del Pueblo* drew social disparity into sharp relief. The paper's pointed and direct criticism of class- and race-based inequity would not be without cost, as *La Voz del Pueblo* would become the object of heated reactionary attacks from within and without the *mexicano* community. Martínez himself was forced to leave Las Vegas in 1898 and moved most of his business interests to El Paso, Texas.

In El Paso he held varied investments in real estate, banking, public works, newspapers, and water-reclamation projects. He also remained owner and principal investor in *La Voz del Pueblo* and continued to invest heavily in English and Spanish newspapers. In Las Vegas, he held stock in the English-language *Optic*, and at Albuquerque he was among the founders of the *Albuquerque Tribune-Citizen* Company. He published the *El Paso Daily News* from 1899 to 1907 and was a founder of the *El Paso Times-Herald*. Martínez's presence in Nuevomexicano journalism turns away from creative, literary, and cultural endeavors and pulls toward the entrepreneurial, political, and business end of such activity. Martínez's work removed writers and journalists from the day-to-day concerns of publishing and afforded them access to an established forum from which they were able to wage a campaign of social and cultural advancement for Nuevomexicanos.

Ezequiel C. de Baca and Antonio Lucero, associate editors of *La Voz del Pueblo*, were lifelong friends and colleagues. As children they attended the same schools, and as young men they studied with the same instructors at the Jesuit College of Las Vegas. They shared similar ideals and sought similar channels to put them into practice. As members of *La Prensa Asociada* they served their community as public spokesmen, leaders, and thinkers. Signing on to the staff of *La Voz del Pueblo* in 1891, Ezequiel and Antonio would find themselves at the center of contentious territorial politics for the next twenty-five years. Both would emerge from the political strife of these years as two of only a handful of Nuevomexicanos holding elected offices in the newly organized state government.

In his initial years at *La Voz*, Ezequiel worked as a reporter and copy editor. Like others of his generation, however, he was particularly interested in fomenting education in the literary and dramatic arts. Ezequiel himself was a member of several educational circles. The Nuevomexicano community in Las Vegas had organized *La Sociedad Literaria y de Ayuda Mutua* (The Literary and Mutual Aid

Society), *La Sociedad por la Protección de la Educación* (Society for the Protection of Education), and *El Club Dramático de Las Vegas* (The Las Vegas Drama Club). As a member of these groups and through *La Voz*, he supported efforts to educate the populace at large in the verbal and dramatic arts.

The altruism, lofty sentiments, and ennobling notions of art and literature fomented by these organizations were offset by cross-cultural conflict, racial strife, and the intrigue of local and territorial politics. Fabiola Cabeza de Baca would later write of her uncle, "He was a slave to the cause of the poor people.... In those days being a member of the political party to which my uncle belonged was indeed martyrdom" ([1954] 1994, 163).

Ezequiel's older brother, Manuel C. de Baca, proprietor and editor of *El Sol de Mayo* from 1891 to 1892, was at the opposite end of the political spectrum. Ezequiel favored the populist sentiments of *La Voz del Pueblo,* which vowed to defend the interest of *"las masas de hombres pobres"* (the masses of the poor) and *Las Gorras Blancas.*

A brief period of reconciliation for the two brothers came on the heels of what would become known as the Billy Green matter. The incident was one of many that strained racial relations in San Miguel County. The disturbance came to a head when Sheriff Lorenzo López and several citizens attempted to apprehend Billy Green, an Anglo ruffian with a history of violence, for the murder of Nestor Gallegos. The authority of Hispano lawmen involved in the arrest was clearly undermined when, according to Rosenbaum, "East Las Vegas Marshall T. F. Clay hurried across the Gallinas River to bring the three (Green and accomplices) into the more congenial custody of Anglo, 'new town'" (1981, 134). Adding injury to insult, a contingent of Army regulars was set against the *mexicano* residents of Las Vegas in what can only be described as a race war (Rosenbaum 1981, 134).

For Nuevomexicanos, the Billy Green matter made apparent the need to set aside factionalism in favor of cultural and ethnic unity that would end such abuse. Hispano leaders urged solidarity. Manuel Salazar y Otero of *El Sol de Mayo* ran an editorial praising the work of Félix Martínez and, in front-page editorials such as *"Unión y prosperidad: El pueblo de San Miguel se une bajo el gremio de un solo partido* (The People of San Miguel Unite Under the Guidance of a Single Party) (4 August 1894), Ezequiel C. de Baca formalized the resolve of *La Prensa Asociada* to steer public sentiment toward unified political and cultural aims.

In his work as journalist and spokesman for the Nuevomexicano community, Ezequiel C. de Baca had been at the center of political life in San Miguel County for twenty years before seeking public office. When finally he did so, it would be as representative and spokesman of the Nuevomexicano community in the context of New Mexico's bid for statehood. C. de Baca wrestled the gubernatorial race from the Republican candidate Holm O. Bursum in November 1916. Unfortunately, Ezequiel C. de Baca died of "pernicious anemia" forty-nine days after taking office as the second governor of the state of New Mexico. Fellow journalist Antonio Lucero delivered the eulogy at the state funeral. Lucero stressed the steadfast commitment Ezequiel had shown to his Nuevomexicano roots. Citing C. de Baca's own words, Lucero invoked the spirit of honor which had guided his friend's life and work: "I die poor, but I lived in honor."

III. Linking Aztlán: Binationalism and *La Prensa Asociada*

With some exceptions, the majority of Spanish-language journalists working in New Mexico at the end of the nineteenth century, as might be expected, were native-born, but the strength and vigor of the press movement drew journalists from other Spanish-speaking regions of the Southwest and other countries. Pedro García de la Lama, editor of Albuquerque's *La Opinión Pública* from 1892–1895, was born in Mexico. Oliveros V. Aoy, who worked for a time at *La Voz del Pueblo,* and José Jordí, who edited *La Bandera Americana* (Albuquerque) and other newspapers in the post-statehood era, were both natives of Spain. Another Spanish immigrant, José Montaner, settled in Taos and served for over a decade as editor of *La Revista de Taos,* a paper with a circulation of 5,000 subscribers. Montaner's assimilation into Nuevomexicano society, coupled with his years as editor of *La Revista de Taos,* laid the basis for a successful career in state politics.

Víctor L. Ochoa, Teófilo Ocaña Caballero, Rafael and Elfego N. Ronquillo, and José Antonio Escajeda were journalists who had a profound identification with northern Mexico and the border area of west Texas and New Mexico, and each left his imprint on Spanish-language journalism on both sides of the border.

La Prensa Asociada's first president was Víctor L. Ochoa. His election came within months of having moved his paper, *El Hispano-Americano,* from El Paso, Texas to Las Vegas, New Mexico. Under Ochoa's direction *La Prensa Asociada* immediately began to press forth a proactive agenda to secure the full participation of the Spanish-speaking in the affairs of government. At its May 9, 1892 meeting in Albuquerque, *La Prensa Asociada* passed numerous measures, among them one petitioning the territorial legislature to require that all legal and judicial documents be published in Spanish, enabling the Nuevomexicano community "to inform itself with knowledge that concerns its rights as citizens" (*se ilustre y esté en conocimiento de todo aquello que atañe en sus derechos de ciudadanos*) (*La Prensa Asociada Hispano-Americana* 1892b).

An activist as well as journalist, Ochoa soon found himself involved in the politics of emerging class struggle in Mexico and did not remain president of *La Prensa Asociada.* Newspapers in New Mexico reported his departure from *El Hispano-Americano* in Las Vegas in 1894. Ochoa, it was reported, had joined the revolutionary struggle in Chihuahua in opposing the Porfirio Díaz regime.

Reports of "the knight errant of the Río Grande," as he became known, continued to appear in New Mexico's newspapers for many years after his presumed death at the hands of *carrancistas*. Some reports had him aiding Villa's cause in the north, others had him serving time in a federal prison in New York for violating intervention laws and for inciting anti-Díaz revolutionary movements along the border.

The newspaper movement in New Mexico was linked to editors throughout the Southwest. In particular, the El Paso and Las Cruces area became important conduits for the exchange of information into north central New Mexico from the border area and beyond. Jesús Enrique Sosa and José Escobar, both born in Mexico, were members of *La Prensa Asociada Hispano-Americana*, and their work and presence contributed greatly to its improvement.

Escobar appears to have immigrated to New Mexico in the late 1880s. Otherwise, little is known regarding his place of birth, education, or formal training as a journalist. José Escobar provided a letter to immigration officials in El Paso on June 1, 1889, in support of the legal immigration of compatriot and journalist, Jesús Enrique Sosa. The letter establishes the fact that Escobar had been living in the United States for a time and that he was inclined to support the immigration of other journalists to the Southwest. Ostensibly, Escobar continued to assist Jesús Enrique Sosa, who went on to found successful newspapers at Las Cruces, Socorro, Albuquerque, Santa Fe, and Mora, New Mexico.

Little is known regarding José Escobar's activities before 1889. Just as perplexing is the abrupt end of any mention of Escobar in New Mexico newspapers after 1898, the year Escobar parted company with *El Combate*, a Socorro, New Mexico newspaper he was editing (Meyer 1978). The paucity of information on Escobar encourages conjecture as to why and to what end Escobar spent some ten or more years in New Mexico, only to vanish from the area with little more ever being said of him. Whether Escobar's move to New Mexico was initially motivated by political, economic, or personal motives remains unclear.

The quality and professionalism of his work suggests that he was trained in journalism and letters before coming to the United States. Entering New Mexico, he would have found a ready and active climate in which to advance his career in journalism. Escobar worked with various publications in towns and cities both in New Mexico and in Colorado and edited no less than fourteen different newspapers in ten separate communities.

Several suppositions can be advanced to explain Escobar's frequent moves and abrupt departures from many of the newspapers with which he associated. As a professional journalist, he was in a position to offer much-needed expertise to fledgling newspapers that were springing up virtually in every Spanish-speaking town in New Mexico and was induced by competing papers to change jobs often. Other evidence, however, suggests that Escobar was a problematic figure and that his ideas brought him into contention with the owners and proprietors of several of the newspapers he was hired to edit (Meyer 1978). Still other news reports from the period paint Escobar in the off-light of a charlatan and a fraud.

Escobar attended the 1891 organizational meeting of *La Prensa Asociada* in Las Vegas in his capacity as editor of the Trinidad, Colorado newspaper, *El Progreso*. After working at several newspapers, he returned to Colorado in January 1896, to become editor of *Las Dos Repúblicas*, a prestigious Denver-based publication bankrolled by Casimiro Barela, an influential and well-to-do member of the Hispanic community of southern Colorado. A state senator from Las Animas County, Barela was appointed Consul General for the Mexican Consulate at Denver in 1896. *Las Dos Repúblicas* obviously benefited from the capital outlay provided by Barela and from the support of the Mexican Consulate. Superior in quality to many English and Spanish publications, *Las Dos Repúblicas* was published on a state-of-the-art press and illustrated with "magnificent engravings," giving Escobar cause to boast:

> I dare say, [these qualities] place this publication, if not in the lead, at least among the first line of publications in the West of this great North American Republic. (*Por último, la idea de ilustrar este semanario con magníficos grabados, complemento es, que viene a colocar al mismo, si no al frente, por lo menos en la primera fila de las publicaciones del Oeste de esta gran República Norte Americana.*) [Escobar 1896a, 1]

Whatever his personal character and temperament, there is no doubt that José Escobar was an editor of great talent and abilities and that he was well-educated and well read. His time at *Las Dos Repúblicas* represents the pinnacle of his activity and achievements as editor, essayist, and poet. While there he managed to publish a superior periodical dedicated to an array of binational issues on the industrial, commercial and scientific potential of trade and exchange between Mexico and the United States, while also managing to systematically publish some of the finest editorial opinions launched by a Spanish-language editor on the condition of the Mexican-origin communities in the Southwest.

In his program for *Las Dos Repúblicas*, Escobar outlines his aspirations, citing the utilitarian function of the paper: "This newspaper will dedicate itself principally to developing to the degree possible, the commercial sectors of these two great republics, [Mexico and the United States] and more particularly those of this state, Colorado, with principal markets in Mexico." While acknowledging that his patronage came from Casimiro Barela and other Mexican and U.S. entrepreneurs, Escobar also declared his objective to publish important works of literature and art, stating,

[W]e are trying to make this weekly a useful and interesting sheet for all social classes, and that, upon its columns the arts, science, literature and novelties each have their appropriate place. (*[H]emos procurado hacer de este semanano una hoja de utilidad é interés para todas las clases sociales, y que, en sus columnas, las artes, las ciencas, la literature y las novedades tienen sus secciones correspondientes.*) [Escobar 1896a, 1]

Las Dos Repúblicas (*"Periódico comercial, de artes, ciencia y literatura"*) [A Periodical of Business, Art, Science, and Literature]) was a six-page, eight-column weekly. Escobar, a published poet, included the following literary-arts departments: "*Plumadas,*" a section of news briefs of an historical, literary, and scientific bent; "*Variedades,*" a series of literary selections, poems, epigrams, etc.; and "*El Folletín,*" which regularly reprinted historical texts from Mexican and New Mexican papers. In its short life, the paper managed to disseminate an impressive number of historical and literary texts, including works by Eusebio Chacón and much of Escobar's own published poetry.[5] That Escobar was directly responsible for the high quality and professionalism of *Las Dos Repúblicas* is apparent in the marked drop in the overall quality of the paper following his departure from the newspaper in July of 1896.

IV. *La Prensa Asociada* in Post-Statehood New Mexico

La Prensa Asociada brought together a diverse cadre of journalists, editors, poets, and writers who were united by a common language and culture, and whose literary agency was keyed to the social, educational, and cultural progress of the Spanish-speaking residents of the Southwest. Nuevomexicanos who had entered journalism with the surge of Spanish-language publication in the 1890s continued to publish well beyond statehood. The long-standing associations and years of shared commitment to the betterment of their community and society created strong and lasting bonds of fraternalism and camaraderie among newspaper editors across the Southwest. The politics of the statehood movement, however, would represent a far more serious challenge to cultural unity then had the ethnic animosities and political cleavages of the territorial period.

After statehood for New Mexico, *La Prensa Asociada* began to experience waning membership, reorganization, inactivity, disunity, and dissolution of purpose. All, however, was not lost. Newspaper historian Porter Stratton affirms that new efforts to revive *La Prensa Asociada* surfaced on the eve of statehood: "Such efforts were renewed in 1911, and an association was formed at Albuquerque. Nestor Montoya of *La Bandera Americana* of Albuquerque was elected president, and Elfego Baca of the Albuquerque *Opinión Pública* became treasurer" (Stratton

1969, 66). The reorganization of *La Prensa Asociada* laid the foundation for the establishment of the present-day press organization in New Mexico: "In 1912 this association in cooperation with eastern New Mexico weekly editors organized a newsmen's organization which later became the present New Mexico Press Association" (Stratton 1969, 66). Conversely, the ideological restraint implicit in the organization's realignment signaled a departure from *La Prensa Asociada*'s original mission to bring to an end "the repeated injuries that are commonly committed against it (the Spanish-speaking community)" (*las repetidas injurias que muy comunmente se le cometen al pueblo hispano americano*) (de Baca 1892). Members were split along ideological lines that pitted cultural guardians against those who viewed assimilation as a positive alternative.

A conciliatory gesture to include eastern New Mexico [Anglo] weeklies in the organization was led by Nestor Montoya of Old Albuquerque. Montoya's paper, *La Bandera Americana,* had a more accommodationist policy with regard to ethnicity and advocated the absorption of Nuevomexicanos into what one editor labeled "*el gran mole que es la ciudadanía de los Estados Unidos americanos,*" or the U.S. melting pot.

A salutation in the first issue of *La Bandera Americana* left no doubt that Montoya espoused the gradual absorption (read assimilation) of Hispanos into the body politic of the United States, an idea echoed in the emblematic patriotism of the paper's name. *La Bandera Americana* promised to advocate for the education of greater numbers of New Mexicans "to bolster as much as possible, as our feeble efforts permit, the education of the masses of the people" (*a alentar en cuanto sea posible, á segun alcanzen nuestras débiles fuerzas, la educación de las masas del pueblo*) (Salutoria 1901).

In saying so, however, Montoya also placed the onus of responsibility for progress on the community itself, asserting that model behavior was necessary

> to prepare our future citizens to firmly take in hand the reins and sovereignty of a state of the American Union and to discharge and enjoy our privileges as citizens of this great Republic. (*para asi preparer á nuestros futuros ciudadanos a empuñar con firmeza las riendas y soberanía de Estado de la Unión Americana y a desempeñar y gozar de nuestros privilegios como ciudadanos de esta gran República.*) [Montoya 1892]

Montoya's stand signaled a change from the generally accepted view espoused by *La Prensa Asociada* regarding the maintenance of the Spanish language and the manner in which Nuevomexicano culture might be situated within plural New Mexico. While earlier journalists and writers never discounted the importance of learning and using English, they nevertheless held to the view that Spanish should have an equal place in the institutions of society—particularly in public education. In Montoya's mind, the language issue had become "*un asunto delicado,*" a matter requiring careful consideration, "*pues este particular merece la más delicada atención en vista de nuestra nacionalidad Americana*" (since this item merits very careful attention in view of our American citizenship) (Salutoria 1901).

La Bandera Americana encouraged the use of English in the public schools and among all classes of Nuevomexicanos, suggesting to its largely monolingual Spanish readership that "we believe that there is not a single man in the Territory that will oppose our assertion to generalize that language" (*creemos que no habrá un solo hombre en el Territorio que oponga nuestro aserto en generalizar tal idioma*) (Salutoria 1901). Likewise, Montoya's pledge to advocate for statehood and seek greater educational advantages for Nuevomexicanos appears more tempered than assertions voiced by *La Prensa Asociada* in the past. In prior decades, editors had seen the establishment of a vigorous press as the means to "educate the populace," but Montoya, noting *La Bandera Americana*'s own "feeble efforts" in this regard, now seemed to substantiate the idea that the press alone could not, in and of itself, enlighten, educate, and inform the masses of Nuevomexicanos. In Montoya's mind, political pragmatism and economic development were the keys to Nuevomexicano opportunity and prosperity in the coming years of the new century. Evoking a kind of economic determinism, Montoya downplayed ethnic and cultural identification, arguing instead for the development of New Mexico's natural resources, since

> *nuestras riquezas en todos los tres ramos aludidos son incalculables y solo se necesita inducir la capital para explotarlos para cambiar la faz y porvenir de nuestro suelo y tracer la felicidad de nuestros habitantes* (it is accepted that our riches in the three areas mentioned are immeasurable and that all that is required to exploit them is the investment of capital which will change the face and future of our land and make its inhabitants happy). [Salutoria 1901]

By the 1920s, Nuevomexicano editors registered pessimism concerning the future of the Spanish-language press in New Mexico and how it might assist in maintaining the sociocultural standing of the community in whose name it spoke. In early 1928, José Montaner, editor of *La Revista de Taos,* acted to counter the apathy and discord among Nuevomexicano publishers. Montaner called for a meeting of Nuevomexicano editors. Representatives from ten of the thirteen remaining Spanish-language newspapers in the state attended an organizational meeting held on February 23, 1928 in Santa Fe. Reorganized as *La Asociación de la Prensa Hispana en Nuevo México,* the group elected José Montaner as the group's interim president, and A. J. Martínez of Las Vegas as interim secretary (*La Unión* 1928).

Given the tenor of the late 1920s and the accumulated frustration at improving the prospects for Spanish-language journalism in the post-statehood period, it is no wonder that the remaining Spanish-language editors in New Mexico continued to express a growing uneasiness and pessimism about the future. In June 1928, Camilo Padilla was elected president of *La Asociación*. Assuming office, he noted several pernicious trends affecting Spanish-language journalism; nonetheless, he made a spirited appeal to bilingualism in the state, repudiating the accusations of assimilationists who contended that the retention of Spanish in public usage was un-American:

> Reading or purchasing periodicals in Spanish does not mean that the official language of this great nation will be damaged in the very least. To think this is to cause injury to ourselves, so much so that [it would be] as if any one of us [once] knowing the two languages mentioned, would refuse to learn French, German, Greek, Latin, etc., at a University. What is abundant does not cause harm, as the well-known adage declares. (*El leer á comprar periódicos en español, no quiere decir que el idioma oficial de este gran país vaya a lesionarse en lo más mínimo. Pensar en esta forma, sería causarnos una injuria nosotros mismos, porque sería tanto que por el hecho que cualquiera de nosotros supiéramos los dos idiomas mencionadas, rehusarnos aprender en una Universidad, el francés, el alemán, el griego, el latín, etc. Lo que abunda no daña, dice un proverbio vulgar.*) [Padilla 1928]

When Felipe Maximiliano Chacón became editor of *La Bandera Americana*, he warned that the Spanish-language press needed to assert its worth or it would disappear. Chacón pointed to *El Independiente* of Las Vegas as an example of the press in decline. Spanish-language newspapers, Chacón cautioned, had become exceedingly reliant on political affiliations for support and advertisement. In Chacón's view the lofty ideals of non-alignment once espoused by the paper's founder, Enrique H. Salazar, were compromised. *El Independiente's* columns, according to Chacón, were now filled with unabashed political diatribe:

> It would seem that Hispano journalism is a means to exploit fools; well, they are satisfied to use the columns of the paper to play local politics and, regrettably, this is out of line and out of time. (*Es de parecer que el periodismo hispano es un medio para explotar bobos, pues se conforman con utilizar sus columnas para hacer juego de política de barrio, y por desgracia, fuera de "olla" esto es, fuera de tiempo.*) [Chacón 1929]

V. Conclusion

Several factors had begun to limit the success of Spanish-language publication in post-statehood New Mexico. Anglo Americans reached a critical mass just as New Mexico entered the Union as a state. Their presence in business, politics, and education became more determinant than at any previous time. Towns such as Las Vegas and Santa Fe, which had large Spanish-speaking populations and which had enjoyed the support of prosperous Hispano businesses, began to experience large population shifts. Advertisement in Spanish-language newspapers shrank in an era that saw Nuevomexicano business ventures close their doors at an alarming rate and Nuevomexicano laborers migrate to other states in search of employment. The Public Education Law of 1890 had made English the language of instruction in the public schools. In time this legislative privileging of Anglo social mores would effect a language shift that reversed whatever gains Spanish-language journalism had made in its attempt to retain Spanish at the center of public life in New Mexico. The Spanish-language press began to show the effects of the hegemonic constriction of Nuevomexicano language and culture by Anglo-dominated social institutions. Felipe M. Chacón, growing caustic at seeing Spanish-language publication in disarray and decline, concluded that Nuevomexicanos had begun to lose ownership and agency of the newspapers they had founded. Seeing the example of *La Voz del Pueblo,* Chacón observed caustically:

> It is in the hands of a Texan who is barely able to write in the language of the nation [English], and who, not even out of courtesy, speaks, however mangled, the language of the Hispano, and yet he publishes a few columns in Spanish for the "Mexicans" who are unfortunate enough to receive his rag. (*Está en manos de un tejano que apenas puede escribir el idioma nacional que ni por cortesía se interesa en masticar el idioma hispano, pero sí publica unas cuantas columnas en español a los "mexicans" que por desgracia reciben su pasquín.*) [Chacón 1929]

Statehood for New Mexico led to a hardening of political borders which, in turn, severed cultural ties to southern Colorado, southern Arizona, and west Texas. A reorganized *Prensa Asociada* now found itself divested of the bold and decisive regional agenda that it had once proclaimed "benefit the Latin race more than any other, that is, the association of the Spanish press in New Mexico, Arizona, California, Texas and part of Mexico" (*puede beneficiará la raza latina más que ningún otro, esto es, la asociación de la prensa española en Nuevo México, Arizona, California, Texas y parte de México*") (*La Prensa Asociada Hispano-Americana* 1892a).

The association was left with a dwindling membership at a statewide level.

But even in hard times the spirit of camaraderie that had sustained the movement in earlier years was not completely absent. The good-natured verses of Ignacio Duarte, the editor of *El Independiente* in 1920,[6] reveal something of the enduring fellowship among the remaining editors in the northern half of the state. In December 1920, Duarte published a Christmas poem in *El Independiente* which he titled, "*Santa Clos nos trajo crismas*" (Santa Brought Our Presents). In it he pokes fun at his colleagues by sketching in verse humorous and farcical caricatures of his fellow journalists. One by one, Duarte embellishes the foibles and penchants of several well-established figures in the press movement of earlier decades. Many of the familiar names in New Mexico's Spanish-language press corps appear in the poem as Duarte's *Santa Clos* visits gifts on Secundino Romero, Antonio Lucero, Nestor Montoya, José Jordí, Ezequiel C. de Baca, Camilo Padilla, and the staffs of *El Independiente* (Las Vegas), *El Boletín Popular* (Santa Fe), *El Progreso* (Trinidad, Colorado), *La Bandera Americana* (Albuquerque), and *La Voz del Pueblo* (Las Vegas).[7]

Spanish-language newspapers continued to be published in several communities in New Mexico into the 1940s and 1950s, but the trends affecting such publication that had begun in the late 1920s became more pronounced and evident after World War II. By the late 1950s, *El Nuevo Mexicano* was the only Spanish-language newspaper established in the 1890s that remained in publication. After sixty-seven years of continuous publication, *El Nuevo Mexicano* ceased publication on April 30, 1958. Pedro Ribera-Ortega, the paper's last editor, was of the opinion that the amalgamation of Spanish and English had made *El Nuevo Mexicano* obsolescent:

> Now, in 1958, when *Raza* heads of household are in most instances as proficient in English as in Spanish, since the younger generations can only read in English, moves toward majority rule have caused many households to receive the paper in English (in place of Spanish). For this reason, this spring, *El Nuevo Mexicano* will become the bride of the *Santa Fe New Mexican* and will even take its name. (*Ahora en 1958 cuando los jefes de familia de "la santa raza," son tan proficientes en inglés como en español, pero como las generaciones jóvenes pueden leer solamente el inglés en lugar del español. Por esta razón, esta primavera,* El Nuevo Mexicano *se convierte en la novia del* New Mexican *y hasta toma su apellido.*) [*El Fin* 1958]

The discontinuance of *El Nuevo Mexicano* signaled to many that ethnic depurations in New Mexico, at least at the level of public culture, were complete. The region's social history as it regarded Nuevomexicanos could now be commuted to non-threatening tricultural motifs that bolstered existing political and economic alignments in the state. But issues of historical redress and inequity would not go unvoiced for long. Less than a decade later, a new movement would spring from the distress of Nuevomexicanos who continued to struggle with social, educational, and political disparity in the land of their *antepasados*. By 1965, grassroots Chicano leaders were employing a bilingual activist press to recast in vibrant articulations many of the same issues that had preoccupied the members of *La Prensa Asociada*, and, in doing so, continued to contest the very same forces that encouraged the social and historical erasure of a *mexicano* presence in the Southwest.

Appendix A

¡Santa Clos nos Trajo Crismas! / Santa Brought Our Presents!

Ayer ya entrada la noche	Late last night
nuestra buena Cucaracha	our good Cucaracha
se puso su mejor hilacha	put on her best tattered clothes
y se fué á pasear en coche.	and went out for a drive.
Muy triste y desconsolada	Sad and full of woe
andaba zurciendo chismes	she went about spreading gossip
y pensando la desdichada	thinking, poor wretched girl,
que nadie le traería "crismas"	that nobody would bring her Christmas.
Eran en punto las dos,	It was two o'clock in the morning
y al cruzar un callejón	and as she crossed an alley
se encontró con Santo Clos	running into Santa Claus
con regalos de montón.	with a pile of gifts for all.
La curiosa Cucaracha	Curious Cuca
quiso al punto averiguar	wanted to know on the spot
á quienes iba á obsequiar	who the old man with the
el viejo barbas de hilacha.	scraggly beard would shower with gifts.
Le siguió los pasos y vió	She followed him and saw
lo que hizo el viejo barbón	what the old beard did
á las casas que entró,	and which houses he visited
y como hizo la repartición.	and how he distributed his gifts.
A Secundino Romero	For Secundino Romero,[8]
que es todavía el "papacito"	still the Big Daddy,
le trajo un chirrión de cuero	he brought a leather whip
rete bien empaquetado.	all nicely wrapped.
A don Toñito Lucero	For Tony [Antonio] Lucero,
le trajo, yo bien lo sé,	for being such a good partner,
por ser un buen aparcero	I know for a fact that he brought
unas medias y un corsé.	some stockings and a corset.

Para Don Nestor Montoya
trajo un grandísimo tanque,
dos cañones y hasta una olla
para que le "atore" al Franque.

To Don Nestor Montoya
he brought a huge tank
two cannons and even a kettle
so he can ram Frank [Hubbel].[9]

Para don Pepe Jordí
que es tan "corto" de nasales,
trajo cincuenta tamales
de chivo y de jabalí.

For Don Pepe Jordí
with the tiny nose
he brought fifty tamales
made from goat and wild boar meat.

De los pobres "independientes"
Santa Clos no se olvidó;
pa que se curen les dió
cien rechinidos de dientes.

Santa did not forget
the wretched staff at El Independiente
and to cure their hangovers
he gave them a hundred gnashing teeth.

A los Voz de los Encierros
Santo Clos le trae sopita,
un "guey" y doscientos "cueros"
y un editor con "pepita."

For "the voice of the shut-ins"
Santa brought bread pudding,
an ox, and two hundred skins
and an editor with pep.

Para Kiko el prominente
escritor, cómico y torero
trajo un peine con un diente
pa meterlo a peluquero.

For Kiko, the prominent
writer, comic, and bullfighter
he brought a one-tooth comb
to make a barber out of him.

Un bolsheviki travieso,
socialista y brabucón
trajo para "El Progreso,"
el pobre viejo barbón.

For El Progreso
the wretched old beard
brought a mischievous,
thick-bearded, socialist, Bolshevik.

Y al "Boletín Popular"
que tanto quiere al "gachuza."
le trajo un hermoso par
de loros y lechuza.

And for El Boletín Popular
which is so fond of the catty one
he brought a pair
of parrots and an owl.

Para el pobre "Anunciador"
vino un frasco con vampiro
para curarle el "ardor"
á su "trampe" que no olvido.

For the poor old Anunciador
came a jar and a vampire
to cure the ache
of its tramp, whom I've not forgotten.

Al viril "Independiente"
le trajo un perrito "cuete"
para que muerda á la gente
demócrata del chisguete.

To the manly Independiente
he brought a drunken dog
to sick on those Democrats
out on the drunk.

Al director (?) de la Banda
al "mestro" don Juan Fachico
le trajo una cara-panda
y un diploma de borrico.

To the director (?) of La Bandera
to "the Master," to foolish Juan
he brought a panda's face
and a sheepskin diploma.

Para Bursum, el odiado	For the much hated Bursum,
cacique, tan temeroso,	so feared a boss,
trajo un carácter templado	he has brought gentleness
y un lomo muy resbaloso.	and a very sleek back.
A Maurilio el surumato,	For Maurilio, from Mexico,
músico de los que hay pocos,	a musician like few others
le trajo un "Fachico" suato	he has brought a foolish "Fachico"
para que le limpie los mocos.	to blow his runny nose.
Para Rechy, el Profesor	For Rechy, the Music
de música, no "Fachico"	Teacher, [he did not bring] a ninny
pa quitarle el hablador	to ebb his endless talking
le trajo un verde perico.	rather he brought him a green parrot.
A las señoras Cacicas	To the women bosses
les trajo una gran receta	he brought a great recipe
pa que pongan de maricas	so they can turn the men into wimps
á los hombres, y hasta en dieta.	and keep them on a diet.
A mi comadre y á Mela	To my *comadre* and for Mela
que de vista no las pierde,	who is never lost from sight
les trajo un dolor de muslo	he brought a muscle pain
y un pollito cola verde.	and a green-tailed chickie.
A todos los comerciantes	To all the storeowners
les trajo un corazón blandito	he has brought a tender heart
para que vendan como antes	so they will sell everything, as
todo, todo, baratito.	in times past, at rock-bottom prices.
Y a la pobre Cucaracha	And to poor Cucaracha
que nunca la puedo olvidar	the one I can never forget
le trajo una linda _____	he has brought her a beautiful _____
para que la vaya á doblar.	so she can fold it up.
Al bueno de Don Camilo	To good Don Camilio
le trajo dos piernas güeras	he has brought him two blond legs
pa que les agarre el hilo	so he might catch on
y pueda hasta jugar carreras.	and can run a race or two.
Al pobrecito de Horacio	To poor old Horacio
le trajo una Margarita	he has brought a Margarita
muy hermosa, re bonita;	very lovely, so beautiful
y él . . . tan fiero y tan lacio.	and he, so ugly, so wispy.
Y para Manuel Gallegos	And for Manuel Gallegos
que es campechado y decente	who is cheerful and decent
trajo cincuenta borregos	he has brought fifty ewes
de la marca "independiente."	of the "Independent" brand.

Para Cobley, el impresor	For Cobley, the most competent
más competente y más activo	and active printer
trajo un gran "componedor"	he has brought a grand composing table
forrado en cuero de chivo.	bound in kid leather.
Y para Manuel Segura	And for Manuel Segura
que de bueno hasta se pasa	who is way too kind
y que por nada se apura	and rushes for no one
trajo una gran calabaza.	he has brought a great pumpkin.
A las pollas de Las Vegas,	For the girls of Las Vegas,
tan lindas como hay pocas,	beautiful as few others,
les trajo muchos pollitos	he has brought many beaux
para que se vuelvan locas.	to drive them crazy.
A Juanito, el velador	For Juanito, the night watchman
y a Toño su compañero	and for his buddy, Tony,
les trajo un despertador	he has brought an alarm clock
porque roncan cual carnero.	since they snore like rams.

Notes

1. In citing the texts from original newspaper sources, I have elected to quote them in their original form, maintaining the idiosyncrasies and variations in punctuation, accentuation, and orthography resulting from the informality of medium and the exigency with which these texts were prepared for publication. All translations are mine.

2. *El Sol de Mayo* of Las Vegas reported in February 1892 that sixteen editors from New Mexico, Colorado, and Texas held membership in the association. Represented at that meeting were the editors of every important Spanish-language newspaper in New Mexico and west Texas. By late March, *La Prensa Asociada* met formally to draft a preamble and to pass resolutions calling for the founding of an association.

3. *El Boletín Popular* began publication in 1885. Absent from existing library collections are issues of the paper for the first two years of its publication. Benjamín Read (1911), however, did record the visit of General Riva Palacio to Santa Fe, indicating in a note that the source of his information was a July 10, 1886 article from *El Boletín Popular*.

4. Francisco Lomelí and other Chicano literary critics have identified Eusebio Chacón as an early exponent of Mexican American literature. Lomelí suggests that Chacón worked to "create the authentic New Mexican novel" (See "Eusebio Chacón: An Early Pioneer of the New Mexican Novel." In *Pasó por Aquí: Essays on the New Mexican Hispanic Literary Tradition, 1542–1988*, ed. Erlinda González-Berry, 131–148. Albuquerque: University of New Mexico Press, 1998, p. 134).

5. For a discussion of Escobar's production in poetry, see my "The Poetics of Self-Representation in Neo-Mexicano Literary Discourse," in *So All Is Not Lost: The Poetics of Print in Nuevomexicano Communities, 1834–1958* (Albuquerque: University of New Mexico Press, 1997).

6. Duarte was one of a succeeding number of editors who occupied the editorship of *El Independiente* after 1910, the year Enrique H. Salazar left the paper after dissolving his partnership with co-owner and political boss, Secundino Romero of Las Vegas.
7. The complete text of *"Santa Clos nos trajo crismas"* and my English translation appear as Appendix A at the end of this article.
8. Secundino Romero at this time was chairman of the Republican Central Committee for San Miguel County. In 1910 he became partnered with Enrique H. Salazar and *El Independiente*. The Romero-Salazar partnership ended in 1910 when Salazar sold his interest in the paper and relocated to Fort Sumner, New Mexico.
9. In the 1920s Frank A. Hubbel was the chairman of the Republican Central Committee of Bernalillo County. He and his brother James held an interest in *La Bandera Americana* and eventually wrenched control of the paper from the heirs of Nestor Montoya after Montoya's death in 1923. The verse alludes to a history of feuding and political squabbling between the Hubbels and Montoya.

Literature Cited

Cabeza de Baca, Fabiola. [1954] 1994. *We Fed Them Cactus*. Albuquerque: University of New Mexico Press.

Chacón, Eusebio. 1929. La Prensa Hispana Se Hace Valer o Desaparece. *La Bandera Americana* (15 August).

de Baca, Manuel C. 1892. La Prensa Asociada. *El Sol de Mayo* (31 March): 1.

El Fin de una Época. 1958. *El Nuevo Mexicano* (30 April).

Escobar, José. 1896a. Nuestro periódico. *Las Dos Repúblicas* (11 January).

Escobar, José. 1896b. Progreso literario de Nuevo México. *Las Dos Repúblicas* (11 July): 1.

La Asociación de La Prensa Asociada Hispano-Americana. 1892. *La Voz del Pueblo* (27 February).

La Prensa Asociada Hispano-Americana. 1892a. *La Voz del Pueblo* (5 March).

La Prensa Asociada Hispano-Americana. 1892b. *El Hispano-Americano* (14 May).

La Prensa Asociada. 1892. *El Sol de Mayo* (31 March): 1.

La Unión de la Prensa Hispana. 1928. *La Bandera Americana* (24 February).

Meyer, Doris L. 1978. The Poetry of José Escobar: Mexican Émigré in New Mexico. *Hispania* 61: 24–34.

Montoya, Nestor. 1892. *El Sol de Mayo* (31 March).

Necrology (Félix Martínez). 1916. *Old Santa Fe Magazine* 61 (July): 286–296.

Padilla, Camilo. 1892. Nuestro patrio suelo. *El Mosquito* (10 December).

Padilla, Camilo. 1894. Carta de un amigo. *El Independiente* (4 August).

Padilla, Camilo. 1928. Un atento llamado a los Hispano-americanos: Manifiesto. *La Revista Ilustrada* (June).

Read, Benjamín M. 1911. *Illustrated History of New Mexico*. Translated by Eleuterio Baca. Santa Fe: New Mexican Publishing Co.

Rosenbaum, Robert. 1981. *Mexicano Resistance in the Southwest*. Austin: University of Texas Press.

Salazar, Enrique H. 1895a. Decadencia de nuestro pueblo. *El Independiente* (16 March).

———. 1895b. Nuestro provenir. *El Independiente* (9 November).

Salutoria. 1901. *La Bandera Americana* (3 August).

Segura, José. 1894. *El Boletín Popular* (31 May).

Stanley, F. 1965. *Ciudad de Santa Fe: Territorial Days, 1846–1912.* Pampa, Texas: Pampa Print Shop.

Stratton, Porter A. 1969. *The Territorial Press of New Mexico, 1834–1912.* Albuquerque: University of New Mexico Press.

Newspaper and Periodical Materials

La Bandera Americana, Semanario Dedicado a los Intereses y Progreso del Pueblo Neo-Mexicano. Albuquerque, New Mexico; weekly; English and Spanish; May 18, 1895–December 3, 1938.

El Boletín Popular, Periódico Político, Literario y de Anuncios. Santa Fe, New Mexico; weekly; Spanish; English and Spanish; 1893; ca. October 21, 1885–ca.1910.

Las Dos Repúblicas, Periódico Comercial de Artes, Ciencia y Literatura. Denver, Colorado and Trinidad, Colorado, weekly, Spanish; January 11, 1896–March 13, 1897.

La Gaceta de Mora and *Mora Gazette.* Mora, New Mexico; weekly, English and Spanish; March 27–November 22; 1890, English and Spanish, January, 1891; March 27–November 22, 1890; January, 1891.

El Hispano-Americano, Organo de la Orden de los Caballeros de Mutua Protección. Las Vegas, New Mexico; weekly; Spanish; April 7, 1892–November 1, 1920.

El Independiente, Dedicado a los mejores intereses del Estado de Nuevo Mexico y en particular del Condado de San Miguel. Las Vegas, New Mexico; weekly; Spanish; March 24, 1894–ca. August 24, 1928.

El Mosquito. Mora, New Mexico; weekly; English and Spanish; November 1891–June 30, 1892.

El Nuevo Mexicano. Santa Fe, New Mexico; weekly; Spanish; August 2,1890–April 30, 1958.

El Progreso. Trinidad, Colorado; weekly, Spanish, 1891–1944.

La Revista de Taos, Periódico Liberal e Independiente, del Pueblo, para el Pueblo y por el Pueblo. Taos, New Mexico; weekly; Spanish; September 24, 1909–1911.

La Revista Ilustrada. Santa Fe, New Mexico; weekly; English and Spanish; March 17, 1917–ca. August, 1933.

El Sol de Mayo, Periódico Independiente, de Noticias, Variedades y Anuncios. Las Vegas, New Mexico; weekly; English and Spanish; January 18, 1894–November 22, 1894.

La Voz del Pueblo, Semanario Dedicado a los Intereses y Progreso Del Pueblo Hispano-Americano. Las Vegas, New Mexico; weekly; English and Spanish; June 14, 1890–February 10, 1927.

Background of New Mexico's Hispanic Literature
Self-Referentiality as a Literary-Historical Discourse

Francisco A. Lomelí

"Bajo tales condiciones tan adversas,
   el mestizaje cultural fue inevitable."

> *Don Pedro Bautista Pino,*
> *Exposición sucinta y sencilla de*
> *la provincia del Nuevo México*

"The Southwest is a mosaic, not a synthesis."

> *Albert J. Guerard*

I. Overview: Hispanic Literature as an Endogamous Tool for Cultural Identity and Expression

UNDERSTANDING THE FULL SCOPE of cultural identity in New Mexico entails the task of recovering a rich and long literary past. With that in mind, much unorthodox, interdisciplinary research has focused on unearthing forgotten archives and manuscripts from diverse and sometimes unexpected sources. Individual attempts are coming together to form a vast diachronic macro-text of past regional writings in order to document a more complete literary portrait of the Southwest. This study aims to create a framework to better understand the evolution of a Nuevomexicano literary consciousness. As a way of illustrating such a framework in a specific narrative, Porfirio Gonzales's novel, *Historia de un cautivo* (1898),will be examined briefly.

To capture the magnitude of New Mexico's literary history, it is important to document Nuevomexicanos' stature in the general society in order to piece together an authentic portrayal of events, social dynamics, and personalities. This larger context can yield a number of important criteria for delineating distinctive characteristics: cultural makeup, participatory agents, politics, economics, gender, worldview, class, language, and, of course, literary traditions.

New Mexico's early Indo-Hispanic writings are unique because a vague but real notion exists among the general populace of possessing a long-standing past. We must remember that the region started to play a major role when incorporated into the larger context of Spanish folklore and myth barely forty-seven years (i.e., by 1539) after Columbus's arrival in the Caribbean. This is certainly not the case in other regions with a strong Indo-Hispanic presence such as California and, to a degree, Texas and Arizona. New Mexico's remarkable qualities and features permit the distinctive confluence of factors that emerged during the early phases of Spanish exploration in the Americas. Although regarded as isolated and remote from pivotal cultural centers like Mexico City or Lima, New Mexico attracted early attention as a new crossroads of human migrations whose potential was fueled by myth, including the myth of largely unrealized riches, and the network of Native American settlements along what is now the Río Grande. These became the foundations of viable social structures where a livelihood was possible within otherwise harsh natural surroundings. The area eventually saw Native American and Hispanic lifestyles blending through time, borrowing from each other to transform their original forms. The literature that developed reflects a cultural dynamics found in no other region with an Indo-Hispanic presence.

The New Mexican enclave developed in isolation from mainstream New Spain as the Hispanic peoples acquired and adapted to their new geographical area, either using Native American pueblos as starting points and social references or by creating parallel colonies near what was already there. Thus, cultural identity has been shaped by the string of communities along the Río Grande much as Mexico City was influenced and fashioned by Tenochtitlan and Lago Texcoco. From this process a regional ethos emerged: The *chilero* cycle—dependent on the cultivation cycles of chiles—permeates virtually all aspects of life, including views of time and culinary habits. Linguistically, a sixteenth-century Spanish (*turbina* for dress or *coyote* for a social caste of mixed bloods) developed into a lingua franca with numerous Native American accents and terminologies (*cusco* for stingy, or *coyaye*, a herb also known as *escoba de la víbora* or snake's broom). Religious worship and iconography conformed to the environment of decentralized institutionalization by forging a sacred mecca, such as the Santuario de Chimayó (a sacred shrine in northern New Mexico), and by religious practices in which the *Penitentes* assumed the role of an ad hoc religious institution. Native Americans' close affinity to the land merged with Hispanics' pastoral economy to promote a notable attachment to place. An architecture, sometimes called Santa Fe-Pueblo, combines Spanish pragmatism in building techniques. At the same time, Native American aesthetics offer harmonious spatial representations between nature and human needs (Lomelí 1987, 81–83).

The singularity of these elements accorded New Mexico an inimitable place in what eventually became the literature and letters of the Southwest. Although attention to New Mexican writings in Spanish has often been superficial, even perfunctory, there is no doubt that the overall production occupies a special place in what the Southwest has to offer. The sheer volume of *crónicas, memorias, relaciones, diarios, historias,* and many other trans-generic writings gives evidence of an obsession with documentation (including incursions into fanciful imagination) for the sake of accountability, and, in some cases, for self-aggrandizement, but fortunately so, for posterity's sake. The magnitude of these writings has gone unheeded mainly due to the materials' dispersion in various archives (e.g., Mexico City, Madrid, Kansas City, and Amsterdam), exacerbated later by their disappearance and by the stigma of Spanish being a "second-class" language. Although startling to many, it is a fact that quantitatively, Hispanic peoples throughout the continental United States far exceeded in productivity all other ethnic and racial minority cultures up to the end of the nineteenth century. And, in the context of Hispanic literature, I would argue that production by Nuevomexicanos is superior in longevity, variety, and abundance.

Literary production by Nuevomexicanos manifests another distinction: it is the first and earliest cluster of Hispanic writings to be dealt with as a corpus unto itself, despite the deficient methodologies to define it as such in *la tierra adentro del vasto norte* (the inner lands of the vast north). Although critical attention to this literature has tended toward the perfunctory (see, e.g., Mary Catherine Prince's "The Literature of New Mexico" [1918] and Mabel Major, Rebecca W. Smith, and T. M. Pearce's renowned *Southwest Heritage: A Literary History With Bibliographies* [1938]), what emerges from such treatments is an undeniable recognition of a body of Hispanic writings—as vague as that recognition might be.

Many years before an organized discourse existed, critical minds often reflected on these writings, contemplating their interrelationships. For example, Gaspar Pérez de Villagrá's 1610 *Historia de la Nueva México* (1992) demonstrates his clear notion of the written literary foundation taking hold in the region. He refers to his chronicle as an enterprise within "nuestro (our) Nuevo México," of which he feels an intimate part. On one occasion he even compares Aztec writings to the contributions of others before him, such as Alvar Núñez Cabeza de Vaca, Francisco Vásquez de Coronado, and Fray Marcos de Niza, obviously suggesting a body of works with a certain regional focus and common features while distinguishing them from mainland Mexican culture. He considers writing in Mexico in the "hieroglyphic mode" in contrast to "*la grandeza y excelencia/Del escribir ilustre que tenemos*" (the greatness and excellence/of the noble writing that we have) (Villagrá 1992, 6).

A sizable number of chroniclers thereafter focused on New Mexico with a particular propensity for comparing both Mexicos, often deviating into either a discourse of disenchantment or embellishments of wishful thinking. But they rarely lost sight of New Mexico as a focal point and axis of literary inspiration. The Río Grande region eventually took on the qualities of an autochthonous natural and human area, serving as a magnet for critical discussions and fanciful recreations in literary works. Hernán Gallegos and Don Pedro Bautista Pino effectively demonstrate this in their respective *Relación y conclusión del viaje y suceso que Francisco Chamuscado con ocho soldados hizo en el descubrimiento del Nuevo México* (Narrative and Conclusion of the Trip and Event that Francisco Chamuscado Accomplished With Eight Soldiers in the Discovery of New Mexico [1581])[1] and *Exposición sucinta y sencilla de la provincia del Nuevo México* (Succinct and Simple Treatise on the New Mexico Province [1812]). Even Miguel de Quintana in 1732, in his semi-mystical poetry, claims a local autonomy vis-à-vis the standards imposed by the local ecclesiastics of Santa Cruz de la Cañada, New Mexico (Colahan and Lomelí 1989). The region's distinctiveness is also reflected in oral tradition and folk theater, which were not limited to the written page. *Los comanches* (1777ca) and *Los tejanos* (1854ca), two popular folk plays, capture local concerns while contrasting them with those found among Plains Indians and Texans.

As early as the 1830s, Manuel Alvarez initiated an embryonic critical appraisal of a specific work, thus continuing the conceptualization of a distinctive regional literature. He highlighted the Native Americans' inclination toward politics and expressed amazement at their ability to import news on far-away events such as Hernán Cortés's conquests. He notes

> *Del [Oñate] dicen de el y todo el efecto que se hizo, que para tanto ruido corto, el Capitán Gaspar de Villagrá que se halló pudiente [sic], escribió un libro en metro castellano.* (Of him [Oñate] they say his colonizing enterprise had great impact, and, when all was said and done, Captain Gaspar de Villagrá stood out as a prudent man, having written a book in Castilian meter.) [Alvarez 1834, 2264]

A cultural self-referentiality was in place during the formative years of the territory's traditions, catching impressions and images of creativity in the region, especially in relation to the conflict caused by the encroachment of Anglo Americans around 1848. One popular example that metaphorically captures the sentiment is the following:

Nuevo México mentado,   Alluded New Mexico,
has perdido ya tu fama,   you have now lost your fame
adonde yo jui por lana   where I (we?) went for wool
y me vine tresquilado.   I returned sheared. [Campa 1946, 526]

We see repeated glances backward at the origins and gestation of a literary expression rooted in New Mexico. Another early assessment of Villagrá's epic poem occurs in 1885 by Mexican critic Francisco Pimentel:

> The *Historia de la Nueva México* has two laudable features, one in the contents, and the other in the form, to wit: the fidelity with which the facts are related, and the simplicity and naturalness of the style and the language. This is really remarkable in the period when gongorism predominated. [Pimentel 1885, 142–143]

Immediately thereafter, in 1887, John Gilmary Shea wrote a groundbreaking essay, "The First Epic of Our Country. By the Poet Conquistador of New Mexico, Captain Gaspar de Villagrá" (Shea 1887), considered the first in-depth discussion of this important poetic text, an important chronicle that unfortunately remained forgotten until the 1990s.

If doubts remained about the legitimacy and importance of early Nuevomexicano literature, they were dispelled by the latter part of the nineteenth century when literary production increased dramatically via newspapers. New Mexico gained in stature and in peculiarity, even leading some historians and politicians to inject it with further elements of myth and thus augment its exoticism. Two examples suffice: William G. Ritch's *Aztlan: The History, Resources and Attractions of New Mexico* (1885) and *An Illustrated History of New Mexico from the Earliest Period of its Discovery to the Present Time, Together with Biographical Mention of Many of its Pioneers and Prominent Citizens of Today* (*Illustrated History* 1895). The two works framed the territory's uniqueness within the confines of the mythic homeland of the Aztecs, that is, Aztlán. No other region has so caught the romantic fancy for its cultural composition and diverse history; even California is known more for its weather and natural resources. If New Mexico conjured up images of Cíbola and Quivira for the early Hispanic explorers, its magic has prevailed to this day, promoted first to attract settlers, and, later, a tourist industry based on cultural voyeurism, whence the emergence in the 1920s of the modern version of what the original explorers sought: the "Land of Enchantment."

In spite of this romanticized past, Nuevomexicanos had to struggle for survival in a society in which the balance of power was against them. By 1878, when the railroad arrived, pastoral life was being interrupted by waves of changes and hostile acquisitions of land, minerals, and agriculture. The railroad introduced new products, facilitated trade, and brought a diversified economy (and, as a consequence, material prosperity). Although economically splintered and politically factionalized, however, Nuevomexicanos made great strides in the field of literature thanks to the proliferation of the printing press and the growth of an audience of readers. Nuevomexicanos began to realize their potential as creators of literary expression, making the easy switch from the backdrop of a rich oral tradition to the written medium. If the concept of a New Mexican literature had been initially latent, almost intuitive, and heavily influenced by the constructs of history, after the 1880s the notion became explicit, unequivocal, and freer in its fancy. A tradition had not been born; this was a renaissance—the first of its kind by any American minority group—where socioeconomic circumstances and human dynamics permitted a florescence, almost an explosion. Suddenly, the written word became accessible to large numbers of people, and a constellation of writers coalesced from individual voices into collective congregations, artistic groups, and even literary societies.

The new incursions into literary expression seem to have spurred a renewed sense of identity and purpose. Publishing outlets afforded Nuevomexicanos the vehicle to articulate what had been repressed since the Mexican-American War, which had left them feeling "voiceless and expressionless" (Paredes 1987, 1079). This newfound freedom of stylized expression, particularly in Spanish, provided the needed impetus to dwell on matters pertaining to the imagination. Newspapers became important instruments of cultural-artistic dialogue. As Nicolás Kanellos notes:

> Besides supplying basic news of the homeland and of the Hispanic world in general, advertising local businesses and informing the community on relevant current affairs and politics of the United States (often through unauthorized translations of the English-language press and/or news agencies), Hispanic periodicals additionally have had to offer alternative information services that present their own communities' views of news and events. At times this information has had to take on a contestatory and challenging posture vis-à-vis the English-language news organizations and U.S. official government and cultural institutions. [Kanellos 1994, 239]

Newspapers assumed the roles of both text and a multifaceted medium of cultural and informational exchange. In them we find the transmission of social values, both overt and subliminal, plus a forum for public debate through polemical editorials and essays. Above all, the newspaper became the meeting ground between the oral tradition of a people and attempts at either experimental or polished writings on a wide assortment of themes and subjects. Newspapers expressed what was in the people's minds and hearts that could be put down in writing. In that sense, they represented an externalization or outpouring of ideas and sentiments, thus serving as a modern form for the long-standing desire to document everything in sight, as evinced in colonial accounts and chronicles. But the newspaper is a fragile medium, and, as a consequence, the Hispanic people's faith in the newspaper as a viable means of expression motivated them to collect and compile newspaper writings as a body of literature.

Regarded by many as useless and cumbersome, newspapers remain the single largest, most comprehensive (and most neglected) stock of daily history constituting the legacy of a people (Grove, Barnett, and Hansen 1975, xv).

It is a well substantiated fact that more Spanish-language newspapers were founded in New Mexico than anywhere else in what became the American Southwest (Stratton 1969, Arellano n.d., Lomelí 1987). Perhaps the greatest proliferation is found in Las Vegas, New Mexico, where newspapers doubled as chronicles of daily events and as literary outlets, serving as the base for the Las Vegas Renaissance. Beginning in the 1870s, the city itself experienced a boom that created and cultivated a readership—a situation propitious for producing literature. Cultured language, verbal wit, and an ingenious flair with words were highly prized abilities, and writers with such skills received social accolades and prompted the creation of literary groups. From this ambience emerged a conglomeration of *sociedades mutualistas* (mutual-aid societies), originally community-based support networks and fringe benefit associations (Amaro Hernández 1983, 3), which evolved into full-fledged literary societies. The objectives of the mutual-aid societies expanded "to investigate and debate questions and subjects of social, literary and moral character" (Arellano n.d., 3). They promoted group consciousness and served as training grounds for politicians, orators, social workers, and literati.

The Las Vegas Renaissance "transversed unprecedented social, class and political affinities with the intent to define their own literary map" (Lomelí 1990, 16). Unlike subsequent minority groupings many years later, such as the Harlem Renaissance (largely directed by white patrons), the New Mexican literary societies were a native mass movement that represented Indo-Hispanic society at all levels, promoting published writings both popular or elite. Powerful and influential persons are indeed known for their contributions, but the salient feature of the Las Vegas Renaissance is the participation of people from all walks of life:

> No one leader stood out nor did anyone in particular direct it. . . .
> [I]t was both a popular and middle-class event. The movement
> became a happening totally apart and separate from Anglo liter-
> ary interests (and circles), and it can be interpreted as a show of
> cultural strength by a conquered people. [Lomelí 1987, 90]

The increase in literary expression mirrored socioeconomic conditions, including an emerging middle class and frequent attempts to internationalize literary tastes and connect locals with cosmopolitan sources. It became commonplace to find writings by New Mexicans alongside those from Mexico, Spain, Germany, Nicaragua, Czechoslovakia, Argentina, and France. A wide range of moods, themes, experimentations, and styles offered variety and sophistication. Indo-Hispanic New Mexico was by then overcoming its image of backwoods illiteracy but remained unrecognized in the literature of the Southwest or, at best, was seen as part of the "sagebrush school of literature" (Martin 1990, 4). A definite movement was in vogue: between 1879 and 1900, 283 newspapers were launched in the state of New Mexico; of these, forty-four were produced in the city of Las Vegas alone (Stratton 1969, 25). Of those forty-four, sixteen were bilingual and thirteen were exclusively Spanish-language newspapers (Stratton 1969, 24), many of which were direct outlets of the literary societies. In 1892 eight of these societies were thriving in Las Vegas, accounting for a remarkable amount of cultural activity. A burgeoning center of creative activity found itself in full bloom, and the Spanish language benefited greatly while gaining new vitality and importance. In 1881 *Revista Católica* detailed the following:

> *La prosperidad física, moral, artística y literaria de Las Vegas pro-gresa a grandes pasos. . . . La cantidad de libros y papeles, que entra en Las Vegas, es pasmosa. Aquí se publican periódicos diarios, heb-domadarios y mensuales. El trabajo de las imprentas no tiene bas-tantes obreros para dar abasto a los muchos encargos que reciben.* (Physical, moral, artistic and literary prosperity of Las Vegas advances in great leaps. . . . The quantity of books and papers that enter Las Vegas is astounding. Daily newspapers, weeklies, and monthlies are published here. The work of printing shops does not have enough workers to supply the many orders received.) [Actualidades 1881, 543]

Amid this cross-national hybridization, Nuevomexicanos continued to develop and promote their own cultural agenda. Hispanic writers were juxta-posed with, even compared to, consecrated authors from other lands, thus plac-ing the former in an illustrious group. The implication is clear: whereas political and economic marginalization characterized their immediate plight in Anglo America, their intellectual and literary prowess empowered them to transcend social restrictions. To emphasize the point, *La Voz del Pueblo* in 1891 highlighted the exceptional talents of an illustrious poet:

> *Don Eleuterio Baca, fiel y digno discípulo de Calderón y Lope de Vega, el primero de los poetas Neo-Mexicanos . . . es uno de esos genios que la madre naturaleza da pocos al mundo."* (Don Eleuterio Baca, loyal and meritorious disciple of Calderón and Lope de Vega, the first among New Mexican poets . . . is one of those geniuses that mother nature gives to the world.) [Arellano & Vigil 1985, 3]

Whereas socially, Nuevomexicanos were experiencing institutionalized segregation, they could metaphorically rub elbows with the classics.

This renewed confidence unchained a variety of literary manifestations, some imitating established forms, some attempting to found new local archetypes, and some melding popular folkloric forms with more purely literary genres. In this context, we can better understand Manuel M. Salazar's picaresque *La historia de un caminante o sea Aurora y Gervacio* (*The Story of a Roamer, that is, Aurora and Gervacio*) from 1881, or some of the historical *cronovelas* (chronicle novels) from the 1890s, such as Manuel C. de Baca's 1896 *Historia de Vicente Silva y sus cuarenta bandidos, sus crímenes y retribuciones* (*History of Vicente Silva and his Forty Thieves, Their Crimes and Retributions*) and his 1892 *Noches tenebrosas en el Condado de San Miguel* (Gloomy Nights in San Miguel County), published serially in *Sol de Mayo,* either of which today might be called a documentary or *reportaje* novel. These novels imitate well-known models, but their principal concern is to provide local substance and content. That is, these adapt a literary form to local reality. Eusebio Chacón, in the *Dedicación* to his two works *El hijo de la tempestad* and *Tras la tormenta la calma,* pinpoints his commitment to the regional novel as a genre: "They (the novels) are a genuine creation of my own fantasy and (are) not stolen nor borrowed from *gabachos* or foreigners. I dare lay the foundation . . . of an entertaining literature on New Mexican soil" (Chacón 1892, 2; my translation). If Chacón's first novel unfolds the perils of a region's ridding itself of totalitarianism and disguised forms of social control, his second work is an imitative exercise in deciphering morality and redefining honor. His main concern is to put fiction at the service of social issues, but part of his fascination is with behavioral ambiguity. While Chacón pioneered the "authentic New Mexican novel," many Nuevomexicano writers, particularly in the 1890s, set out to captivate a readership anxious for stories relevant to their social milieu, offering a wide range of poetry, *coloquios* (dramatic pieces) or *actos* (skits), short stories, and literary essays that contrasted the starkness of current events with aesthetic intrigue and verbal ingenuity.

The 1890s saw the greatest production of literary pieces, many of which are yet to be read and studied. The dilemma becomes how to extract from these texts a viable corpus of Nuevomexicano writings, for many of these works were not archived and were thus lost. More problematic than faulty storage were social stigmas and linguistic biases. Spanish-language newspapers suffered the same destiny as many of the important documents from colonial New Mexico: Most American scholars in the nineteenth century concentrated more on preserving English-language materials, thus contributing to the destruction, disfigurement, or dispersal of Spanish-language documents. That is precisely why any endeavor to recover the bits and fragments of Nuevomexicano literature, from whatever sources and through whichever means, is so vital to reconstruction of a forgotten past.

II. *Historia de un cautivo* by Porfirio Gonzales: A Turn of the Century Narrative

An author who exemplifies some of my previous arguments is Porfirio Gonzales (1863–1920), a renowned pioneer educator from the Las Vegas area who suffered a fate similar to many Nuevomexicano writers of his time—*postergación* or relegation. Others worthy of critical consideration are Apolinario Almanzares, José Escobar, Vicente or Luis Bernal, Secundino Baca, Josefina Escajeda, Eleuterio Baca, Jesús María H. Alarid, José Inés García, and Higinio V. Gonzales.

Gonzales's short novel, *Historia de un cautivo,* which appeared in 1898 in the Las Vegas, New Mexico newspaper, *La Voz del Pueblo* as a ten-part weekly serial, encapsulates many of the sentiments of Indo-Hispanics at the turn of the century when their condition oscillated between continuity as an unstable territory and official statehood. The uncertainty produced ambivalent allegiances that often bordered on the contradictory. Gonzales's novella, like many written during this era, seems simple and straightforward. An almost nostalgic romanticism shapes the central theme of granting a person something that rightfully belongs to him, with some luck involved. The work in part captures a regional history of past conflicts by telling a captivity story within the *indita* tradition in which the central focus is rectifying the captive's social condition. The narrative framework offers identities that are layered and mixed; intrigue is paramount and harmony is reinstated. The storyline, at least on the surface, presents the problem of double identities and the natural outcome of inevitable wealth for the survivors. Gonzales's hero, Esteban Stankiwicks, is a rich Swede adopted by a Norwegian family. Stanki befriends and falls in love with a Mexican maiden, Margarita Molina, who had been captured in childhood by the Apaches. Esteban also becomes a victim of captivity and is eventually mortally wounded by the Apaches and dies in the arms of an unsuspecting traveler who relates the unfolding events.

The plot offers a Cervantes-style narrative in which reality is muddied by the use of deliberate ambiguities and confused identities; Gonzales provides a series of leads (literally a trail) that takes the reader in many directions beyond the simple reunification of a family. First, the blending of historical and literary contexts results in ambivalence. Further, the allegorical aspect of the story defies either realism or romanticism. In addition, the narrative mixes fantasy (e.g., inherited riches) and desire (e.g., finding an identity lost through circumstances).

Part of its intrigue rests on its *sui generis* qualities and resonance, but the novella contains much more: its explicit reference to important historical markers grants it some authority. For example, it establishes a parallelism between 1898, the time of its publication (which also forebodes the turn of the century into modernity), and 1842, the fictional time of the novella in which the old order of Mexican rule foreshadows Anglo American domination. Either way, double preparations for a changing future—in which peoples of diverse origins will commingle—seem to be in progress. If the primary fears in 1842 were of violence, lawlessness, and Indian raids, in 1898 the greatest anxiety is about long-overdue statehood and a troubled integration into an Anglo-American world. The novella is a way to comment on the significance of such landmarks in history.

Don Eduardo Pérez de Molina, the narrator, main character, and patriarch is the "Apache maiden's" father; he is the touchstone of reality who tries to achieve social harmony by bringing the loose pieces together. Not by coincidence, Don Eduardo is a colonel who lost his daughter to the Apaches some fourteen years before the action of the novel; he measures all events by the degree of Apache threat in the Southwest. To Don Eduardo, the region is a place of strife that demands domination—that is, a place still in the process of becoming. The process of recovering his daughter Margarita, by extension, can be taken as a symbolic act of reclaiming what is rightfully his—equivalent to the retrieval and possible redemption of his homeland and honor. The novella's title, *Historia de un cautivo,* is ambiguous. One might think that the romantic motif of captured Europeans or *mestizos* confines the story within the *indita* tradition or that the captivity alludes only to Esteban Stankiwicks's situation. The reference is a generic one, for each character is living out a kind of captivity. In other words, the work encompasses what might more appropriately be termed *"historia de un pueblo cautivo"*—the history/story of a captive people—suggesting shifts in affinities within the context of a conquest.

Esteban is discovered to be a nobleman who, unknown to him, is the heir to a huge estate. Margarita then manages, with meticulous documentation, to convince her lover's relatives that she is the true benefactor of Esteban's inheritance. Esteban's relatives are caught in a web of some intrigue, forced to turn Esteban's inheritance over to Margarita. Thus, Margarita goes from being a "primitive" (an Apache maiden) to a modern corporate owner who renounces her double past—Apache and Mexican. By marrying Esteban's brother, she completes the circle of assimilation into monied mainstream American society. The question that emerges is, Is there a price to pay for such quick social mobility in a region in which identities are still in flux?

Gonzales's short work embodies a number of other interesting considerations. For example, the term *"historia"* can mean either history or story (or both, as Cervantes might have preferred), thus representing a double-edged commentary on the social evolution of the times. Clearly, this work romanticizes social relations with the histrionic techniques of shifting identities to achieve a felicitous suspense, but it lacks the superficiality of nineteenth-century dime novels and the caramelized content of Helen Hunt Jackson's 1884 *Ramona.* Narrative perspective is expertly handled by Gonzales as the story unfolds around Don Eduardo, much like a whirlwind of discoveries and revelations that soon evolve into new opportunties. Although Native Americans cause physical harm and are described as "savages" and antagonists, facile monolithic polarizations between them and others are generally lacking. Margarita, after all, has become Apache by living with them for fourteen years and she never belittles them. The traditional cowboy-and-Indian framework is missing because the characters recognize an implicit process of assimilation and blurring of difference as well as the value of upholding a *mestizo* culture.

The novella, then, foreshadows changes that were about to take place in the twentieth century—analogous to the kinds of changes experienced by Mexicans in the late 1840s. The text contains a prophetic note of sweeping transformations. Even though the ending seems to be a happy one, a doleful mood permeates the narrative, recalling Eusebio Chacón's *El hijo de la tempestad* (1892) and its symbolism of disharmony and social turmoil. The work presents closure and resolution, but it also suggests quandary, misgivings, and skepticism.

Porfirio Gonzales, in the final analysis, delivers an ambivalent novel with competing messages: He comments on the tribulations of the past as he intimates radical, fundamental changes in the near future. *Historia de un cautivo*, therefore, encases the discourse of a region's self-referentiality as it comes to grips with its turbulent history and begins to negotiate with elements of the outside world and inevitable influences. In that sense, the work is both entertaining and mildly foreboding.

Judging from the various sources cited, including *Historia de un cautivo*, New Mexico has been a major presence in Hispanic texts since the colonial period. Nuevomexicano literature very early is recognizably localized, specific to the region. By tracing texts from various historical epochs, we can appreciate the development of a Nuevomexicano literary ethos. *Historia de un cautivo*, as an example from a well sustained literary tradition, has remained overlooked, and the unresolved dichotomies and troubling dilemmas that the novel brings to light have often been misunderstood or misinterpreted. What is required now is to retrace the steps of the Nuevomexicano literary tradition, unearthing texts that remain hidden in early newspapers or that lie unread in archives. Further research into and careful critical discussion of these narratives will unravel meanings that have heretofore been compromised, and will, at last, allow a comprehensive history of our Nuevomexicano literary heritage to emerge.

Notes

1. Hernán Gallegos's "Relación y conclusión del viaje y suceso que Francisco Chamuscado con ocho soldados hizo en el descubrimiento del Nuevo México" appears in Vol. 15 of Joaquin Pacheco and Francisco Cárdenas's edited *Colección de documentos inéditos, relativos al descubrimiento, conquista y colonización de las posesiones españolas en América y Oceanía, sacados, en su mayor parte, del Real Archivo de Indias* (42 Vols., Madrid: Imprenta de Manuel B. de Quirós, 1864–1865).

Literature Cited

Primary Sources

Actualidades. 1881. *Revista Católica*. 2 December:543.

Alvarez, Manuel. 1834 (24 December). *Memorandum Book of Manuel Alvarez*. Manuel Alvarez Papers, Center for Southwest Research, Zimmerman Library, University of New Mexico, Albuquerque.

Amaro Hernández, José. 1983. *Mutual Aid for Survival: The Case of the Mexican American*. Malabar, Fla.: Robert E. Krieger.

Arellano, Anselmo F. n.d. The Rise of Mutual Aid Societies Among New Mexico's Spanish-Speaking During the Territorial Period. Unpublished manuscript.

Arellano, Anselmo F. and Julián Josué Vigil. 1985. *Las Vegas Grandes on the Gallinas, 1835–1985*. Las Vegas, N.Mex.: Editorial Teleraña.

Campa, Arthur L. 1946. *Spanish Folk-Poetry in New Mexico*. Albuquerque: University of New Mexico Press.

Chacón, Eusebio. 1892. *El hijo de la tempestad; Tras la tormenta la calma; dos novelitas*. Santa Fe: La Tipografía de *El Boletín Popular*.

Colahan, Clark and Francisco A. Lomelí. 1989. Miguel de Quintana: An Eighteenth-Century New Mexico Poet Laureate? In *Pasó por Aquí: Critical Essays on the New Mexican Literary Tradition, 1542–1988*, ed. Erlinda Gonzales-Berry, 65–78. Albuquerque: University of New Mexico Press.

de Baca, Manuel C. 1896. *Historia de Vicente Silva y sus cuarenta bandidos, sus crímenes y retribuciones*. Las Vegas, N.Mex.: Las Vegas Normal University.

Gonzales, Porfirio. 1898. *Historia de un cautivo*. Serialized in *La Voz del Pueblo* (Las Vegas, N.Mex.) 4 June–3 September.

Grove, Pearce S., Becky J. Barnett, and Sandra J. Hansen, eds. 1975. *New Mexico Newspapers: A Comprehensive Guide to Bibliographical Entries and Locations*. Albuquerque: University of New Mexico Press.

Illustrated History of New Mexico from the Earliest Period of its Discovery to the Present Time, Together with Biographical Mention of Many of its Pioneers and Prominent Citizens of Today. 1895. Chicago: The Lewis Publishing Co.

Kanellos, Nicolás. 1994. A Socio-Historic Study of the Development of Hispanic Community Newspapers in the United States. In *Handbook of Hispanic Cultures in the United States; Sociology*, ed. Félix Padilla, 239–256. Houston: Arte Público Press.

Lomelí, Francisco A. 1990. Hispanic Literary Legacy in New Mexico, 1880–1930. Unpublished manuscript.

———. 1987. New Mexico as a Lost Frontier: A Cultural and Literary Radiography. In *La línea: ensayos sobre literatura fronteriza mexico-norteamericana/The Line: Essays on Mexican/American Border Literature*, eds. Harry Polkinhorn, Gabriel Trujillo Muñoz, and Rogelio Reyes, 81–92. Mexicali/Calexico: Universidad Autónoma de Baja California/San Diego State University.

Major, Mabel, Rebecca W. Smith, and T. M. Pearce. 1938. *Southwest Heritage: A Literary History With Bibliographies*. Albuquerque: University of New Mexico Press.

Martin, Russel. 1990. Sagebrush School of Literature. *Los Angeles Times*, 1 April:4.

Paredes, Raymond. 1987. Early Mexican-American Literature. In *A Literary History of the American West*, sponsored by the Western Literature Association. Fort Worth: Texas Christian University Press.

Prince, Mary Catherine. 1918. The Literature of New Mexico. Unpublished manuscript.

Center for Southwest Research, Zimmerman Library, University of New Mexico, Albuquerque.

Pimentel, Francisco. 1885. *Historia crítica de la literatura y de las ciencias de México. Desde la Conquista hasta nuestros días.* México: Librería de la Enseñanza.

Ritch, William G. 1885. *Aztlan: The History, Resources and Attractions of New Mexico.* Boston: D. Lothrop & Co.

Shea, John Gilmary. 1887. The First Epic of Our Country. By the Poet Conquistador of New Mexico, Captain Gaspar de Villagra. *United States Catholic Historical Magazine* (April):1–16.

Stratton, Porter A. 1969. *The Territorial Press of New Mexico, 1834–1912.* Albuquerque: University of New Mexico Press.

Villagrá, Gaspar Pérez de. 1992. *Historia de la Nueva México, 1610: A Critical and Annotated Spanish/English Edition.* Translated and edited by Miguel Encinias, Alfred Rodríguez, and Joseph P. Sánchez. Albuquerque: University of New Mexico Press.

Secondary Sources

Gonzales-Berry, Erlinda, ed. 1989. *Pasó por Aquí: Critical Essays on the New Mexican Literary Tradition, 1542–1988.* Albuquerque: University of New Mexico Press.

Gutiérrez, Ramón and Genaro Padilla, eds. 1993. *Recovering the U.S. Hispanic Literary Heritage.* Houston: Arte Público Press.

Herrera-Sobek, María, ed. 1993. *Reconstructing a Chicano/a Literary Heritage: Hispanic Colonial Literature of the Southwest.* Tucson: The University of Arizona Press.

Construction of Identities:
A Regional Ethos

Retratos de Mestizaje
A Photographic Survey of Indo-Hispanic Traditions of the Río Grande Corridor

Miguel Gandert

CHICANO, LATINO, HISPANIC—the debate over cultural identity is an important issue for all Hispanos in the United States, but within the four-hundred-year heritage found in New Mexico, the definition of who we are can be confusing and often controversial.

Growing up in Santa Fe, New Mexico, I was taught that Nuevomexicanos, especially those from the north, were Spanish-American. *La Raza* from southern New Mexico and other Hispanos in the region were thought to be more Mexican than the "Spanish-Americans" from the north.

Culture can be examined in more critical ways than ethnic or national labels imply. The camera, far from being an objective observer, can be a catalyst for self-examination and visual comparison, especially in cultural, spiritual, and ritual traditions. The focus for this project is a visual examination of several community rituals and what they share with similar cultural communities in the region of the Río Grande del Norte.

In 1540 the Hispano *mexicanos* first appeared in what is now New Mexico. San Gabriel, located near San Juan Pueblo, became one of the most remote outposts of the Spanish diaspora. During that time, the miscegenation occurring between native peoples and the descendants of Hispano *mexicanos* evolved unique cultural traditions, many of which continue today.

Who are the arbitrators of these cultural traditions? Who are the guardians of the *herencia*? Clues to our cultural identity can be found in fiestas, feast days, and rituals, during which time the communities of the Río Grande corridor reflect on their historical and spiritual traditions. In many of the communities examined in this survey, great efforts are made by members of the community to create elaborate pageants based on traditions that have evolved from the combination of colonial Spanish and Amer-Indian traditions.

During the last several years I have been photographing the urban and rural Hispano experience found along the Río Grande corridor. Some of the images in this survey have been edited to create a visual discourse, an experience found along the Río Grande corridor, an examination of who we are, and perhaps a more realistic look at our *mestizaje* heritage. My interest is in photographing the blurring of ritual between Indian culture and that which has been traditionally described as Hispanic culture in the Southwest. For the sake of this discussion I will describe these traditions using the term "Indo-Hispano," a term that perhaps embodies the best representation of the culture heritage of this region. Images in this survey were taken in communities as far north as Amalia, New Mexico, a village a few miles from the Colorado border, and continuing to the south to Ciudad Júarez, a Mexican border city of over a million people.

Prior to discussion of the images in the survey, it is important to examine the methodology under which my images were created. I consider myself a documentary photographer. My work is part of a continuing tradition in photography that is as old as the medium. Documentary photography is, simply stated, the fair and reasonable presentation of the "real" world with images that communicate ideas. My primary concern is people and their relationship to their environments.

In the photographic history of New Mexico, the visual history of the state has traditionally been portrayed by white males, and the interpretation and dissemination of images have been controlled by the same. At the turn of the century, much of what was known about Nuevomexicanos was based on the writings and images of Charles Lummis, a white man who photographed the *hermanos penitentes* while protected by an armed guard. The visual history of the depression era in New Mexico is seen through the images of John Collier and Russell Lee, who visited the state while on assignment for the Farm Security Administration.

I feel it is important at this time that Nuevomexicanos assert their own cultural identity as image-makers and scholars by examining critically the Indo-Hispano perspective and the traditions that make New Mexico a culturally rich and complex place.

In the kind of photography I practice, certain issues are vital. Perhaps the primary one is my lack of enthusiasm for the journalistic fallacy of objectivity. I do not claim to be an objective observer of events, but I do make the effort to be fair and honest. My objective is not to manipulate the truth; rather, I strive to create images that are both informative and compelling. There is a large amount of portraiture in the photographs I make. Through this confrontational method of picture-making, the subjects of the imagery are given some control over the way they are perceived on film.

A photograph should possess creative tension and a sense of drama; it should provide a satisfactory aesthetic experience. Theatrical qualities within the frame have always been an important factor during my editing process. The pictures that are exhibited or published are only a small percentage of the images that are actually created during specific events.

Theatrical qualities in documentary imagery have often been criticized. Postmodernist photographic theory claims that documentary photographers presume to offer their work as a "verifiable reality," presenting the images on film as automatically authentic despite the possibility of theatricality or hyperbole. As an artist attempting to understand that which changes and disappears, I would hope that my images would extend beyond the simplistic issues of voyeurism. The subjects in the photographs are in the theater of the world, presenting their own ritualistic pageantry. I respond to the theatric performance by recording and therefore preserving it in the form of imagery. This is my method of documentary photography.

I seek to create images that viewers will study and question. In the strongest images there needs to be a tension, or at least empathy, for the subjects in front of the camera. As a Chicano I believe my pictures reveal a unique viewpoint and a level of intimacy that is seldom seen in regional photographs. In other more traditional academic pursuits, such as history, political science, and anthropology, Hispano scholarship has created new insights into the ways New Mexico's regional culture is viewed.

The camera and the photographer are constantly framing and editing images out of the world. In my work, single images are less important than larger groups of images. The photographs are conceptually linked; they relate to well-defined themes and issues. In this survey, I have gone from showing very specific events to the presentation of political, religious, and cultural activities in a regional context. The pictures examine commonalities in spiritual community Hispano rituals. The purpose of this survey is to create dialogue. Upon viewing these photographs, Nuevomexicanos may address the issue of their *mestizaje* heritage and Indo-Hispano culture. I am hopeful that this will support new dialogue about post-Spanish colonial heritage, which is a product of the miscegenation between Europeans and the native peoples of the Americas.

There is a specific thesis for the selection of photographs in this survey. I seek to create visual conjecture, namely that the culture of the native peoples of this region, both Hispanos and Amer-Indians, is an Indo-Hispano culture. Based on that shared heritage, the cultural delineation between Nuevomexicanos and Southwest Amer-Indian is more political than spiritual.

When we look at how Nuevomexicanos define their cultural legacy, the question needs to be asked: How much of our image is formed through the mainstream media. Was it not politics that defined the role of Nuevomexicanos in territorial New Mexico? In terms of land grants and the Treaty of Guadalupe-Hidalgo, it appears that white conquerors needed a justification to distinguish between the legal rights of Indians and *mexicanos*. Indians have been perceived as citizens of sovereign nations, protected by both the United States and New Mexico's territorial governments; if the same sovereign rights had applied to Nuevomexicanos, there would have been little prime land available to settlers from the east.

The spirituality of the land and the comprehension of injustice against the land grant claims of Nuevomexicanos based on the Treaty of Guadalupe-Hidalgo is where this survey begins. This treaty, signed between Mexico and the United States in 1848, ended the Mexican-American war and ceded the northern frontier of Mexico, including New Mexico, Arizona, and California, to the United States. A major provision of the Treaty of Guadalupe-Hidalgo was to insure that the land grants made to Indians and Hispanos, under decrees from the king of Spain, were respected.

One hundred and forty years later the treaty is still an issue. In 1988 I documented the land occupation by followers of Amado Flores in the northern New Mexico community of Tierra Amarilla. Based on the Treaty of Guadalupe-Hidalgo, Flores wrote a deed, filed it at Río Arriba county, and paid taxes on the land. Later, a land speculator from Arizona claimed the land and New Mexico's district court told Flores the land was not his and he would have to leave. Flores refused and was jailed, and a group of armed supporters occupied the land. Pedro Archuleta, a veteran of the Reies López Tijerina land-grant campaign twenty years earlier, led the occupation. During the time I was conducting my field work, a *New York Times* interviewer asked Archuleta why Hispanos should have any claims to the land, why shouldn't they return the land back to the Indians. Archuleta answered with a single sentence in Spanish, "*¿Quién es mi mamá?*" Who is my mother?). This was a reflective reference to the miscegenation between Spanish male colonists and the region's native people.

When we contemplate the spirituality of Indians in the Southwest, we think of traditional religion based on a reverence for the ancient ones, the past and the sanctity of land. In many ways, our Indian *vecinos* (neighbors) had a profound effect on how the Hispanos regarded the land, as the original land grants with community ownership were structured much like pueblo land holdings. Continuing struggles in northern New Mexico to preserve water rights and the traditional agrarian lifestyle demonstrate that Nuevomexicanos' fidelity to preserve and survive continues.

The issues of land grants and spirituality come together each year during Easter in Tomé, a Hispano village located about thirty miles south of Albuquerque. In 1966 the courts were petitioned to dissolve the original Tomé land grant, and a lump sum was paid to their heirs. A volcanic mountain called El Cerro is the heart of the grant and is sacred to the community. The land was sold to the Horizon Corporation, which held the title to the property and posted signs prohibiting trespassers. It was not until January 1993 that El Cerro was returned to the community. Yet despite the Horizon signs about trespassing, over the years Nuevomexicanos have appropriated the hill as their own during Holy Week.

"*Los Peregrinos de Tomé*" (The Pilgrims of Tomé) is a series of images that documents the spiritual pilgrimage to El Cerro. It is a vital center of worship for this part of New Mexico. Years ago the community *morada,* a meeting place for the *hermanos penitentes* (a lay Catholic brotherhood), was located at the base of the hill. Although the most recent *morada* has been abandoned, the *hermanos* still have a profound influence on the spirituality of the hill. Many people, in the tradition of the *hermandad,* carry crosses on their backs and climb the hill barefoot or on their knees.

A revealing image in this series is of Edwin Berry, a *penitente* and the *hermano mayor* of the Tomé brotherhood. In the photograph, Berry is shown singing traditional *alabados* (Spanish religious hymns) as he plays a drum. When Berry was asked the significance of the drum, he says it is because of his Indian heritage. Like many Nuevomexicanos, Berry considers himself a *genízaro,* a descendent of detribalized Indians dating back to the colonial period. Berry acknowledges cultural miscegenation as central to his Indo-Hispano heritage, and like Pedro Archuleta, is proud of that *herencia.*

When one examines the content of images in the survey, there are many that contain references to *Nuestra Señora de Guadalupe.* Her symbolism is important to an understanding of the cultural identity of this region. She is the most widely venerated symbol in the northern portion of the Spanish diaspora. *La Guadalupana* is the spiritual symbol of the miscegenation of the colonial Spaniard and the Amer-Indian.

The history of the *virgen* is almost as old as the history of the Spaniards' arrival in the New World. The apparition of Our Lady of Guadalupe (*la Morenita* or "the little dark one," as she is often called) was first recorded in the Americas on December 9, 1531, thirty-nine years after Christopher Columbus landed. She appeared on a remote hilltop of Tepeyac, now Mexico City. Tepeyac was the sacred place of the pre-Columbian goddess Tonantzín, the Earth Mother. The young dark-skinned *virgen,* wearing a blue-green mantle filled with stars, was seen by the Amer-Indian peasant, Juan Diego. She left her image on his cloak.

With the early Spanish and *mestizo* settlers, the *virgen* and her influence came north through the Río Grande corridor. She has since become the symbol of peace and justice for minorities along the Río Grande as well as for other Indo-Hispanos of the region.

Los matachines, a ritualistic dance, is another point in the visual analysis of these photographs. This ceremonial dance is an important part of numerous Hispano and Amer-Indian communities. Although the origin of the word "*matlachín*" is unknown, the choreography and symbolism are thought to have come to the Americas from Spain, and may date from the Moorish invasion of Spain in the eighth century. Although the dancers and the rituals vary from community to community, there are many characters which remain constant within all the different presentations. In New Mexico the *matachines* pageant is considered primarily a Hispano tradition, although several pueblos, including Taos, Picurís, San Juan, and Jemez, perform the ritual dance. In Mexico and along our southern border with Mexico, the *matachines* are performed by numerous indigenous groups, including the Yaquis in southern Arizona and the Tarahumaras who live in the remote areas of *Barranca del Cobre* in northern Mexico. Both are Amer-Indian. The dance of the *matachines* does not have a specific day on which it is to be performed. The ritual performance varies from community to community.

Hispanos who dress as Indians are a third subject in this survey. From northern New Mexico to Juárez, many communities perform dances and rituals during which Hispanos use face paint, feathers, drums, and noisemakers that resemble bows and arrows. In this visual survey, the importance of Amer-Indian objects is seen in numerous rituals. In the north, New Mexico Hispanos call themselves "Comanches." In Juárez, Mexican performers who dress as Indians call themselves "Apaches," and, at the Tortugas celebration in Las Cruces, the Nuevomexicanos who perform costumed as Indians are known as *matachines* or Tewas. Tewas are another group of dancers whose dress is similar to that of the *matachines* in the northern communities of New Mexico; they are called "*danzantes.*"

Certain characters are important in the *matachines* ritual. A partial list of the roles is important to the analysis of these images. The *abuelo* (grandfather) or, in Mexico, *el viejo* (the old man), is a masked trickster whose role is to keep order during the rituals. A fur-masked figure appears in Amalia, New Mexico, where the *abuelo* dances alone during the mid-winter Masquerades. In other communities the *abuelos* are just some of the many characters who participate in the ritual dances.

In Picurís, a small Tiwa pueblo north of Española, New Mexico, Indians dance the *matachines* on Christmas Eve and Christmas Day. There are two *abuelos*, one dressed as a male and a second in female drag. Both wear rubber masks.

In Bernalillo, a town north of Albuquerque, the *matachines* perform on the Feast of San Lorenzo. The *abuelos* wear black hats, and, although they keep order, they are not masked. In Alcalde, where the *matachines* dance on the 27th of December, the *abuelo* mask is made of fur, much like the ones in Amalia.

In Juárez, *el viejo* is like the *abuelos* in Picurís, where rubber masks or Mexican wrestling masks are worn and the characters not only play the trickster, the fool, who keeps order, but also play tricks, while *mexicanos* dressed as Indians dance to the steady beat of the Indian drums.

The Malinche is usually played by a young girl dressed in white. She is the symbol of purity, named after the Indian mistress of Hernán Cortés. She dances in ceremonies in many communities including Alcalde, Picurís, Albuquerque, Bernalillo, Tortugas in Las Cruces, and San Antonio, a small village on the east side of the Sandias where the *matachines* dance for the Fiesta de Nuestra Señora De Mapimí.

The *monarca* is the lead dancer in the *matachines* ceremony. It is this character to whom the Malinche pays tribute. He is an important character in all the typical *matachines* rituals.

The December 12th Fiesta de Nuestra Señora de Guadalupe is key in this survey in that three of the Indo-Hispano pageants in this project, as well as a pilgrimage similar to Tomé, are celebrated on that day. Barrio San José, Albuquerque's largest Hispano barrio, celebrates with *matachines* as a part of their community ritual. Community parish members dress up as Juan Diego and Nuestra Señora de Guadalupe. It is interesting to note that the *matachines* in San José are not from the community, but from the East side of the Sandia Mountains.

In Las Cruces, the celebration is large and spectacular. The feast begins with pilgrims climbing a mountain to the east of Las Cruces. Although the mountain is covered with radar antennas, this pilgrimage, like the one in Tomé, is an example of Nuevomexicanos reappropriating spiritual land rights. Later at the church in Tortugas, the *Guadalupana* is celebrated by Hispanos dressed as Indians and dancing to the beat of drums. There are four groups of dancers at Tortugas—three dress in Indian clothing, although the *danzantes,* the dance group that most resembles the northern *matachines* dancers, complete with a *monarca* and Malinche, do not call themselves *matachines.*

The parallels between Tortugas in Las Cruces and the celebrations in front of the cathedral in Juárez are notable. At both places, *mexicanos* dressed like Indians participate in devotion to *la Guadalupana.* At Juárez the structure of the dance is nearly identical to Tortugas, with the exception of the role played by the *abuelo* or *viejo.* His role as trickster is a significant one.

The tradition of Hispanos dressing as Indians exists in northern New Mexico as well. In this survey I include images from Alcalde, where community men dress as Indians in order to do battle against the Spaniards in a New World version of the historic drama, *Los Moros y Cristianos.* The pageant is also performed in the traditional version at Santa Cruz, New Mexico, a Hispano community near Chimayó. Throughout the Americas, *Moros y Cristianos* is also performed by Hispanos and *indios.*

How is cultural identity lost? In *Nuevo Mexico* there was first the loss of the land, and this tendency continues even today. After land is lost and the lifestyles have changes, traditions are threatened. Next the language is lost. How many young Chicanos no longer speak Spanish or have learned the language only in school? With the loss of Spanish we lose much of the oral history and the spiritual traditions. Finally, there is the loss of culture. This is the battle that all cultures struggle with in the modern world. This is especially important in the reconstructing of an Indo-Hispano cultural legacy.

Ritual performances are community celebrations that explore the complexity of cultural diversity. These images are meant to examine the confluence of traditions illustrating the ways in which Hispanos share much with our Amer-Indian neighbors. The photographs in this survey are part of a regional examination in which the camera reveals a profound Indo-Hispano cultural identity in the Southwest, one that pays tribute not only to miscegenation and complex intercultural traditions, but to the understanding of what it means to be Nuevomexicano. We have asked, are still asking, "*¿Quién es mi mamá?*"

fig 2   Pedro Archuleta, Tierra Amarilla, New Mexico, 1988.
Photo: Miguel Gandert.

fig 3   Amador Flores and another prisoner, Río Arriba County Jail,
Tierra Amarilla, New Mexico, 1988. Photo: Miguel Gandert.

fig 4   Guadalupe Rael, Tomé, New Mexico, 1989. Photo: Miguel Gandert.

fig 5   Edwin Berry, Tomé, New Mexico, 1992. Photo: Miguel Gandert.

fig 6   Moctezuma y su Hija, Tortugas, New Mexico, 1996.
Photo: Miguel Gandert.

fig 7   Danzantes de la Plaza, Juárez, Mexico, 1996. Photo: Miguel Gandert.

fig 8   Armas de los Tiguas, Tortugas, New Mexico, 1996.
Photo: Miguel Gandert.

fig 9   Alegría de los Matachines, Picurís Pueblo, New Mexico, 1996.
Photo: Miguel Gandert.

fig 10　Malinche y Abuelo, Picurís Pueblo, New Mexico, 1995.
　　　　Photo: Miguel Gandert.

fig 11   Abuelo con Chicote y Toro, Alcalde, New Mexico, 1996.
          Photo: Miguel Gandert.

fig 12   Dolor del Abuelo, Juárez, Mexico, 1993. Photo: Miguel Gandert.

fig 13 Orgullo de Cuerno Verde, Alcalde, New Mexico, 1994.
Photo: Miguel Gandert.

fig 14   Soldado de la Santa Cruz, Santa Cruz, New Mexico, 1993.
Photo: Miguel Gandert.

Ni de Aquí ni de Allá
The Emergence of the *Mexicano*/Chicano Conflict

Ana Perches

"*Por más que la gente*
me juzgue tejano
Yo les aseguro
que soy mexicano
de acá de este lado"
(No matter if people think I
am Texan I assure them
that I am Mexican, from
this side of the border)

THE ABOVE *"Corrido del Norte"* by Pepe Guisar expresses what many Mexican nationals living in the United States have felt at one time or another in regard to their Mexican ethnic identity. Guisar does not want people to view him as a Mexican American or Chicano, insisting that he was born on the Mexican side of the border.[1] This ethnic self-consciousness was reflected in several *corridos* of the 1920s as well as in some of the journalistic writings published in Spanish-language newspapers in the United States. Whereas *corridos,* as a popular oral form, reflect the point of view of the *campesino* or working classes, some of the writers of the 1920s to be discussed here were of upper- or middle-class origins. Some of these writers did not participate actively in the economic struggles of their Mexican compatriots.

The three writers to be discussed here—Benjamín Padilla (Kaskabel), Julio Arce (Jorge Ulica), and Daniel Venegas—are classified as Chicanos by most current critics and academics.[2] My focus is on the perception that these Mexican writers had of their special Other, not with reference to their Anglo American co-resident, but to the "Chicano" or American of Mexican descent. They fit into a category of Mexicans who misunderstand, misrepresent, or mistrust the Chicano and *pocho,* with varying degrees of intensity.

In fact, I argue that many of these Mexican nationals insisted on preserving the cultural heritage of the *mexicano* and not of the Chicano, in contrast to Luis Leal's comments in reference to cultural maintenance of Spanish-language newspapers of the period:

> All Spanish-language newspapers published in the United States . . .
> have had one important function: to preserve the Mexican cultural
> heritage of the Chicano, and to stimulate a sense of identity. Most
> important, they have contributed to keeping the Spanish written
> language alive. [Leal 1989, 161]

It is impossible to state how many Mexicans immigrated to the United States during the 1920s or how many chose to remain permanently (Reisler 1976, 56). The fluctuation in numbers reflects economic conditions in both countries, including the rise in Mexican immigration in the 1920s and its dramatic decline in the 1930s, due to the American Depression. Mexican laborers who came to work in the U.S. were generally labeled "chicanos" (Villanueva 1980, 7). Such immigrants were usually associated with low-paying, "unskilled" labor such as agriculture or railroad work.[3]

The period of the Mexican Revolution (1910–1917) and the decade following represent a contrast between middle-class conformist values of some Mexican writers and the anarchist views of the Flores Magón brothers (often known as the "*revoltosos*"), and such revolutionary women as Leonor Villegas de Magón, who organized women's groups and defended Mexican language and culture in Texas (Lomas 1994).

Manuel Gamio, in a study of Mexican immigration carried out in 1926–1927, was among the first scholars to map out the various social classes found in the Mexican immigrant population. Some "[came] to the United States to escape the disorders of the revolutionary periods" (Gamio 1969, 1). While many came from the peasant class, a number of these Mexicans came from middle- to upper-classes and some, such as the writer Daniel Venegas, not only witnessed the deplorable conditions suffered by the immigrant but also worked with the railroad or in other manual jobs (Kanellos 1984, 15). Writers like Kaskabel and Ulica belonged to a social category more attuned with the *ricos* or *gente de razón,* distinct from the large numbers of laborers and *campesinos* who desperately fled Mexico for the U.S. in search of better economic opportunities. That they belonged to the educated middle-class (in both Mexico and the U.S.) provided them with socioeconomic advantages. Ulica and others who had published in Mexico prior to coming to the United States rapidly established themselves in the journalism business, thus escaping much of the physical hardship and discrimination suffered by workers in menial jobs. In other ways, they also fit into Gamio's category of "the Leader and the Intellectual," specifically as urban writers or journalists (Gamio 1969, 183–224).

This period in history, marking the onset of the twentieth century, witnessed a large influx of Mexican immigrants who were more assimilated than the "chicanos" (Villanueva 1980). It is, in part, due to class self-consciousness and a conservative ideology that writers like Ulica and Kaskabel profess a negative attitude toward the "U.S. Mexicans" (*pochos*) of the time. However, the middle class and the *ricos* who fled Mexico were as distinct from the laborers in the U.S. as they had been in Mexico. These writers perceived themselves as exiles, not immigrants, who "wanted to continue to see themselves as Mexican citizens in exile and not as Mexicans accommodating to their new environment" (García 1991, 53). According to Nicolás Kanellos:

> In the U.S. Southwest, educated political refugees of the Mexican Revolution played a key role in publishing. From their upper class, expatriate perspectives, these intellectuals and entrepreneurs created and promoted—and here the newspaper was essential—the idea of a Mexican community in exile, or a "México de afuera" (Mexico on the outside), in which the culture and politics of Mexico could be duplicated until Mexico's internal politics allowed for their return. [Kanellos 1993, 110]

During the 1920s, there were at least four major categories of "Mexicans" throughout the Southwest: (1) the Nuevomexicano or Neomexicanos, the descendants of the Spanish explorers and mestizo settlers from New Mexico and Southern Colorado, with its various social classes; (2) the descendants of Spanish and Mexican settlers from California, Arizona, and Texas, each with distinctive characteristics; (3) the offspring of first- or second-generation Mexicans comprising an upper middle class (often called *gente decente*), a middle class, and a lower class; and (4) immigrants and exiles from Mexico, composed of urban and rural people, mainly Chicanos from *campesino* or working-class roots and educated middle- to upper-middle-class individuals (with variations within each group). The first three categories would be generically lumped into the category of "*pocho*" by many Mexicans from Mexico.

Mexican nationals such as Ulica, Kaskabel, and Venegas did not become aware of their ethnicity until they were confronted with a population of Mexican origin that did not self-identify with Mexico in the expected way. Concerning cultural preservation, Kanellos says that the "*México de afuera*" campaign "was markedly nationalistic and militated to preserve Mexican identity in the United States" (Kanellos 1993, 110). Referring to San Antonio's *La Prensa,* Bruce-Novoa states that "it was the voice of the Mexican exile group. And exiles, having to face the trauma of exodus, often react by reproducing the homeland in a representational form of their own choosing and one that serves their needs" (Bruce-Novoa 1989, 151).

The distinction between Mexicans from Mexico and Mexicans from the United States was progressively more marked with each decade that passed. With the exception of a group of Nuevomexicanos writing during the twenties and thirties, many of the writers in the Southwest who were writing in Spanish for the

Mexican and Mexican American community were originally from Mexico, not the United States.

At the time, writing and publishing were limited to the educated middle or upper classes, and those able to publish in Spanish language journals were an educated middle class. A recent book by Gabriel Meléndez points to the impact of Spanish-speaking newspapers from the turn of the century to the 1950s (Meléndez 1997). In the case of New Mexico, the Spanish language among native Nuevomexicanos was a strong cultural force up to about the 1930s.[4] Antonio Ríos-Bustamante also argues that, during the first decades of the twentieth century, the distinction between *mexicano* and Mexican American was not as marked as it is today. Rather, people identified in terms of their region. For example, "California-born Mexicans were called *californios*" (Ríos-Bustamante 1993a, 246). If the concept of the provincial *patria chica* of the seventeenth and eighteenth centuries prevailed before state demarcations (Ríos-Bustamante 1993b, 4), it can be assumed that continued differences would come about upon the beginning of massive immigrations into the Southwest that brought Mexicans from various cultural regions of Mexico, many of whom were not aware of the unique characteristics of the inhabitants of the region. Regional nomenclature became more complex as certain terms designated specific class standing within the region, such as the term *"californio,"* which was used especially to refer to the old *hacendados* from California.

Although there were variations among the different regions or states, there were middle-class Mexican Americans who identified with Mexico, as in the case of residents from the Texas Lower Valley whose ancestors settled in the region in the 1700s and who, even in the twentieth century, sang the Mexican national anthem in their private schools in Texas (Tatum 1989, 131). As Raymund Paredes points out:

> Thousands of campesinos came north because the fighting had all but destroyed the country's agriculture. Other immigrants were political refugees. Many Mexicans, from every social class, left because they found the prevailing atmosphere of random violence intolerable. But in no sense did the immigration movement represent a widespread rejection of Mexican culture. These people saw themselves as exiles, and many dreamed of returning home. In the meantime, they held as best they could to their traditions and deplored those who did not. [Paredes 1978, 80]

In fact, the onset of the Mexican Revolution brought a new ethnic consciousness that would forever mark the Mexican idiosyncrasy, although, like all idiosyncrasies, it is dynamic and contradictory. The complexity of defining a Chicano identity stems from the fact that such identity is defined not only in defiance and contrast to "Anglo" culture but also by the perception of the Chicano held by the

Mexican national. Although Chicanos from the 1960s and beyond have insisted on self-nomenclature and self-affirmation, many U.S. Mexicans (or Mexican Americans) still refuse to identify with such a term. However, many Mexican Americans self-identifying as "mexicanos" would find that their Mexican national counterparts would not accept them as such, but instead would consider them as Chicano or *pocho*. Such categorization on the part of the Mexican national is usually based on linguistic observation, albeit unconsciously. Therefore, in addition to the Chicano defining himself, it is also the Mexican national, by excluding the Chicano from Mexican identity, who defines who is a Chicano. If it were not for the Mexican national monitoring the Mexicanness of Chicanos, Chicanos would have kept on feeling very Mexican or Mexican enough. It is through opposition, through contrast, through sameness, through dichotomy, that Chicanos define themselves vis-à-vis Mexicans.

The three Mexican writers, Kaskabel, Ulica, and Venegas, often categorized within Chicano literature, exemplify a sentiment of ethnic self-consciousness that combines such factors as *malinchismo*, ideology, and class.[5] By insisting on their Mexicanness, these writers disassociated themselves from the *pochos,* whom they viewed as culturally inferior.[6] The old saying "*no son ni de aquí ni de allá*" (they're neither from here nor from there) is still commonly heard in Mexico when referring to Chicanos. The denigration, "they speak neither English nor Spanish," usually follows.[7]

Two writers with similar backgrounds and views reflect a chronic attitude assumed by many contemporary upper- and middle-class Mexicans: a misunderstanding of the Mexican American often accompanied by a paternalistic attitude of pity toward him.

Kaskabel: The Ultra-Mexican (*mexicanista*) in the First Stage of Chicanoization

Benjamín Padilla, here referred to by his pen-name Kaskabel, was a businessman and a part-time journalist. In 1906, he founded a magazine in Guadalajara, *El Kaskabel,* which was published until 1915 (Rodríguez 1982, 20). Kaskabel met Julio Arce in Guadalajara, became his good friend, and was also exiled in San Francisco in the 1920s. While in San Francisco, Kaskabel continued to write satirical vignettes (*estampas satíricas*) published in various Mexican American newspapers: *La Patria* in El Paso, *Eco de México* from Los Angeles, *El Cronista del Valle* from Brownsville, and *Hispano-América* from San Francisco.

Juan Rodríguez maintains that some of Kaskabel's articles remind us of contemporary Chicano literature because he wrote on such topics as loss of culture and assimilation to Anglo society (Rodríguez 1982, 20). However, it is not these topics themselves that give Kaskabel a Mexican American perspective. In fact, the attitude professed by Kaskabel attests to his lack of comprehension of Mexican American perspectives or empathy with Mexican American people. What Kaskabel confuses as the Mexican's desire to assimilate into American society is actually the necessity for survival that recently arrived Mexican nationals experienced in the United States. Kaskabel accuses his compatriots on the other side of being *malinchistas* or victims of assimilation. *Malinchismo* projects disdain for and denial of one's own culture and promotes admiration for the imitation of another culture.

In the essay *"Los que llegan hablando trabado"* (Those Who Return [to Mexico] Speaking All Jumbled Up) Kaskabel lists seven rules that apply to the Mexican immigrant who desires to pass for an American when he returns to Mexico. He describes *"el vendido"* (the sell-out) as someone who shaves his mustache, wears a cap instead of a sombrero, smokes cigars, and pronounces Spanish with difficulty, including the name of his own country, Mexico. In addition, Kaskabel states that these *"agringados"* (Anglicized Mexicans) do not even speak English because they live side by side with other Mexicans in a Mexican barrio, and because they *"sudan gotas mexicanas de sudor amarguísimo"* (sweat bitter Mexican sweat) (Kaskabel 1923, 363). Kaskabel, like his contemporaries, criticizes the exploitation suffered by the Mexican workers at the hands of the American bosses who chew tobacco and makes them work endlessly. The technique of caricature, although humorous, creates a stereotype of the Mexican immigrant, a stereotype held by many Mexicans vis-à-vis the Mexican American or Chicano. In fact, Kaskabel's rendition of the *"pocho"* dialect resembles the speech pattern of an Anglo trying to learn Spanish more than it does the everyday speech of the *pocho*. The following passage is unrealistic, especially given the fact that the speaker, according to Kaskabel, doesn't even speak English:

> *Oh . . . bueno . . . tú sabes. Yo mucho tiempo fuera de mi país . . . sabes. Oh, mucho gusto sienta volver Meksico . . . !* (Oh . . . well . . . you know. I much time out my country . . . you know. Oh, very happy feels return Meksico . . . !) [Kaskabel 1923, 362]

Kaskabel believes that these U.S. Mexicans or *pochos* speak no English and a very broken Spanish. By reiterating his disdain for the Mexican American population's loss of Spanish, he reaffirms his own Mexicanness. He assumes an anti-*malinchista* position but fails to understand not only the linguistic reality of the Chicano, but also his vulnerable position in a society that stresses assimilation.

In an interesting twist to Kaskabel's ethnic ideology, we find the position of the Mexican residing in the U.S. who experiences a detachment from his mother country, and therefore undergoes an initial process of Chicanoization. This is seen in his reference to the fact that he feels more Mexican than Mexicans from Mexico:

Los que por acá luchamos para ganarnos la vida, sentimos amar más hondamente nuestra tierra. Somos más mexicanos que los que viven en el propio México. (Those of us here who struggle to earn a living feel deeper affection for our country. We are more Mexican than those who actually live in Mexico.) [Kaskabel 1923, 364]

However ironic or contradictory this may seem, such a comment makes Kaskabel in some ways more "Chicano" or *"mexicano de este lado"* (Mexican from this side), and less Mexican because he is identifying with a sector of the population (*somos*) that resides in the United States and is ethnically at odds with his Mexican counterparts. The sector of the population with whom he identifies is composed of individuals like himself who continue to feel much more Mexican than Mexican American. His attitude toward Mexicans from this side is generally negative, and his writing displays a sense of cultural superiority.

Ulica: Devil's Advocate or Devilish Chronicler?

Coming from a similar background, Julio G. Arce, better known by the pseudonym Jorge Ulica, has received more critical attention than Kaskabel perhaps because he stayed in the United States until his death in 1926. The son of a medical doctor, Ulica was born in Guadalajara in 1870. From an early age, he took a strong interest in journalism and published his first newspaper at the age of fourteen (Rodríguez 1982, 9).[8] He studied pharmaceutical science and moved to Mazatlán, Sinaloa, to work at a friend's pharmacy, but suddenly took an interest in journalism. Among the newspapers that influenced him was *El Correo de la Tarde*, which published poetry by two Mexican Modernistas, Amado Nervo and Enrique González Martínez. Using the pseudonym "Jorge Ulica," he began to write controversial literary criticism. He then moved to the state capital, Culiacán, and joined the only newspaper in the city, including the inauguration of Teatro Apolo in 1892 (Rodríguez 1982, 10–11).

Ulica was encouraged by his colleagues to start a literary magazine, inviting his friend, Manuel Bonilla, to be co-editor of *Bohemia Sinaloense*. The first issue appeared on September 15, 1895 and was a success during its two years of existence. Ulica was also active in politics and served in various positions that were awarded to him for his support of the Porfirio Díaz government (Rodríguez 1982, 12). In 1901, Ulica published a newspaper, *Mefistófeles,* which ran for seven years. Soon afterwards, as Francisco Madero was gaining political ground against the Díaz dictatorship, Ulica was writing against Madero's political beliefs in *El Diario del Pacífico*. Back in Guadalajara, he found it difficult to find a steady job and teamed up with some friends who had also fled Sinaloa. He then started an evening newspaper, *El Diario de Occidente,* and founded an association of journalists who had become targets of the revolutionary forces. In 1915, Ulica fell into the hands of the revolutionaries and was jailed for two-and-a-half months (Rodríguez 1982, 14).

Desperate to leave Mexico, Ulica embarked on the first ship leaving Mexico, not knowing of its destination. As it turned out, the ship was headed for San Francisco, where he arrived in October 1915. Like many other Mexicans in his situation, he took a job as a laborer in the American Can Company, but soon found placement in one of the Spanish language newspapers, *La Crónica*. He assumed the position of the editor in November 1915 and remained in charge for two years (Rodríguez 1982, 15).

Ulica's collection of *Crónicas diabólicas* (Rodríguez 1982) comprises humorous essays on various aspects of American life, with an abundance of commentaries dealing with the Mexican population residing in the United States and its desire to assimilate into mainstream American culture. Ulica pokes fun at the increasing use of English words or anglicized Spanish words, which formed a hybrid language that he defined as "*pocho*," a common derogatory term used mostly by Mexican nationals to describe the way Mexican Americans/Chicanos spoke Spanish. In his *crónica* "Do You Speak Pocho . . . ?" Ulica sarcastically suggests that a Pocho Academy (like the Royal Academy of the Spanish Language) be established with its own dictionary of "*español-pocho*" and a list of vocabulary items in the *pocho* dialect ("*vocabulario de pocherías*"). Using a play on words, Ulica states that he will be one of its most diligent students (*uno de los alumnos más aplicados*) and that his application is on its way ("*Y en seguida irá mi 'aplicación'*")[9] (Rodríguez 1982, 155).

Ulica is a master of satire. He strikes a linguistic chord in bilinguals who have experienced a momentary loss of a word, whether in English or in Spanish. In "Do You Speak Pocho . . . ?" Ulica deliberately writes the title in English in order to make the point that the dialect spoken by many "Spanish" people from California is "*un revoltijo, cada día más enredado, de palabras españolas, vocablos ingleses, expresiones populares y terrible* 'slang'" (a scramble, more mixed-up by the day, of Spanish words, English words, popular expressions, and terrible slang) (Rodríguez 1982, 153). In this *crónica*, Ulica reproduces a letter written to him by Mrs. Skinejon, who once was Señora Pellejón. This letter is basically written in Spanish with an abundance of words that Ulica places between quotation marks. Such words or phrases are either English words written with Spanish phonics (*posofis*=post office, *lob y quises*=love and kisses, *jiven*=heaven), false cognates ("*aplicación*" instead of *solicitud* for application, *papeles* instead of *periódicos*) or idiomatic expressions that do not translate literally from English to Spanish (*levantar infierno* for "to raise hell"). By having Mrs. Skinejon misspell English words such as *aromovil* (automobile), *don Taun* (downtown), *especial de liver* (special delivery), Ulica is not necessarily implying that people such as Mrs. Skinejon do not master either language, but rather that these people have such a tremendous urge to assimilate that they purposely choose to speak this way. Such seems to be the case with Mrs. Skinejon, who, within a few months after leaving Mexico, *"habla perfectamente pocho"* (speaks *pocho* perfectly) (Rodríguez 1982, 153). Ulica exaggerates the intensity of the longing to assimilate, calling attention to the "problem" and achieving a comical caricature of the *pocho*. Ulica demonstrates a superiority complex vis-à-vis Mexican (Americans), many of whom lacked the educational opportunities of middle-class exiles such as himself. In reference to the educational situation of the 1880s, Antonio Ríos-Bustamante points out that:

> Research on literacy appears to indicate that more recent Mexican and Latin American immigrants tended to have a higher literacy level than native Mexican Californios who tended to have a more rural heritage and lifestyle. [Ríos-Bustamante 1993a, 262]

Ulica, although a self-proclaimed *"defensor de la Raza"* (defender of the Mexican people), makes no attempt to extol qualities found in the Mexican population (Lomas 1978, 48). There is a contrast between his self-representation and the representation of the Mexican population in the U.S. Lomas argues that Ulica takes an elitist stand, flaunting a privileged economic status that makes him acceptable within Anglo American society in general (Lomas 1978, 48). She also critiques the way in which Ulica conveniently slides between a position that criticizes the acculturation process to which the Mexican is subject and a position that condones various Anglo American traits of the middle class.

Ulica's elitist attitudes are based on his own experience as a member of the middle-class of Mexico, however. He, like Kaskabel, does not want to be "confused" with the "masses" and therefore makes a point of constantly ridiculing people of Mexican descent who have undergone a certain degree of transculturation or biculturalism. Forgetting that the Spanish language is viewed by him and others as a sign of the non-educated, Ulica's perception of *"pocho"* language and lifestyle may have been somewhat different had he settled in northern New Mexico, where Spanish was more prevalent, as opposed to San Francisco. However, in his attempt to resist becoming "Chicano" or Mexican while on this side, Ulica undergoes the first state of Chicanoization, which is recognizing that such a process is a possibility and even a cultural "threat" to someone who prides him/herself on being, as the popular Mexican expression goes, *"más mexicano que el nopal"* (more Mexican that the prickly pear cactus) and never a *"vendido."*

Venegas: Slapstick Social Commentary

Daniel Venegas published the novel *Las aventuras de don Chipote o cuando los pericos mamen* (*The Adventures of Don Chipote or When Parrots Suckle Their*

Young) in 1928 in a Los Angeles based Spanish-language newspaper, *El Heraldo de México*.[10] Nicolás Kanellos, who rediscovered this novel, once referred to it as "the first Chicano novel" (Kanellos 1984, 8),[11] but it is more accurate to see it as a novel dealing with the Chicano experience from a Mexican perspective.

Daniel Venegas was a newspaper editor for *El Malcriado* (The Brat), a satirical weekly from Los Angeles during the 1920s. Kanellos describes the paper as "chatty periodical which employed worker's dialect and openly identified with Chicanos, the term used both in the newspaper and in his novel." Venegas also wrote plays and directed a vaudeville company in Los Angeles whose audience was working class.[12]

In a similar manner, Daniel Venegas is quick to criticize Mexicans who forget their native language and who show off the minimal English they know to their compatriots:

> *[A]lgunos mexicanos, nomás cruzan la línea divisora y ya no saben hablar su idioma; presumen de gringos, principalmente cuando encuentran paisanos recién desempacados, a quienes les presumen de su sabiduría en el toke inglis.* ([S]ome Mexicans, as soon as they cross the dividing line, can no longer speak their language. They pretend arrogantly to be gringos, especially when they meet recently arrived countrymen, to whom they show off their knowledge of "tok inglis" [English]. [Venegas (1928) 1984, 45]

Venegas's novel begins and ends in the same place, in a peaceful *ranchería* (small ranch) probably in the central state of Michoacán.[13] The protagonist, don Chipote de Jesús María Domínguez, and his wife, doña Chipota (the don/doña title, used for the upper classes or people highly respected by their community, injects an ironic tone), work hard to feed their "*chipotitos.*" The scatological tone of the novel begins in the first chapter, where Chipote (a made-up name that, for Mexicans, refers to a temporary protruding bump on the head caused by a blow) works as an oxen-driver, "*picándole la cola al buey*" (poking the ox's ass). Chipote, Venegas tells the reader, "*tenía que seguir a la retaguardia del cornudo, aspirando de vez en cuando las poco confortadoras emanaciones del conducto trasero del animal*" (had to follow in the rearguard of the horned one, occasionally inhaling the not-so-comforting emanations from the animal's posterior conduit) (Venegas 1984, 16). Throughout the novel, a combination of linguistic registers, ranging from the most formal Spanish to the most colloquial, creates a humorous, slapstick adventure with occasional double-entendres and many picaresque elements. Don Chipote is impressed by Pitacio, who returns from the United States in a fancy outfit (yellow shoes, silk socks, and cowboy hat), weaving story after story of riches and economic opportunity up North. Don Chipote begins his journey, accompanied by his faithful dog, Sufrelambre (he who suffers hunger), and arrives in Juárez, referred to by the narrator as one of the most perverse cities in Mexico, a place where people from the United States, unable to consume alcoholic beverages because of prohibition laws, find solace in bars and brothels. The narrator laments the fact that, because of this, Americans are quick to judge as ignorant all Mexicans of *"el interior de nuestro país"* (the interior of our country), or what some call the "real Mexico."

Don Chipote arrives at the border crossing on the U.S. side, but before being considered for a visa, is forced to bathe and have his clothes disinfected, thus suffering the first humiliation of many to come (Venegas [1928] 1984, 29). Not being granted permission to cross to the United States, he meets with a *coyote* (middleman) who exploits him and the others. Finally in El Paso, don Chipote and his new friend, Policarpo, get drunk at the hotel and are robbed by a prostitute. Not having money to pay for the food at the restaurant, they are forced to wash dishes. Afterward, they work for the Union Pacific Railroad, which exploits them through their *"suplai"* (supply or company store) system. After a series of jobs at *traque,* laying railroad lines in Arizona and New Mexico, and after recovering from a railroad injury, don Chipote finds a job as a dishwasher in Los Angeles while Policarpo works as a cement mason. After a few paychecks, they buy the latest-style clothes and frequent the vaudeville theaters and movie houses.[14] Don Chipote begins an affair with a waitress, a flapper referred to as his *pelona* (a term that refers affectionately to someone with short hair, but which became the Spanish term for "flapper"). Meanwhile, doña Chipota becomes impatient waiting for her husband to come back and, without telling him, arranges to travel north with all of the *"caravana chipoteril"* (chipotesque offspring). Pitacio, who supposedly had been in charge of the land, goes with them at doña Chipota's expense. Riding on four burros, they finally reach the United States and encounter difficulties similar to those of most immigrants. Doña Chipota tries her best to haggle with the *coyote* to no avail. Finally, they make their way to Los Angeles. Doña Chipota, wanting to have some fun, goes to a theater one night, and, to her surprise, finds that her husband is one of the performers. She begins to shout at him and to hit him while the audience believes that it is part of the show. When the *chipotitos* also climb up on stage and make a racket, the audience complains and the chipotesque family is sent to jail. They are subsequently deported back to their *rancho.* On the way home, doña Chipota forgives her husband and they return to the peaceful setting of their *campesino* surroundings. They are met with enthusiasm by neighbors who believe they have returned with plenty of money in their pockets. Don Chipote asks his former boss for work, sells him a few burros, and begins to work the land as before. The Epilogue repeats the idyllic setting found in the first chapter, including the description of driving oxen. But it adds the memories of bitter adventures and amorous moments coupled with the constant disillusionment and *fracasos* (failures) experienced by "chicanos ... who leave their country, inspired by the many tales of those who have been to the United States, supposedly to sweep the streets of gold" (Venegas [1928] 1984, 155). The last paragraph contains Venegas's thesis, which appears several times throughout the novel:

> *Y pensando en esto, [don Chipote] llegó a la conclusión de que los mexicanos se harán ricos en Estados Unidos: CUANDO LOS PERICOS MAMEN.* (And thinking about this, [don Chipote] came to the conclusion that Mexicans in the United States will become rich: WHEN THE STARS FALL FROM THE SKY.) [Literally, when parrots breast feed.] [155]

The message found in Venegas, Ulica, and Kaskabel regarding the assimilated Mexican or "*pocho*" parallels that found in some *corridos* of the period. Raymund A. Paredes calls attention to a piece appearing in Los Angeles in the 1920s ("The Renegade") wherein a Mexican national living in the United States deplores the Mexican who yearns to appear American in his big car, all dressed up like a dandy, when in his *rancho* back home he didn't even own a pair of *huaraches*. On the other hand, he also claims that he will never forget his country, and it is because of the unfortunate political situation of his homeland's "*continuas revoluciones*" (ongoing revolutions) that he finds himself far from home. A good Mexican never disowns his homeland, because there is nothing worse than a renegade *("no hay nada en el mundo tan asqueroso como la ruin Wgura del renegado")* (Paredes 1978, 80).

Of the three, Venegas is the most critical of the United States' exploitation of Mexican workers. He does not criticize feminism and, in fact, his only female protagonist shows initiative and determination in her actions. Venegas sympathizes with Chicanos largely because he had worked side by side with them. Whereas Kanellos and Meléndez argue that Venegas uses the "Chicano language," it can be argued that neither Chicano nor Mexican dialect is monolithic. Venegas's novel contains various linguistic registers, among them a very formal Spanish. In fact, the examples given by both Kanellos and Meléndez as "Chicano" words are Mexican as well, and therefore not exclusively Chicano. Moreover, the linguistic patterns of the Chicanos in the novel are very different from those of the narrator. The few dialogues between the *campesinos* are in classic "rural" Spanish. The narrator, on the other hand, is educated in formal Spanish as well as in informal (urban) slang. The narrator's discourse, while on the whole an interesting blend of highly formal words, colloquial expressions or *modismos*, *dichos* (sayings), and *caló* (argot) expressions, does not correspond to that of the typical Chicano of the twenties, nor to that of the present-day Chicano for that matter.[15] In addition, the "Anglicisms" that both Kanellos and Meléndez consider elements of Chicano speech are used very differently by Venegas than by contemporary Chicano writers. Venegas places the English words in italics or in quotation marks to signal a deviation from his own speech. On the other hand, English is used in contemporary Chicano literature as either the predominant narrative language or part of a code-switching and is therefore a natural linguistic process that precludes italics or quotation marks.

The Malinche complex is observed in Venegas in his insistence that "chicanos" (meaning Mexicans who cross over to the United States for work) not venture into the United States. Mexicans should stay in their own country, avoiding not only discrimination, but becoming that despised monster, the *renegado* or traitor. The confusion that the modern reader may have is that Venegas continuously uses the term "chicano" as originally intended, to refer to a Mexican from Mexico who plans to return as soon as he earns enough money to take home. One could argue that don Chipote is a Mexican who ventures into the United States temporarily in search of a job and not a Chicano who is either born in the United States or who immigrates in order to stay. He fits into a category that is difficult to classify. He would not self-classify as Chicano yet his Mexican counterparts would label him as such if he had stayed in the United States. Although Venegas's novel can be regarded as a Mexican novel published in the United States, it should be considered as part of a Chicano literary patrimony because it raises issues of Chicano identity although not from a Chicano perspective.

Feminism as *vendidismo/malinchismo*

Both Jorge Ulica and Kaskabel express patriarchal attitudes throughout their essays. They are appalled by changes taking place in the United States regarding women's rights. Ulica regards the Mexican American woman as someone who has been influenced by American feminism. His aversion to "assimilation" is further intensified when he witnesses changes in the gender status quo. In *"Arriba las Faldas,"* Ulica functions as a "shoulder to weep on," sympathizing with Mexican men who complain to him of a spouse's reluctance to be the obedient *mosquita muerta* (weakling) wife she was back in Mexico: *"En mi tierra, podía haberle tumbado los dientes a manazos; pero aquí, si hace uno eso, lo cuelgan en San Cuintín, como le dicen a la cárcel"* (In my country [Mexico] I could have knocked her teeth out with blows but here, if you do that, they'll hang you in San Cuintín [*sic*], as they call the prison here) (Rodríguez 1982, 145). Ulica satirically describes how gender roles are completely reversed in the U.S., making American women the happiest in the world because their husbands do all the housework, change diapers, do the grocery shopping, wash and iron, and obey their wives in everything. He describes a married couple (Rufina and Castro) getting into an argument because Rufina comes home late one night, drunk, her dress burned by a cigar. She proceeds to scold her husband and beat him physically. Ulica states that there are many Rufinas in these lands, referring to the United States (Rodríguez 1982, 146–147). In another *crónica, "Inacia y Mengildo"* (Rodríguez 1982, 89), Ulica suggests that Mexican men leave their wives in Mexico, as far as possible from the United States, lest they find out that *"aquí mandan ellas"* (women are the ones who give the orders). Ulica presents Mexican women as desiring assimilation and social mobility much more than their male counterparts. Inacia tries to "civilize" her husband, making him cut his hair in the latest style and criticizing his insistence on eating such Mexican foods as chorizo, sopes, tostadas, chicharrones, menudo, and pozole. She, on the other hand, prefers to eat clam chowder, bacon, liver and onions, beef stew, and hot dogs (Rodríguez 1982, 90).

Kaskabel's perspective is very similar to Ulica's, but his misogyny is not necessarily tied to the assimilation process, as is the case in Ulica. However, he expresses his contempt for marriages between Mexican women and Anglo men, labeling it *"el peligro yanqui"* (the Anglo threat). These "gringos," he states, take advantage of what "should be exclusively ours, something intimate that belongs to us (from Mexico), the virgin hearts of our 'chicks': the ineffable love of our Mexican girls" (Kaskabel 1923, 97). In *"Novias y esposas"* (Girlfriends and Wives) (Kaskabel 1923, 113), Kaskabel criticizes modern girlfriends (*"las novias de hoy en día"*), who are more preoccupied with their looks than with their domestic duties (115). Yet, when they get married, they neglect both their looks and their household duties (115). The solution is for the husband to educate his wife in the manner that her "mustached" mother (*"la bigotona mamá"*) should have done, *"a golpes con su cónyuge"* (through physical force) (Kaskabel 1923, 115).

Although Kaskabel usually addresses a male audience, there are cases in which he clearly addresses women. Through the fictitious voice of a priest, he advises married women to continue being coquettish and not to become stinky, uncombed, and sloppy (*"hediondas, desgreñadas y malfajadas"*) (Kaskabel 1923, 235). He adds that, unless married women shape up and be coquettish, there will be many "enemies" who will win the heart of their husbands.

Daniel Venegas presents a more balanced portrait of gender roles. He prescribes less judgment on the actions of his characters in regards to sex roles. He neither condemns nor condones don Chipote's extramarital affair with *"la Pelona,"* and, in the second half of the novel, it is his wife who assumes a more active role in their relationship: she acts independently and assertively without being ridiculed by the narrator. When she travels to the United States to look for her husband, she finds him at the night club doing his act. Instead of portraying her as a passive *campesina,* Venegas has her confront her husband. Having stayed in Mexico while her husband worked in the United States, Mrs. Chipota had not been influenced by American feminism. Therefore, Venegas does not make a connection between the two and shows respect and understanding for doña Chipota.

The authors discussed here are examples of writers who should be categorized within both Mexican and Chicano literary traditions. As scholars recognize the vast differences among a growing ethnic group in the United States, we will have an increasing need to invent new terminology and create new methods of interpretation. It will be insufficient to say that Ulica, Kaskabel, and Venegas understood the "Chicano" experience when in fact they distinguished themselves from the Chicanos of the time. By unveiling these writers' ideologies, we increase our awareness of the immense heterogeneity of the Mexican American experience.

Notes

1. Raymund Paredes interprets *"acá de este lado"* as being the United States: "While the tejano (in *"Corrido del Norte"*) ardently proclaims his allegiance to Mexico despite his American origins, the Mexican-born composer of *"El renegado"* recognizes the easy temptations of American life . . ." (Paredes 1978, 80). I argue that *"acá de este lado"* (this side) in *"Corrido del Norte"* refers to Mexico, not the United States. The singer's attire *(sombrero vaquero, chamarra de cuero, mascada roja)* is often perceived as that of a cowboy, when in fact, he is a *vaquero*. *"Porque uso de lado el sombrero vaquero/porque uso pistola y chamarra de cuero/porque acostumbro mi cigarro de hoja/y anudo a mi cuello la mascada roja/ me creen otra cosa"* (Because I wear my cowboy hat sideways/ because I carry a gun and wear a leather jacket/because I roll my own cigarettes/ and I wear a red bandanna around my neck/ because of those things people take me for something that I am not) (Paredes 1978, 80).

2. Clara Lomas has rightfully argued that Ulica was a "Mexican journalist and a political exile who wrote from that perspective. [He] does not view himself as part of an oppressed minority, and his short satirical pieces reveal more insights about his ideological position than they do about the community he is depicting and satirizing" ("Jorge Ulica," *Dictionary of Literary Biography: Chicano Writers*, Vol. 82, eds. Francisco A. Lomelí and Carl R. Shirley, 268–270, [Detroit: Gale Research, Inc.], 270).

3. For this time period, Nicolás Kanellos uses the term "Mexican(-American)" to designate the general population of Americans of Mexican descent because the term "Mexican-American" did not appear until later. In other contexts, I have proposed the use of the word "chicano" with a lower-case "c" to designate the first definition of the term (a Mexican who emigrates to the United States) in opposition to capital-C "Chicano," which emerged in the 1960s to designate Americans of Mexican descent. The lower-case form is the correct usage for adjectives of ethnicity or nationality in Spanish. Lower-case "chicano" was usually used in a Spanish-language context during the first decades of the twentieth century.

4. Meléndez points out that: "[I]f Neo-Mexicanos and Neo-Mexicanas wished to remain a part of the public discourse that expanded around them, they were obliged to write in English, and within a modality of expression that precluded references to a social history of conquest and subordination" (1997, 205).

5. *Malinchismo* refers to the proclivity of many Mexicans to overly admire foreign culture, specifically American and European, and to denigrate or reject indigenous peoples or their culture.

6. *Pocho* is a derogatory term used mostly by Mexican nationals or Mexican-identified

Mexican Americans to describe what they view as an assimilated Mexican who wants to adapt to American lifestyle, and who often makes a fool of himself in the process. Mexicans are repulsed by the *pocho's* "contaminated" Spanish or his lack of Mexicanness. "*Pocho*" is used as an adjective or noun to describe a hybrid Spanish or dialect. Also, as a verb *("apocharse")* and adjective *("apochado").*

7. Margarita G. Hidalgo's research on language attitudes of residents of Juárez vis-à-vis Chicano Spanish points to a disapproval and rejection of the Chicano dialect often associated with the use of Spanish-English code-switching (24–25). Many respondents emphasize the ugliness and incorrectness of the Spanish spoken in El Paso, stating that "no one should speak that way" *(Nadie debería de hablar así).* (See Hidalgo's *Language Attitudes and Language Use in Ciudad Juárez, México* [El Paso: Center for Inter-American and Border Studies, 1984.]) A survey of Mexican attitudes toward Chicanos, "Unwelcome Home: Chicanos in Mexico," was presented by Erlinda Gonzales-Berry at the Simposio Sobre Estudios Internacionales de la American Association of Teachers of Spanish and Portuguese, Pamplona, 1985.

8. As Juan Rodríguez states in his *"Prólogo"* to *Crónicas diabólicas,* these articles originally appeared in San Francisco's Spanish-language weekly, *La Crónica,* which began publishing in 1914. Ulica served as editor-in-chief from 1915 to 1917. During his absence, *La Crónica* changed its name to *Hispano-América,* and in 1919 Ulica became its sole proprietor and editor-in-chief, a post he held until his death in 1926 (Rodríguez 1982, 15–16).

9. *Aplicación* is an Anglicism for "application"; the Spanish word for application is *solicitud.*

10. Translation of title by Nicolás Kanellos (1993, 114). The title refers to a situation that will never happen, such as "when pigs fly."

11. Francisco Lomelí credits Eusebio Chacón as a pioneer of the "Hispanic novel of New Mexico" (See Lomelí's "Eusebio Chacón: An Early Pioneer of the New Mexican Novel" in Erlinda Gonzales-Berry's edited volume, *Pasó por aquí: Critical Essays on the New Mexican Literary Tradition—1542–1988* [Albuquerque: University of New Mexico Press, 1989], 149–166, p. 149.) Chacón published two short novels in 1892, *El hijo de la tempestad (Son of the Storm)* and *Tras la tormenta la calma (Calmness After the Storm).* Rosaura Sánchez and Beatrice Pita, however, have brought to my attention a novel published in 1885, María Amparo Ruiz de Burton's *Squatter and the Don,* edited by them and reissued by Houston's Arte Público Press in 1992. As we continue to recover the Chicano literary heritage, the title of "first" must remain flexible.

12. Kanellos lists the names of Venegas's plays (all have been lost): *Quién es culpable (Who is to Blame),* 1924; *Nuestro egoísmo (Our Selfishness)* (consisting of three acts and dedicated to Mexican women), 1926; and *Esclavos (Slaves),* 1930. Kanellos also points out a number of magazine articles among Venegas's contributions such as *"El maldito jazz"* (That Darned Jazz), *"El establo de Arizmendi"* (Arizmendi's Stable, which celebrated the boxer, Baby Arizmendi), and *"El con-su-lado"* (The Consulate—a play on words referring to an opinionated or biased Consulate). Referring to the premiere of *Esclavos, La Opinión* (8 January 1930) printed that *"El autor cuenta con muchas simpatías entre el elemento obrero mexicano de Los Angeles, por lo que seguramente tendrá casa llena esta noche"* (The author has many fans among the Mexican laborers from Los Angeles and will therefore have a full house this evening) (Kanellos 1984, 15).

13. The narrator refers to a nearby town by the name of Nacatecuaro. Many towns in Michoacán have the ending "cuaro" as in Pátzcuaro. The "naca" in Nacatecuaro is per-

haps used to connote a poor environment: "naco/a" are derogatory adjectives used to designate lack of sophistication in working-class Mexicans or to refer to persons with "tacky" taste. Michoacán is one of the states from Mexico from which many Mexicans emigrate.

14. Douglas Monroy indicates that "in the new land, even with low wages, one could buy commodified things of great iconic value. Seductive images encountered in movie houses and in fashion advertising provided compelling new models of behavior for Mexican youth" ("'Our Children Get So Different Here': Film, Fashion, Popular Culture, and the Process of Cultural Syncretization in Mexican Los Angeles, 1900–1935," *Aztlán: A Journal of Chicano Studies*, 1988–1990, 19(1):79–108, p. 79.)

15. One could argue that the language found in Venegas is not common to current Chicano speech. An exception may be found in the work of Miguel Méndez, who writes in a formal and "flowered" Spanish, mixed with expressions of *caló* (Mexican/Chicano slang). Because Méndez's (like Venegas's) dominant language is Spanish, however, Méndez represents a small minority within the current Chicano population.

Literature Cited

Primary Sources

Bruce-Novoa. 1989. La Prensa and the Chicano Community. *The Americas Review,* 17(3–4):150–156.

Gamio, Manuel. 1969. *The Mexican Immigrant.* New York: Arno Press and the New York Times.

García, Richard A. 1991. *Rise of the Mexican American Middle Class: San Antonio, 1929–1941.* College Station: Texas A&M University.

Kanellos, Nicolás. 1984. Introduction to *Las aventuras de don Chipote o cuando los pericos mamen by Daniel Venegas.* Mexico City: Secretaría de Educación Pública-Cefnomex.

———. 1993. A Socio-Historic Study of Hispanic Newspapers in the United States. In *Recovering the U.S. Hispanic Literary Heritage,* eds. Ramón Gutiérrez and Genaro Padilla, 107–128. Houston: Arte Público Press.

Kaskabel [Benjamín Padilla]. 1923. *Un puñado de artículos: Filosofía barata.* Barcelona: Casa Editorial Maucci.

Leal, Luis. 1989. The Spanish-Language Press: Function and Use. *The Americas Review* 17(3–4):157–162.

Lomas, Clara, ed. 1994. *The Rebel by Leonor Villegas de Magón.* Houston: Arte Público.

Lomas, Clara. 1978. Resistencia cultural o apropiación ideológica: Visión de los años 20 en los cuadros costumbristas de Jorge Ulica. *Revista Chicano-Riqueña* 6(4):44–49.

Meléndez, A. Gabriel. 1997. *So All Is Not Lost: The Poetics of Print in Nuevomexicano Communities, 1834–1958.* Albuquerque: University of New Mexico Press.

Monroy, Douglas. 1998–1990. "Our Children Get So Different Here": Film, Fashion, Popular Culture, and the Process of Cultural Syncretization in Mexican Los Angeles, 1900–1935. *Aztlán: A Journal of Chicano Studies,* 19(1):79–108, 79.

Paredes, Raymund. 1978. The Evolution of Chicano Literature. *Melus* 5(2):71–110.

Reisler, Mark. 1976. *By the Sweat of their Brow: Mexican Immigrant Labor in the United States, 1900–1940.* Westport: Greenwood Press.

Ríos-Bustamante, Antonio. 1993a. Nineteenth Century Mexican Californians—A Conquered Race: From Landowners to Laborers and "Tenants At Will." In *Regions of La Raza:*

Changing Interpretations of Mexican American Regional History and Culture, ed. Antonio Ríos-Bustamante, 237–269. Encino, Calif.: Floricanto Press.

———. Antonio. 1993b. Preface, Introduction, and Observations: Regions and Raza. In *Regions of La Raza: Changing Interpretations of Mexican American Regional History and Culture,* ed. Antonio Ríos-Bustamante, 1–12. Encino, Calif.: Floricanto Press.

Rodríguez, Juan, compiler. 1982. *Crónicas Diábolicas (1916–1926) de Jorge Ulica.* San Diego: Maize Press.

Tatum, Charles. 1989. Rolando Hinojosa. In *Dictionary of Literary Biography; Chicano Writers,* Vol. 82, eds. Francisco A. Lomelí and Carl R. Shirley, 130–139. Detroit: Gale Research Inc.

Venegas, Daniel. 1984. *Las aventuras de don Chipote o cuando los pericos mamen.* Los Angeles: El Heraldo de México, 1928. Reprint, México: Secretaría de Educación Pública-Cefnomex.

Villanueva, Tino, ed. 1980. *Chicanos (selección).* México: Secretaría de Educación Pública.

Secondary Sources

Bruce-Novoa. 1990. *Retrospace: Collected Essays on Chicano Literature, Theory, and History.* Houston, Tex.: Arte Público Press.

Gonzales, Phillip B. 1991. "Ethnic Diffidence" and "Categorical Awareness": Aspects of Identity Among a Set of Acculturated Blue Collar Mexican Americans." University of New Mexico. Unpublished manuscript.

Kanellos, Nicolás (Daniel Venegas). 1989. *Dictionary of Literary Biography: Chicano Writers,* Vol. 82, eds. Francisco A. Lomelí and Carl R. Shirley, 271–274. Detroit: Gale Research, Inc.

Meléndez, A. Gabriel. 1986. *Camellando en los Estamos Sumidos. The Bilingual Review* 13(3): 87–93.

Paredes, Raymund. 1993. Mexican-American Literature: An Overview. In *Recovering the U.S. Hispanic Literary Heritage,* eds. Ramón Gutiérrez and Genaro Padilla, 31–51. Houston: Arte Público.

Ulica, Jorge. *Treinta años de galeras periodístas: 1881–1911.* Reproduction of a collection of Ulica's newspaper articles. Chicano Studies Library. University of California-Berkeley.

La Alianza Hispano-Americana, 1894–1965
An Analysis of Collective Action and Cultural Adaptation

Olivia Arrieta

⟡ MUTUAL-AID SOCIETIES WERE widespread during the nineteenth century among the laboring classes in Mexico and among different ethnic groups in the United States.[1] Mutual-aid societies were organizations of cooperative assistance for life insurance, but frequently had additional functions. While *sociedades mutualistas* (mutual-aid societies) were particularly popular among *mexicanos*[2] in the Southwest (Rivera 1984), this organizational form had earlier become popular in Mexico around the 1850s. The stated purpose of *sociedades mutualistas* was to provide some degree of grassroots, cooperative economic security for members and their families, primarily through life insurance. Many *sociedades,* however, provided unstated, but equally significant support in religious, educational, legal, political, cultural, and social arenas. *Sociedades* differed in activities, functions, and emphases. Their orientations were predicated on local or regional cultures and on particular social, historical, political, and economic circumstances.

The *Alianza Hispano-Americana* began as a local *sociedad mutualista* in 1894 and grew to be the first national organization for people of Mexican descent in the United States. In 1896 the *Alianza* registered in the state of Arizona as a fraternal insurance society, allowing it to branch out into affiliate lodges and also bringing it under external regulation by the state. Fraternal organizations serve the same basic functions as *sociedades mutualistas,* but have a more sophisticated organizational structure with a complex ritual system and affiliate lodges accountable to a centralized executive branch.[3]

The following discussion includes an overview of the purpose, structure, and maintenance of this *mexicano* organizational effort at adapting to changing conditions in an Anglo-dominated society.

Early in the organizing effort, other local *sociedades mutualistas* were incorporated as lodges of the *Alianza.* These independent local organizations, along with newly formed lodges, were brought together under the fraternal society's over-arching purpose of uniting its membership under its common philosophy, organization, and special rituals.

When the *Alianza* reached its peak in the late 1930s, it consisted of about three hundred lodges and included between 17,000 and 20,000 members in the United

States and Mexico. The initial successful launching of the *Alianza* had been done through organizational efforts and cooperation between Arizona and New Mexico *mexicanos* and the *Alianza*'s executive functions continued to be centered in these two states.

Cultural Foundations of the *Alianza Hispano-Americana*

The fundamental principles of the *Alianza Hispano-Americana* were summarized in the motto *Protección, Moralidad, e Instrucción* (Protection, Morality and Instruction) and no doubt emerged from a social and cultural matrix in place before the creation of the organization. The meaning of each of these principles, described by Tomás Serrano Cabo (1929) in *Las Crónicas* (The Chronicles) of the *Alianza,* is expressed in the very formal and dramatic style of Spanish common to *mexicano* public discourse at the turn of the century. Serrano Cabo was a regional organizer for the early *Alianza* who took it upon himself to record and describe the history of the organization's development in *Las Crónicas.* The meaning of the *Alianza* principles can also be inferred from their use in other forms of *Alianza* discourse, such as conference discussions and correspondence or in the *Alianza*'s monthly publication.

Protección was seen as the primary principle and cornerstone of the organization (Serrano Cabo 1929, 27). In conflating the principle of *Protección* with fraternalism, Serrano is, in effect, presenting a cultural expression of *mutualismo* or mutual aid. Serrano Cabo states in *Las Crónicas:*

> The fraternal man . . . is always ready to sacrifice himself for his neighbor. It is he who imparts benefits to others, without hesitating on details, nor assessing those persons whom he protects and assists. He is beholding to all in general and in particular to the most needy. And there is no time when he is called upon that he does not respond, that one looks for him and he is not found, and that a request is put to him and he does not what he can. The fraternal person suffers with those who suffer and cries with those who cry, rejoicing with those who rejoice. It is essential to have a great heart, in order to be able to store therein the humanitarian sentiments which should imbue the fraternal person. It is not self-interest that guides the fraternal person, nor is self-glorification his goal, nor the desire to gain the attention of others; he has as his objective right for the sake of right. [Serrano Cabo 1929, 28]

The second major principle was *Moralidad,* or morality, which was defined in a social sense rather than through any religious dogma (e.g., general Christianity,

Roman Catholicism, or Protestantism). Like politics, religion and religious debate within the organization was forbidden. Ironically, however, one of the requirements for membership was that the person had a belief in God. *Las Crónicas* generally presents the principle of *Moralidad* as social norms to be followed by worthy members of the community.

The third part of the *Alianza* motto, *Instrucción* (instruction) was interpreted in *Las Crónicas* in terms of the general value of acquiring knowledge as a means of self-improvement and becoming a good member of society (Serrano Cabo 1929, 34–37). This is basically the Mexican view of *educación* as contrasted with the Anglo American view of education as limited to academic learning. In the Mexican view, persons with *educación* know how to handle any social situation to the satisfaction of all concerned; that is, they are polite and well-mannered and adhere to acceptable social forms of behavior and decorum. Serrano Cabo adds that the acquisition of basic knowledge on how to live will especially prepare "our people," for living in a foreign land (i.e., the United States) and becoming better citizens (Serrano Cabo 1929, 35).

The principle of *Instrucción* was also extended to the promotion of Spanish-language maintenance, particularly through formal education. In the early 1900s, for example, an *Alianza* lodge in Metcalf, Arizona, sponsored after-school classes in Spanish for Mexican American students. Later, the *Alianza* promoted Spanish-language instruction nationally as part of maintaining Spanish-English bilingualism. Because the inevitability of English-language incursion into the Mexican American community had become apparent by the 1940s, the idea was apparently to assure the continuation of Spanish along with English. In a 1943 edition of the publication named *Alianza,* the results of their language survey was explained in these terms:

> The object of the survey is to determine as nearly as possible the educational needs of this great area; to crystallize our bi-lingual [*sic*] policy in order to stress the need for the increased teaching of Spanish in all public schools. We believe the teaching of English alone is not sufficient to answer the living problems in this area. In the light of present a future world developments and the growth of the Pan-American idea, we believe formal education must realize the necessity of teaching Spanish in the early school years. [Alianza January 1943, 12]

In general, the same over-arching principle of *mutualismo* was behind the *Alianza* motto of *Protección, Moralidad e Instrucción.* It was meant to guide all activities so that mutual support and assistance promoted the unity and integrity of the ethnic community.

Initial Organization and *Mutualismo*

Initial organizing efforts for enlisting affiliate lodges are thought to have been directed at the elite in different *mexicano* communities (Briegel 1974, 48). The two main researchers of the *Alianza,* James Officer, an anthropologist, and Kay Briegel, a historian, agree that the purpose for the initiation of the *Alianza* was to maintain a degree of political power for the *mexicano*/Hispano elite within the Anglo dominated system in Tucson (Officer 1964, Briegel 1974). With the coming of the railroad to Tucson in 1880 and the accompanying surge of Anglo settlers, entrepreneurs, and investors, the socioeconomic and political status of the Tucson Hispano elite began to be eroded. It has been suggested that the *Alianza* was organized in response to the emergence of the American Protective Association lodge in Tucson in 1894—a carrier of Anglo attitudes of social superiority current at that time in the form of "American nativism" (Officer 1964, Briegel 1974). The *Alianza* was not merely established as a reactive measure to Anglo organization, however, as it also came out of the pre-existing concept of *mutualismo* and the *sociedad mutualista* as an organizational form filtering into the Southwest from Mexico.

The seeds of *mutualismo* had been germinating in Tucson and the surrounding area for about twenty years before the advent of the *Alianza* was formed. By 1875 two *sociedades* existed in Tucson,[4] and between 1886–1893 four other *sociedades mutualistas* arose in other Arizona communities.[5] It is no coincidence that Carlos Velasco, the principal founder of the *Alianza Hispano-Americana,* had been an honorary member of two *sociedades* and honorary president of another (Sheridan 1986, 109) or that the first affiliated lodges of the *Alianza* were established in two of these communities.[6]

Furthermore, much of the groundwork for organizing among *mexicanos* in the Southwest at the turn of the century was done through Spanish-language newspapers.[7] The conceptualization of the *Alianza* was put forth to the community in the Spanish-language newspaper *El Fronterizo,* published by Carlos Velasco, recognized as the founding father of the *Alianza.* Other Spanish-language newspapers throughout the Southwest later became the major means, aside from the *Alianza*'s own publication, for disseminating *Alianza* news and meeting announcements.

Between 1894 and 1913, during what is called the early "mobilization stage" of organizations (Márquez 1993, 6), the *Alianza* organized mainly in Arizona and New Mexico. In 1904 the *Alianza* began organizing in New Mexico by establishing lodges in the mining towns of Silver City and Hillsboro near the southeast Arizona border. By 1942, the *Alianza* had thirty-five lodges in Arizona and forty-five lodges in New Mexico.

Organization based on the concept of *mutualismo* or mutual aid had existed in New Mexico for centuries preceding the nineteenth-century form of Mexican *sociedades mutualistas* (Hernández 1983, 15–29).[8] Earlier Nuevomexicano organizational forms of *mutualismo* were based on cooperation within a farming economy, but the nineteenth-century form of the *sociedad mutualista* offered a modern means of adapting to changing conditions under industrialization (Hernández 1983, 30–32).[9]

As with events in Arizona, the arrival of the railroad in New Mexico in the 1880s brought with it disruptions of the established system of *mexicano* political-economic relationships, and the *mexicano* elite responded in similar ways.[10] *Alianza* lodges were established in New Mexico communities where members were generally part of a mobile population working in the mines and on the railroads, and in communities where local Nuevomexicano leaders needed to adapt to competition from Anglo economic enterprise.

Structure of the *Alianza Hispano-Americana*

Like other fraternal organizations, the *Alianza Hispano-Americana* was governed by statutes that defined the roles of members and officials, delineated procedures for the acceptance and dismissal of members, and prescribed the conduct of meetings and elections. At the national level, the tone of the general organization was set by the Supreme President and through national conventions. The membership was otherwise united through the organization's monthly publication, *Alianza.* General business and many national conventions were held in the organization's national headquarters building completed in 1916 in downtown Tucson.

Of the thirteen Supreme Presidents who held office from 1896 until 1965, nine were born or lived in Arizona, and two were from New Mexico. Arizona Supreme Presidents governed for a total of forty-five years, and the two Supreme Presidents from New Mexico governed for fifteen years. Altogether, the seventy-one-year life-span of the *Alianza Hispano-Americana* was dominated by sixty-nine years of Supreme Presidential leadership from Arizona and New Mexico. (See Table 1.)

The national conventions of the *Alianza Hispano-Americana* afforded a forum for setting the national agenda of the organization. Here, representatives of the hundreds of lodges gathered to elect officials and to discuss and decide on major issues of general concern. Although any member could attend, direct participation in the Supreme Conventions was restricted to delegates from each of the lodges, with the number of delegates determined by the size of each lodge's membership.

Because national conventions could not bring together the entire *Alianza* membership, the primary vehicle for unifying them was the organization's publication, *Alianza,* which was disseminated to all members. The publication remained in newspaper form until about the mid-1930s, when it went into newsletter format; the *Alianza* then moved into magazine format in the 1940s. The publication reported national, state, and local news items in addition to *Alianza* issues, activities of affiliate lodges, literary writings, and visual images.

Table 1

Alianza Hispano-Americana *Supreme Presidents*

NAME	TERM	PLACE OF ORIGIN
Carlos Velasco	1894–1896	Tucson, Arizona
Pedro Pellón	1896–1897	Tucson, Arizona
Mariano Samaniego	1897	Tucson, Arizona
Samuel Brown	1897–1927	Tempe, Arizona
Antonio Sedillo	1927–1933	Socorro, New Mexico
Jesús Siqueiros	1933	Nogales, Sonora
Emilio Apodaca	1933–1941	Socorro, Texas
Candelario Sedillo	1941–1950	Socorro, New Mexico
Gregorio García	1950–1951	St. Johns, Arizona
Arturo Fuentes	1951–1954	Glendale, Arizona
Ralph Estrada	1954–1962	Tempe, Arizona
Carlos McCormick	1962–1963	Santa Barbara, California
J. M. Romero	1963–1965	Trinidad, Colorado

Cultural Symbolism and Regional Variation

Throughout its existence, the *Alianza* publication emphasized key cultural meanings and symbols. In the early period from the early 1900s until World War II, stress was on "Mexicanismo," on Mexican identity and meaning as popularly known in Mexico, on the meaning of being Mexican, and on the symbolism used to support that identity. The *Alianza* presented "Mexicanismo" principally through literary genres and editorials in this early period. From the 1940s onward, symbolic representation was more common through visual images and illustrations on the *Alianza* cover page. Many symbolic elements used by the *Alianza* were also those being generally employed by Mexican Americans in the process of developing a cultural-ethnic identity in the United States during the same period. Mexican cultural symbolism and American national symbolism were commonly used, although Spanish and Southwest regional images were also represented.

Lodges differed in their activities and in the different aspects of cultural identity that they emphasized. For example, Arizona lodges were more likely to sponsor *Fiestas Patrias* (Mexican national celebrations) than were the Nuevomexicano lodges, where Spanish rather than Mexican symbolism was emphasized. Nuevomexicanos are generally known to identify more with their Spanish ancestry than with a mixed Spanish-Indian heritage and, for historical-political reasons, disavowed a kinship with *mexicanos* from Mexico particularly after the Treaty of Guadalupe Hidalgo.[11]

This Hispano/*mexicano* dichotomy in cultural identification is expressed among New Mexico lodges according to type of membership. For example, Lodge 37 of Albuquerque, with a membership of native Nuevomexicanos, held an annual event called *Baile en España* (Dance in Spain) in commemoration of the entry of Coronado in 1542 into the region that became the Southwest (*Alianza*, December 1945). A precedent for this was set in 1911 when Lodge 43 of Santa Fe "furnished all the men for the Vargas procession" celebrating the Spanish conquest of New Mexico and "spared neither their time nor their purses to make the pageant beautiful and 'historically correct'" (*Santa Fe New Mexican* 1911, 1). In comparison, Lodge 178 of Albuquerque, established later in the century and consisting principally of recent Mexican immigrants and their children, emphasized Mexican national symbolism and celebrations.

In both Arizona and New Mexico the most elaborate cultural activities were the *Alianza* dances and balls, particularly in the 1940s and 1950s in Tucson and Albuquerque.[12] Balls were initiated with a coronation ceremony of the festivity's *reina* [queen] in which local and regional dignitaries participated. The ceremony was followed by a formal procession led by the *reina* and her attendants. Many dance events were attended by a large representation of the Mexican American community including non-members of the *Alianza*. In both Tucson and Albuquerque, many people knew of the *Alianza* only through this activity and were unaware of any of its other service functions. In sum, these dances encouraged a wide-based participation of people of different ages, including non-members, and thus served as both a cultural symbol and a social bonding mechanism. It solidified social links among the membership and between the membership and the wider ethnic community.

The social dance is a very strong and central feature of *mexicano* culture and society. Three key types of dance events include theme balls (like *Alianza*-sponsored balls), wedding dances, and *quinceañeras* or debutante balls, all of which are key community events that serve to initiate and reinforce social relationships. These events enhanced community collectivity in a multifaceted manner, primarily encouraging courtship and marriage under the auspices of the extended family and other respected community elders. Women, girls, men, and boys of all ages were brought together in a socially appropriate context by the *Alianza*, despite American society's norms of age-segregation and individualized lifestyles and Mexican American society's tendency toward gender segregation. In the *Alianza*, the social dance was a prime way to assure participation of the entire family in the organization.

Language is significant not only as an indicator of the assimilative process among the Mexican American population, but also as a cultural symbol for that population. A diachronic examination of the *Alianza* magazine gives us a sense of the changes in the proportionate use of Spanish and English through time. The issues dating from the late nineteenth century until June 1942 are completely in Spanish. In the July 1942 issue the Supreme President states:

> In our last issue we stated that the *Alianza* magazine would gradually begin to print articles in English as well as in Spanish at the request of many of our members. In this article will appear the first words of English in thirty-five years of publication. For this moment we have chosen some of the most significant words in the English language—the Preamble of the Constitution of the United States. [Sedillo 1942, 3]

The November 1942 magazine cover title is presented for the first time in both Spanish and English–*Alianza/Alliance*. Of all *Alianza* magazine covers, this one is a drawing displaying the whole gamut of cultural images of Spanish colonization, *mestizaje* (mixed Spanish-Indian heritage), "new" Mexican culture, and life in the U.S. Southwest. Drawn by Juan Menchaca of Denver, Colorado, the rendering includes an Indian (Navaho); a Spanish conquistador; a Mexican *charro;* a Pueblo Indian house; a Spanish mission; a saguaro cactus; cattle, horses, and sheep; and the three ships associated with the Spanish conquest. The accompanying textual explanation of the cover reads:

> We have become bilingual for the benefit of a great number of our readers. However, our position regarding the issue of bilingualism is clear. In order to be happy a person residing in the southwestern United States should read, write, and understand both languages, Spanish and English. This applies to both English speakers and Spanish speakers. [*Alianza*, November 1942, cover copy]

In 1950, when the new Supreme President, Gregorio García came into office, the magazine returned to Spanish only, until at least April 1954. In 1955, the contents were once again in both Spanish and English, and continued in this format until at least the early 1960s.

The emphasis on binationalism and biculturalism is seen in the deliberate juxtaposition of Mexican national symbols with the national symbolism of the United States, although this involved using "folkloric" images conforming to Anglo stereotypes and perceptions of Mexicans. *Alianza* activities often bore the stamp of its cultural identity in this fashion, particularly during World War II. For example, at one national fund-raising event for a war effort called *Alianza*

Por La Victoria, some *Alianza* members dressed in Mexican national costumes, and "The World's Largest Tamale" was displayed (*Alianza,* January 1944). During the war period, bicultural symbolism was most prominently featured on January issue covers featuring one New Year's baby dressed in an Uncle Sam costume and another in a *charro* (Mexican horseman) costume. Like the increased emphasis on English over Spanish, however, the trend in cultural symbolism became increasingly Anglo-assimilative, as exemplified on the cover of the November 1955 *Alianza* issue featuring a Pilgrim couple.

The Mexicano Family and Organizational Success

The organizing principle of Morality included strong support for the integrity of the family and is expressed in the *Alianza's* ritual as follows: "(members should) maintain inviolate the sanctity of our co-members' homes, considering their honor and that of their families, as sacred and worthy of respect as our own" (Serrano Cabo 1929, 33). *Alianza* activities, particularly at the lodge level, encouraged participation of the entire family. The first anniversary of the *Alianza's* existence was celebrated with a formal dinner and dance for two hundred people, including "members, their families, and other guests" (*El Fronterizo* 1 January 1895).

The place of the family was defined along conservative lines based on middle-class values of either the United States or Mexican cultures. For example, the "*Alianza* Family" on the cover of the July 1949 issue of *Alianza* is a photo depicting parents and two children (daughter and son) sitting in the living room reading *Alianza* magazine. This cover reflects the middle-class American ideal of the family, rather than middle-class Mexican culture, which valued a larger, extended family over the nuclear family.

Because *sociedades mutualistas* were usually adult male organizations, the *Alianza's* extension of membership and participation to adult women and young adults indicates a commitment to "whole family involvement" that Tirado (1970) identifies as an indicator of organizational success. The definition of members' roles, other than those of adult men, varied over time. In 1913 women were accorded full membership rights in the *Alianza* (Serrano Cabo 1929, 87). Women were to "enjoy all the privileges enjoyed by men" (Serrano Cabo 1929, 87).[13] However, by the period from the 1940s to the 1960s, women in the *Alianza* seemed to function principally in an auxiliary role parallel to their Anglo counterparts in fraternal organizations.

Participation of young people was also organized through *Legiones Juveniles* (Youth Legions), separate, affiliated clubs of youngsters' lodges, benefits, rituals, and activities paralleling the adult lodges (Serrano Cabo 1929, 352–355).[14] During the period of the 1940s through the 1960s, young men were more directly involved in the political activities of the older *Alianza* men. They seemed to be undergoing grooming to assume leadership positions in the *Alianza*. In contrast, young women's affiliates seemed to function as social clubs which organized dances and otherwise helped in charitable and fundraising activities (Officer 1964, 248), thus paralleling the older women's activities.[15]

The most notable presence of young women was in competitions for *reina* (queen) of the organization, of large dance events, or of one of the lodges, a role for women more in keeping with the Mexican customs.

Alianza Political-Economic Philosophy

Like many *sociedades mutualistas* and fraternal organizations at the turn of the century, the *Alianza* statutes forbade "political discussions" within the organization. The *Alianza Hispano-Americana* tended to be issued-oriented rather than an organization with a long-term vision of collective action with respect to the general status of *mexicanos* in U.S. society. Although the *Alianza* has been credited with fomenting the 1903 strike in the copper mines of the Morenci-Clifton area (Hernández 1983, 13, 38–42), evidence to support this contention is not substantial and the involvement of the *Alianza* in direct support of labor organizing is questionable (Arrieta 1991, 72; Sheridan 1986, 112–113). In fact, at the 1918 national convention, in response to a question raised by the Metcalf and Morenci Arizona mining camp lodges, the *Alianza* disavowed any role in intervention in labor disputes (Briegel 1974, 10). This position is explained in *Las Crónicas* as follows:

> [I]t was concluded that it was not an issue for the organization since it had to do with differences between unionists and non-unionists and [the matter] was dropped and given no further attention. Camilo Padilla spoke on this matter in general advising the conventioneers that mexicanos should take great care in union affairs when they are against the interests of the government, because the United States regards these movements as provoked by enemies of the nation. [Serrano Cabo 1929, 118]

Direct *Alianza* involvement in Mexican American civil rights was on a case-by-case basis, particularly in the 1950s. In 1921 the *Alianza*, along with other *mexicano* organizations, advocated for Aurelio Pompa, accused of killing an Anglo. The governor of California was asked to commute his death sentence (Briegel 1974, 169), an intervention that did not meet with success (Acuña 1988, 174). Concerted *Alianza* efforts at fighting discrimination were begun in 1950 and followed by the creation of a Civil Rights Department in 1954. *Alianza* lawyers took cases concerning segregation of public facilities, criminal justice, and citizenship and immigration (Briegel 1974, 168).

From almost the beginning, the *Alianza*'s "political" involvement had consisted of inviting Mexican and Anglo civic and political leaders to its local and national festivities and ceremonies. However, in the 1960s, the *Alianza* leadership escalated this practice to political influence peddling among candidates in local, state, and national politics.

Leadership and Organizational Maintenance and Demise

A strong sense of *mutualismo* and sense of cultural/ethnic unity maintained the organization through some very difficult crises and in spite of pressures from within and outside the organization survived until the 1940s. At this point, because of general social change caused by World War II and the subsequent assimilative effects on most American ethnic groups, the *Alianza* began to take on a less *"mexicano"* character. By the 1960s the fundamentals of fraternalism and *mutualismo* had been abandoned in favor of self-interest by the leadership. The membership had not, for reasons still to be determined, kept the leadership accountable and the *Alianza* ended as an organization in 1965.

The *Alianza Hispano-Americana* was started in 1894 by elite members of the *mexicano* community in order to maintain their leadership role in that community, and to secure a place for themselves in the new political-economic structure imposed on all *mexicanos* by the arriving wave of Anglo Americans. The *Alianza* continued to maintain a centralized, hierarchical structure and had at the locus of control a middle-class leadership.

There had always been an underlying philosophy of individual progress in the *Alianza*. However, in the early period, personal advancement was balanced more against the greater good. The leadership made the affiliate lodges feel that their opinions and interests were being taken into account. The membership also demanded that they be kept informed about Executive Council actions and decisions, and the officers worked for, and often spoke of, the interests of the larger body. In the later period of the 1950s to 1960s, the leadership seemed less accountable to the membership and used the *Alianza* as a means of personal and political advancement. This attitude and subsequent actions by the leadership hastened the demise of the *Alianza* as an organization in 1965.

The capacity of a single leader to inspire or maintain solidarity among the membership and mobilize the organization in the direction of the greater good was no doubt a positive factor in the maintenance and growth of the *Alianza* until 1939. Sometime thereafter, we begin to see a shift in leadership style that seems to be correlated with cultural style. For example, with the election of Candelario Sedillo in 1941, "the *Alianza* began to operate new programs based on the idea of assimilation" (Briegel 1974, 153). When Sedillo was declared the winner of the 1948 election, the results were hotly contested by his opponent, Gregorio García, who strongly promoted a return to a cultural maintenance philosophy. A costly, drawn-out legal battle ensued, which resulted in the declaration of García as the Supreme President in 1950. By then the process had tarnished the *Alianza*'s image and depleted its finances.

The faltering *Alianza* should also be viewed in terms of the destabilizing effects of World War II on *mexicano* communities in the United States in general. Because American patriotism was at its zenith in the 1940s and great numbers of *mexicanos* served in the armed forces during that time, this population acquired a bicultural identity and a strong sense of American citizenship, becoming the "Mexican American Generation" (Álvarez 1973). During and after the war, we see an *Alianza* leadership more interested in Anglo American notions of "progress," the English language is increasingly used, and the old *mexicano* style of doing business is abandoned. Thereafter, the Supreme President as a single, strong leader seems to become more and more detached from the general needs of the membership and from a strong sense of promoting group unity based on cultural maintenance.

The beginning of the demise of the *Alianza* becomes apparent during the administrations of two of the last three supreme presidents, Ralph Estrada (1954–1963) and his son-in-law, Carlos McCormick (1962–1963), who was half Mexican. They increasingly involved themselves as individuals in new activities outside the usual realm of the organization, and, by association, the *Alianza* also became involved.

During the 1950s the *Alianza* leadership had increasing contact with local, state, and national political figures. The organization may also have been a vehicle for promoting a number of political careers. For example, Raúl Castro was featured in the *Alianza* during the 1950s as an active participant in key organizational activities including some with the *Legiones Juveniles.* He later became the first Mexican American governor of Arizona in 1974. Campaign advertisements for both *mexicano* and Anglo politicians were common in the *Alianza.* In 1956, four of six candidates with campaign advertisements in the July issue were *Alianza* members.

A great deal of effort and publicity was directed at hosting political notables in the mid-1950s. For example, receptions were given by the *Alianza* central lodge in Tucson for senators Dennis Chávez and Joseph Montoya of New Mexico. In New Mexico *Alianza* Lodge 178 of Albuquerque gave a special dinner for Chávez and had New Mexico Governor Thomas Mayberry crown its *Alianza* queen. In the late 1950s and early 1960s, official positions in the *Alianza* and participation in national politics positioned both Estrada and McCormick for federal political appointments (Briegel 1974, 203–204).

Estrada's and McCormick's involvement in the national political arena occurred at a time when the *Alianza* was experiencing difficulties in finances and new membership recruitment. The organization at this point would have benefited more from their concentration on internal affairs such as bolstering membership rosters and organizational solvency perhaps through some of the means used by LULAC during its period of decline (Márquez 1993). Instead, the *Alianza* went into the last stage of its decline.

The final blow was the indictment of McCormick in 1965 on fifteen counts of grand theft related to embezzlement of organizational funds, after which the *Alianza* was forced into receivership (Briegel 1974, 207–208). The structure of the *Alianza Hispano-Americana* was obviously very decentralized with a strong presidency invested in a single individual. The locus of control was maintained in the central offices in Tucson, where all of the conventions were held from 1944 to 1963. The type of consensual process based on *mutualismo* that occurred in the early days of the *Alianza* was gone and could have occurred in later days only at the local lodge level.

Analysis and Conclusions

Mexicanos in the United States, like other national ethnic groups, have had a variety of options for adapting to mainstream society and culture either individually or collectively. Adaptations are based on the principles of cultural maintenance and assimilation to Anglo society and culture. Many choose either of these two extremes, while others combine both principles and develop a third adaptation: biculturalism. The *Alianza*'s history reflects some of these patterns of reaction, definition, and transformations of cultural and ethnic identity among *mexicanos* in the United States. Knowledge of the *Alianza*'s development can greatly contribute to an understanding of cross-culturally based change in the context of political-economic domination.

The creation of the *Alianza* is an example of how members of a dominated group can react and take the initiative in the form of collective action. Although the *Alianza* was basically accommodationist in the political-economic realm, its very foundation was predicated upon a strong ideology of cultural maintenance and in this sense demonstrated a form of resistance. The characterization of the *Alianza* here assigns a central role to traditions or "culture" as forming the base for *Aliancista* actions and for guiding their organizational expression.

Some important points should be kept in mind when assessing "successful" adaptation to domination. First, cultural adaptation should be considered as separate from political-economic adaptation. That is, dominated peoples often want political or economic advancement without giving up their ancestral culture. Secondly, political-economic success for individuals does not mean political-economic success for the dominated ethnic group as a whole.

In assessing the success of the *Alianza* in enhancing the position of the ethnic group in general, it is best to focus on its maintenance of social and cultural integrity in the face of tremendous assimilative pressures on *mexicanos* from mainstream American society. In assessing the success of the *Alianza* in terms of its political-economic benefit to the ethnic group in general, its main accomplishments were in the area of individual civil rights cases in the 1950s.

The impetus for the *Alianza*'s development into a national ethnic organization came both from dynamic interactions within the ethnic group and from reactions to external pressures from the dominant society. The degree to which *Alianza* efforts were primarily aimed at benefiting the membership and ethnic group rather than benefiting the leadership varied at different points in time under different administrations.

Although the *mexicano*/Hispano elite of the nineteenth century were organizing to protect their political-economic interests, they also recognized the racial/ethnic factor that had been introduced into class dynamics and into socioeconomic mobility for all *mexicanos* in the United States. It was this consciousness, coupled with a call for cultural solidarity, that constituted the basis for early recruitment of the majority of the *Alianza*'s membership.

The *Alianza*'s emergence fits the classic explanation that collective behavior occurs during periods of rapid social change including industrialization. Under such conditions, people engage in collective behavior "when attempting to repair and reconstitute a ruptured social structure" (Morris 1984, 275). The *Alianza* was not merely an emotional reaction to rapid economic change as suggested by classic collective action theory, however, but was also a political action or strategy used in dealing with a culturally different and dominant society. Furthermore, mainstream explanations of social movements and collective action also underplay the active role of the participants and, when referring to ethnic groups, completely deny the rootedness in the ethnic communities' social and cultural forms.

Non-mainstream interpretive frameworks such as Morris's (1984) discussion of the "indigenous approach" to collective action, Tirado's (1970) explanation of Mexican American political organizations, and Márquez's (1993) analysis of LULAC (League of United Latin American Citizens), another major *mexicano* organization, are more useful for analyzing the initiation and maintenance of the *Alianza*.

Aliancistas exemplified the "ability of groups to organize, mobilize, and manage valuable resources" (Morris 1984, 279), and "to take collective action out of pre-existing social structures and political processes" (Morris 1984, 280). They used extant networks among *mexicano* elites, Spanish language newspapers, and the *sociedad mutualista* organizational form. The *sociedad* was conceptually one of the "mass-based institutions" that were of primary significance in the initiation of collective action according to the "indigenous" approach (Morris 1984, 282).

In a study of Mexican American political organizations, Tirado (1970, 53–78) identifies six characteristics common to those groups that endure: (1) is multifunctional; (2) involves the entire family; (3) deals with single-area issues; (4) has personalistic, consensual leadership; (5) has a decentralized structure; and (6) makes effective use of ethnic symbolism. With two exceptions, these were all characteristics of the *Alianza Hispano-Americana*. Exceptions include the *Alianza*'s centralized and hierarchical structure and its "non-consensual" leadership.

According to Márquez's (1993) use of incentive theory, the *Alianza*'s incentive structure mainly included material benefits in the form of life insurance and "solidary benefits" defined as "socially derived rewards created by the act of association, such as fun, camaraderie, status of prestige" (Márquez 1993, 5). "Solidary rewards"—what Tirado (1970, 77) calls "effective use of ethnic symbolism" (1970, 77) and Morris refers to as "cultural factors" in collective action(1984, 280)—were largely responsible for the cohesion and continuity of the *Alianza Hispano-Americana* during times when it may have otherwise collapsed.

It is debatable whether or how the *Alianza* offered "purposive or expressive rewards"—that is, those "derived from advocating a particular cause or ideological orientation" (Márquez 1993, 5). The *Alianza* remained issue-oriented rather than becoming a vehicle for collective action for the whole ethnic group. In this sense, it was completely unlike the Chicano Movement of the 1960s and 1970s, which was ideologically driven and which challenged the existing power structure for the benefit of all ethnic group members.

In the end, the *Alianza* suffered a loss of membership that might have been remedied by adopting new strategies and adapting "incentives to a changing context" (Márquez 1993, 6). More significantly, there was a loss of interest *and* participation on the part of the membership, along with reduced accountability of the leadership. The use of an organization to advance personal agendas was not unique to the *Alianza*, but was also recently experienced by LULAC (Márquez 1993, 115).

The *Alianza Hispano-Americana* was strongly guided, particularly in the early period, by the ideal of providing for *mexicanos* in the United States through institutionalized means not available to them in Anglo society. The *Alianza* afforded members stabilization of their socioeconomic base and the promotion of upward mobility without abandonment of culture. As assimilative pressures increased, the *Alianza* facilitated the development of a bicultural society and affirmed members' identity as Mexican Americans. The move toward biculturalism developed with the gradual addition of Anglo American symbolism, events, and activities, until, toward the end, the *Alianza* had developed into a mechanism for promoting assimilation into mainstream U.S. society and culture.

Notes

1. Some of the discussion in this chapter derives from my thought processes and analysis as I examined issues of the *Alianza* publication that spanned the period between July 1940 and February 1960. Unless otherwise indicated, all translations from Spanish in this article are my own.

2. The term "*mexicano*" is used here to encompass the ethnic terminology of Hispano, Mexican, Chicano, and Mexican American. When referring to mexicanos in New Mexico, I use the term "Nuevomexicano" in recognition of that strong, unique regional identity and in conformity with some historical usage and with regional acceptance of that term of self-identification.

3. Briegel (1974, 54–57) explains at length the difference between a mutual-aid society and a fraternal insurance society.

4. These two *sociedades* were the "Mexican Society for Mutual Benefit" and the Club Union, identified by Sheridan (1986, 108–109) from English language sources.

5. *Sociedades* in surrounding communities were:

Date	Organization	Community
1886	Sociedad Hispano Americana de Beneficencia	Florence
1888	Sociedad de Beneficencia Mutua de la Raza Latina	Phoenix
1889	Sociedad Hidalgo	Solomonville
1893	Sociedad de la Protección Mutua	St. Johns

6. In 1895 the first affiliated lodge was established in Florence, Arizona (*Alianza Hispano-Americana Ledger 1894–1900,* 301; the *Ledger* tracked lodges, members, and dues payments for the years 1894–1900).

7. See Meléndez and Lomelí in this volume for further elaboration on the role of Spanish-language newspapers.

8. In New Mexico, the concept of organization based on mutual aid preceded the *Alianza Hispano-Americana* in the forms of the *Acequia Penitente* religious brotherhood of the seventeenth and eighteenth centuries and the classic nineteenth-century *sociedad mutualista.* The earlier forms extended mutual assistance of all kinds to the community in general. These forms were most active in northern New Mexico, which may account for the emergence of relatively few *Alianza Hispano-Americana* lodges in that region.

9. The *Asociación de Mutua Protección y Mutuo Beneficio,* which was incorporated in 1885 for Cerro de Guadalupe in northern New Mexico (see Carolina R. Sánchez, *Cerro de Guadalupe Indigenous Social Service Organizations,* Master's Thesis, New Mexico Highlands University, 1979, p. 25), appears to have functioned as a land-rights organization. The *Orden de Protección Mutua* (*La Voz del Pueblo,* 1892) organized in Alamagordo in 1891, and the *Sociedad Nuevo Mexicana de Mutua Protección,* organized in Albuquerque in 1896, were *sociedades mutualistas* in the organizational form of the *Alianza.*

10. Jesús Romero, for example, a central business and political figure in Albuquerque, New Mexico, organized the *Sociedad Nuevo Mexicana de Mutua Protección* in that town in 1896.

11. John R. Chávez has amply discussed Hispano identity in New Mexico in *The Lost Land: The Chicano Image of the Southwest* (Albuquerque: University of New Mexico Press, 1984).

12. In Tucson, dances were held in the *Alianza*'s downtown Club La Selva. In Albuquerque, Lodge 37's dances took place in the downtown Hilton (*Alianza,* December 1943) or at the University of New Mexico's Carlisle Gym (*Alianza,* June 1945).

13. This was done presumably in keeping with the women's suffrage movement in the United States. However, *Alianza* men's early support for admitting women as equal members stands in contrast to the strong opposition of Anglo American men to allowing women into their fraternal organizations during the same period. See, e.g.,

Mark C. Carnes, *Secret Ritual and Manhood in Victorian America* (New Haven: Yale University Press, 1989), 79–90; 117–121.

14. A *Departamento Juvenil* was started in 1924 for youngsters ranging from ages two to sixteen. According to Briegel, no further information is available on the *Legiones Juveniles* after 1931, when the membership had risen to 1,500 (Briegel 1974, 88). However, I have since found more information. The *Legiones Juveniles* were organized to allow parents to buy insurance policies for their children but also to prepare youngsters to be future *fraternalistas* (*Alianza* 1940, 32[7]:2). The idea was to "prepare them for civic life" so that "they learn to be loyal and patriotic, to love their friends, their country, and the Society" (*Alianza*, 33[10]:2). In 1939, when the adult membership was 17,366, the Juvenile Department reported a membership of 3,240 (*Alianza*, 33[10]:1). There is also a report of an *Alianza*-sponsored Christmas party for *Legiones Juveniles* youngsters and their parents (*El Tucsonense*, 19 December 1939).

15. Young women's lodges were organized as *Alianza* lodges as follows: Club Mavis organized as Tucson Lodge 126 in 1949; in 1954, Club Orquídea became Lodge 110, and Club Azalea and Club Cienna together formed Lodge 38.

Literature Cited

Acuña, Rodolfo. 1988. *Occupied America: A History of Chicanos.* 3rd ed. New York: Harper and Row Publishers.

Álvarez, Rodolfo. 1973. The Psycho-historical and Socioeconomic Development of the Mexican American People. *Social Science Quarterly* 53:929–944.

Arrieta, Olivia. 1991. La Alianza Hispano-Americana *in Arizona and New Mexico: The Development and Maintenance of a Multifunctional Ethnic Organization.* Renato Rosaldo Lecture Series Monograph Vol. 6, Tucson: Mexican American Studies and Research Center, University of Arizona.

Briegel, Kaye. 1974. *Alianza Hispano-Americana, 1894–1965: A Mexican-American Fraternal Insurance Society.* Ph.D. diss., University of Southern California.

Hernández, José A. 1983. *Mutual Aid for Survival: The Case of the Mexican American.* Malabar, Florida: Robert E. Krieger.

Márquez, Benjamin. 1993. *LULAC: The Evolution of Mexican American Political Organization.* Austin: University of Texas Press.

Morris, Aldon D. 1984. *The Origins of the Civil Rights Movement: Black Communities Organizing for Change.* New York: The Free Press.

Officer, James. 1964. *Sodalities and Systemic Linkage: The Joining Habits of Urban Mexican-Americans.* Ph.D. diss., University of Arizona.

Rivera, José A. 1984. *Mutual Aid Societies in the Hispanic Southwest: Alternative Sources of Community Empowerment.* Research Report submitted to U.S. Department of Health and Human Services, Washington, D.C.: Albuquerque: Southwest Hispanic Research Center, University of New Mexico.

Sedillo, Candelario. 1942. La voz del Presidente Supremo. *Alianza* 35(7) (July):3.

Serrano Cabo, Tomás. 1929. *Las Crónicas de la Alianza Hispano-Americana.* Tucson: Alianza Hispano-Americana.

Sheridan, Thomas. 1986. *Los Tucsonenses: The Mexican American Community in Tucson 1854–1941.* Tucson: University of Arizona Press.

Tirado, Miguel. 1970. Mexican American Community Political Organization. *Aztlán* 1 (spring):53–78.

Newspaper and Periodical Materials

Alianza, various issues, July 1940 through February 1960.
El Fronterizo, 1 January 1895.
El Tucsonense No. 77, 19 December 1939.
La Voz del Pueblo 12 March 1892.
Santa Fe New Mexican, Vol. 48, 5 July 1911.

Cultural Forms, Agencies, and Discourse:
New Mexico's Coming of Age

Las Hijas de la Malinche
Mexicana/India Captivity Narratives in the Southwest, Subverting Voices

Tey Diana Rebolledo

IN ANGLO AMERICAN LITERATURE of the seventeenth through the nineteenth centuries, "captivity narratives" formed a subset of the colonizing literature. These narratives, told by both men and women, illustrated the alleged barbarity of Indian tribes and inhumanity to their captives, rationalizing the subsequent taking of native lands and annihilation of native peoples. The captivity narratives recounted by women were a special genre of "horror stories" that included infanticide, rape, violence, and barbarism. If the women survived, it was, they believed, a tribute to their faith in the Christian god, who had answered their prayers. These narratives, often recounted to someone who put the story into writing, were sensational and sold well. Beginning in the colonial period, these narratives appealed to and reinforced the fear and hatred of colonists toward native peoples. In *The Narrative of the Captivity and Restoration of Mrs. Mary Rowlandson, 1682*, Mary Rowlandson described her captors as murderers and barbarians. In 1692 Mary Renville wrote her *Thrilling Narrative of Indian Captivity*, emphasizing the "thrilling," while in 1859 the *New York Times* reported the cases of seventeen children rescued by the Commissioner of Indian Affairs. Moreover, the *Times* and other newspapers often informed their readers of Indian "uprisings," "atrocities," and continued captivities of whites. Of prurient interest to the reader was whether or not the "White" women had sexual relations with their captors, although often this was only hinted at in the tales. These sensationalized accounts of intercultural violence and conflict not only justified the colonizers' right in the economic sphere, but reinforced the concept of the spiritual superiority of a Christian god.

As Glenda Riley has noted:

> these captivity narratives fulfilled various functions throughout the nearly three centuries of their existence. During the colonial period they were largely religious documents concerned with the issue of salvation for those who had escaped the savagery and debasement of their lives as captives. By the end of the eighteenth century, they became more strongly an expression of anti-Indian sentiment and as such began to deviate increasingly from factual accounts. . . .

> Throughout their history, captivity narratives deviated little in
> form. The unifying pattern was that of an odyssey. Whether male or
> female, the captive followed a sequence of separation from family
> and civilization, detention by the savage captors, and eventual
> reunion with white society. Yet the return to their former civilization
> was not always a happy one. Some women experienced particular
> difficulties in adjustment because they missed their native children,
> because they found themselves rejected by white society due to their
> "contamination" by their Indian captors, or because they lacked
> financial means to support themselves. [Riley 1984, 19]

Cultural conflict and the dichotomous conqueror/conquered aspect also existed in the Hispanic Southwest, reinforced by native tribes' rebellion against the destruction of their traditional lands and pathways. From the sixteenth century until the late 1880s, capture and slave trading were not unusual occurrences in the Southwest. The native tribes captured each other and captured *mexicanos*, and *mexicanos* captured and enslaved the natives. From the Spanish, Mexican, and, later, the Anglo perspective, the burden and blame for these captivities was put on the native peoples as the detentions were called barbarous "Indian depredations." When native peoples were captured and forced to work as servants, however, it was considered to be for their benefit as they were Christianized.

Official accounts kept by Spanish, Mexican, and, later, Anglo chroniclers and journalists are filled with descriptions of native and *mexicana* women and children who were captured. Primarily women and children were kept as captives by the native peoples to replace their own children who had been killed or captured, to serve as ransom, or because they would pose fewer problems than men. Men who were taken prisoner were often killed. Native peoples, both women and men, were taken captive by *mexicanos* for use as labor or to be sold to others.

Separation from family, community, and familiar things can cause devastating, lifelong effects. It is surprising, therefore, that there is not more literature about the lives of these captives. It is astonishing because hundreds of accounts tell of men, women, and children being carried into captivity—and into oblivion. Many families never knew if their loved ones were dead or remained alive as captives. We have occasional glimmers of what may have happened because some were rescued, others were ransomed, and still others were sometimes even returned to their families. Although some fictionalized narratives exist, such as *La historia de un cautivo* by Porfirio Gonzales, serialized in *La Voz del Pueblo* in 1898, there are few first-person accounts of captivities, especially by women, in the literature of the Southwest.

In this essay, I discuss the captivities of nine women—six *indias* and three *mexicanas*—as depicted in stories and narrative songs told about them. Theirs are voices that are subverted into the narratives of other voices—those of their

children, their families, of those who rescued and felt responsible for them, or of
women who knew them and were trying to subsume their voices under one collective voice. I have found no stories told by the women themselves. This silenc-
ing of women by redirecting their personal accounts from narratives into
"remembered" historical voices is not unusual. If they were *indias* still living in the
mexicano community, they would have continued to guard themselves. In fact,
one *mexicana* who had a Navajo grandmother told me that her grandmother had
been forbidden to speak of her childhood to the family. If they were *mexicanas*
who had been restored to their own community, they would be considered
"suspect," perhaps impure, and were not likely to tell their stories openly, as was
the case of Inez González. That their voices and their stories have survived at all
speaks to the admiration of those around them for their survival through the
hardships and deprivations they suffered.

These voices from the past also speak to social relations that we as Chicanas/os
and native peoples would rather put to rest. That we traded people as slaves, that we
were inhumane to each other, that we could be the oppressor as well as the oppressed
are issues that we would prefer to leave dormant. Yet there is historical evidence for
such interactions, and the voices of these women serve as reminders not only of the
evils of societies, but also of the survival of the races and their redemptions.

The history of the captivities and of the slave trade in the Hispano Southwest,
which began in the 1600s, is a complex web of mutual hostility, of constant warfare, of raids and campaigns in reprisal by both Spanish/*mexicanos* and *indios*.
The seizure of captive children and women from enemies undoubtedly had been
practiced by the Apachean and other tribes before Coronado's time (1642), and
the Spanish practice of the use of *repartimiento*, Indian labor given to certain
people, was common in Mexico and South America before the Spanish entry into
the Southwest. Very few *encomiendas*, the grant of land and the use of the people
on it, were granted in New Mexico, and the *repartimiento* system was theoretically
designed to be as benevolent to the Indians as it was practical to the Spaniards.
Although the enslavement of Indians was forbidden by Spanish law, the slave
trade flourished in the seventeenth and eighteenth centuries, was continued by
the Mexicans in the nineteenth, and was tolerated by the Americans who arrived
in 1848. As one historian has noted, "Although illegal, the custom flourished
openly, rationalized by the supposed benefit conferred on the victims by exposure
to Christianity" (McNitt 1990, iii). Traffic in Indian slaves was not only enjoyed by
the upper levels of secular and religious authority, but also extended into every
home of moderate means. Another historian notes:

> Records of various New Mexican parishes reveal that during a fifty
> year period—from 1700–1760—nearly 800 Apaches were anointed
> with oil and holy water, and baptized into the Catholic faith. These

were not willing converts. . . . They were women and children, taken against their will by slave raiders, and distributed by lot among the captors. In accord with Catholic tradition, the individuals were baptized into Spanish families. Although they bore Spanish names, these Apaches would never be a part of the family of their captors. Their status remained that of menials and servants. [Bailey 1973, 19]

The use of these Indian servants was rationalized, unlike the African slave experience, by the fact that they were "adopted into the family" and their souls saved by Christianizing. These "slaves" were kept within the family, were not sold from person to person, and were sometimes able to barter for their freedom. Many of those released became detribalized Indians, called *genízaros*, who later formed townships such as that of Abiquiu, New Mexico.

During the colonial period, as slave raids were made on native peoples, the natives retaliated, increasing the frequency and intensity of raids and reprisals on the Spanish/*mexicano* settlers. A great deal of confusion exists in early Spanish documents regarding who is causing the reprisals—the Apache or the Navajos. There was so much harassment from native tribes in San Gabriel, the first Spanish settlement of 1598, that the inhabitants were forced to move to Santa Fe in 1610. The official Spanish policy toward native tribes was one of divide and conquer, trying to keep the tribes distracted by using one against the other. This policy worked to some extent. While the Pueblo tribes were generally allied with the Spanish/*mexicanos* against the more nomadic tribes, the Navajos suffered most of all from Spanish raids. During the 1640s, the Pueblos and the Navajos alternated between fighting each other and forming alliances to drive out the colonists. For example, Frank McNitt states, "According to one authority, Pueblo herders employed by Spanish *encomenderos* from time to time turned over large herds of horses to Navajos. Conversely, Navajos all but halted trade between the pueblos of Zuni and Hopi and the Rio Grande settlements" (McNitt 1990, 11).

By 1650, Navajo raids were increasingly concentrated in driving off Spanish and Pueblo horses—later sheep would also be a target. In the period between 1650–1660, Fray Alonso de Posada described a situation in which the colonists lived in fear—men were killed "atrociously," and women and children were carried off as captives (McNitt 1990, 12). Fear of captivity continued to be seen in the literature and the oral tradition as late as the early 1900s. It should also be noted that while native aggressions, raids, and depredations were recorded promptly, Spanish aggressions were almost never recorded. This anti-native perspective continued when the Americans took over.

From the 1740s to the 1800s, the Navajo, a farming and sheep-raising people, were subjected to increasing pressure and harassment by the Utes and Comanches from the North, and, in 1778, it was the Apaches who held the vast area of New Mexico and Arizona in terror. These tribes only barely survived calculated destruction by the Spaniards' alternating wars and treaties. In 1800, however, the Spanish aggressively began to push their frontier west into the grazing country held by the Navajos, all of which led to more raids and escalating reprisals. Pressures from the Americans moving westward and the Spanish moving north led to increasingly desperate attempts by the natives to maintain their traditional lands. After 1848, when the Americans took control of the territory, matters were no better. Because the native peoples were considered barbarous by the Americans, they had neither rights nor feelings worthy of consideration. After one or two rays of hope at the start, treaties drafted by Americans became progressively worse than anything conceived under Spanish rule. Finally, the Comanche tribes, one of the most feared and mobile of all native groups, succumbed in 1874–1875. Although there are recorded incidents of captives being taken as late as the 1880s, the practice had ended by the early 1900s; the native peoples had been defeated and were either put on reservations or annihilated.

What are the stories, the remembered history of the women who were captured and taken from their culture into another? Because all the discourses are submerged into other discourses, many of which have a specific authorial intention, it is difficult to discern or to speak in any authoritative manner about "truths," veracity, or precision in these texts. Nevertheless, at times we can discern the intent of the texts in which these voices are submerged and see glimpses of what the lives of these women may have been like.

We actually know more about the reactions of the families the captives left behind. For example, Josephine Córdova of Taos tells of her grandmother Josefa's reaction to the loss of her young son Manuel in 1867 to either Navajos or Mescalero Apaches. Josefa nearly lost her mind with grief, blaming her husband because he had not searched enough for the child. In her grief she pleaded with the statue of Baby Jesus in the Arroyo Seco Church to restore her child. When he did not, she stole the statue and hid it in a crevice in the mountains. She neglected her other six children, three of whom died, and she continued to grieve until she too died in 1927 (Córdova 1976, 26–27). Another tragic story of a mother who lost her child but later found him was reported in the *Tucson Citizen* on 6 January 1875:

> A woman named Francisca Rosa went out to Apache pass this week in search of her son who was made captive by the Apaches near Arispe over ten years ago. The poor woman said that she did not know whether he had entirely forgotten his mother tongue or not, but that she hoped to be able to induce him to quit his wild life and come and live among his relatives once more. It is very doubtful if he leaves the Apaches, as he could have done so at any

time during the past two years if he had been so disposed. Her son is undoubtedly married and has children among them, and to all intents and purposes he has become an Apache. But it will be a hard trial for his poor mother if he refuses to come home with her. During all the long absent years she has constantly thought of and prayed for him, and now to find him a savage and an enemy to her people will be heart breaking for the poor woman.

Similar stories were told about Navajo and Apache women who were captured. One Apache text is included in a group of stories told by Apaches to anthropologist Grenville Goodwin in the 1930s and compiled by Keith Basso in 1971. Several, including the stories told by John Rope, an Apache scout for the Americans, and one by David Longstreet, tell about women's captivities. I also include the story of Mrs. Andrew Stanley, a White Mountain Apache who was captured by Chiricahuas in the 1880s, because it is one of the few that gives us a native woman's perspective on the alienation caused by her captivity and the difficulties she faced in integrating herself back into her community of origin.

When John Rope was scouting for the Americans around 1877, he reported finding a Chiricahua woman who was near starvation. She told of being captured by Mexicans and kept in a jail for about a year. She was befriended by a *mexicana* who would come to see her and bring her things. One time the *mexicana* asked her if she had thought about escaping, assuring her that she would help her. There was to be a dance, and the Chiricahua prisoners were made to clear a path from the town to where the dance was to take place. The *mexicana* brought the Chiricahua two dresses, one white to wear to the dance and one brown to wear in her escape. She told the Chiricahua woman to shake her arms and legs and run around inside the building so she would not be weak. As she tells her story through Rope:

> The next night of the dance it was bright moonlight. She (the Chiricahua) could hear the drums and horns over where the dance was. She put on the white dress and pretty soon the Mexican girl came and got her. They started to walk down the path that the prisoners had cleared. There were lots of Mexicans going along the path, but it was too dark and the Chiricahua woman was dressed like the other Mexican women. The Mexican girl was carrying the parcel with her food and the brown dress under her arm. There were two girls in front of them so the Mexican girl and the Chiricahua woman went from side to side pretending to look at things and let the other people get ahead, as well as the two girls. . . . The Mexican girl and the woman dodged in behind one of the piles of brush at the side of

the trail. Here the woman put on her brown dress and took the food. The Mexican girl walked out and caught up with three other girls in front and went on to the dance. [Basso 1971, 114–115]

The Chiricahua woman escaped and survived until the Apache scouts found her. This narrative leaves us with many unanswered questions: what languages did the women speak and how did they understand each other? Why did the *mexicana* help her? How did she get out of the jail and so on? Such questions, however, are never answered.

The following story is that of David Longstreet, who tells of his mother's capture by American soldiers around 1865 and her subsequent escape and return to her own people. The mother, never named in the narrative, was aided in her escape by another White Mountain Apache who was the wife of an Apache Manso chief, a scout for the American troops. Longstreet's mother was taking care of her niece who was also captured and never returned to the tribe. Longstreet's mother cries for the little girl who is "adopted" by an American officer. When Longstreet's mother approaches the officer "he told her to stay away from the little girl, so my mother had to do as he said." And Longstreet adds, "I think this little girl must still be living with the White people someplace" (Basso 1971, 192). She is told, "Don't cry. Your sister-in-law and your nephew got killed—you should feel sorry for them. But that little girl will be raised just like a White person" (Basso 1971, 195). Later she is told that the little girl was still with that officer and his family and no longer spoke Apache, but only English.

Another narrative from a native perspective is the tale of Mrs. Andrew Stanley, a White Mountain Apache, captured by Chiricahuas in the 1880s. It is one of the few texts that give us a native woman's perspective and the only narrative that tells us what emotions were going through her mind as she was captured and as she returned home. Her tale is remarkable for its description of the way she defended herself with revolvers, rode wild horses, survived a long trip home without knowing the territory, often got lost, and was afraid to talk to anyone. During her journey she finally meets some people with a wagon, Tonto Apaches, who had been captured as children by *mexicanos* and raised by them. These people had befriended each other in earlier days, so the ex-captives help her. She ultimately returns to her people, but remains apart from them for six days before she approaches them. As she recalls her travails, she cries. She is recognized by her uncle and cousin, and all the people gather around her, but she has a violent personal reaction to her own homecoming. As she tells her story, she remembers that

a lot of people gathered about me. But I had been so long alone that they all smelt bad to me, and I could not stand it. I vomited because of it. They gave me food to eat, but I could not swallow it.

I was not used to this. I slept a ways apart from the rest, so as to avoid being too close to them. [Basso 1971, 218]

The next day, however, she finds herself abandoned because her people fear she may have led the enemy to them. The tale, nevertheless, ends with this resolution:

These people thought that I was dead long ago, and now when I came back, it was like a ghost coming back to them. But the next day my maternal uncle came back here to see how things were and saw my horse there now. So all the rest came back to their camps now. That's the way it used to be in the old days; whenever a person returned who had been captive to the enemy, their relatives were always afraid that he would lead the enemy to them. This has happened before. [Basso 1971, 219]

The reticence of American Indian women to tell their stories (especially to outsiders) comes from various cultural traditions: the first is the subordination of the individual to the collective; and the second is that, as Gretchen Bataille and Kathleen Mullen Sands tell us: "American Indian women's autobiographies . . . may seem understated to those unaccustomed to the emotional reserve of Indian people. There is little self-indulgence on the part of Indian women narrators; events occur and are articulated in words conservative in emotional connotation" (Bataille and Sands 1984, 18).

Two other compelling native captivities are described by two Hispana/ Nuevomexicana writers: one is a "true" story of a Navajo woman told by Dora Ortiz Vásquez, the other a literary creation about a Navajo slave told by Fabiola Cabeza de Baca Gilbert.

Dora Ortiz Vásquez writes about the Navajo slave, Rosario, who was a servant to the famous Padre Antonio José Martínez in Taos. Vásquez' book *Enchanted Temples of Taos: My Story of Rosario* was written in the early 1930s but not published until 1975. Vásquez was a granddaughter of the famous New Mexican priest and had known Rosario when the writer was a little girl. The discourse in this book is a curious one in which the narrative shifts between sympathy and nostalgia for the woman she had known, on the one hand, and a sympathetic portrait of Padre Martínez, Rosario's captor, on the other.

Rosario, whose Navajo name was Ated-Bah-Hozhoni (Happy Girl), known also as Ma-Ya-Yo, is represented as fortunate to have such good "owners," but she also has a roving spirit. The narrative is a discourse of colonial nostalgia that attempts to picture the conditions of these slaves as happy and amiable. Nevertheless, a consciousness about their position on the part of the narrator also leaps out from the text:

In the Padre's home there were several maids, but the most outstanding one was Rosario, the young Navajo slave, who was about
twenty-five years of age. Padre Martínez had bought her for one
hundred and fifty pesos. She went about her duties wishing and
watching for a good chance to free herself and go back to her own
people, although she had no complaints, for fate had been good to

fig 15   Rosario, the "young Navajo slave" Ated-Bah-Hozhoni. "She went about
her duties wishing and watching for a good chance to free herself . . .
although she had no complaints, for fate had been good to her" (Dora
Ortiz Vásquez 1975). Used by permission of the Kit Carson Historical
Archives, Taos, New Mexico. Courtesy Taos Historic Museums.

her. She had a good home, but she had the characteristics of her own people, restlessness and a desire to roam rather than stay in one house and be ruled. [Vásquez 1975, 9]

Rosario's desire to be free is acknowledged throughout the text: "[S]he could not endure this captivity much longer; she so longed to run to the country and climb those mountains in the distance and enjoy the outdoor, free life.... [S]he was one of the luckiest of her friends and she felt quite privileged, for to be a slave to the good Padre was to her an honor" (Vásquez 1975, 100). Vásquez vacillates between describing the "good home and good luck" that Rosario has in being a slave in the household of good Padre Martínez and acknowledging her right to be free. On various occasions Rosario tries to escape. One time she is so grumpy that she "misbehaves" by ruining some blue corn tortillas, which she usually made deliciously. Her behavior concerned Father Martínez (whose name is always preceded in the narrative by the word good or some other benevolent adjective), and he decided that she must be unhappy because she was separated upon captivity from her daughter who was around one year old. Martínez decides to try and buy the daughter also, thinking that would make Rosario "happy." When they go to see the family who owns her daughter, the little child flies into her mother's arms. An emotional scene follows: "So deeply stirred were they all, that they forgot their selfishness. They all shed a few tears, even Doña Manuela (the daughter's owner) with all her pride began to cry, for she too had known sorrow when she had lost her only child years ago" (Vásquez 1975, 16).

The narrative seems to find Rosario reconciled to her fate, but when she hears that Navajos are coming to attack Taos, she resolves to flee and return home. Joined by several other Navajo slaves, Rosario is soon captured by the Nuevomexicanos. When they find Rosario, a boy tells her, "Padre Martínez has sent for you; he wants you back. You belong to him; already you are costing him over three hundred pesos." Upon her return, Padre Martínez behaves so well to her that she is ashamed because the family is so "good" to her.

During the remainder of the narrative, Rosario's story is subordinate to that of Padre Martínez and Taos; Rosario appears only from time to time until near the end. In a chapter entitled "Rosario Gets Her Freedom Too Late," Padre Martínez breaks the news to Rosario that she is free after President Lincoln delivers his Emancipation Proclamation. Padre Martínez tells Rosario that she may return to her people if she wishes and that he will pay her for the years she served him. In an interesting aside, when Rosario sees a picture of Abraham Lincoln, she thinks he "looks a bit Navajo." Faced with the choice of going back to a people she no longer knows and to a society where she no longer has a place, she decides to stay with Martínez, saying, "I have all I need—I am a part of you; I cannot leave you. Will you let me stay?" To emphasize her freedom of choice, Rosario weaves a serape, which she gives to Padre Martínez. The serape is an icon of her captivity and of the changes in her life that symbolize this captivity:

> "I'll weave a serape for the good Padre as a token of appreciation for all that he has done for Soledad and myself." She was making a plan of it in her mind as she carded and spun the wool. What colors would she use? "I'll make it a bit Navajo and the rest Spanish, for I am both now. I'll use more white for the pureness, nobleness and sincerity of the Padre, and I'll use black for the sorrow I caused them and for the sorrow I too went through many years ago. And I'll put red for the courage we all have to have."
> [Vásquez 1975, 69]

This serape becomes a symbol for "the loyalty of a faithful servant and how she felt toward the one family who so patiently overlooked all her faults and gave her a home" (Vásquez 1975, 70). Of cultural importance here is the practice of weaving in New Mexico what are known as "captivity," "servant," or "slave" blankets. These were blankets woven by Navajo slaves that incorporated both Spanish and Navajo elements—that is, Navajo designs with Spanish loom work (Fisher 1979, 33). These blankets represent a syncretization of cultural elements and are represented as a feature of transculturation in Rosario's blanket.

Although Vásquez uses her narrative about Rosario as a way to illustrate the benevolence of Padre Antonio Martínez, the narrative is always a conflicted one. Vásquez's sympathies often lie with Rosario and are articulated in the poignant descriptions of Rosario's longing to be free. In addition, Vásquez contributes her own value judgments as seen in the title "Rosario Gets Her Freedom *Too* Late" (italics mine). The reader is forced to ask, Too late for what? To have her own life and family?

In *The Good Life* (1982), first published in 1949, Fabiola Cabeza de Baca Gilbert wrote about the Turrietas, a family representative of village life in northern New Mexico, where she had worked with both Hispanic and native women as a home economist. In a section titled "The Herb Woman," Cabeza de Baca Gilbert introduces Señá Martina, a Navajo woman who had been a slave. The mother of the Turrieta family, Doña Paula, is preparing food for drying when Señá Martina drops by the house, and in the ensuing dialogue the relationship between these two women is presented as an example of Spanish/*india* conviviality. In the story, told from the perspective of Doña Paula, the women work alongside one another, helping each other mutually, sharing domestic knowledge and the preparation of food. Señá Martina is the *curandera* (healer) of the area, visiting families with her herbs. Throughout the narration, Señá Martina remains a mysterious person, even to Doña Paula:

The medicine woman seemed so old and wrinkled to Doña Paula and she wondered how old she was. No one remembered when she was born. She had been a slave in the García family for two generations and that was all any one knew. She had not wanted her freedom, yet she had always been free. She had never married, but she had several sons and daughters. Doña Paula had heard many tales about Señá Martina. Some said the children belonged to the patrón, the master, under whom she had worked; others said they were his grandchildren. Doña Paula thought, "What right have I thinking of such things? They are children of God and they have been good sons and daughters. That is all that matters." [Cabeza de Baca Gilbert 1982, 140]

As Señá Martina's story unfolds, it is evident that she is a servant because she is always helping prepare meals and doing other chores. When Señá Martina dies, Doña Paula thinks, "She died as she lived, contented, helping others to the end and causing no one any inconvenience with a lingering illness" (Cabeza de Baca Gilbert 1982, 42). At the end of the narration we are again reminded that Señá Martina is, after all, an Indian woman:

Next morning the priest arrived by eight o'clock to say the Mass for the departed one. The men carried the body on a litter as there was no coffin for Señá Martina; she had asked to be given an Indian burial. She had often said to Doña Paula, "I do not want a coffin. There is no need for pomp and expense because once we are dead nothing matters anymore. The coffin rots and we return to the earth as was intended. . . ." Doña Paula was the chief mourner for Señá Martina, who had been closer to her than even her own mother. She had depended on her since she came to El Alamo as a bride and theirs had been a silent friendship, deeper than words could express and only the heart could feel. [Cabeza de Baca Gilbert 1982, 43]

The Señá Martina and Rosario captivity narratives are texts embedded in colonial discourse. They are narratives divided between sympathy for the plight of these captives and a lack of remorse for the colonizer's having enslaved them. They are stories that invent or describe an idealized politics of "cultures in harmony" in which the dominant discourse presents women of different classes and races working in harmony together (Cabeza de Baca Gilbert 1982), or, when there is disharmony, the captive's restless ways are blamed, as when Rosario tries to escape, causing "trouble to the family." In the narrative about Rosario, the discourse of domination is one in which Padre Martínez is praised for his sympathetic attitude, his good treatment of the slave, and his patience. Whether his attitude was socially just or not is never questioned. In fact, the entire perspective about slavery and captivity is never questioned by the narrators. What does peek through the text is a strange ambivalence about the desire to be free, an ambivalence about the nature of the cultural other.

What do we, as readers, learn about these *indias* who were captured? That eventually they learned to conform and to adapt to an alien culture, that they tried to escape, that they longed for their people and their culture. We learn, too, that they survived, that they cried, and that they invoked a wistfulness in the people who observed them that was difficult to ignore.

Now I turn to the captivity tales of *mexicanas* who were captured by American Indians: the story of Inez González, an unpublished narrative about Refugio Gurriola, and an *"indita"* (a song) about the capture of Plácida Romero.

The tale of Inez González is unusual because of her rescue by U.S. Government Officials and their subsequent interest in her life. In September of 1850, Inez González, who lived in Santa Cruz, Sonora, went with other members of her family on a religious pilgrimage to the town of Magdalena for the Fiesta of San Francisco. She was fifteen at the time. In their party, besides the young Inez, was her uncle, Pacheco; her aunt, Mercedes Pacheco; her cousin, Francisco Pacheco; and a young married woman, Jesús Salvador. They had an escort of ten soldiers under the command of an Ensign Limón. On September 30 the party was attacked by Pima Apaches from east-central Arizona. The three women and the boy were taken captive. Mercedes Pacheco was apparently sold by the Apaches to Navajos and never heard from again. Jesús Salvador remained a captive until she escaped with a child. Inez remained an Indian captive for about ten months until 1851 when she was sold by her captors to a party of *mexicano* slave traders from Santa Fe. In the summer of 1851, a group from the American Commission sent to survey the new boundary line of the Treaty of Guadalupe Hildalgo arrived in the area. Its leader was a Rhode Islander, John Russell Bartlett, who had with him an interpreter, John Carey Cremony. One evening, the members of the commission noticed the young woman and discovered that she was a captive being conveyed for re-sale in Santa Fe. The Americans demanded that she be freed. She is described by Bartlett in the following manner:

> The girl herself was quite young, artless, and interesting in appearance, prepossessing in manners, and by her deportment gave evidence that she had been carefully brought up. Her purchaser belonged to a people with whom the system of peonage prevails, and among whom, as a general thing, females are not estimated as with us, especially in a moral point of view. . . . I therefore deemed

it to be my duty—and a pleasant one it certainly was, to extend over her the protection of the laws of the United States, and to see that, until delivered in safety to her parents, she should be 'treated with the utmost hospitality' that our position would allow. [Bartlett (1854) 1965, 306–307]

Bartlett's perspective toward the Mexican traders is one of condescending racism, perhaps even more strongly articulated because they traded in human beings. It is a racism that does not, however, display itself toward Inez throughout the narrative.

Inez consequently tells them her story, and Bartlett claims, "no improper freedom was taken with her person; but she was robbed of her clothing, save a skirt and under linen and was made to work very hard" Bartlett [1854] 1965, 308). As Inez was being led back to her home, they were met by a group of men, among whom was one of Inez's uncles and her step-father, Jesús Ortiz. The wildly emotional scene that ensued is described by Bartlett:

The joy of the father and friends in again beholding the face of her whom they supposed was forever lost from them, was unbounded. Each in turn (rough and half naked as many of them were), embraced her after the Spanish custom; and it was long ere one could utter a word. Tears of joy burst from all; and the sun-burnt and brawny men, in whom the finer feelings of our nature are wrongly supposed not to exist, wept like children, as they looked with astonishment on the rescued girl. She was not less overcome than they; and it was long before she could utter the name of her mother, and ask if she and her little brothers yet lived. The members of the Commission who witnessed this affectionate and joyful scene, could not but participate in the feelings of the poor child and her friends: and the big tears as they rolled down their weather-beaten and bearded faces, showed how fully they sympathized with the feelings of our Mexican friends. [Bartlett (1854) 1965, 399]

When Inez is reunited with her mother the description is even more emotionally charged, even for Bartlett the narrator:

Mr. Cremony helped Inez from the saddle, when in perfect ecstasy she rushed to her mother's arms. Words cannot express the joy manifested on this happy occasion. Their screams were painful to hear. The mother could scarcely believe what she saw, and after every embrace and gush of tears, she withdrew her arms to gaze on

fig 16   Doña Inez. "At the tender age of fifteen she had seen her relatives murdered before her eyes. . . ." Original line drawing by J. Ross Browne from his book, *Adventures in the Apache Country: A Tour Through Arizona and Sonora with Notes on the Silver Regions of Nevada.*

the face of her child. I have witnessed many scenes on the stage, of the meeting of friends after a long separation, and have read highly-wrought narratives of similar interviews, but none of them approached in pathos the spontaneous burst of feeling exhibited by the mother and daughter on this occasion. Thanks to the Almighty rose above all other sounds, while they remained clasped in each other's arms, for the deliverance from captivity, and the restoration of the beloved daughter to her home and friends. Although a joyful scene, it was a painfully affecting one to the spectators, not one of whom, could restrain his tears. [Bartlett (1854) 1965, 403]

Inez returns home and goes about trying to pick up the pieces of her life, but it is soon clear that its course has been irrevocably altered. The following year, 1852, when the Commission returns to Santa Clara, they find Inez living at Tubac with Captain Gómez, the commander of the Presidio. Bartlett demands to see Inez.

> The poor girl seemed very glad to see us. She was not ill, but evidently felt under some restraint, as the Captain remained during the interview. She seemed very sad and unhappy; and when asked if she would accompany us back to the States, as we had before invited her, she knew not what to say, and, fearing to give offense to her new captor, looked to him for a reply. The interview was a very unsatisfactory one, and we were all quite reluctant to leave her in such a position. [Bartlett (1854) 1965, 303]

The indignation felt by Mr. Bartlett is commented upon by J. Ross Browne, another member of the party:

> It was admitted by all that Mr. Bartlett had manifested a most praiseworthy and chivalrous interest in the misfortunes of this young woman. At the tender age of fifteen she had seen her relatives murdered before her eyes; had been dragged over mountains and deserts by ruthless savages; had suffered the most cruel barbarities at their hands; and was now once more, by the exertions of this humane American, restored to her friends and to civilization. The delicate and chivalrous conduct of Mr. Bartlett toward the fair captive can not be too highly estimated, considering her beauty and the peculiar circumstances of her career [Browne 1869, 178].

This ethnocentrism felt by Browne toward *mexicanos* is not extended to Inez, whom he describes as "the fair Inez, the divine Inez." He explains, however, that Gómez could not marry Inez because he already had a wife. This fact angered Bartlett "who had rescued the divine Inez," and he wrote an official protest to the governor of Sonora, Mexico as well as to the Bishop. These officials acquitted Gómez of bad conduct upon receiving his explanation that he was already married and his wife would "be very unhappy if he married another woman" (Browne 1869, 179). Cremony later recorded that Gómez married Inez after his wife died, and legitimized their two sons. She was later to marry again, this time the mayor of Santa Cruz (Mahr 1989, 14).

The last episode in the story is again related by Browne who visited Inez in 1865:

Doña Inez is married and settled at Santa Cruz. Her husband is not Captain Gómez. . . . On the subject of her treatment by the Apaches she was somewhat reserved. . . . Doña Inez is now about twenty-seven years of age, though she looks older. Her features are thin, sharp, and care-worn, owing to ill-health. Possibly, she may have been pretty in her youth. Mr. Bartlett thought so and he ought to be a judge. He saw a great deal of beauty unadorned in his tour of exploration. [Browne 1869, 179]

Browne goes on to state that

my trip to Santa Cruz offered me the opportunity to visit Inez, whom I found to be the wife of the chief and most influential man in that little community. She has an affectionate husband . . . is surrounded by a fine and promising family of three boys and a girl and is universally esteemed for her many excellent qualities. [Browne 1869, 180]

Thus, Inez is seen through the eyes of her self-styled redeemer, Bartlett, as a fair, innocent angel of captivity. His narrative is the romantic story of a chivalric American hero saving a fair maiden from barbarism. That, in his opinion, she had fallen into sin and was being taken advantage of by Gómez angered him no end. Her reticence in speaking about her situation illustrated, perhaps, her own acceptance of her moral position. Later, she became a "respectable wife and mother" and was in her late twenties when J. Ross Browne made the sketch of her (Radbourne 1979, 75). While this narrative of captivity focuses more upon the restoration and its aftermath than upon the captivity itself, we do not know what became of Inez in later years.

The Kit Carson Archives in Taos, New Mexico holds an unpublished manuscript entitled *"La cautiva,"* the "true story" of Refugio Gurriola, held captive from about 1858–1864. It was written by Jacobo M. Bernal of Taos, whose mother told him the story. It was finally put on paper in 1971, in Spanish, by Mr. Bernal when he was eighty-two years old. A second, more creative version of the story exists in English, written by Bernal's wife, Myrtle Rendón Bernal. Refugio Gurriola had married Teófilo Martínez who was the granduncle of Jacobo Bernal.

Refugio Gurriola, too, came from near Magdalena, Sonora where she lived with her family. She was about fifteen when she was captured by Yaqui Indians and later sold (along with her horse) to Apaches. She lived for five years among the Apaches, learning to hunt, to dry meat, to fish, and to make clothes. Refugio met Tomás, another captive who spoke Spanish. He helped her to escape, traveling together through Navajo country, until finally they reached the trading post of Juan José Trujillo in Tierra Amarilla. At last, Refugio arrived at Fort Union, New Mexico (near Las Vegas), where she was taken in by the Captain and his wife Juanita. While at Fort Union, she met Teófilo Martínez, a soldier in the army, and they fell in love. Teófilo wrote a letter to his mother, Luz Lucero de Martínez, telling her that Refugio had been an Indian captive and that he wanted to marry her. Apparently, Teófilo was very timid with women, so the family was happy that he found someone to marry. Teófilo's two older brothers, Nestor and Inocencio (Jacobo Bernal's grandfather), went from Taos to take Refugio to live with the family until Teófilo was mustered out of the army.

All the people in Taos had heard of Refugio's plight and were awaiting her arrival with great anticipation. They had posted lookouts to notify townspeople of her arrival, and, when the party was spotted, the church bell of Taos began to ring. When Refugio approached and dismounted her horse, she was embraced by the people and they threw pieces of silver at her as a sign of welcome. As Refugio neared the church, she entered to give thanks for her salvation. Because this story comes from the viewpoint of a Taoseño and because Refugio was to marry into

fig 17   Refugio Gurriola, *"La Cautiva."* Used by permission of the Kit Carson Historical Archives, Taos, New Mexico. Courtesy Taos Historic Museums.

his family, the narrator shows the people of Taos in a favorable light. Unlike Inez's story, no prejudice was shown toward Refugio because she had been a captive. Indeed, according to the story, it did not take Refugio long to be a *"verdadera"* Taoseña. She married Teófilo and, because she was an expert seamstress, she became a dressmaker. As well adjusted as she became to life in Taos, she always refused to go to a ritual play put on by the Taoseños called *"Los comanches"* in which the men of the village enacted hostilities between the Comanches and Nuevomexicanos. Refugio was too afraid to attend the play.

After the "happy" ending of this story, there is an epilogue. One day, as Inocencio Martínez was walking around Taos plaza, he came upon a man playing a musical instrument up to then unknown in Taos. The musician was a *mexicano* from Sonora and Inocencio invited him to visit at the house of his mother, Luz. He was interested in the musician because he himself was a violinist well known in the Taos area. At dinner Refugio asks the musician:

"What part of Mexico are you from, Sir?"

"I am from Sonora, from the town of Magdalena." Refugio's face turned red as much from happiness as from curiosity.

Refugio: "Do you know don Guadalupe Gurriola and his wife, Josefa Flores Gurriola?"

"Yes," said the man, "yes, yes I know them. They had two daughters, Refugio and Elena, affectionately called 'La nena' because she was the youngest."

Refugio: "Did you know Refugio?"

"Yes, yes I knew her but she was very young when I saw her last, just before she was kidnaped by Yaqui Indians."

"Look at me carefully to see if you recognize me," said Refugio.

The man looked intently at her and said, "Your face is almost the face of Mercedes Flores." (Bernal 1971, 24)

He then tells her that her mother had died and her father had left Magdalena. Refugio cries from love and sorrow and tells him, "The hope and great desire of my life was someday to return to my country and embrace my parents, especially my mother who loved me so much" (Bernal 1971, 24).

This Spanish version of the story is corroborated by place names and the names of the people who helped Refugio along the way. We hear the names and details of canyons, mountains, rivers, towns, army posts, trading posts, streets, people, and clothing indicative of the oral tradition from which it came. It is documented with the placement of other people who could corroborate the evidence of this extraordinary tale. Yet also included are clearly fictive inventions, such as conversations with the captive Tomás, who helped Refugio escape, and the appearance of the musician.

That the story is generally true is of no doubt. There is even a photograph of Refugio in the archives that shows us how she looked when she was older. The lineage of the Martínez family is also included to document Refugio's relationship to the narrator. The English version of the story, however, written by Bernal's wife, begins to transform the facts. Although her manuscript was never completed, further elements of introspection and conjecture about Refugio's life would have been likely to enter the narrative. In Myrtle Rendón Bernal's version, Refugio is more religious than in the previous story; she is accepted into the family before she falls in love with Teófilo; the captive who helps her is named Felipe, not Tomás; and, in the end, she is reunited with her sister (whose name becomes Jesusita). The story begins to demonstrate more of the characteristics of Anglo/American captivity narratives, such as descriptions of Indians as cruel and savage, elements not included in the Spanish version. In the few chapters that are completed, the motivation and the introspection become more acute, and romantic elements are added. It is clear that this English version was on its way to becoming a romanticized captivity narrative. However, the Spanish version rings true and gives us more clues as to what Refugio Gurriola's life may have been like. One detail in the story that lends veracity is that, when Refugio was left at Fort Union, she removed her Indian clothes, a buckskin dress, deciding to save the dress as a reminder that the clothing served her well during her captivity. Moreover, her fear of the *"Comancheros"* play and the details about her family at the end all lend a certain believable pathos to the tale. While the Yaqui Indians are seen as cruel at the beginning of the story (they kill her younger sister Nene), the Apaches do not treat Refugio in a particularly cruel manner, except for keeping her tied at night so she won't escape. Of particular interest is the emphasis in the story on Refugio's whiteness of skin and her beauty. This is given as the central explanation as to why she is treated so well. An examination of Refugio's picture, however, shows that Refugio looks very much like a *mestiza*.

Finally, I want to examine a captivity tale in the form of an *"indita,"* a commissioned ballad, the *"Indita of Plácida Romero."* For this information I am indebted to the work of my colleague, Enrique Lamadrid, who collected the *indita* and has examined its history, legend, and performance traditions. Of particular importance to Lamadrid is the fact that this *indita* has been sung by five generations of the women of the Romero and Gallegos families. Thus, the singing of this ballad by the women who are descendants of the original *cautiva* restores and reinforces the memory of her ordeal for the family. As Lamadrid comments, these ballad forms of the *inditas* "share a thematic fascination with disasters, natural and historical, and the personal dimension of human tragedy" (Lamadrid, this volume). While many *inditas* deal with a variety of themes, the *"Indita de Plácida Romero"* deals specifically with a *cautiva*. Plácida Romero was captured in 1881, and the song was written by an anonymous local poet six months later. In his excellent article on this particular *indita*, Lamadrid traces the different versions of the song and its entry and transformation into the oral tradition. In the narrative, Plácida and her daughter are captured by Gileño Apaches. During the fight, Plácida's husband is killed. Separated from her daughter, Plácida is able to escape and make her way home. After returning, she gives birth to a daughter by a young Apache, whom she names Trinidad, after her lost daughter (Lamadrid, this volume). The ballad is full of emotive elements meant to capture the sympathy of the audience for the captive woman. In the refrain, the pain of separation from her known life is expressed in an emotional repetition of her lament as she is led away into captivity, *"Adiós, ya me voy."* She says good-bye to her daughters, to her ranch, to her town. Even the trees and the rocks weep to see her go into captivity. The word *"Adiós"* is repeated twelve times. As Lamadrid notes (this volume), this reinforces the speaker's attitude, and "the repeated interjections of *'adiós'* re-emphasize the tragic absence of the abducted speaker while simultaneously projecting her presence and concern back to her family." This *indita,* while being the most emotional of all the captivity narratives discussed here, is also almost totally lacking in blame toward the Indians who captured Plácida, nor does it describe them in barbaric terms. As Lamadrid points out, even the descendants of Plácida Romero talked about how well she had been treated by the Apaches.

These captivity narratives of *indias* and *mexicanas* are illustrative of the underside of cultural conflict and hostility. These are the great tragedies and the great adventures of their lives. The voices and travails of these women were never initially public ones; their stories became public when told by others with various motives. In the case of the *indias* captivities told from the Indian perspective, we see kindness on the part of individual *mexicanas*, support on the part of others who had been captives, and reunion, after initial suspicion, on the part of their kinsfolk and relatives. The *indias* captivities as related by the Hispana writers had a different goal. In the case of Dora Ortiz Vásquez, the tale of Rosario is used to show the nobility of Father Martínez and to illustrate what a kind, sympathetic, and forgiving man he was. This text is a complicated one, however, in which the subverted narrative, that of the desire for freedom on the part of Rosario, keeps popping forth. The text of Fabiola Cabeza de Baca Gilbert is meant to express the way Indian and *mexicano* cultures were able to work together mutually. There is certainly no hostility expressed here because it was the political ideology and wish of Cabeza de Baca Gilbert that this harmony be true. Nevertheless the colonizing discourse is evident.

The *mexicana* captivities offer an interesting contrast. The famous case of Inez González deals with the ideology of the Americans who rescued her. Because she was their "fair" and "divine" heroine, they saw themselves as her "saviors." Doubtless they were anti-slavery advocates as well as chivalric heroes. And although Inez is a *mexicana,* their prejudice does not come out against her, but against the traders who bought her and, later, against Captain Gómez, who, in their opinion, did not do the honorable thing by her. Thus did they see their "noble victory" tarnished.

The story of Refugio Gurriola is interesting because once again she is the "fair maiden" who has lived an adventurous life. Through her skill of survival she is ennobled by her family; at the same time, she is made "feminine" by her fear of the ritual play. The story also distinguishes the people of Taos in their generosity toward and acceptance of her.

Finally, the *"Indita of Plácida Romero"* reminds us of the heart-wrenching agony and displacement suffered by all these captives. That any survived at all is due to their strength as women, to good luck, and to their own abilities to escape, not to the help of God. In these aspects, the native and *mexicana* captivity narratives differ from those in the Anglo/American tradition. Perhaps it is because the native and *mexicano* cultures continued to struggle and survive together in a "real" way, sharing the perspectives of both the colonizing and the colonized.

Literature Cited

Bailey, L. R. 1973. *Indian Slave Trade in the Southwest.* Los Angeles, Calif.: Westernlore Press.

Bartlett, John Russell. 1965. *Personal Narrative of Explorations and Incidents in Texas, New Mexico, California, Sonora and Chihuahua.* New York: D. Appleton, 1854. Reprint, 2 Vols. Chicago: The Rio Grande Press, Inc.

Basso, Keith H. 1971. *Western Apache Raiding and Warfare. From the Notes of Grenville Goodwin.* Tucson: University of Arizona Press.

Bataille, Gretchen M. and Kathleen Mullen Sands. 1984. *American Indian Women: Telling Their Lives.* Lincoln: University of Nebraska Press.

Bernal, Jacobo M. 1971. *La Cautiva.* Unpublished manuscript, "Bernal Papers," Kit Carson Historical Archives, Taos, New Mexico.

Browne, J. Ross. 1869. *Adventures in the Apache Country: A Tour Through Arizona and Sonora with Notes on the Silver Regions of Nevada.* New York: Harper and Brothers.

Cabeza de Baca Gilbert, Fabiola. 1982. *The Good Life. New Mexico Traditions and Food.* Santa Fe: San Vicente Foundation, 1949. Reprint, Santa Fe: The Museum of New Mexico Press.

Córdova, Josephine. 1976. *No lloro pero me acuerdo.* Dallas, Tex.: Mockingbird Publishing Co.

Fisher, Nora, ed. 1979. *Spanish Textile Tradition of New Mexico and Colorado.* Santa Fe: Museum of International Folk Art.

Mahr, Aaron P. 1989. Women on the Mexican Frontier: The Case of Inez González. *Best Student Essays* (University of New Mexico) 1(2) (fall): 9–15.

McNitt, Frank. 1990. *Navajo Wars. Military Campaigns, Slave Raids, and Reprisals.* Albuquerque: University of New Mexico Press.

Radbourne, Allan. 1979. Ambush at Coscopera Canyon: The Story of Inez González. *The English Westerners' Tally Sheet* 4 (July):63–76.

Riley, Glenda. 1984. *Women and Indians on the Frontier, 1825–1915.* Albuquerque: University of New Mexico Press.

Vásquez, Dora Ortiz. 1975. *Enchanted Temples of Taos. My Story of Rosario.* Santa Fe, N.Mex.: The Rydel Press.

Magical Realism in Nuevomexicano Narrative

Luis Leal

To Rudolfo Anaya

ᐒ IN SPITE OF CRITIC Theo L. D'haen's statement about magical realism and postmodernism—that "[t]hey now seem almost the only short-hand available to categorize contemporary developments in Western fiction" (1995, 193)—literary critics have indeed claimed that Chicana/o literature to some degree has affinities to postmodernism, but rarely to the magical-realistic mode. In the analyses and reviews of the works of several authors, however, passing references are made to the magical-realist nature of the work under discussion. In addition, Rosaura Sánchez (1987) examined the influence of Latin American magical realism on modern Chicano writers, and Roland Walter (1990) studied magical realism in Miguel Méndez's novel *El sueño de Santa María de las piedras* (1986). Some critics have also mentioned the related mode, *lo real maravilloso*. Sánchez, for example, in "Postmodernism and Chicano Literature," states that: "Burlesque realism *à la* García Márquez is now beginning to appear (in Chicana/o literature), as have 'magical' elements, in the Carpentier mode of the 'marvelous real,' common in the works of Rodolfo [*sic*] Anaya, Genaro González, and Alejandro Morales" (Sánchez 1987, 8–9).

More recently, Manuel M. Martín-Rodríguez stated that "[A]nother narrative trajectory that utilized some of the essential characteristics of Magic Realism and the Latin American *nueva novela* appears to have been more fruitful. *The Road to Tamazunchale*...by the Californian, Ron Arias, is the first example that we have" (Martín-Rodríguez 1983, 116). The phrase "more fruitful" refers to Martín-Rodríguez's discussion of the failed attempt by Anaya and Estela Portillo Trambley to produce an integrated mythical and social reality. He does, however, acknowledge that Anaya, Portillo Trambley, and Orlando Romero are "the best exponents of this recovery of myth or legends for the purpose of incorporating them in a current context" (Martín-Rodríguez 1983, 116).

It is my purpose in this presentation, which I dedicate to Rudolfo Anaya, to bring to light the *real maravilloso*—the magical-realistic elements in Nuevomexicano narrative—and the contributions of both to postmodernist American fiction. I will touch upon some of the most important early works in this mode and concentrate on two novels, Anaya's *Bless Me, Ultima* ([1972] 1994) and Orlando Romero's *Nambé—Year One* (1976), early examples not only of the mythical approach, as several critics have stated in the case of Anaya, but also of magical realism.

Magical Realism

What is the relationship between magical realism and *lo real maravilloso*? Both literary modes have been amply studied in recent years, but much controversy and misunderstanding remains about them. Of the two, the term "magical realism" is perhaps the most important.

The term "magical realism" was coined by the German art critic Franz Roh in 1925 to refer to the post-expressionist movement that appeared in Europe about that time, a movement that was essentially a return to figurative representation in art. According to Roh, however, such a movement did not "acknowledge that radiation of magic, that spirituality, that lugubrious quality throbbing in the best works of the new mode" (1995, 20). Today, the term "magical realism" is applied to a literature (or art) that is non-realistic, or rather, that is concerned with a reality that is considered to be magical.

Roh's book was translated by Fernando Vela into Spanish (Roh 1927) and, in that same year, published in abbreviated form in the *Revista de Occidente,* the famous periodical edited in Madrid by José Ortega y Gasset. The term became popular in Latin America. The first to use the term in literary writing, however, was Venezuelan novelist Arturo Uslar Pietri, who wrote in 1948: "What predominated in the short story and left an indelible mark there was the consideration of man as a mystery surrounded by realistic facts. A poetic prediction or a poetic denial of reality. What for lack of another name could be called a magical realism" (161–162).

In the United States, the first to write about magical realism in Spanish American literature was Puerto Rican critic Ángel Flores who, in 1955, published an article entitled "Magical Realism in Spanish American Fiction." Without mentioning Roh or Uslar Pietri, Flores states that magical realism began with Franz Kafka in Europe and Borges in Latin America. His definition, however, cannot be accepted, since for him magical-realistic literature is a mode practiced by the elite only. He says: "[T]he magical realists do not cater to a popular taste, rather they address themselves to the sophisticated, those not merely initiated in aesthetic mysteries but versed in subtleties. Often their writings approach closely that art characterized by Ortega y Gasset as 'dehumanized'" (1955, 191). Flores's article was beneficial, however, because he was the first to apply the term to contemporary Spanish American narrative fiction, and this started a controversy that has not ended yet after almost half a century.

In spite of its novelty, Flores's article did not have an impact on Latin American literary criticism. By 1966, however, a student announced that he was writing his dissertation on magical realism in contemporary Argentinean literature. Motivated by that announcement, I decided to write an article defining magical realism in a more precise form than Flores. In my study, published in 1967 in Spanish in *Cuadernos Americanos* (Leal 1967) and translated as part of an English-language anthology on magical realism in 1995, I mention Roh and Uslar Pietri and consider magical realism to be an attitude toward reality that can be expressed in popular or cultured forms, in elaborate or rustic styles, and in closed or open structures, and that can be separated from fantastic and oneiric literature and from surrealism. I go on to say that, in magical realism, "the writer confronts reality and tries to untangle it, to discover what is mysterious in things, in life, in human acts" (Leal 1995, 121). Since the 1960s, and especially during the 1980s and 1990s, magical realism has gained respectability in American and European mainstream literary criticism as a component of postmodernism (Faris 1995, D'haen 1995), cultural studies, and postcolonial discourse (Slemon 1995), and has been extended to cover film (Jameson 1986).[1]

Lo Real Maravilloso

In order to present a total picture of magical realism I will point out how it differs from *lo real maravilloso* and give some examples from early Nuevomexicano narrative. This is necessary because critics often confuse the two modes and accept them as synonymous. The phrase *lo real maravilloso* was coined by the Cuban novelist Alejo Carpentier and first appeared in the "Prólogo" to his 1949 novel, *El reino de este mundo* (*The Kingdom of this World*). An expanded version of the "Prólogo" was published as the essay *"De lo real maravillosamente americano"* in Carpentier's 1964 collection, *Tientos y diferencias;* note the word *americano* in the title. By 1943 Carpentier had visited Haiti and was fascinated by what he saw there—that is, "*algo que podríamos llamar lo real maravilloso*" (something we could call the marvelous real) (Carpentier 1964, 13). In the 1949 version of the "Prólogo," translated and republished in 1995 by Zamora and Harris, Carpentier defined the term in these words:

> The marvelous begins to be unmistakably marvelous when it arises from an unexpected alteration of reality (the miracle), from a privileged revelation of reality, an unaccustomed insight that is singularly favored by the unexpected richness of reality or an amplification of the scale and categories of reality, perceived with particular intensity by virtue of an exaltation of the spirit that leads it to a kind of extreme state. [Carpentier 1995, 85–86]

A few paragraphs later, however, Carpentier localizes the term, making *lo real maravilloso* a characteristic of Latin American culture. He wrote:

I thought, the presence and vitality of this marvelous real was not the unique privilege of Haiti, but the heritage of all of America, where we have not yet begun to establish an inventory of our cosmogonies. The marvelous real is found at every stage in the lives of men who inscribed dates in the history of the continent and who left the names that we still carry: from those who searched for the fountain of eternal youth and the golden city of Manoa to certain early rebels or modern heroes of mythological fame from our wars of independence, such as Colonel Juana de Azurduy. [Carpentier 1995, 87]

The difference between *lo real maravilloso* and magical realism can be derived from that quotation. *Lo real maravilloso* is to be found in nature and in citizens of the Americas who provoke a reaction called "marvelous;" that is, causing wonder or astonishment. On the other hand, in magical realism the important characteristic is the mystery found in people, nature and objects, a mystery that eludes the understanding of the observer.[2] In *lo real maravilloso* only certain events are considered to be marvelous; in magical realism all reality is magical.

Abundant examples of *lo real maravilloso* in New Mexico and other areas of the Southwest can be found in the chronicles of the explorers who came to the region during the sixteenth and seventeenth centuries, as well as in the many folktales brought by settlers from central Mexico. Famous early *cronistas* whose works are rich in marvelous experiences in New Mexico are those of Cabeza de Vaca, Fray Marcos de Niza, Coronado, Fray Alonso de Benavides, and others. When Fray Marcos de Niza came in search of the Seven Fabulous Cities, of which Cíbola is the most important, he described the homes in superlative terms, saying that the façades of the principal houses have "much turquoise stonework" (de Niza 1865, 340), of which there was great abundance. His account of the richness of Cíbola, although not actually observed by him, inspired Coronado's expedition into New Mexico.

Fray Marcos was guided in his expedition by a *real maravilloso* character, the black man Estevanico, a companion of Cabeza de Vaca, who met his death in New Mexico. Also known throughout the Southwest is the story of the Lady in Blue—that is, the Spanish nun Sor María de Agreda (1602–1665) who, as her story was retold by Alonso de Benavides, brought the gospel to the natives and preached to them in their native tongues without ever leaving Spain (Colahan 1994).

Magical Realism and Postmodernism

Wendy L. Faris, Theo D'haen, and other contemporary literary critics have suggested that magical realism is an important component of postmodernism. Faris argues that "magical realism, wherever it may flourish and in whatever style, contributes significantly to postmodernism" (Faris 1995, 166). Other critics go so far as to say that the two terms are equivalent. For the Canadian critic Geert Lermout they are interchangeable. In "Postmodernist Fiction in Canada," Lermout observes that "what is postmodern in the rest of the world used to be called magic realist in South America and still goes by that name in Canada" (as quoted by D'haen 1995, 194).

How the terms "magical realism" and "postmodernism" first came to be associated is not clear. This matter, however, is inconsequential. The real problem is not to prove the relationship, which is now taken for granted, but how it has contributed to shape postmodernism. As D'haen says: "If magic realism, then, seems firmly established as part of postmodernism, the question remains as to *what* part it plays in this larger current or movement, and where and why" (1995, 194). It is not our purpose to answer that question, but to demonstrate how Chicana/o fiction in New Mexico, in its magical-realistic aspect, contributes to that movement, keeping in mind that some features of postmodernism apply to Chicana/o literature, and others do not.[3]

Magical Realism and Nuevomexicano Fiction

Chicana/o literary criticism has identified very few texts that fall within the magical-realistic mode or that have aspects that can be considered as such. The first to consider some Chicana/o works as magical-realistic were Francisco A. Lomelí and Donald Urioste (1976), although they define magical realism not in the text but in the glossary ("a vision of reality in which true and unbelievable events may be found in the same plane without seeming incongruous. Natural phenomena (are) closely associated to supernatural beliefs, thus creating a magical atmosphere" [1976, 113]). They also do not say why the works designated as magical realistic belong in that mode.

Among the New Mexican works Lomelí and Urioste consider magical realistic are, of course, Rudolfo Anaya's *Bless Me, Ultima* ([1972] 1994), which they call "a rich reservoir of myth and legend," adding that it is a "Chicano-style magical realism of wizardry and dreams as dimensions of reality that foretell happenings and reveal otherwise unknown occurrences" (Lomelí and Urioste 1976, 40). The other work mentioned in this category is Orlando Romero's novel *Nambé—Year One* (1976), which they call "a fascinating work of magical realism" (Lomelí and Urioste 1976, 47). Unfortunately, Lomelí and Urioste do not explain such terms as "Chicano-style magical realism" or how magical realism is expressed in the books they mention.

Catherine Bartlett, in her "Magical Realism: The Latin American Influence on Modern Chicano Writers," includes only one Nuevomexicano author, Orlando

Romero, whose *Nambé—Year One* she considers "a flowery, sugar-coated imitation" of new Latin American techniques (1986, 28).

Earlier Nuevomexicano texts of magical realism have not yet been identified, although they may exist. *The Texans,* a play composed in New Mexico around 1846, may be one example. Based on the actual invasion of New Mexico by a Texan army in 1846, the play includes a character, Don Jorge Ramírez, who is believed to have magical powers. According to another character, "The Indian," Don Jorge, "can take a stone and turn it into gold. He can tear up a piece of cloth and then make it like new. He can turn you into a chicken in the twinkling of an eye" (Espinosa and Espinosa 1943, 305). Don Jorge is introduced by means of a literary motif common in magical-realistic texts, a song in the distance. The Indian says, "The one who is singing is Ramírez" (Espinosa and Espinosa 1943, 306), a statement the reader has to accept without objective confirmation.

Another New Mexican early text in which some critics have found magical realism is the novelette *El hijo de la tempestad* (1892) by Eusebio Chacón. According to Lomelí and Urioste, this early fiction "is a combination of folklore beliefs, *novela caballeresca,* adventures and magical realism" (1976, 42). Although these critics do not give any examples of magical realism in the novel, motifs of this nature can be found in the two female characters, the Gypsy girl and her mysterious enemy, Sombra de la Luz. Of interest here is this early reference in Chicano literature about the earth that parts and swallows those who are sinful. With the help of her monkey, transformed into the devil, the Gypsy girl conquers her enemy: *"Lanzó una carcajada el diablo y la vieja cayó muerta a sus pies, y la tierra se abrió y se la tragó"* (The devil busted out laughing and the old lady fell down dead at his feet; the earth opened up and swallowed her) (Chacón 1892, 12).

It is, however, during the contemporary period that Chicana/o fiction has produced several magical-realistic texts that fall within the definition now accepted as characteristic of the mode. Among recent authors producing magical-realistic texts in New Mexico the following have to be considered: Fray Angélico Chávez, Sabine Ulibarrí, Rudolfo Anaya, Orlando Romero, and Denise Chávez. Even if not born in New Mexico, Ana Castillo has to be included, for she has written a magical-realistic novel that takes place in New Mexico, *So Far from God* (1993).

In the fiction of Fray Angélico Chávez (1987) there is a special kind of magical realism, for he combines it with religious imagery. His magical-realistic topics and images are usually associated with the figure of the *santero,* as can be seen in "Hunchback Madonna," in which Mana Seda, caught in a rain storm in the forest, finds refuge in the adobe hut of a mysterious *santero,* a fact she attributes to having prayed to the Holy Lady. Religious images are introduced to recreate the legend of the Virgin of Guadalupe. In "The Bell That Sang Again," the death of the rivals Capitán Pelayo and Joaquín, Ysabel's husband, causes the bell to magically lose its silvery tone, which is regained when Ysabel gives birth to her child. The religious imagery here is presented in the context of a hagiographic legend, that of Saint Ysabel, mother of John the Baptist. When Saint Ysabel meets her namesake, the girl Ysabel, who, after her husband's death, is about to commit suicide, she tells her that she heard the movements of the baby she is carrying in her womb, and saves her. In the context of Nuevomexicano religious culture, the opinion of Father Bartolo regarding New Mexico is significant: he believes that New Mexico is like the Holy Land and that its soil is red because of all the blood spilled from Saint John's head.

Magical-realistic topics like those mentioned can be found in Chávez's "The Fiddler and the Angelito," in which humor, also present in other stories, is an essential element; the burro's owner has to receive help from the wise little angel to make his beast of burden move. In "The Black Ewe," the girlfriend of the *patrón* is transformed into a ewe. In the story "The Colonel and the Santo," the Colonel visits the mother of a soldier to tell her that her son has been killed, but does not reveal that he was also crucified. The Colonel is mystified when he sees a painting in her home of a crucified saint dressed as a soldier. There are, in Chávez's stories, instances of mysticism. Whether they should be considered as a special aspect of magical realism is a question that has not been resolved. Clark Colahan, in his study of the mystical journey of Sor María Agreda, states that "in view of contemporary Latin American fiction's magical realism, which incorporates much of traditional Hispanic mysticism, perhaps the time has come to argue against the other side of the question" (1994, 99).

In his 1964 collection of short stories, *Tierra amarilla*, Ulibarrí included "*Mi caballo mago*" ("My Wonder Horse"), which can be classified as a tale of magical realism. This characteristic is found in the attitude of the narrator, a fifteen-year-old young man, toward a wild white horse and the environment wherein he roams. The wonder horse, who fills the boy's imagination, is called mysterious and talismanic. When he is seen by the boy, nature is suspended:

> I sit drowsily still, forgetting the cattle in the glade. Suddenly the forest falls silent, a deafening quiet. The afternoon comes to a standstill. The breeze stops blowing, but it vibrates. The sun flares hotly. The planet, life, and time itself have stopped in an inexplicable way. For a moment, I don't understand what is happening. Then my eyes focus. There he is! The Wonder Horse! [Anaya (1988) 1993, 2]

The young man's whole being is fused with that of the horse. "I was going in search of the white light that galloped through my dreams." When he finally faces the horse, he says: "We saw one another at the same time. Together, we turned to stone." When he is able to rope the horse, "The whole earth shakes and shudders"

(Anaya [1988] 1993, 3–4). He brings the horse home and lets him roam in the pasture, from which it soon escapes. Before letting him loose in the pasture, the young man had asked him: "What shall I do with you, Mago?" (Anaya [1988] 1993, 5). He knows that a magic horse like Mago cannot be kept prisoner, that it belongs to the wild range, that it is part of the landscape.

In Rudolfo Anaya's essay, "An Author's Reflections: The Silence of the Llano" (1983), Anaya refers to his short story "The Village Which the Gods Painted Yellow," set in Mexico, as "that strange tale." He continues, saying that he will return to Yucatán and Guatemala, "armed with magic," and ends by saying that Aztlán is also a land where "[p]ower flows through the land and the people, (where) dimensions of reality quickly evaporate under the sun, (and where) the visions and the dreams compel as much as any other force" (Anaya 1983, 17). The two great natural forces are, of course, the *llano* and the river where the *llaneros* and the people of the valley live. Anaya's stories "The Road to Platero" and "The Silence of the Llano" reflect the mystery of the *llano,* and "The Place of the Swallows," that of the river. Anaya gives both motifs a full treatment in *Bless Me, Ultima* ([1972] 1994). But the great mystery, of course, is life itself, "the deep sense of the mystery of life which pulsed along the dark green river" (Anaya 1983, 14). The color green seems to be symbolic of mystery.

In *Bless Me, Ultima,* the magic of the color green is precisely what the boy Antonio, Ultima's protégé, experiences through her power. He says: "She took my hand, and I felt the power of a whirlwind sweep around me. Her eyes swept the surrounding hills and through them I saw for the first time the wild beauty of our hills and the magic of the green river" ([1972] 1994, 12).

A great novel lends itself to numerous interpretations, and that is what has happened with *Bless Me, Ultima.* The many interpretations to which the novel has been subjected are summarized by Roberto Cantú in his article "Apocalypse as an Ideological Construct: The Storyteller's Art in *Bless Me, Ultima*" (1990). To those interpretations I want to add one more, the magical-realistic perspective, which is based on the sense of mystery present throughout the work.

In the opening paragraph, Antonio mentions the two key motifs, the *llano* and the river, and wraps them around the word mystery:

> Ultima came to stay with us the summer I was almost seven. When she came the beauty of the llano unfolded before my eyes, and the gurgling waters of the river sang to the hum of the turning earth. The magical time of childhood stood still, and the pulse of the living earth pressed its mystery into my living blood. [Anaya (1972) 1994, 1]

The reference to the image of the turning earth brings to memory the use of the same image in a magical-realistic Mexican novel, *Pedro Páramo,* by Juan Rulfo: "As dawn breaks, the day turns, stopping and starting. The rusty gears of the earth are almost audible: the vibration of this ancient earth overturning darkness" (Rulfo [1955] 1994, 109).

For Cantú, the landscape in the opening paragraphs of *Bless Me, Ultima* "is integrally rhetorized in an apocalyptic mode according to the ideal landscape literary tradition" (1990, 31). In the following statement, however, Cantú comes close to describing a magical-realistic experience, but attributes it to a different mode: "The revelatory experience undergone by Antonio is extraordinary in the sense that he reaches a peculiar level of cognition better known in apocalyptic literature as a vision trance" (1990, 31). An alternative interpretation would be the magical-realistic one, which can be applied to most of Antonio's experiences. Throughout the novel, the words "mystery" and "mysterious" recur frequently.

Four years after Anaya's novel appeared, Orlando Romero published *Nambé— Year One* (1976), a novel that has much in common with *Bless Me, Ultima*. Both narratives take place in the same region. The narrators, Antonio and Mateo, are remembering events that began at the magical age of seven years; and, most important, the authors' attitudes toward reality can be called magical realistic. In Anaya's novel, Ultima inspires Antonio; in *Nambé—Year One*, it is the green-eyed Gypsy. Unlike Eusebio Chacón's Gypsy in *El hijo de la tempestad* (1892), a mere traditional stereotype, Romero's is idealized and becomes a New Mexican Dulcinea. Some critics have thought that to create his Gypsy girl, Romero was inspired by García Márquez. More likely is Cervantes's Preciosa, the young Gypsy with the "ojos de esmeralda" ([1613] 1938, 33) from the novelette *La gitanilla*, the beauty who had also inspired Victor Hugo, who renamed her Esmeralda.

The landscape in both Anaya's and Romero's novels is mysterious and magical, as are the two women, Ultima and the Gypsy. They have hypnotic powers, although their powers emanate from different sources. A bond is established between Antonio and Ultima, as takes place between Mateo and the Gypsy girl. The motifs through which these bonds are established are an owl and a golden chain. Both motifs have magical powers—the owl represents Ultima, and the golden chain transforms feet into wings. Both Antonio and Mateo are strongly attached to the land and to the people of their communities. The central magical motif in *Bless Me, Ultima* is the golden carp; the corresponding one in *Nambé— Year One* is a giant salamander. The difference between these two motifs is to be found in the fact that Antonio sees the golden carp. When that magical moment comes, Antonio's reaction is typical of that of a person who experiences *lo real maravilloso*. "'The golden carp,' I whispered in awe. . . . I knew I had witnessed a miraculous thing" (Anaya [1972] 1994, 114). The carp looks at Antonio and is cognizant of his presence. On the other hand, the giant salamander appears to Mateo in a vision, talks to him, and advises him never to leave his native land, advice Mateo accepts without question.

This attachment to the land, for Mateo, is centered on the old house inherited from his great-grandfather, a house that

> kept hidden and forgotten secrets within its worn floorboards.
> Every step taken on them was recorded and memorized. . . . It
> caught time itself, made it stop, and its haunting memories were
> left as reminders. Other times as well as these were only echoes,
> vibrations and waves of energy that, as if by accident, had been
> thrown into the earth that went to make these walls as well as phys-
> ical and spiritual beings. [Romero 1976, 9]

The source of mystery in Romero's novel is ethnicity and the landscape. The
title itself, from the Tewa and meaning "the people of the roundish earth" (García
1978, 26), is expressive of those two elements. Mateo feels that he is the incarnation of his grandfather, "of his wild blood, that hybrid of solar-maize plant
blood" (12), and finds his *mestizo* nature to be a source of mystery. He says, "There
is Indian in us, of ancient forgotten peoples that roamed the world before there
was history" (12), a reference to the second part of the title, the year one. Like
Antonio, Mateo becomes conscious of this mystery the night he is seven years old
(12)—again the magical number. Both novels make references to *"La Llorona."* In
Romero, she is a real person called *La Bartola*. As García tells us, *"La Llorona* is
very much a part of New Mexico's culture; and physically *La Bartola* in her old age
becomes indistinguishable from the soil" (1978, 22). As Mateo says: "She looked
like her adobe house" (Romero 1976, 59). And so does Mateo himself, who is
strongly attached to the earth and feels that "[t]he adobe earth, dampened by the
street rain" (Romero 1976, 9) is pulling him. These two novels are perhaps the best
examples of magical realism in Nuevomexicano fiction.

Conclusion

If any literature outside of the Latin American and Caribbean regions lends itself
to analysis from the perspective of magical realism, it is Nuevomexicano literature,
for even in the fiction of social realism there are motifs, symbols, and images that
can be identified as belonging to the magical-realistic mode. As stated before, I
want to argue that Nuevomexicano literature is rich in magical-realistic features
and is, therefore, a contributor to postmodernism, as is evident in the novel *The
Milagro Beanfield War* (1974) by John Nichols and in the work of other important
novelists. By focusing on these features in Nuevomexicano letters, it is possible also
to consider this literature as both a part of the larger Latin American literary sphere
and as an aspect of postmodernist American literature. Magical realism offers an
alternative theory helpful in analyzing Chicana/o literature. With magical realism,

myth and other aspects of imaginative literature can be considered an aspect of the mode, for it combines the two worlds, the real and the imaginary, both so rich in New Mexican culture.

An analysis of fiction from the perspective of magical realism does not require a consideration of structural, generic, or stylistic elements in the text, since magical realism is a mode that can be expressed in any structure, any style, and in any genre. At the same time, it is not necessary to study Chicano or any other Hispanic literature as a separate entity, for magical realism allows the critic to see it in the context of Latin American literature, even if it is written in English. Nor is it necessary to separate popular literature from scholarly literature or to dwell on the racial background of the writers or the racial contents of the text. *Y en fin,* magical realism is most appropriate to study Hispanic and indigenous literatures, as it is a methodology born from the American soil, just like the texts to which it is applied.

Notes

1. For the most recent studies on magical realism see Zamora and Faris (1995).
2. On *lo real maravilloso,* see also Alejo Carpentier, "The Baroque and the Marvelous Real" in Zamora and Faris (1995, 89–108).
3. Some of the most important books dealing with postmodernity in literature are: Steven Connor, *Postmodernist Culture: An Introduction to Theories of the Contemporary* (Cambridge, Mass.: Basil Blackwell, 1989); Douwe Fokkema, *Literary History, Modernism, and Postmodernism* (Amsterdam and Philadelphia: John Benjamins, 1986); Ihab Hassen, *The Dismemberment of Orpheus: Towards a Postmodern Literature* (New York: Oxford University Press, 1982); Brian McHale, *Postmodernist Fiction* (New York and London: Methuen, 1987); and Frederic Jameson, *Postmodernism or, The Cultural Logic of Late Capitalism* (Durham, N.C.: Duke University Press, 1991).

Literature Cited

Anaya, Rudolfo. 1983. An Author's Reflections: The Silence of the Llano. *Nuestro* (April):14–17, 49.

———. 1994. *Bless Me, Ultima.* Berkeley, Calif.: Quinto Sol Publications, 1972. Reprint, New York: Warner Books.

———, ed. (1988) 1993. *Voces: An Anthology of New Mexican Writers.* Albuquerque: University of New Mexico Press.

Bartlett, Catherine. 1986. Magical Realism: The Latin American Influence on Modern Chicano Writers. *Confluencia* 1(2) (spring):27–37.

Cantú, Roberto. 1990. Apocalypse as an Ideological Construct: The Storyteller's Art in *Bless Me, Ultima.* In *Rudolfo Anaya: Focus on Criticism,* ed. César González-T, 13–63. La Jolla, Calif.: Lalo Press.

Carpentier, Alejo. 1949. *El reino de este mundo.* México: EDIAPSA.

———. 1964. *Tientos y diferencias.* México: UNAM.

———. 1995. On the Marvelous Real in America. In *Magical Realism: Theory, History,*

Community, eds. Lois Parkinson Zamora and Wendy B. Faris, 75–88. Durham, N.C.: Duke University Press.

Castillo, Ana. 1993. *So Far from God.* New York: W. W. Norton.

Cervantes Saavedra, Miguel de. [1613] 1938. *La gitanilla.* In Vol. 1 of *Novelas ejemplares,* edited by Pedro Henríquez Ureña. Buenos Aires: Losada.

Chacón, Eusebio. 1892. *El hijo de la tempestad / Tras la tormenta la calma.* Santa Fe: El Boletín Popular.

Chávez, Fray Angélico. 1987. *The Short Stories of Fray Angélico Chávez.* Edited by Genaro Padilla. Albuquerque: University of New Mexico Press.

Colahan, Clark. 1994. *The Visions of Sor María de Agreda: Writing Knowledge and Power.* Tucson: The University of Arizona Press.

de Niza, Fray Marcus. 1865. Descubrimiento de las siete ciudades por el P. Fr. Marcos de Niza. In *Colección de documentos inéditos, relativos al descubrimiento, conquista y colonización de las posesiones españolas en América y Oceanía, sacados, en su mayor parte, del Real Archivo de Indias,* eds. Joaquin Pacheco and Francisco Cárdenas, 325–351. First Series, Vol. 3. Madrid: Imprenta de Manuel B. de Quirós.

D'haen, Theo L. 1995. Magical Realism and Postmodernism: Decentering Privileged Centers. In *Magical Realism: Theory, History, Community,* eds. Lois Parkinson Zamora and Wendy B. Faris, 191–208. Durham, N.C.: Duke University Press.

Espinosa, Aurelio M. and J. Manuel Espinosa, eds. 1943. The Texans. *The New Mexico Quarterly Review* 13.3 (autumn):299–308.

Faris, Wendy B. 1995. Scheherazade's Children: Magical Realism and Postmodern Fiction. In *Magical Realism: Theory, History, Community,* eds. Lois Parkinson Zamora and Wendy B. Faris, 163–190. Durham, N.C.: Duke University Press.

Flores, Ángel. 1955. Magical Realism in Spanish American Fiction. *Hispania* 38:187–192.

García, Nasario. 1978. The Concept of Time in *Nambé—Year One. Latin American Literary Review* 7(3) (fall–winter):20–28.

González-T, César, ed. 1990. *Rudolfo Anaya: Focus on Criticism.* La Jolla, Calif.: Lalo Press.

Jameson, Frederic. 1986. On Magical Realism in Film. *Critical Inquiry* (winter):301–325.

Leal, Luis. 1967. El realismo mágico en la literatura hispanoamericana. *Cuadernos Americanos* 43(4):230–235.

———. 1995. Magic Realism in Spanish American Literature. In *Magical Realism: Theory, History, Community,* eds. Lois Parkinson Zamora and Wendy B. Faris, 119–124. Translated by Wendy B. Faris. Durham, N.C.: Duke University Press.

Lomelí, Francisco A. and Donaldo W. Urioste. 1976. *Chicano Perspectives in Literature: A Critical and Annotated Bibliography.* Albuquerque: Pajarito Publications.

Martín-Rodríguez, Manuel M. 1983. Aesthetic Concepts of Hispanics in the United States. In *Handbook of Hispanic Cultures in the United States: Literature and Art,* ed. Francisco A. Lomelí, 109–133. Houston, Tex.: Arte Público Press.

Méndez, Miguel. (Miguel Méndez M.) 1986. *El sueño de Santa María de las piedras.* Guadalajara, Jalisco: Universidad de Guadalajara.

Nichols, John. 1974. *The Milagro Beanfield War.* New York: Random House.

Roh, Franz. 1927. *Realismo mágico, postexpresionismo: Problemas de la pintura europea más reciente.* Translated by Fernando Vela. Madrid: Revista de Occidente.

———. 1995. Magic Realism: Post-Expressionism. Translated by Wendy R. Faris. In *Magical Realism: Theory, History, Community,* eds. Lois Parkinson Zamora and Wendy B. Faris, 15–31. Durham, N.C.: Duke University Press.

Romero, Orlando. 1976. *Nambé—Year One.* Berkeley, Calif.: Tonatiuh International.

Rulfo, Juan. 1994. *Pedro Páramo*. Translated by Margaret Sayers Peden. New York: Grove Press. Original edition, México: Fondo de Cultura Económica, 1955.

Sánchez, Rosaura. 1987. Postmodernism and Chicano Literature. *Aztlán* 18(2) (fall):1–14.

Slemon, Stephen. 1995. Magic Realism as Postcolonial Discourse. In *Magical Realism: Theory, History, Community*, eds. Lois Parkinson Zamora and Wendy B. Faris, 407–426. Durham, N.C.: Duke University Press.

Ulibarrí, Sabine. 1964. *Tierra amarilla: Cuentos de nuevoméxico*. Quito, Ecuador: Editorial Casa de la Cultura Ecuatoriana.

Uslar Pietri, Arturo. 1948. *Letras y hombres de Venezuela*. México: Fondo de Cultura Económica.

Walter, Roland. 1990. Social and Magical Realism in Miguel Méndez' *El sueño de Santa María de las Piedras*. *The American Review* 18(1) (spring):103–112.

Zamora, Lois Parkinson and Wendy B. Faris, eds. 1995. *Magical Realism: Theory, History, Community*. Durham, N.C.: Duke University Press.

History, Faith, and Intercultural Relations in Two New Mexican *Inditas*
"Plácida Romero" and "San Luis Gonzaga"

Enrique R. Lamadrid

⊂℞ THE INDO-HISPANO *cultura popular* or folk culture of New Mexico is an excellent index of the dynamics of cultural resistance, accommodation, and assimilation in the region. The evolution of this tradition reveals a great deal about the nature and history of intercultural relations between Nuevomexicanos and distinct groups of Native Americans, including *naturales*—allies from neighboring nominally Christianized Keresan and Tanoan Pueblos; *bárbaros* or *herejes*—"barbarian" or "heretic" nomads such as Apaches, Comanches, Utes, and Navajos often in conflict with these others; and *genízaros*—detribalized, hispanicized Indians, incorporated into Nuevomexicano society mostly as war casualties, slaves, and captives taken from the enemy groups of *bárbaros* (Gutiérrez 1991).

Musical forms such as the *indita* ballads and regional dance/dramas such as the Matachines and the Comanches are sung and celebrated in both Pueblo Indian and Nuevomexicano communities across the state. These cultural expressions contain explicit references and implicit structures, which in performance reenact and redefine political and cultural relations between both groups (Rodríguez 1996). A complex profile of New Mexican *mestizaje* or cultural synthesis emerges from an analysis of these traditions. At the core is a dynamic concept of alterity: the construction and negotiation of cultural otherness and its dialectical relation to cultural identity (Lamadrid 1992).

After the United States occupation of New Mexico in 1846, yet another powerful factor comes into play in the heightening struggle for power over politics, resources, culture, and identity. The Territorial period between the 1846 military invasion and statehood in 1912 is an especially turbulent and decisive time in which the fundamental paradigms of contemporary social and cultural relations emerge. Since the flourishing of the *indita* ballad in New Mexico corresponds to the Territorial period and so closely expresses this struggle, it is the particular focus of this study. Two examples typical of the narrative and the religious veins of the *indita* will be examined here. "*La Indita de Plácida Romero*" is a captivity ballad dating to the Apache wars of the 1880s, and "*La Indita de San Luis Gonzaga*" is a miracle ballad from the 1898 Spanish-American War.

II. The New Mexican Indita: An Intercultural Tradition

The *inditas* of the late nineteenth century are New Mexico's unique contribution to the history of Hispanic balladry in the Southwest. Their origins can be traced to the colonial literature of New Spain, including popular songs, church hymns, and the bilingual *villancicos* or Christmas plays of Sor Juana Inés de la Cruz, which incorporated Spanish and Nahuatl (with code-switching) into song lyrics, dialogue, and a dance style called *Tocotín* (Méndez Plancarte 1952, 14–17, 41–42). Like the Iberian *Romances,* their millennial root-stock, and the greater Mexican *corrido* ballads to which they are closely related, the *inditas* share a thematic fascination with disasters, natural and historical, and with the personal dimensions of human tragedy. The folk term *"indita"* can be translated as "little Indian girl" or "little Indian song," and it is applied to a variety of musical and poetic forms, including a large corpus of historical narrative ballads, a smaller corpus of burlesque love songs, a few intercultural religious song/dances, and even a popular social dance performed to the instrumental music of the previous forms. As the term *indita* implies, there is usually some connection to Indians or Native American culture in the songs, both thematically and musically. The historical ballads appear only in the Nuevomexicano repertory, but the burlesque and religious *inditas* are also occasionally performed in the Indian Pueblos.

In formal terms, almost all *inditas* feature the *copla,* the ubiquitous quatrain of popular poetry, characterized by its octosyllabic lines and alternating assonant rhyme scheme. A few use the sextain and even the *décima,* or ten-line stanza. As with the *corrido* ballad, the narrative conventions of the *indita* include the naming of participants, dates, and places; the rhetorical foregrounding of key acts of the protagonist; and a loosely strung sequence of decisive dramatic scenes (McDowell 1981). A particularly poignant characteristic of the *indita* is the highly reflexive use of a *refrán* (refrain) or chorus between verses, and the common use of first-person narration. Sometimes the use of the word *"cuándo"* (when) in choruses prompts many to use the New Mexican folk genre called the *"Cuándo"* to refer to these ballads (Robb 1980, 481).

In terms of the music, several Native American melodic elements have been identified in the *inditas* (Mendoza and de Mendoza 1986 and Robb 1980). Of particular interest is the frequent use of vocable choruses with melodic lines that emulate and approximate the pentatonic scale of Native American music. Vocables are the non-lexical seed syllables characteristic of Indian songs, a dramatic manifestation of musical interculturality. *Inditas* are often sung *a cappella* as with *"Plácida Romero."* *"San Luis Gonzaga"* is often sung with a *tombé* or Indian drum to accompany the dancing that is performed with it.

Although long eclipsed by *corridos,* and only rarely performed at present, *inditas* are by no means an archaic form belonging solely to another time, but rather

fig 18   Adorando a San Luis Gonzaga, San Luis, New Mexico, 1993.
Photo: Miguel Gandert.

what can be defined as a residual form, "effectively formed in the past, but still active in the cultural process" (Williams 1977, 122). Most musicians and singers who have *inditas* in their repertories present them as cultural "demonstrations" or "presentations" (Hymes 1981, 138–141), examples of what New Mexican singers themselves term *"la música de antes"* (music from before), compositions from a bygone day. Both *inditas* discussed here, however, still derive from their original performance contexts, through the direct descendants of the captive woman in the case of *"Plácida Romero"* and the prayer vigils of the devotees of the saint in the case of *"San Luis Gonzaga."*

III. *"Plácida Romero"*: The Power of Lamentation

The suffering of women captives on a war-torn frontier is a story heard all too often in the history of New Mexico. The last tragic chapter dates to the 1880s and the coordinated American and Mexican military campaigns against the Apaches, the last Native Americans of the Southwest to be defeated. What is exceptional about the story of the captive, Plácida Romero, is the powerful way it has been told and retold in poetry, music, folk drama, and oral narrative, each form relating the details of the murder of her husband and of her nine-month ordeal among the Gileño or Warm Springs Apaches.

The consequences of the actual events reached far beyond the realm of Nuevomexicano-Native American relations. Upon her return, a controversy broke out in which the Bureau of Indian Affairs and the Federal Government were accused in the Spanish language press of unfair treatment of Nuevomexicanos, especially those who had suffered in the Apache wars (*Río Colorado Chronicle* 17 June 1882). Repercussions were felt in statehouses in both the United States and México, and legislation was quickly passed by the Territorial Legislature (*Acts of the Legislative Assembly 25th Session*, 2 March 1882), authorizing the governor to correspond with the governor of the state of Chihuahua concerning the reimbursement of ransom money for the redemption of Plácida Romero and two children. Mrs. Romero was also granted a widow's pension for her misfortunes. These incidents have long since been forgotten. What is remembered is the emotional content and those events that determined it. As in the captivity ballads of Medieval Spain, superfluous details drop away, leaving behind the "emotional core" for the sympathetic contemplation of the folk (Coffin 1961, 246).

To the extended Romero and Gallegos families of Cubero, New Mexico, the *indita* tradition still commands the signifying power that it had as a fully emergent form more than a century ago. For five generations, the women of these families have maintained an unbroken performance tradition of "*La Indita de Plácida Romero*," a captivity ballad as rich in personal emotion and religious faith as it is in historical detail. Their verbal art finds its expression in performances that include not only the sung ballad, but the distinctive narratives and pedagogical discourse that always accompany it. As descendants of their "Nana (grandmother) Plácida," they invoke the spiritual strength of the captive woman, and deliver not "demonstration" but what has been described as "authoritative performance" (Hymes 1981, 138–141).

Of the six different versions studied (see Appendix A for a complete listing), only three were recognized by family members as authentic or authoritative— the original 1882 *indita*, which has been lost, and incomplete versions consisting of family recollections of it. When the ballad was incorporated into oral tradition, it was often masculinized. One version is named for Domingo Gallegos, Plácida's husband, and the others change the captive's name itself into the masculine form, Plácido. Verses are truncated and reconstituted, but the poignant fragments of the lament of a woman in a powerful first-person voice shine through.

Fieldwork in the Cubero area finally resulted in locating a group of female descendants of Plácida Romero, including her granddaughter, the late Rosa Trujillo; a great-granddaughter, the late Feliz Bustamante; Margarita Aguilar Johnson and Verónica Aguilar Rickert, two great-great nieces who conserve the "family authorized" version of the ballad that they grew up singing. This family takes great pride in being direct descendants of Plácida Romero and in criticizing the versions of the *indita* that are "unauthorized" or masculinized. In Rosa's words: "*Todavía lo cantan mucho—pero no, no cantan más de como les parece, o no, de versitos que agarraron de aquí y allí*" (They still sing it a lot—but no, they only sing what they please, only the verses that they have gotten here and there) (Trujillo 1985).

The family also placed the events squarely in 1881 and produced historical photographs including an exceptional portrait of their "Nana Plácida." Subsequent historical research has uncovered contemporary archival and military records, newspaper accounts, and books on the Apache campaigns of which the family was unaware, but which corroborate their oral histories and the events in the *indita* (Ball 1970, Lekson 1987). The Aguilar-Trujillo 1985 version is as follows:

1

El día de San Lorenzo　　　　The day of Saint Lawrence
era un día poderoso,　　　　　was a powerful day,
que me llevaron cautiva　　　 when they took me captive
y mataron a mi esposo.　　　　and killed my husband.
El año de ochenta y uno,　　 In the year of eighty one,
cerca de las diez del día,　 close to ten in the morning,
así sería yo pienso　　　　　 that was when it was I think
cuando esto nos sucedía,　　 when this happened to us,
que mataron a mi esposo　　　when they killed my husband
y al hombre Jesús María.　　 and the man named Jesús María.
Refrán:　　　　　　　　　　　Chorus:
Adiós, ya me voy,　　　　　 Farewell, I'll be gone,
voy a padecer.　　　　　　　　gone into suffering.
Adiós, mis queridas hijas,　Farewell, my beloved daughters
¿cuándo las volveré a ver?　when will I see you again?

2

Adiós Rancho de la Cebolla,　Farewell, La Cebolla Ranch,
¿por qué te muestras esquiva?　why have you turned away?
Los palos, las piedras lloran　The trees, the rocks are weeping
de verme salir cautiva.　　　　to see me go into captivity.
Adiós, Cubero afamado,　　　　 Farewell, my famous Cubero,
se te acabó lo valiente.　　　your bravery was finished.
Quizás no tenías parque,　　　Maybe your ammunition was gone,
o te ha faltado la gente.　　 or your people failed you.
Refrán:　　　　　　　　　　　　Chorus:

3

Manuelita la mayor,
cuida de tus hermanitas
que ya les faltó el calor,
se quedaron huerfanitas.
Adiós, plaza de Cubero,
adiós, mi hogar y mi casa,
adiós, paderes [*sic*] y esquinas,
adiós, madre Marucasia.
Adiós, madrecita fina,
duélete de mi desgracia.
Refrán:

Manuelita the oldest,
take care of your little sisters
they have lost all our warmth,
they were left orphans.
Farewell, town of Cubero,
farewell, my house and my home,
farewell, walls and corners,
farewell, mother Marucasia.
Farewell, finest little mother,
may you feel my grief.
Chorus:

4

Adiós, Domingo Gallegos,
adiós, fino compañero,
quizás no tenías hermanos,
ni parientes allí en Cubero,
que se quedaron tus huesos
en un triste gallinero.
Refrán:

Farewell, Domingo Gallegos,
farewell, fine companion,
perhaps you had no brothers,
nor relatives there in Cubero,
since your bones remained
in a sad chicken house.
Chorus:

5

En la sierra de Galeana,
allí terminaron mis días.
Lo que reconocí,
que era gente la que veía.
Le dije a mi muchachito,
"no te retires de mí,
oyes, Procopio García."
Llegué al Ojito Salado
y me puse a devisar [*sic*],
a ver si veía venir
a mi padre o a mi hermano.
También si veía venir
a mi hermano Cayetano.
Refrán:

In the mountains of Galeana,
there my days of captivity ended
What I recognized,
was that I was seeing people.
I said to my little boy,
"don't stray from me,
do you hear, Procopio García."
I got to Salt Spring
and started looking,
to see if I could see
my father or brother coming.
Also to see if my brother
Cayetano was coming.
Chorus:

6

Mi Señora de la Luz
fue la que reina en Cubero,
pidiéndole al Santo Niño
que salga del cautiverio.
Refrán:

My Lady of Light
was she who reigns in Cubero,
asking of the Holy Child
my escape from captivity.
Chorus:

The historical events and context reconstructed from the *indita*, the family narrations, and contemporary sources are as follows: On the feast of San Lorenzo, August 10, 1881, the Rancho de la Cebolla, in Cebolletita Canyon, thirty miles south of Cubero, New Mexico, was raided by a war party of the Ojo Caliente (Warm Springs) band of Gileño Apaches, the Tchihene ("red paint people") or eastern-most band of the Chiricahua. Their aging leader was named Nana, known in Spanish as Nané, successor to the famous chief Victorio, killed the previous year in México, the subject of another well known *indita*. In a disastrous series of forced relocations, these Apaches had been promised, then denied, a reservation near their homeland area along the Black Range east of the Río Grande in South Central New Mexico. Groups of local militia and African American units of the United States Army "buffalo soldiers" were already pursuing Nané's band when it attacked a remote ranch and killed a young Navajo ranch hand named José María and the rancher, José Domingo Gallegos. Plácida Romero de Gallegos, his wife, and a young nephew and daughter were abducted. Two daughters were left behind unharmed.

Nané, his band, and the captives fled south, raiding ranches and killing a number of other people before finally crossing the Mexican border into the Casas Grandes area of northern Chihuahua. According to family accounts, on the way, Plácida's daughter, Trinidad, was left with a group of Navajos that Nané's band met at a spring. No more than a toddler at the time of her abandonment, she was young enough to assimilate into Navajo culture. Plácida found her again after more than a decade of searching, but Trinidad chose to remain a Navajo and stayed with her adoptive family. Meanwhile, in the Sierra Galeana near Galeana, Chihuahua, a detachment of the Mexican army attacked Nané's band by surprise sometime in the spring of 1882. The warriors fled, leaving behind several women and captives including Plácida Romero and her nephew, allowing their escape. They were taken into protective custody by local authorities and later accused of being Apache spies. Finally, they befriended some local people who helped them escape from the jail by digging a hole through the ceiling.

Whatever her means of escape, Plácida Romero then made her way to El Paso and wrote her family to come and get her. Her father and brother left Cubero in a horse-drawn wagon on a month-long journey to El Paso to bring her home. After returning, she gave birth to a daughter by "Tato" (possibly the historical Chato), a young warrior in Nané's band. The little girl was named Trinidad after the daughter that was lost. For some time after her return to Cubero, Plácida Romero desperately sought some form of justice for the death of her husband and the separation from her daughter, Trinidad. In her futile appeals to U.S. authorities for help, she was quite specific in her accusations, since she had learned the identities not only of her Apache captors, but of several local Navajos who had assisted them and who were still living in the area between Grants and Gallup.

Charges against these local Navajos were never successfully filed, much to the dismay of local Nuevomexicanos, whose letters of protest were found in newspapers as far away as Santa Fe and San Luis Río Colorado east of Las Vegas. Plácida's concerns, however, soon turned to matters of faith.

While in captivity, Plácida made a promise to the *Virgen de la Luz* (Virgin of Light) and *Santo Niño de Atocha* (Holy Child of Atocha) that, if she succeeded in escaping, she would make her testimony known to others as an example of faith and perseverance. Her pilgrimage of thanksgiving led her to churches along the route of her journey and as far north as Cuba, New Mexico where special masses were said for her. Years after her return, a *"comedia"* or dramatic presentation of her abduction and captivity was presented in front of the church in Cubero, New Mexico. Off-duty soldiers from nearby Fort Wingate played the part of the Apaches.

Rosa Trujillo recalls playing the role of Trinidad, Plácida's lost daughter, in the commemorative *comedia* or folk drama that was staged annually for a period of years (Trujillo 1985). With soldiers dressed as renegade Apaches, firing their rifles as they "abducted" her, she experienced the most intense fear in her life: *"Tenía miedo—estaba llorando . . . que venían los apaches . . . yo sí, me llevaban llorando* (I was afraid—I was crying . . . the Apaches were coming . . . and they took me away crying)" (Trujillo 1985). Thus she was introduced to her grandmother's ordeal not only by listening to family stories and singing in the first-person voice of the *indita,* but by reenacting the events themselves.

Besides teaching family history, the other pedagogical intent of this discourse is the idealization of the trials of Plácida. An example of faith, perseverance, and determination to survive, she inspires the pride and emulation of her entire family and community. In their emphasis on spiritual strength, rather than vengeance or hatred, the narratives relating Plácida Romero's suffering coincide with only the very earliest captivity narratives of the Anglo-American tradition. Puritan women such as Mary Rowlandson interpreted their ordeals from a religious framework as an opportunity that God was granting them to progress spiritually as well as to set an example for others (Levernier and Cohen 1977, xvii). Captivity was the symbolic equivalent of a journey into Hell or Purgatory, and surviving was deemed a sign of God's favor.

Later, when more negative stereotypical views of Indians became useful to American society, captivity narratives became more secularized and were used for "propaganda purposes" in times of Indian warfare or territorial expansion. The same August 11, 1881 issue of the *Albuquerque Daily Journal* that reported Plácida Romero's abduction contained a disturbing editorial that graphically described and applauded the lynching and burning of two Apache youths sixty miles south of Albuquerque, advocating the act as an example of how to deal with the "Indian problem." In a political context such as Territorial New Mexico,

fig 19   Rosa Trujillo, Grants, New Mexico, 1986. Photo: Miguel Gandert.

it is truly remarkable that this *indita* and accompanying narratives would emphasize spiritual aspects rather than indulge in the racist diatribes of the day.

According to family tradition and textual evidence from the 1929 version, when Plácida returned from captivity, a local poet composed the ballad at the family's request. He refrains from including his name into the verses, as many poets would do, but does reveal that he is from Rinconada, a village near Cubero. The ballad has since been performed in the family by five subsequent generations of women. The minimal narrative framework of action verbs in the *indita*: *mataron* (they killed), *me llevaron* (they took me), *me voy* (I'm going), *veía* (I saw), etc., are linked to the key events in the following chronology: the killing of Plácida's husband, her capture and departure, her constant vigilance for signs of her rescuers, and her eventual escape. In the six versions studied, the only basic information common to all is that someone named José Domingo Gallegos was killed, and that the woman narrating the story was taken captive. Five of the six versions give the first name of Plácida as protagonist and three offer her last name, Romero. The "emotional core" of the *"Indita de Plácida Romero"* is probably invested in these poignant verses:

> Los palos, las piedras lloran   The trees and rocks weep
> por verme salir cautiva.   seeing me in captivity

If the plight of *la cautiva* (the captive woman) arouses sympathy even from her natural surroundings, how can it fail to move a listener? Of all six versions involved in this study, this particular verse is the one that occurs in them all. The pathetic fallacy so prevalent in nineteenth-century romanticism also had a firm hold on the hearts and popular imagination of Nuevomexicanos.

If a single word were to be chosen as the most representative of the *indita*, emerging straight from its "emotional core," it would have to be the word *adiós* (farewell). In the nine-stanza Trujillo-Aguilar version, it occurs a total of nineteen times, in part because of the chorus. *La cautiva* takes leave of all that is most intimate and familiar: her life on the Rancho La Cebolla, the town of Cubero, her home and house, its very walls and corners, her mother, and her murdered husband twice in the same verse. The most insistent and excruciating *"adiós,"* the pathetic separation of a mother from her orphaned daughters, is repeated a total of twelve times in the chorus. Such extensive reiteration within such a limited text generates a metanarrative dimension where "repetition not only raises the repeated words and their referent to a different level, making it 'present,' it also calls our attention to the act of 'presenting'" (Babcock 1977, 72). More so than any of the operative verbs or verb aspects, the insistent and plaintive *"adiós"* makes present Plácida Romero's voice through the voices of her descendants.

This most simple and effective rhetorical device allusively echoes the farewell and the final verse of the refrain of a popular prayer to the Santo Niño de Atocha *"¿cuándo te volveré a ver?"* (when will I see you again?) (Espinosa 1985, 113). Highly esteemed in New Mexico, Santo Niño de Atocha is the patron saint of pilgrims, travelers, and prisoners, who in this and other *inditas* is the central spiritual figure who mediates the deliverance of captives.

The repeated plea of Plácida thus carries the power of prayer as well. The repetition and emphasis of the word *cuándo* (when) in each chorus is notable because it is also a characteristic of the *"Cuándos,"* a particularly Nuevomexicano folk genre of ballads that use the word over and over to emphasize despair, longing, and perseverance (Robb 1980, 481). Although the ballad of Plácida Romero is popularly known as an *indita*, some singers refer to it as a *corrido* or even a *Cuándo* ballad.

Although the wealth of historical detail in the family's oral history and performance tradition is an important contextual contributor to the viability of this ballad, its survival has not depended entirely upon the personal esteem of the descendants of Plácida Romero for their ancestor. The powerful textual features of this and other *inditas* also play a major role in their duration. When the *indita* left the family on its journey into the oral tradition, these features emerged in the natural winnowing process of oral transmission, revealing the ballad's "emotional core." Underlying the repeated farewells and the central image of a sympathetic landscape of weeping rocks and trees is the powerful *indita* strategy of first-person narration, which creates a unique linguistic synthesis of lyric, exordial, and epic modes.

Further analysis of the rhetorical structure of the *indita* reveals the power of what Jakobson defines as the "conative" function, expressed through the use of the second person vocative and imperative verbs (Jakobson 1960, 354). In the third stanza, Plácida exhorts her eldest daughter, Manuela (Rosa Trujillo's mother) to assume the maternal role and care for her sisters. Unlike declarative sentences that can always be converted into questions, the imperative mode is not liable to a truth test. Historical ballads use a formidable battery of testimonial conventions and rhetorical devices to entice the belief of the listener. In her desperation, with all that is dear and familiar slipping away before her, Plácida's plaintive exhortations animate her surroundings, her ranch, the walls of her house, and, finally, even the rocks and trees.

The conclusion of this analysis concurs with Briggs's assertion that the form and content of performances are simultaneously shaped by structural and contextual factors, and it is the act of connecting these two sides that generates the power of performances (Briggs 1985, 289).

The elemental yet poignant vitality of the *"Indita de Plácida Romero"* is a synthesis through performance of text and context. The simple power of Plácida's *"adiós, ya me voy"* (farewell, I'm already leaving) evokes a sympathy still to be felt in the stark landscapes of western New Mexico and embodies a voice that still transforms the speech of her great-great-granddaughters into song.

IV. *"La Indita de San Luis Gonzaga"*: Text, Miracle, and Sacred Dance

"La Indita de San Luis Gonzaga" is another example of an *indita* still emergent, still functioning within its original performance tradition. (See Appendix A for a complete listing of versions studied.) It is sung regularly not by performers or musical specialists, but by devotees of the saint as part of yearly cycle of observances culminating in his fiesta on June 21, celebrated with processions, *velorios de santos* (prayer vigils for saints), and devotional dancing. Although *"La Indita de San Luis Gonzaga"* originated as a ballad concerning the Spanish-American War, the original historical connection has become obscured. After the war, it evolved into a sacred hymn sung while the devotees of the saint danced for him to honor their personal petitions for good health and the protection of youth.

There is historical evidence that there was a popular devotion of San Luis Gonzaga by the early nineteenth century, since he is depicted in *retablos* (painted wooden panels) from this period (Keleman 1983, 25). With the arrival of the Jesuits in 1868, the order promoted the devotion in its New Mexico missions since Aloysius was one of their own (McKevitt 1992, 378). The young Jesuit died at age twenty-four in 1591 in Rome while attending to the sick during an epidemic. Canonized in 1726, San Luis became the patron saint of youth and the protector of soldiers, and was attributed with special healing powers (Hoever [1955] 1959, 235–237). In his most recent ministry, he is the patron saint of people with HIV and AIDS as well as of Catholic hospice workers.

In New Mexico, Luis Gonzaga has also acquired a second appellation, *Amarant,* or *Abaranda,* as it is sometimes spelled, signaling a phenomenon not uncommon in folk Catholicism, the conflation of saints and their attributes. Gonzaga is the homophonic link to Gonzalo, the first name of Gonzalo de Amarante, a thirteenth-century Portuguese saint so obscure he is associated with no particular cause, but whose iconography includes an aureole of clouds and a bridge he built with his own hands near Amarante, Portugal (Giffords 1974, 103). There are no New Mexican *retablos* portraying Gonzalo de Amarante and only very few in Mexico. In the folk imagination, however, both his attributes are transposed to the popular Italian saint, Luis Gonzaga, the clouds to dramatize his appearance, and the bridge to symbolize passage over troubled waters.

In the folk tradition, Luis Gonzaga also became the patron saint of dance—somewhat ironic because the historical Aloysius spent several unhappy years in the court of Felipe II and was known to detest courtly pursuits and distractions such as dancing. The popular logic behind the attributes of saints is often convoluted. The origins of devotional dancing for the saint are still obscure and seem to be localized in New Mexico.

The earliest reference to the existence of this tradition is a promise to dance for the saint in the text of the *indita* itself, composed in 1898 (Espinosa 1985, 131–132). The first description of dancing at the June 21st Fiesta de San Luis (in Córdova, New Mexico) was compiled by Lorin W. Brown in his 1939 report to the Works Progress Administration survey on New Mexico folklore and folklife:

> San Luis Gonzaga is the patron saint of the dance. His day falls on the 21st of June. In some places a vigil is held in his honor. This in itself is not so unusual, but the nature of the ceremony is different from the usual vigil in honor of any special saint. For since he is the patron saint of the dance, a dance is given in his honor.
>
> The saint is seated between the musicians, usually a guitar and a violin player. San Luis's hymn is sung and, after praying the rosary, dancing is the order of the night. Instead of singing couplets in honor of the different dancers, the musicians dedicate their verses to San Luis Gonzaga, coupling his name with some one of the dancers on the floor. The individual so honored is expected to give the musicians a coin in acknowledgment of the honor. The dance lasts until daylight, when the saint is joyfully carried back to the church. [Brown, Briggs, and Weigle 1978, 187]

The "hymn" sung after the rosary is the *"Indita de San Luis Gonzaga."* Although Brown, Briggs, and Weigle make no particular reference to dancing during the singing of the hymn itself, subsequent descriptions dating to the 1940s and 1950s in the Albuquerque area emphasize the devotional dance performed to the singing of the *indita* (Pacheco 1988). Fiestas in recent years in Los Griegos, Bernalillo, and San Luis, New Mexico, have also featured devotional dancing, which follows the rosary and precedes the social dance, when there is one.

The concept of dance as devotion or holy exercise does not seem to be a particularly European introduction to New Mexico, given the local indigenous traditions of sacred dance (Ortiz 1979). Several verses in the *indita* attest to Native American participation in the cult to San Luis, specifically people from Mogollón, an Apache area in the southwest mountains of the state. Oral histories mention the regular visits of Pueblo Indians for feast days and prayer vigils to dance for San Luis (Sargeant and Davis 1986, Jaramillo 1991).

Whatever the devotional practices to San Luis were like prior to 1898, the Spanish-American War was the occasion for a renewed dedication to San Luis. The war with Spain incited heated controversies in New Mexico. Since recruitment for the armed forces was not well organized and the hostilities lasted less than three months, only limited numbers of Nuevomexicanos were involved (Arellano 1985). Anglo-controlled English language newspapers questioned their loyalty to the United States and criticized their continued use of the Spanish language as subversive and un-American. There were over thirty Spanish-language newspapers in the state at the time. Editorials and popular poetry appeared in their pages to defend both the Spanish language and the loyalty of the New Mexicans, so thoroughly tested in the Civil War, in which the Federal militia in New Mexico was over 90 percent Nuevomexicano (Chacón and Meketa 1986). But the Spanish-American War was more problematic. The irony that the "sons of conquistadors" were now fighting Spaniards was not lost on the people of the day.

Popular Sabinal, New Mexico poet, Norberto M. Abeyta, was one writer who participated in this public debate by defending the Spanish language in one of his poems. Soon after the war with Spain began on April 25, 1898, he also wrote a series of verses entitled "*A San Luis Gonzaga*" in a poetic petition to San Gonzaga de Abaranda and the Virgin to intercede for a merciful end to the conflict (Espinosa 1985, 131–32). The reference to the "*mes florido*" (flowery month) historically places the narrator of the poem in May 1898. The poet's source of inspiration was the report of a miracle on the high seas—a ship of Nuevomexicano soldiers, on the way to fight Spain, is saved by San Gonzaga who quells a terrible storm.

1
San Gonzaga de Abaranda
aparecido en el mar,
concédeme mi salud;
luego te voy a bailar.

Saint Gonzaga of Abaranda,
who appeared on the high seas,
grant me my good health;
and later I will dance for you.

3
Ahora en tu mes florido,
en el que todos te claman,
pídele, santo glorioso,
por América y España.

Now in your flowery month [May]
when all seek your blessing,
intercede, oh glorious saint,
for America and Spain.

4
Por esos pobres soldados,
que están en guerra peleando;
pídele, santo glorioso,
que la paz vaya triunfando.

For those poor soldiers
who are fighting in the war;
ask, oh glorious saint,
that peace will be triumphant.

6
Dicen que la golondrina
de un volido pasa el mar.
En las Islas Filipinas
comenzaron a pelear.

They say the swallow
in one flight crossed the sea.
In the Philippine Islands
they began fighting.

This initial literary text of the *indita* is the only version that retains any specific reference to the war and the suffering of its soldiers. Other poems commemorating the short but pivotal conflict appeared in the Spanish-language press. The poem *"A la Unión Americana"* (To the American Union) by Eleuterio Baca of Las Vegas is representative of these. The same poem was published once in 1898, and again in a revised version in 1899, with appropriate changes in wording and verb tense to reflect both the United States' victory and the diplomatic consequences.

Magnífico astro de Imperio	Magnificent star of Empire
Que con tu luz iluminas	Who with your light illuminates
El lóbrego cautiverio	The lugubrious captivity
De Cuba y las Filipinas.	Of Cuba and the Philippines.
Hoy felicitan mis voces	Today my voice congratulates
A tu enseña victoriosa	Your victorious ensign
En la lengua majestuosa	In the majestic language
De los dones y los dioses.	Of gentlemen and gods.
. . . .	. . . .
¡Oh Iberia, tu hidalgo trono	Oh Iberia, your noble throne
Bamboleará en la impotencia	Will bumble on in impotence
Mientras no aprecies la ciencia	As long as you don't appreciate
Del siglo décimo-novo!	The science of the nineteenth century.
Deja las quijoterías,	Leave your Quixotic ways,
Despierta a la realidad,	Wake up to reality,
Y ve aquí las maravillas	And see here the marvels
Que ha obrado la libertad.	That liberty has wrought.
	24 de junio de 1899 [Arellano 1976, 87]

Despite its lofty diction, the allusion to Don Quijote, and its aspiration to a more literary *redondilla* (abba) rhyme scheme, this poem uses the same popular octosyllabic meter as the *indita*. Besides the religious content and genre self-identification of Abeyta's verses as an *indita*, the major difference between the poems is the continuing persistence of the ballad versus the instant literary oblivion of Baca's patriotic poem.

The main reason the Spanish-American War left such a limited impression in the popular imagination was its brevity and lack of military heroics. More narrative would have surfaced in these poems and ballads had the war been more momentous. The most dramatic single loss was the sabotaged battleship the *U. S. S Maine,* whose sailors died in their sleep. Yellow Fever took many more lives than Spanish bullets. And the First Regiment of the U.S. Cavalry, Teddy Roosevelt's famous "Rough Riders," in which New Mexican volunteers rode, arrived in Cuba without their horses. They were obliged to storm San Juan Hill on foot as *infantería* (infantry) rather than *caballería* (cavalry), not exactly an inspiring feat to a culture that associated warfare with equestrian prowess. In the mercifully short conflict, the enemy was quite simply overextended, undersupplied, and outgunned. This was not the kind of gallantry that was commemorated in *inditas* or in the *corridos* that would eventually replace them. Hispanic balladry has a marked preference for the truly heroic, whether it be the feats of war or courage in the face of suffering.

More than an occasion for action, the war was an opportunity for reflection on identity, on community, on loyalty, and on nationhood. The editorial debates and commemorative poems in the newspapers are ample evidence of this process. An exhaustive newspaper search failed to turn up Norberto Abeyta's poem; we can only speculate that its fame and diffusion were due instead to its efficacy as a devotional text. Abeyta chose the right saint to end the war. The poem was undoubtedly recited or sung at the Fiesta of San Luis Gonzaga in the summer of 1898 as a prayer of hope and, in the summer of 1899, as a prayer of thanksgiving. Word would spread in the communities of the Río Abajo (Down River or central and southern New Mexico) as devotion to San Luis grew. This special power of the saint has been called on and danced for in every war since.

Within a few years, as Abeyta's *indita* entered the oral tradition, it and the dance that accompanies it became the principal vehicle of devotion in the popular cult to San Luis Gonzaga. After all, the poetic petition had succeeded and the miracle was granted. The boy saint and the Virgin had interceded to stop the bloodshed. The war came to a swift conclusion with minimal carnage. Because of this miracle, the poem itself achieved devotional status as its power grew to foment additional miracles.

The cries of the soldiers are only heard in the earliest versions of *"La Indita de San Luis."* Because there was nothing memorable to narrate, the story of the war became a pilgrim's prayer for health, parents' hopeful pleas for their sons to return. The text itself came to be regarded as miraculous, a literary object of devotion. Since the saint appreciates dancing, people offer their physical movement. Because Hispanic tradition has no sacred dances, Native American tradition supplies the steps and the vocable chorus. Vocables are the non-lexical, non-referential syllable sequences sung or chanted in Native American music whose meaning resides on an associational and symbolic level. As they sing, some dancers join arms and step back and forth in unison before the image of the saint. Many women dance with bare feet, their arms outstretched and palms up. In special vigils for the health of individuals, side steps in a circle around the saint and the ailing person are performed in a style somewhat reminiscent of the Plains Indian round dance.

After the war, verses appeared that refer to the participation of Indians in the cult, and several versions of the *indita* attribute its authorship to "an Indian from Mogollón." It is unknown, however, whether this is actually the case, or whether the word "Mogollón" was chosen simply because it rhymes with *corazón* in the verse that is matched to it: *"San Luis de mi corazón"* (Saint Aloysius of my heart).

As with other saints, the faithful make devout *promesas* (promises) to the saint in return for favors and blessings and miracles, which include everything from bringing rain to curing sickness and protecting soldiers. Again, the most unique feature of this cult is the fulfillment of promises by dancing for the saint on his feast day of June 21.

John D. Robb's 1950 recording of *"La Indita de San Luis"* (Robb 1980, 444–445) and its striking *"yo heyana"* vocable choruses, provided little clue that devotion to this lesser-known saint would become as widespread as it currently is. However, shortly after Robb's recording, a new recording of the *indita* was made with the father of Nadine Mirabal, a student whose brother had been cured by San Luis when he was hopelessly ill with rheumatic fever as a child in the 1950s (Lamadrid 1994, CD3, Track 27). In his account of the family miracle, the late Manuel Mirabal of San Luis, New Mexico, explained that after all hope had been lost and the doctors had given up, and after a fruitless pilgrimage to the holy earth shrine of Chimayó (Kay 1987), he took his son back to the village of his birth to seek its patron saint's help. The child was placed on the ground in front of the saint, and several singers danced around him in a circle to petition for the miracle. Of the twenty verses of Mr. Mirabal's version, two are identical to the 1898 Abeyta poem: the two mentioning the saint's appearance on the high seas and the swallow's flight to relay the news. Another four verses share imagery and the promise to dance. Other religious figures, notably the Santo Niño de Atocha and the Guardian Angel, appear in this and other versions to accompany San Luis and the Virgin.

1

De mi casa he venido
a pasear este lugar,
dénme razón de San Luis
que le prometí bailar.
Coro:
Yana jeya jo,
yana jeya jo,
yana jeya jo.
Yana jeya jo,
yana jeya jo,
yana jeya jo.

From my house I have come
to visit this place,
tell me about Saint Aloysius
since I promised him a dance.
Chorus:
Yana heya ho,
Yana heya ho,
Yana heya ho.
Yana heya ho,
Yana heya ho,
yana heya ho.

2

En el marco de esta puerta
el pie derecho pondré,
denme razón de San Luis
y luego le bailaré.
Coro:

In this doorway
I will put my right foot,
tell me about Saint Aloysius
and then I'll dance for him.
Chorus:

5

San Luis Gonzaga de Amarante	St. Aloysius Gonzaga of Amarante
aparecido en un puente,	appeared on a bridge,
esta indita te compuse	I composed this *indita* for you
cuando mi hijo andaba ausente.	when my son was away from home.
Coro:	Chorus:

8

Dicen que la golondrina	They say the swallow
de un volido pasó el mar,	in one flight crossed the sea,
de las Islas Filipinas	from the Philippine Islands
que acabaron de pelear.	which they have just fought for.
Coro:	Chorus:

14

Santo Niñito de Atocha	Holy Child of Atocha
tú solito no más sabes,	you and you only know
el corazón de cada uno	the heart of each of us
también todas sus necesidades.	and all our needs.
Coro:	Chorus:

[Lamadrid 1994: 155–157]

In his performance (as opposed to the written version in his hand) in Stanza 5, Mirabal replaced the word *"inocente"* (innocent or helpless) with *"ausente"* (absent) to refer to the desperate physical state of his stricken son. The word *"ausente"* is used for other petitions involving the absence of a son who has gone away to war or on a journey. Besides the Mirabal version, only a few other contemporary versions have preserved the reference to the Philippines (Stanza 8), and singers invariably assume that it dates from World War II. No one interviewed in this survey seemed to have any clue of its origins in the war with Spain. From oral historical accounts, the *indita* was heard frequently during World War II, when families leaving their sons at the Army Depot in Albuquerque visited a private chapel of the Martínez family on Teodoro Road, in the nearby village of Los Griegos, to sing and dance for San Luis (Jaramillo 1991).

The musical configuration of this *indita* juxtaposes Spanish lyrics and melodies with Native American vocable choruses, which, although not strictly pentatonic, nevertheless emulate the Native style. There is no better musical demonstration of the unique New Mexican style of pluralistic *mestizaje* or cultural blending. The *indita* is not a case of appropriation, but rather of synthesis, yet another example in a millennial tradition of interculturality in which borrowing and code-switching are strategies of everyday life. Despite the chauvinism of monarchs and statesmen, the peoples of the Iberian Peninsula and their descendants have tolerated each other's religions and cultures across the centuries. In medieval times, the *jarcha, zéjel,* and Mozambic *haragat* lyrics were sung bi- or even trilingually with Arabic, Hebrew, and/or Latin verses interspersed with refrains in the Ibero-Romance dialect (Hall 1974, 117). In New Spain, in the last five centuries, Native American languages and music were simply added to the mixture. That the power of a miracle that saved New Mexican soldiers fighting Spain on behalf of the United States would come home to combine with *mestizo* spiritual healing traditions to heal the sick and bring rain to the desert is a tribute to the syncretic power of Indo-Hispanic popular culture in New Mexico.

Appendix A

Versions of "La Indita de Plácida Romero."
1. ca. 1882—Rinconada (Grants area). Anonymous composer, original version lost.
2. 1929—Taos. Performed by Pascual Martínez, *"La Indita de Plácido Molina,"* collected by Arthur L. Campa, November 1929 (Robb 1980, 606).
3. 1937—Santa Fe. Performed by Juanita Chávez González, *"Corrido de José Domingo Gallegos,"* also known as *"Murió Saburia famosa,"* collected by Lolita Pooler, May 1937 (Mendoza and de Mendoza 1986, 406).
4. 1984—Gallup. Performed by Feliz Bustamante, *"Corrido de Plácida Romero,"* collected by Herman Bustamante, May 1984.
5. 1985—San Fidel. Performed by Trinidad Chávez, *"Indita de Plácida Romero,"* collected by León Tafoya, June 1985.
6. 1985—Grants. Performed by Rosa Trujillo and Margaret Aguilar Johnson, *"Indita de Plácida Romero,"* collected by Herman Bustamante and Enrique R. Lamadrid, November 11, 1985 (Lamadrid 1994: 31–3).

Versions 4–6 are from the personal archives of Enrique R. Lamadrid.

Versions of *"La Indita de San Luis Gonzaga."*
1. 1898—Sabinal. Composed by Norbeto Abeyta (Espinosa 1985, 131–32).
2. n.d.—Sevilleta. Collected by Ernestina Armijo, family *cuaderno.*
3. 1938—No place given. Collected by Manuel Berg—WPA Files, NM State History Library.
4. 1930s—Atarque (Gallup area). Performed by Feliz Bustamante, collected by Herman Bustamante.
5. 1930s–1940s—Los Duranes (Albuquerque area). Performed by Cosme Trujillo.
6. 1940s—Ranchitos de Albuquerque. Collected by Consuelo Pacheco (1988).
7. 1950—Tijeras. Performed by Helen Little, Elfego Sánchez, and M. García (Robb 1980, 444).
8. 1987—Santa Fe. Performed by Elvira Montoya, collected by Lucy Narvaiz.
9. 1989—San Luis (Bernalillo area). Performed by Manuel Mirabal (Lamadrid 1994, 155–157).
10. 1991—Los Griegos (Albuquerque area). Performed by Juanita Martínez de Jaramillo, collected by Félix Torres and Enrique R. Lamadrid.

Video recordings of the San Luis Gonzaga Fiesta were made on June 21, 1991 at Los Griegos, by Félix Torres; and in San Luis, by Melissa Salazar. These and version numbers 2, 4, 5, 8, 9, and 10 are from the personal archives of Enrique R. Lamadrid.

Literature Cited

Arellano, Anselmo F. 1976. *Los pobladores nuevo mexicanos y su poesía, 1889–1950.* Albuquerque, N.Mex.: Pajarito Publications.

———. 1985. Las Vegans and New Mexicans During the Spanish-American War, 1898. In *Las Vegas Grandes on the Gallinas 1835–1985,* eds. Anselmo F. Arellano and Julián Josué Vigil, 56–60. Las Vegas, N.Mex.: Editorial Telaraña.

Babcock, Barbara. 1977. The Story in the Story: Metanarration in Folk Narrative. In *Verbal Art as Performance,* ed. Richard Bauman, 61–80. Rowley, Mass.: Newbury House Publishers.

Ball, Eve. 1970. *In the Days of Victorio: Recollections of a Warm Springs Apache.* Tucson: University of Arizona Press.

Briggs, Charles L. 1985. Treasure Tales and Pedagogical Discourse in Mexicano New Mexico. *Journal of American Folklore* 98:287–314.

Brown, Lorin W. with Charles L. Briggs and Marta Weigle. 1978. *Hispano Folklife of New Mexico: The Lorin W. Brown Federal Writers' Project Manuscripts.* Albuquerque: University of New Mexico Press.

Chacón, Rafael and Jacqueline Meketa. 1986. *Legacy of Honor: the Life of Rafael Chacón, a Nineteenth Century New Mexican.* Albuquerque: University of New Mexico Press.

Coffin, Tristam P. 1961. Mary Hamilton and the Anglo-America Ballad as an Art Form. In *The Critics and the Ballad,* eds. MacEdward Leach and T. P. Coffin, 245–256. Carbondale, Ill.: Southern Illinois University Press.

Espinosa, Aurelio M. 1985. *The Folklore of Spain in the American Southwest,* edited by J. Manuel Espinosa. Norman: University of Oklahoma Press.

Giffords, Gloria K. 1974. *Mexican Folk Retablos: Masterpieces on Tin.* Tucson: University of Arizona Press.

Gutiérrez, Ramón. 1991. *When Jesus Came the Corn Mothers Went Away: Marriage, Sexuality, and Power in New Mexico, 1500–1846.* Stanford, Calif.: Stanford University Press.

Hall, R. A. 1974. *External History of the Romance Languages.* New York: American Elsevier.

Hoever, Rev. Hugo, S. O. Cist. [1955] 1959. *Lives of the Saints: For Every Day of the Year.* New York: Catholic Book Publishing Co.

Hymes, Dell. 1981. *"In Vain I Tried to Tell You": Essays in Native American Ethnopoetics.* Philadelphia: University of Pennsylvania Press.

Jakobson, Roman. 1960 Linguistics and Poetics. In *Style in Language,* ed. Thomas A. Sebeok, 350–377. Cambridge: Massachusetts Institute of Technology Press.

Jaramillo, Juanita M. 1991. Interview by author. Los Griegos, New Mexico, 11 September.

Kay, Elizabeth. 1987. *Chimayó Valley Traditions.* Santa Fe: Ancient City Press.

Keleman, Pál. 1983. Icon and Santo—In Remembering. In *Hispanic Arts and Ethnohistory in the Southwest: New Papers Inspired by the Work of E. Boyd,* ed. Marta Weigle, 15–28. Santa Fe, N.Mex.: Ancient City Press.

Lamadrid, Enrique R. 1992. *Los Comanches: The Celebration of Cultural Otherness in New Mexican Winter Feasts.* Forty-six-page report, eight audio tapes and transcripts, one video tape, thirty-nine transparencies. Washington, D.C.: 1992 New Mexico Festival of American Folklife Archive, Smithsonian Center for Folklife and Cultural Studies.

———. 1994. *Tesoros del Espíritu: A Portrait in Sound of Hispanic New Mexico,* and accompanying 3-CD set. Embudo, N.Mex.: Academia/El Norte Publications, distributed by University of New Mexico Press.

Lekson, Stephen H. 1987. *Nana's Raid: Apache Warfare in Southern New Mexico, 1881*. El Paso: Texas Western Press.

Levernier, James and Hennig Cohen, eds. 1977. *The Indians and Their Captives*. Westport, Colo.: Greenwood Press.

McDowell, John Holmes. 1981. The Corrido of Greater Mexico as Discourse, Music, Event. In *And Other Neighborly Names: Social Process and Cultural Image in Texas Folklore*, eds. Richard D. Bauman and Roger D. Abrahams, 44–78. Austin: University of Texas Press.

McKevitt, S.J., Gerald. 1992. Italian Jesuits in New Mexico: A Report by Donato M. Gasparri, 1867–1869. *New Mexico History Review* 67(4) (October):357–392.

Méndez Plancarte, Alfonso, ed. 1952. *Sor Juana Inés de la Cruz. Obras completas*. Vol. 2: *Villancicos y letras sacras*. México: Fondo de Cultura Económica.

Mendoza, Vicente T. and Virginia R. R. de Mendoza. 1986. *Estudio y clasificación de la música tradicional hispánica de Nuevo México*. México: Universidad Nacional Autónoma de México.

Ortiz, Alfonso, ed. 1979. *Handbook of North American Indians, Southwest*. Vol. 9. Washington, D.C.: Government Printing Office.

Pacheco, Consuelo. 1988. Sana, Sana, Colita de Rana. *Sin Embargo / Nevertheless: A Woman's Journal* 1(1):4–15.

Robb, John Donald. 1980. *Hispanic Folk Music of New Mexico and the Southwest: A Self-Portrait of a People*. Norman: University of Oklahoma Press.

Rodríguez, Sylvia. 1996. *The Matachines Dance: Ritual Symbolism and Interethnic Relations in the Upper Río Grande*. Albuquerque: University of New Mexico Press.

Sargeant, Kathryn and Mary Davis. 1986. *Shining River, Precious Land: An Oral History of Albuquerque's North Valley*. Albuquerque: The Albuquerque Museum.

Trujillo, Rosa. 1985. Interview by author. Grants, New Mexico, 11 November.

Williams, Raymond. 1977. *Marxism and Literature*. Oxford: Oxford University Press.

The Taos Fiesta
Invented Tradition and the Infrapolitics of Symbolic Reclamation[1]

Sylvia Rodríguez

EVERY YEAR DURING the third week of July, the town of Taos celebrates its traditional fiestas of Santa Ana and Santiago. This two-and-a-half-day festival is held on a weekend and is marked by several features. To begin with, the downtown plaza is closed off to automobile traffic and concession booths are set up all around on the street, along with Taos's antique merry-go-round, known as Tío Vivo. The celebration begins on the evening before the first day with a vespers mass at the Catholic church located just off the plaza, followed by a procession and coronation of the fiesta queen. For the next two days a constant stream of music and dance entertainers perform atop the gazebo platform near the center of the plaza. There is a children's parade on one day and an adult "historical-hysterical" parade on the next, and dance balls on at least two nights. Thousands of locals crowd onto the plaza to watch the coronation and parades, enjoy the entertainment, sit, walk around, visit, eat, drink, and generally have a good time.

The Taos fiesta is smaller, less complex, and less spectacular than the Santa Fe fiesta, which has been studied by Ronald Grimes (1976). But like its fancier counterpart to the south, the Taos fiesta is nonetheless of interest as a public cultural event that can be examined for insight into the larger sociocultural and political milieu within which it occurs.

This article traces the persistence and vicissitudes of the Taos summer fiesta from its invention by an elite group of Anglo boosters in the 1930s to its control by a select Hispanic fiesta council in the 1990s. The fiesta offers a window onto the changing face of intra- and interethnic relations and cultural politics over six decades of an evolving tourism economy in Taos. The character and management of the fiesta at different points in time register social concerns, political climate, and the balance of local power. Rhetorical-symbolic, organizational, and spatial control over the fiesta, including its site on the Taos plaza, defines a field of contestation that reflects the larger context of sociopolitical struggle between and among ethnic groups, classes, intragroup factions, and cross-group sectors.

This reflection involves a symbolic link between fiesta and plaza, an inversion in their meaning, and a shift in control. Whereas at its inception, and for decades thereafter, the fiesta as spectacle was orchestrated and dominated by Anglo artists and entrepreneurs, in the 1960s a gradual transition began toward Hispanic control and predominance, such that today the organizers are high-status Hispanos, and the fiesta itself is attended almost exclusively by Hispanos/Mexicanos from the greater Taos area.[2] During this transition, fiesta-council rhetoric went from a romantic celebration of "tricultural harmony" to a self-conscious "preservation of Hispanic tradition." The complete Hispanicization of the fiesta occurred during a phase of resort development in which the plaza changed from a center of commerce for locals to a reconstructed and gentrified site geared exclusively to tourist consumption.

Today, the fiesta is the only time during the year when local Hispanos, through sheer numbers, physically reoccupy and thus symbolically reclaim the public space that was once the center of their community, but is now a kind of theme mall from which their daily social lives are effectively banished. This reclamation signals, ironically, a form of resistance occasioned and defined by the very hegemonic process it seeks to undermine. It is this metamorphosis, and the symbolic link it implies between fiesta and plaza, that initially piqued my interest and inspired me to undertake research on the Taos summer fiesta.

This essay presents a chronological narrative of how the fiesta came to be and how its organization, features, and character have both persisted and changed during the past sixty-plus years. My account is based upon a review of Taos newspaper archives, examination of various organizational records and ephemera, interviews, and my own memory, as a Taos native who grew up watching and participating in the fiestas during the 1950s and early 1960s. The approach here is strictly diachronic or historical. It lays the foundation for future ethnographic description of the fiesta. My initial inquiry arose from the casual observation, made over the course of my lifetime, that the Taos fiesta had shifted from Anglo to Mexicano control. Here, I will show how that transition took place, tracing the sequence of events and elucidating their significance.

History

As old-timers recall, more than sixty years ago no "fiesta" was held on the Taos plaza in July, but only one at the end of September, when people from all over came for the San Gerónimo feast day at the Tiwa-speaking Taos Pueblo roughly four miles north of Taos. *Vecinos* from the outlying communities attended the vespers procession at the pueblo, where a foot race, pole climb, and dances were also held the next day. The crowd flowed into town to watch horseback races and parades, and to gamble, trade, visit, drink, and enjoy music and dancing on the plaza. Occasionally a traveling carnival added excitement to the event.

The custom of celebrating the pueblo's feast day with special events in town probably arose from Taos's history as a regional trade center, which, during the eighteenth century, saw a lively traffic in goods and produce, livestock, and genízaro slaves (detribalized, Hispanicized Indians). San Gerónimo day comes at the height of the fall harvest, and it seems plausible that a September trade fair could have perdured throughout the Mexican and Territorial periods, registering cultural modifications with every sociopolitical shift. By the turn of the century, in any case, town merchants were organizing and promoting a program of events that preceded and followed the pueblo's feast day on September 30. A 1902 flyer contains the following commentary and three-day schedule for "San Geronimo Feast and Taos Carnival; To Be given in the old and Quaint Town of Taos":

September 29, 1902:
10 A.M. Rock Drilling Contest
12 P.M. Band Concert on the Plaza
2 P.M. Indian Dance
5 P.M. Sun Dance at the Indian Pueblo in honor of the Setting Sun.
In the afternoon and evening the Sisters of Loretto will hold a Bazaar at the Convent.
Band Concert.
Dances in the evening.
Sept. 30
The San Geronimo Feast at Taos Pueblo.
The Most unique and original of Indian Ceremonies.
Wonderful relay race in which fifty braves take part.
Strange Ceremonial Pueblo Indian Dances.
In the afternoon the Chifonetes perform their queer pranks.
DO NOT FAIL TO SEE THIS.
Band Concert.
Several Grand Balls in the evening.
October 1
9 A.M. Foot Race, 100 yd. dash. Purse $10.00; entrance fee $1.00.
11 A.M. Matachine Indian Dance by Taos Pueblo Indians.
12 P.M. Band Concert
2 P.M. Boxing Contest. Queensberry Rules. Private Purse.
4 P.M. Indian Dances by Pueblo Indians in the Plaza.
5 P.M. Sack Race. Purse $5.00; entrance fee 50 cents
Band Concert.
Grand Balls in the evening.[3]

Organization of the town program for San Gerónimo seems to have resided during the 1920s in the hands of the predominantly Anglo Commercial Club, a precursor of today's Chamber of Commerce. By the 1930s a parade and other entertainment had been added to the town routine, but it was not until after the incorporation of the Village of Taos in 1934 that a group of businessmen and artists established formal organizational control over the San Gerónimo events in town. For the most part, these were individuals who had business interests on the plaza. They also decided to institute a separate but similar fiesta in July, for the explicit and unabashed purpose of attracting tourists. This was because one drawback had emerged in the town's otherwise commercially opportune celebration of the San Gerónimo feast day: It came two months late to capture the peak tourist season.

Judging from the fragmentary newspaper record for the period, it appears these promoters decided on a late-July date after experimenting with both a springtime "Taos Fiesta Fair" and a gala Fourth of July celebration. The proximate saints' days of Santiago (July 24) and Santa Ana (July 25) offered amenable dates for the new fiesta, especially inasmuch as they are celebrated at Taos Pueblo with so-called Corn Dances (Parsons [1936] 1970, 85, 88). New Mexico lore holds that women would parade or race on horseback on Santa Ana's day while men would ride for Santiago. While these days may have been observed accordingly in the region, neither appears to have been the occasion for a community festival until the late 1930s. The entrenched Catholic ritual practice of religious processions for certain saints' days posited an ideal legitimizing format. A combination of these elements, including the presence of local and outside concessions around the plaza and several dance balls, seems to have crystallized around 1938–1939, more or less in anticipation of and conjunction with the 1940 Coronado Cuarto Centennial Celebration.[4] No doubt the Taos fiesta was inspired also by the Santa Fe fiesta, which had been invented or "revived" (as a celebration of the de Vargas reconquest entrada) by a comparable group of mostly Anglo boosters in the second decade of the twentieth century.

In 1939, ten Taos citizens, eight of them Anglo and eight male, all with local business interests, formed Taos Fiesta, Incorporated. According to the Articles of Incorporation, their purpose was "to promote, manage, and conduct Fiestas, Feasts, Fairs, Bazaars, Carnivals, Celebrations and other public entertainments, and to raise, by the sale of stock and other means, monies for this purpose."[5] A special committee, composed of corporation board members and other citizens, assumed responsibility for organizing both the July and September fiestas. Individual members took charge of specific practical and organizational tasks for each event. The two-day schedule for the 1939 midsummer fiesta included Spanish dancing, singing and games, the Matachines dance, a clown contest, and a "Billy the Kid episode" in town, with late-afternoon "Indian Dances" at the pueblo (*Taos News* 22 July 1939).

Apart from the town's San Gerónimo Fiesta, the corporation's next major undertaking was the Coronado Cuarto Centennial Fiesta held on July 25-26, 1940. This event involved much planning and preparation, as well as the publication of a special twenty-eight-page "Kit Carson Edition" of *The Taos Review* on 18 July

1940, featuring advertisements and promotional literature about the scenic won-
ders of local exotica. It virtually inaugurated the July fiestas as an invented tradition. A pageant entitled "Ayer y Hoy," an outline of which is still discernible in the
adult parade today, depicted the stages of local interethnic history as a procession
of Indians, conquistadores, Franciscans, nobles, colonists, mountain men, and
Anglo settlers and artists. Also featured were displays of "modern" Taos by agencies or clubs such as the Forest Service, National Guard, or Lions Club, precursors
of modern "floats." The fiesta queen and her attendants, all Hispanas, or "Spanish,"
as many New Mexicans call themselves, led the parade around the plaza. The
queen's coronation was a central feature of the celebration. The LULAC (League
of United Latin American Citizens) staged the equestrian drama of Los
Comanches, which was followed by a dramatic enactment of a wagon-train attack
and cavalry rescue. A "kangaroo court" for exacting fines was instituted, along with
a children's parade. In 1941 the religious folk drama Los Reyes Magos was added to
the program (*El Taoseño* 26 June 1941), and special fiesta costumes for men and
women, allegedly based on "A. L. Campa's investigation of an old manuscript,"
were designed and promoted by Ruth Fish (*El Taoseño* 3 July 1941). The July fiesta
had solidified as an annual event, even though the corporation would struggle to
sustain it, and San Gerónimo continue to outshine it, for at least another decade.

The strong promotional momentum of the late 1930s was cut short by World
War II, which subjected northern New Mexico in early 1941 to a massive draft of
its National Guard to the Philippines, where these soldiers met with military dis-
aster (battle survivors spent the remainder of the war in Japanese prison camps).
The fiestas took on a muted, patriotic tone during the war years. In 1942, an "old-
time, non-commercial," patriotic summer fiesta was planned, featuring horses and
wagons but no motor vehicles in the already routinized historical theme parade. A
prayer mass was held for the men overseas. Two months later, military equipment
was displayed in the San Gerónimo fiesta parade. In 1943 the July fiesta was short-
ened to one Sunday, despite some preference among plaza merchants to hold it on
a Monday. The San Gerónimo celebration featured a victory fair, auction, races,
and an archery contest between an Anglo doctor and some Taos Indians.

Tío Vivo had come into being at around the same time the fiesta itself was
born. This old carousel had been found, dismantled and in dilapidated condition,
in a corral in Peñasco, where it had been abandoned some years before by a traveling circus. It was already about a hundred years old and originally had been
powered by horses. The Lions Club purchased it for ninety dollars and hired a
local carpenter to refurbish it. Its wooden horses were farmed out to Taos artists
who painted them in whimsical colors, a maintenance practice that continues to
the present. The merry-go-round was hand-cranked through the 1940s; a motor
was finally hooked to its axis around 1952.

By 1944, problems had developed between the town and the fiesta corporation over fees and renewal of the fiesta franchise. The financially strapped fiesta corporation had to pay the town a $225 fee and was therefore "practically forced to allow an outside carnival to come in, which took thousands of dollars out of the community and in no way replaced the usual fiesta" (*El Taoseño* 28 June 1944). The franchise was renewed the following year, but problems continued. Despite the fact that its explicit purpose was to stimulate local business, the fiesta corporation had difficulty mustering much support among the merchants for the July fiesta. In 1946 they threatened to cancel the event for lack of attendance at the initial planning meeting. A burst of rekindled enthusiasm led largely by Anglo volunteers, however, made it possible for a one-day celebration to be organized at the last-minute.

Plans for the San Gerónimo fiesta the same year were lavish by comparison, and centered around the centennial theme of Kearney's 1846 "bloodless conquest" of New Mexico. Writer Blanche Grant urged public participation in the pageant, and ordered special costumes, including dozens of cavalry uniforms, much as in 1940. She was the official narrator of the carefully choreographed pageant, which followed a circuitous route through the center of town and culminated in the raising of the "flag of 1846" on the plaza by a man from Taos Pueblo. Kearney's army featured Anglo, Hispano, and Taos Indian men on horseback, all dressed as soldiers. The program included Spanish and Mexican folk dances, and the plaza was decorated with farolitos. The fiesta drew "thousands" of people, and afterwards *El Taoseño* declared it "the most successful and truly traditional San Geronimo fiesta in many years" (*El Taoseño* 3 October 1946).

Enthusiasm for both fiestas waxed even more in 1947, when, interestingly, the July parade theme was the 1598 Oñate entrada (settlement colony) into New Mexico. The shift from the U.S. conquest entrada to the Spanish settlement entrada (in a year that marked the never-celebrated centennial of Taos's bloody insurrection against New Mexico's first Anglo governor, Charles Bent), suggests that a subtext of interethnic contest was already being played out in the symbolic discourse of parade behavior. Once again, "record crowds attended." Prizes for the fiestas, including best costumes, totaled $345. In the spring of that year Tío Vivo, by now a "traditional fiesta attraction," was rented out by the Lions Club to a Hollywood studio for the making of a movie *(To Ride a Pink Horse)*. The fiesta corporation raised money by assessing its members according to categories ranging from five to one hundred dollars. They even adopted an official song, entitled "Fiesta in Taos," written by Marjorie Pickett of Albuquerque (*Taos Review* 24 July 1947).

By the end of the 1940s, several areas of contestation over the fiesta had emerged; they would persist and grow more complex and intense during subsequent decades. These included resentment by local business against outside concessions over economic benefits and tension between the town council and the fiesta corporation over franchise fees, between the board and plaza merchants over shopkeepers' contributions to the event, and between Anglo and Hispano perspectives in the cultural discourse embodied in fiesta events such as the historical pageants and the language of public address. This last issue was raised, for example, by Félix Valdez, the Spanish-page editor of Taos's (English-language) newspaper *(El Taoseño/The Taos Review)*, who maintained that public announcements during the fiesta should also be in Spanish, since so many in the audience, even though they understood English, appreciated hearing their own language and did not want to see it disappear from public discourse. Accordingly, he urged:

> *Que los programas se anuncien por micrófono en español, no nomás en inglés y así la mitad de los oyentes no se quedarán en ayunas; a pesar que año tras año mencionamos esto, aquellos que están a la cabeza de la celebración todavía no realizan la necesidad del cave y mientras no lo realizan le hacen gran injusticia a Taos y a millares de sus moradores que aunque comprendan el inglés, todavía aprecian su idioma y no quieren que desaparesca de entre nuestra sociedad.* (That the programs be announced over the microphone in Spanish as well as in English, so that half the listeners are not left wanting; even though year after year we mention this, those in charge of the celebration still do not see the need for it and meanwhile do not realize that they do a great injustice to Taos and its thousands of inhabitants who, although they understand English, nevertheless appreciate their own language and do not want to see it disappear from our society. [*El Taoseño* 31 July 1947; my translation]

Another theme, only obliquely reflected in the newspaper, was Taos Pueblo's nonengagement in the town's fiesta activity and public discourse (despite participation by individual Taos Indians), which nevertheless still relied heavily on the promotion of Indians as cultural symbols.

During the early 1950s both fiestas continued to become bigger and fancier. The issue of who should control the microphone during the two days of events was resolved by installing a Hispano Lions Club member as the master of ceremonies. This garrulous, bilingual individual, who had moved to Taos as an adult and learned Spanish as a second language, had originally helped acquire Tío Vivo. He held the emcee post for several years, followed thereafter by another Spanish speaker. He announced the program primarily in English but laced his banter with Spanish. Privately, he considered Valdez's position extremist. In 1951, Spud Johnson, the celebrated voice of Taos's bohemian art colony (or Anglo cultural elite), complained in his *Taos News* column, "The Horse Fly," that this announcer's loud, incessant commentary spoiled the solemnity and beauty of the July fiesta's religious procession. He also ridiculed the new reviewing platform constructed in the center of the plaza atop semi-subterranean offices, nicknamed "la kivita" (*Taos*

News 24 August 1951). That year the San Gerónimo program featured a dramatic reenactment of the alleged Civil War episode in which the American flag was torn down in Taos plaza by Confederates and then nailed back up by a local (Anglo) Union loyalist. The three-day celebration drew an estimated crowd of five thousand, causing a traffic jam on the road to the pueblo so large that the newspaper editor called afterwards for the establishment of a parking plan.

Although the fiesta board remained predominantly Anglo, by the late 1950s more Hispanos were slowly being elected to it, and a gradual infusion of self-consciously Hispanic symbols (such as papier-mâché parade figures of "El Abuelo" and "La Bruja" fashioned by an Anglo artist) was taking place. Another figure added to the parade during this era was "El Viborón," a long, colorful snake train, supposedly derived from the legend of a large serpent kept in a pueblo kiva.

Events were underway that would ultimately extinguish the town's San Gerónimo fiesta. In 1957 the town council unanimously approved a truck bypass that cut northeast of the plaza behind Kit Carson Park and along the southern perimeter of Taos Pueblo. The town did not bother to consult the pueblo, which was quick to oppose the plan, gaining instant support from the Anglo cultural elite. By 1959 the pueblo was so incensed over the plan that it advertised Corn Dances for both days of the July fiesta in order to draw people away from the plaza (*Taos News* 25 July 1959).[6] The town's San Gerónimo fiesta fizzled, and, in 1960, the September fiesta was celebrated only at the pueblo. In the end the bypass was blocked by a wealthy Anglo landowner who built a large motel in what would have been its path. But the town's San Gerónimo fiesta never revived, and the pueblo continued contentedly to celebrate its feast day separately.

The 1960s brought major change to Taos and its fiesta. In abandoning the San Gerónimo fiesta, the corporation ceased to fulfill its original charter, the precise terms of which had been forgotten anyway. In 1962, Taos Fiesta, Inc. lost its charter, having failed for several years to submit an annual report to the State Corporation Commission. At the time of its official dissolution, the president reported that apart from the treasurer's ledger, the board possessed only fragmentary records, and no copy of its original charter or bylaws. It had been functioning for years as three interrelated bodies: an elected board of directors; an elected advisory board; and a special committee made up of board members and volunteers who were in charge of various organizational tasks, such as finance, publicity, program, entertainment, parade, queen selection, concessions, decorations, and so on. The board reorganized itself more or less along the same lines and continued to operate for the next twenty years without official corporate status. The July fiesta was now the sole reason for the board's existence as well as the town's only "traditional fiesta." It was well on its way to being more popular among local residents than among the plaza merchants.

Critics nevertheless continued to complain each year about the fiesta's chaotic disarray, boring program, poor sanitary conditions, bad timing, low quality, crass commercialism, and so on. They also regularly bemoaned the small native (Hispanic) involvement in its working organization. Public discussion about the fiesta reflected internal division within the Anglo community and a patronizing attitude toward Hispanos. In 1961, for example, an anonymous letter writer, responding to an earlier editorial that had complained of low native participation and had criticized "certain Anglos who sing badly in Spanish" (*Taos News* 30 March 1961), defended the latter: "[I]n short, these people [Anglos] are helping the Spanish-Americans do what they don't seem to have the inclination to do, but which ninety-nine percent of them support and appreciate" (*Taos News* 20 April 1961). This exchange invoked the familiar stereotype of the passive, apathetic Mexican in contrast to the executive Anglo, whose initiative and energy made the fiesta happen.

One important feature of the July fiesta that underwent elaboration during the 1960s was the queen's selection, coronation, and royal court, a phenomenon that paralleled the post-war baby boomers' entry into adolescence. It was heralded in 1959 when "old Castile-style" brocaded velvet gowns were made for the queen and her two attendants or princesses. For the first time it seems, they visited the Santa Fe fiesta as guests of that city's "royal court," a reciprocal courtesy extended today among a network of local fiesta councils. Intensification of the queen motif, like the pageantry in general, was doubtless inspired in part by the bigger and more elaborate Santa Fe fiesta. In any case, the queen has always been "Spanish," although, beginning in the late 1960s, the fiesta board tried to integrate her court. The queen's coronation and procession follow a vespers mass the night before the fiesta begins, a practice maintained since the 1940s. This aspect of the program with its ethnoreligious associations has constituted, along with the Spanish-Mexican music, dancing, and an overall party atmosphere, the major source of the fiesta's enduring popularity.

During the 1960s the Jaycees, a recent and comparatively integrated (Anglo-Hispano) service club, became the annual sponsors of the fiesta, which meant they raised the money and organized the event. Their expanding costs included the queen and her court. In 1965, the Taos News reported that the board not only paid the queen and her attendants and gave her a one-hundred-dollar college scholarship, but also footed the food and liquor bills for her party. That year was publicized as the "350th Anniversary"—although it is not altogether clear of precisely what. The theme was to be "Taos Blends Three Cultures," and the tone declared was religious rather than commercial, so no concession booths would be allowed. One Anglo woman wrote a letter to the editor complaining that, despite the theme of three cultures, the queen was always Spanish but there really ought to be three queens, one from each group (*Taos News* 15 July 1965). This was actually accomplished in 1969, and for a few years in the early 1970s the Hispana queen was accompanied by an Anglo and an Indian counterpart.

By 1967 the Jaycees felt the financial and organizational strain of being the only fiesta sponsors. That year every head of a task committee was Hispanic. In 1968, both the Jaycees and the fiesta board reached exhaustion, and the Chamber of Commerce salvaged the event at the last minute with what was dubbed an "instant fiesta." The "Great Hippie Invasion" had begun, and, by the following year, the resentment and open hostility toward these thousands of youthful, mostly middle-class newcomers was so intense that the board and other civic clubs decided to cancel the fiesta, due, they said, to the "Three Ds: Dirt, Drugs, and Disease" (*Taos News* 24 March 1969). In August they changed their minds, however, and decided to have a one-day fiesta just before San Gerónimo. It was sponsored by the Optimists, Taos's newest integrated (Hispano/Anglo) service club. The decision to have triethnic queens was an effort to paint a prettier face on what had become a bitter and overtly violent situation.[7]

The hippie crisis in Taos had unmistakable ethnic-racial overtones, but the lines of antagonism were not merely interethnic. In general, Chicanos were the most resentful and openly hostile toward the hippies, but community divisions over the counterculture invasion were multiple. It internally divided all three groups along complex combinations of class, subcultural (business vs. cultural elites), and political (conservative vs. liberal) orientations. It also created intergenerational conflicts, and took on strong local vs. outsider overtones. Each sector perceived a slightly different threat. The business community was for the most part virulently anti-hippie because it saw them as a threat to Taos's tourist appeal. In the long run, of course, the counterculture was absorbed into Taos's ever-marketable neo-bohemian mystique. But their influx, contemporaneous with the rise of the national and regional Chicano movements, marked a turning point in the character of local ethnic politics.

Thereafter the customarily subtle undercurrent of Hispano resentment against Anglos became more overt, a trend since intensified by the social pressures generated by increasing Anglo immigration and progressive resort development. Taos's first tourism boom, roughly between World War I and World War II, was based on Indianism and the art colony. The second major tourism boom began in the late 1960s and continues to the present, with fluctuations along the way. The contemporary boom is based on the ski industry, which was established in the Río Hondo watershed some twenty miles north of Taos in the late 1950s. The ski industry was instantly embraced by local businessmen as the panacea for Taos's winter doldrums, but it took at least a decade to become a major force in the local economy. This transformation became manifest during the 1970s and its impact grew exponentially during the 1980s. Both decades saw a concurrent, progressive Hispanicization of the Taos fiesta—both in terms of who was in charge of organizing the event and of explicit symbolic focus.

After 1969, the fiesta board or council was predominantly Hispano-Chicano, with only a few and indeed ever fewer Anglos—the reverse of its composition when it began and for the first decades of its existence. This transition began almost imperceptibly during the early 1960s but was apparent by 1970. During the 1970s it crystallized while the symbolic rhetoric and cultural style of the fiesta became increasingly Hispanicized.

A major aspect of this process was the glamorization and growing importance of the fiesta queen complex. During the first few years of the decade, the board espoused and several times managed to have three queens, one from each ethnic group. But this innovation soon faltered, and, by 1974, the custom had reverted to a single queen who was Hispana, and the board was beginning to experiment with eligibility rules that would effectively ensure such an outcome without necessarily appearing to do so. The selection procedure seems to grow more complex as the stakes got higher. In 1973, the last year there were three queens, they were to be selected at a fashion show, but ended up being chosen at a ball instead. The manner of selection was ostensibly by chance, in that the candidates were instructed to pick corsages from a tray, three of which contained slips of paper indicating the winners. The candidates themselves had been chosen by the senior class of Taos High School based on talent and scholastic standing. Each queen received a $200 college scholarship. The corsage selection had been rigged, but somehow the wrong Hispana candidate picked the winning corsage. The queen's committee later asked the winner's mother to abdicate her daughter's claim to the crown, but she indignantly refused.[8] Royal courts from Santa Fe, Española, and Peñasco attended the fiesta. The official theme was Taos's ancient tricultural roots, touted in the special brochure printed by the Taos News. Afterwards the event was called a huge success, even though it exceeded its allotted budget.

In 1975 and 1976, proclaimed bicentennial years, fiesta pageantry was up, and the queen complex enjoyed a new infusion of religiosity, status, and glamour. In 1975, the archdiocese's bicentennial year, Archbishop Robert Sánchez of Santa Fe performed the queen's mass. The candidates, drawn from an ostensibly open (but implicitly Hispanic) pool of young women between seventeen and twenty-two, appeared before the fiesta board at a tea, and each made a speech. The winner received a $600 college scholarship. The 1976 fiesta was a four-day extravaganza. That year the queen was selected at a beauty pageant that featured evening gowns, street clothes, and a talent contest. Six of the judges were from out of town. This general format continued into the 1990s.

The evening mass before the first day of the fiesta was referred to in the paper as the "traditional Queen's mass." By the late 1970s, Spanish had become the dominant language and cultural idiom at the fiesta. The program was a combination of Spanish-Mexican-Latino, some Indian, and popular mainstream musical elements, with "traditional Spanish-Catholic-family" as the reigning cultural theme.

The process of Hispano-Mexicano reclamation of the fiesta's symbolic, social, linguistic, and physical space paralleled the progressive gentrification of that space, the plaza and heart of town, into what is today a kind of Southwest theme mall for tourists. This process started in the early 1970s with the relocation of the county courthouse to a new building nearly a mile south of the plaza. Gradually, the last businesses catering to local needs, such as drug, hardware, and clothing stores, cafes, barber shops, cantinas, and so on, gave way entirely to souvenir shops, art galleries, boutiques, and restaurants for tourists. The growing majority of such businesses were owned by recently arrived Anglos. In 1976, the center of the plaza was remodeled from an encircled area containing grass, flagstones, and exposed dirt to a landscaped, bricked, fully paved surface. The transition to a plaza-mall became absolute during the 1980s. As this happened, the living, day-to-day presence of native Hispano-Mexicano people on the plaza diminished, and it became a place most natives and locals preferred to avoid. The 1970s saw a further dramatic shift in demographic proportions: Taos County's population went from 86 percent Hispanic in 1970 to 68 percent in 1980, while the Anglo population increased by roughly 18 percent, largely through amenity migration.[9]

In 1980 the theme was once again "Fiesta de la Gente." The council and town instituted a new policy against drinking and open containers on the plaza, and arrests were made for illegal liquor sales to minors as well as for a drunken attack on one of the entertainers. Afterwards, a letter to the newspaper, written by an Anglo art gallery owner, called the fiesta "the most shoddy, tawdry, boring, dirty (no, filthy) I have witnessed in the 24 years I have spent in Taos!" The author ridiculed the appearance in the parade of "a 1964 Chevy lowrider" as an inappropriate expression of Taos plaza's historic heritage, called for a public accounting of the fiesta committee's collections and expenditures, and demanded,

> if indeed there is any justification for continuance of the summer Taos fiestas, that the community begin immediately seeking people with education, taste, culture and sensitivity to plan any future fiestas, or, relegate the whole thing to the garbage cans where it evidently belongs from the looks of the downtown area on Friday, Saturday, and Sunday nights of the fiestas. [*Taos News* 7 August 1980]

Not surprisingly, this letter provoked a number of indignant responses. One Hispana wrote that obviously the author "or her tourist friends have no idea what a fiesta is really all about" (namely, the writer argued, a time for native people to celebrate the saints' days of Santa Ana and Santiago and to come to the plaza to visit):

> It was the "Fiestas de la Gente." It wasn't called "La Fiesta de el Dinero" or "La Fiesta de los Touristas." It was our fiesta, a tradition

that we have had before people like you came in to let us know how we could sell our culture for the American dollar. [*Taos News* 14 August 1980]

Another response, from a member of the car club, "Los Low Riders de Aztlan," objected that the author of the infamous "filth" letter strongly implied that the *carros bajitos* didn't quite coincide with the history of the community.

> Our carros flemantitos represent a color pride mixed with a true carnalismo, low and close to sierra madre. Historically, La Raza Chicana has been a tight and cohesive group, holding on to our language and culture despite Anglo criticism and exploitation. Our carnalismo is a philosophy that has survived through the decades of our history, a concept too abstract and complex for an Anglo to comprehend. Yes, our carros bajitos illustrates the unity, pride, and closeness to nature of our people—indeed a historical representation of our community. [*Taos News* 14 August 1980]

Two weeks later, an Anglo resident accused the newspaper of fanning the flames of racism by printing such letters in the first place and urged the editor to refrain from doing so in the future: "I personally don't feel that we Taoseños need any more blatant evidence of racism than we already have to deal with" (*Taos News* 28 August 1980).

This series of letters shows that racism and ethnic anger were "out" in the public arena in a way that would have been unthinkable before the late 1960s. It signals the loss of Anglo hegemony over the fiesta and further reveals a heightened expression of Hispano-Chicano differentiation, idealized essence, and opposition to a likewise essentialized, ubiquitous Anglo Other.

The following year the fiesta council met early and was better organized. And finally, after a lapse of twenty years, it once again incorporated. The council decreed that candidates for queen had to be between seventeen and twenty-five, single, childless, and a native of Taos County of Hispanic descent. Moreover, her parents had to be of Spanish descent, and at least one of them a Taos native. Entry into the pageant required a twenty-dollar fee. Selection was based on poise, talent, personality, appearance, bilingual speech, skits, and a research paper on the history of Taos.

There was also a Pueblo queen in 1981, apparently selected independently, which the council proudly publicized. The evening coronation ceremony, however, revealed that gifts donated by local businesses had not been provided for Indian members of the royal court. Thus the Indian queen and her attendants stood empty-handed while their Hispana counterparts were lavished with presents.

By the middle 1980s the council was solidly Hispanic and dominated by several couples who became pillars of the event. New members had to be nominated or sponsored by established members and became permanent only after a year of probation. This general constituency remained in charge through the end of the 1990s, representing an elite, conservative, civically active, devoutly Catholic sector of local Hispano society. This new council constitutes more a status elite than an economic elite, because, although middle-class, its members are by no means the wealthiest Mexicanos. Their status derives more from their roles and respectability in the community and the values they embody than from explicit financial power. They define their role as organizers but also as custodians of Taos's "religious fiesta tradition."[10]

Another visible change that emerged during the 1980s was a progressive shift from what had once been a generally ethnically mixed fiesta crowd to a predominantly, indeed almost exclusively, Hispanic one. As Hispanicization of the fiesta progressed through the 1970s to deepen in the 1980s, Anglo participation and attendance steadily dwindled. With some exceptions, the crowds at the two-day event had become, by the middle of the decade, virtually "pura raza." This audience includes older people from the communities surrounding Taos and many who have moved away for employment but come home during fiesta to visit, as well as lots of *pleve* or youth.

Tourist attrition is probably encouraged by Santa Fe's cannily competitive timing of Spanish Market the same weekend as the Taos fiesta (this was the case in 1992, 1993, and 1996, but not in 1994 or 1995). The two frequently concurrent events pose an interesting contrast as tourist experiences of the Hispanic/Mexican Other. The visitor to Santa Fe encounters an ordered and tasteful market display of carefully crafted and selected Spanish colonial artifacts, typically presented by the artists themselves. In Taos, however, one is engulfed in a massive crowd of Mexicanos milling around the plaza, where concessions sell fast food and cheap carnival trinkets. In 1992 one saleswoman in an upscale clothing shop located just north of the plaza affably told me the fiesta stimulated tourist flight in her direction. Many plaza shop owners even close for fiesta weekend, while others complain of increased traffic, especially if it rains (which it almost always does), security risk, and either neutral or negative impact on sales. The few downtown bars, on the other hand, do extremely well. A few business owners advocate moving the fiesta off the plaza altogether. Thus, ironically, the festival originally invented to promote plaza business now impairs it.

Analysis

The period from 1940 to 1990 showed a gradual but absolute reversal in ethnic control over the Taos fiesta. The fiesta represents a cultural field in which local interests compete and boundaries are symbolically enacted. The event, defined and controlled by Anglos for about thirty years, began as a promotional gimmick to attract tourists. Assertion of Hispanic symbols and the struggle for linguistic parity at the microphone were present from the beginning, but the shift away from Anglo predominance did not become manifest before the mid-1960s. Two concomitants of the fiesta's gradual Hispanicization-Mexicanization are noteworthy: the dissolution of its tie with the San Gerónimo fiesta and Taos Pueblo involvement, and the expansion and prominence of the queen complex. Each affirms a different boundary. The progressive disengagement of Taos Indians from the town fiesta asserts the pueblo boundary against perceived municipal appropriation, encroachment, and effrontery. Elaboration of the queen complex, with emphasis upon her figure as a symbol of Hispanic female beauty and chastity, expresses an ethnic boundary through gender. Expansion of control over the fiesta registers the rise of a Hispano middle class, but also signals, and symbolically inverts, concomitant native loss of geographic and demographic control of and access to the heart of town—especially its symbolic center, the plaza. By the early 1980s, the fiesta had become a nativist, tacitly anti-tourist event, dominated by the Spanish language and saturated with symbols of Hispanic ethnicity and tradition.

In his introduction to *The Invention of Tradition*, Eric Hobsbawm noted three types of invented tradition in the industrial world: "those establishing or symbolizing social cohesion or the membership of groups, those establishing or legitimizing institutions, status or relations of authority, and those whose main purpose [is] socialization, the inculcation of beliefs, value systems, and conventions of behavior" (1983, 9). The Taos fiesta has performed all three of these roles at different stages in its history, beginning with the second and today fulfilling the other two as well. But apart from its fit with Hobsbawm's typology, another feature of the Taos fiesta is the amnesia-like erasure of its original commercial motive and concomitant reappropriation in the name of "Hispanic tradition."

The meaning of "traditional" varies according to use. During the first two decades of the July fiesta's existence, the term "tradition" or "traditional" was invoked by promoters to convey a sense of Taos's "colorful tricultural" past as well as a cluster of romantic pastoral values from the implicit viewpoint of a dominant outsider who suffers from what Rosaldo (1989) calls imperialist nostalgia. After 1970, the struggle of the fiesta board became to retrieve or construct some essence of Hispano-Nuevomexicano-Taoseño cultural heritage, identity, or "tradition" from the tacit point of view of those who have lost or are on the verge of losing it. The same platitudes were invoked, but their implicit meanings had changed.

Differences in ethnic perspectives notwithstanding, one universal consistency in the use of the term "tradition" remains its basic opposition to the term "commercial." Thus, for Anglos and Hispanos both "tradition" connotes authentic as opposed to fake, and community-oriented as opposed to tourist-oriented. From the start, the term "tradition" dressed the naked truth in a perfect suit of clothes. That a tourist town contrived an event to lure customers seems less remarkable than the fact that locals would become enthusiastic proponents of its "authenticity." Different ethnic constituencies have organized the fiesta during different periods and have controlled its public rhetoric. Each has subscribed to the fiction according to its own lights and needs as well as the exigencies of the period.

Perhaps their common investment in the great fiction of tradition derives from the fact that, whereas the fiesta board's ethnic proportion gradually reversed itself over the years, its class composition has remained much the same. After 1970, Chicanos began to enter the business class in significant numbers in Taos. This is reflected in the emergence of integrated service clubs like the Jaycees and Optimists, whose constituencies occupied the fiesta as well as other arenas of local power. By 1990, the fiesta board exerted absolute control over selection of its permanent membership. In short, the architects of public ethnic boundary construction are the rising middle class.

The Taos fiesta exhibits several interesting features. It has come to defeat the very purpose for which it was invented, stimulus of commerce on the plaza. The fiesta may benefit liquor sales and outside vendors, but not boutiques or art galleries. As a "genuine artifact of tourism," the fiesta embodies, enacts, and symbolizes an impulse of local resistance as well as capitulation to the relentless advance of capitalism. Native reclamation of the plaza affirms the reign of tourism by agreeing to interrupt it but once a year. As Stanley Brandes (1988, 1) observes, fiestas paradoxically are agencies of social control even while they provide momentary release from normal constraint. Herein lies the interest and power of any given fiesta. The fiesta exerts control along the conventionally symbolized lines of ethnicity, gender, religion, family, class, and the state. Every major symbol is hierarchical, regulatory, and conservative. But the fiesta is also one big drunken party: a nonordinary, ineffable moment of abandon, reversal, and communitas. The fiesta stages this transcendent moment by transforming the public space to which it is, by definition, bound.

Acknowledgments

Research for this article was initiated in 1992 and was made possible by the UNM Center for Regional Studies, through its sponsorship of the Southwest Hispanic Research Institute (SHRI)-Anthropology Harwood field station, plus a Faculty Development grant (1992-1993). The latter funded the able archival research assistance provided by Mo Palmer. Fieldwork in 1993 was supported in part by a Rockefeller grant through SHRI, and, in 1994, by a grant from the New Mexico Endowment for the Humanities. I wish to thank Genaro Padilla, Víctor Sorell, and other members of the SHRI Rockefeller scholars group for their helpful comments on earlier drafts of this paper.

Notes

1. This article first appeared in *The Southwest Review,* 39(1), spring 1997.
2. The nomenclature for Spanish-speaking peoples of Mexican descent in New Mexico (as elsewhere in the United State) is notoriously problematic in that no single term is universally acceptable. Several terms are therefore employed here, including Hispano, Mexicano, Chicano, Hispanic, Spanish, Spanish American; and La Raza. For the most part, my use of a particular term in any given context reflects what would seem acceptable to the people being referred to.
3. From the "Taos Fiesta" archives of the Taos Historical Museum, formerly the Kit Carson Museum.
4. The 1940 Coronado Cuarto Centennial year was intensely promoted in New Mexico and provoked mixed responses. For example, Raton reportedly began preparing for the celebration in 1937 (*El Taoseño* 12 June 1940). Yet the Santa Fe newspapers complained that LULAC was not helping with the Coronado celebration. George I. Sánchez responded by saying that the whole thing was organized by outsiders who got big credit for it while ignoring the knowledge and local customs of the Spanish Americans (*El Taoseño* 17 April 1940). Another dissenting voice was the seventy-seven-year-old president of the All-Pueblo Indian Council, Pablo Abeyta, who refused to honor Coronado because he had killed Pueblo people and forced them into war (*Taos Review* 6 June 1940).
5. Article II, Articles of Incorporation of Taos Fiesta, Incorporated, March 9, 1939. Obtained from the Corporation Commission of New Mexico in Santa Fe.
6. These so-called Corn Dances no doubt provided an original incentive for the summer fiesta instigators to pick July 24th and 25th for the feasts of Santa Ana and Santiago. Parsons refers to them as konli or saints' day dances, known to whites as Corn Dances ([1936] 1970, 85, 88, 97-98). The pueblo continues to perform these dances on the actual saints' days whereas the town fiesta is now always on a weekend.
7. During this period, hippies were in several instances physically attacked by gangs of local Chicano youth. Some were beaten up or shot at; several women were gang raped and arson took place. This was perhaps the first time since 1847 that certain Anglos became the target of open physical aggression by groups of Mexicanos.
8. This queen was my first cousin, who told me the story.
9. The term "amenity migrant" refers to the migration of tourists and retirees who take up full- or part-time residence in a locale they formerly visited as tourists. That is, they relocate because of the "amenities" that originally drew them as tourists. The term usefully distinguishes "amenity migrants" from current tourists as well as from labor migrants. The dramatic population increase in both Taos and Santa Fe in recent decades is due primarily to amenity migration.
10. The new council came into being around 1980 when the mayor of Taos instigated the organization of a permanent group that would dedicate itself to organizing the annual fiesta. All but two of Taos's mayors have been Hispanos. Both Anglo mayors were elected in the years surrounding World War II.

Literature Cited

Brandes, Stanley. 1988. *Power and Persuasion: Fiestas and Social Control in Rural Mexico.* Philadelphia: University of Pennsylvania Press.

Grimes, Ronald. 1976. *Symbol and Conquest: Public Ritual and Drama in Santa Fe, New Mexico.* Ithaca, N.Y.: Cornell University Press.

Hobsbawm, Eric. 1983. Introduction: Inventing Traditions. In *The Invention of Tradition,* eds. E. Hobsbawm and T. Ranger, 1-14. Cambridge, Mass.: Cambridge University Press.

Parsons, Elsie Clews. [1936] 1970. *Taos Pueblo.* Reprint, New York: Johnson Reprint Corporation.

Rosaldo, Renato. 1989. *Culture and Truth.* Boston: Beacon Press.

Guadalupe's Emblematic Presence Endures in New Mexico
Investing the Body with the Virgin's Miraculous Image

Víctor Alejandro Sorell

I. Introduction: Sacred Power
Vested in Cloth, Clothing, and Skin

    LITERAL AND FIGURATIVE REFERENCES to cloth and clothing abound in scripture, popular religious belief, legend, and tradition. According to Genesis, Adam and Eve received garments of skin directly from God (Genesis 3:21). In Revelation, the apocalyptic Virgin Mary appears as "a woman clothed with the sun" (Revelation 12:1). In sixteenth-century Mexico, the Virgin of Guadalupe appeared to a Christianized Aztec, Juan Diego, in several ephemeral, miraculous apparitions. A palpable "absence" punctuated her ensuing four exits. Only her visual likeness, miraculously imprinted on Juan Diego's cloak—supplanting the Castille roses bundled and carried at Guadalupe's own request—would capture the Virgin's "presence" in perpetuity. Juan Diego's *tilmatli* (Escalada 1995, 101–108), made of *ayate*[1] fibers from the maguey plant (aloe family), became a "canvas" for *la Guadalupana*'s "portrait" and fourth apparition. "Present" before the faithful multitudes for centuries thereafter, that enduring, mystical icon—impressed on *"un pobre paño de tosco material"* (a humble cloth of coarse material [Escalada 1995, 101])—recalls both Christ's own face (*vera icon*) allegedly impressed on Veronica's Veil and his body's presumed imprint indelibly inscribed on the sacred Shroud of Turin. The veil has been likened to a large handkerchief, while the shroud has been said to resemble a bedsheet, a *"Sábana Santa"* (Escalada 1995, 101).

Historian of Amerindian clothing, Patricia Rieff Anawalt documents the importance of the *tilmatli* in Aztec society (1981, 30–31). Also referred to as a *manta* in *Codex Magliabechiano,* one of a number of painted books or codices, a *tilmatli* was likened to a sheet denoting the power and status of the wearer. One *tilmatli* in particular was worn by a litter bearer for the human impersonator of the fertility god *Xochipilli.* Consequently, this garment and others came to be associated with powerful deities. According to the Dominican missionary Fray Diego Durán (writing in Mexico City between 1576 and 1581), various *tilmatli* were

fig 20   Inviting the Virgin's intervention in his grandmother's battle with
cancer, artist Dickie Ray García depicts la Guadalupana's fourth
apparition to Juan Diego. (Exterior adobe wall, García residence,
near Sunset Gardens, Albuquerque, N.Mex.) Photo: Miguel Gandert.

elaborately decorated with the very figures of the gods. Arguably, Juan Diego was himself empowered and ennobled by the Virgin when she chose to invest his *tilmatli* with her singular and symbolic aura or presence. Was this a sign acknowledging her own liminality between two antagonistic worlds, one pre-Columbian and the other Christian? Writing about *El rebozo en el estado de México* (The Shawl in the Mexican Republic), author Gustavo G. Velázquez argues that *"algunos aseguran que la Virgen de Guadalupe quiso estampar su imagen en una tilma para expresar su identiWcación con las penas y esperanzas de los indios"* (some assert that the Virgin of Guadalupe wanted to stamp her image on a *tilmatli* to convey her empathy with the natives' struggles and hopes) (1981, 40). Others would be skeptical of such a view. Scholar William B. Taylor makes splendidly clear the complexity and density of the multivocal symbol *la Guadalupana* represents. To claim her as the Virgin of the conquered Indians is, in his opinion, a simplistic conclusion unsupported by the historical evidence unearthed to date (Taylor 1987). In the end, popular perception of her role as champion of the disenfranchised further underscores her multivocality and may win the day even in the face of historical caution and doubt.

That this goddess would emanate incarnate from mere fabric is hardly incidental or insignificant. Rather, the unexplained phenomenon appears symbolically fitting. Consider that the Virgin's *esplendor* or radiance is not unlike the *mandorla*, an almond-shaped figure formed by two intersecting circles, the two spheres of heaven and earth. Morphologically, the *mandorla* is also cognate with the spindle of the *Magna Mater* (Great Mother) and with magical spinners of thread (Cirlot 1962, 127, 194). Revealingly, special deities regarded as patrons of spinners, weavers, and embroiderers were venerated in every pre-Hispanic culture, and weaving was regarded as a sacred occupation among women (Lechuga 1982, 35–37, 55). Significantly, one of these patron deities was *Xochiquetzalli,* a name meaning "plumage of roses." A day celebrating the cultivation of roses was observed and documented by Fray Diego Durán (Lechuga 1982, 35–37). Thus, just how untenable is the notion, albeit metaphysical, that the Virgin "wove" her own self-portrait, what cultural historian David Freedberg calls an acheiropoietic image (1989, 110), one not believed to be made by human hands?

Jungian scholar Erich Neumann has ably demonstrated that the nexus between weaving and the goddess is of global proportions and is archetypal or primordial in its foundations.

> Thus the Great Goddesses are weavers, in Egypt as in Greece, among the Germanic peoples and the Mayans. And because "reality" is wrought by the Great Weavers, all such activities as plaiting, weaving, and knotting belong to the fate-governing activity of the woman, who . . . is a spinner and weaver in her natural aspect. . . .

It is said of the Great Goddess: *Clother* is her name. [Neumann (1955) 1963, 227, 230]

   In the words of Mircea Eliade, arguably the most encyclopedic scholar among researchers of the world's religions, Juan Diego's *tilmatli* constitutes an example of an "elementary hierophany," a "receptacle for a manifestation of the sacred" (Eliade 1964, 32).
   Notwithstanding the extensive body of literature devoted to Our Lady of

fig 21   The Virgin's imprint on Juan Diego's cloak/*tilmatli* persuades the Bishop to believe Juan Diego's accounts of the miraculous apparition and commands the prelate's reverence. (Miguel Cabrera, *Juan Diego Before Bishop Zumárraga* [1752], oil on canvas.) Photo: Ludwig Iven.

Guadalupe, it would appear that nobody, including Father Stafford Poole, possibly the most rigorous and definitive of the recent contributors (1995) to this evocative subject, has tried to acknowledge, let alone explain what is a symbolic, if not causal link between the Virgin's visual incarnation and the fiber surface on which it made its mark. That emblematic relationship lies at the very center of this paper's argument and should be scrutinized as more than anecdotal happenstance. Sustaining the argument for a causal relationship is the historically telling fact that several Amerindian goddesses were themselves named for their vestments: *Chalchiuhtlicue*—"lady of the jade skirt"; *Citlalinicue*—"lady of the luminous starry skirt"; *Coatlicue*—"lady of the serpent skirt"; and *Tecolliquenqui*—"lady of the black attire" (León-Portilla [1963] 1990, 98). Consistent with these iconographic associations, which foreground vestments, is the Amerindian belief, already cited, that weaving was a sacred occupation among women. Conforming to this precedent, Guadalupe can be characterized as lady of "*[la] prenda de liberación para los pobres y los conquistados*" ([the] liberating garment for the poor and conquered) (Escalada 1995, 104). Should readers harbor reservations about the revelatory and rhetorical power of vestments and their attendant vestiary images, semiotician Roland Barthes would remind them that "the costume must be an argument," that it has "a powerful semantic value" and should be "read" as well as seen. For him, costume communicates "ideas, information, or sentiments." In short, Barthes invokes the vestimentary sign and its politics (Barthes 1972, 46–47).

In her *Viva Guadalupe! The Virgin in New Mexican Popular Art,* noted New Mexican *Guadalupana* scholar Jacqueline Orsini Dunnington has demonstrated the widespread popularity of Our Lady in New Mexico, including her emblematically encoded presence on cloth and skin (Dunnington 1997, 34, 59, 66). Mass-produced cotton T-shirts emblazoned with the powerful, talismanic Mediatrix are donned by believers, and commonplace handkerchiefs illuminated with her image—conceivably modern and contemporary allusions to the veil of the compassionate Veronica—are sent to loved ones on the outside by prison inmates doing time in the New Mexico State Prison near Santa Fe. Those same inmates and others outside prison walls have their own bodies—a "first skin" as compared to cloth's "second skin" (Horn and Gurel 1981, 5)—inscribed with her radiance (Dunnington 1997, 72). Empowerment, lamentation, mediation, penance, remembrance, reverence, and revelation in her name unfold on plain fabric and appear inscribed on human skin.

It is the larger purpose of this essay to document and critically interpret Nuevomexicano popular devotion to Our Lady of Guadalupe—irrespective of strict ethnic boundaries—encoded on human skin and the medium of cloth, the latter arguably a material emblematic of the Virgin herself. That is, to speak of her material presence would be tantamount to an invocation of sacred cloth, and, by inference, weaving as a sacred occupation among women. Metonymically put, a part or attribute of the Virgin can substitute for the whole, especially in iconographic terms. That is certainly true for *Coatlicue,* whose animated "serpent skirt" immediately connotes in its totemic totality the splendid monumental sculpted monolith for which it stands. Amerindians seem to place an even greater premium on metonymy in the sphere of language through the device of *difrasismo.* Below, we will revisit this subject in relation to Guadalupe.

II. The Multivalent Veil: Mantles of Oppression, Liberation, and Empowerment

How much more effectively or conspicuously could the Virgin have endowed her subject, Juan Diego, with her own mantle of power than to have literally dressed him in/with her own image? In a manner of speaking, she unveiled herself—thereby divesting herself of a modicum of her own power?—to veil him. Vesting and unvesting come to be understood as conscious or unconscious ritual engaged in by those who venerate *la Guadalupana.* The act of putting on clothes or other accessories bearing her image is, in one respect, a veiling and empowering of the body, and, in another respect, a public unveiling of the Virgin. To take the clothing off is to remove her presence from public view, and, consequently, to disempower oneself. Conversely, a believer tattooed with her image reveals her presence every time s/he uncovers the tattoo—a perpetually empowering talisman—and renders her invisible (and less potent?) when the tattoo is concealed under clothing. The veil's multivalent essence is an aspect Erich Neumann appreciated, although he would choose to read the veil as a mantle. There exist, he pointed out, "numerous (Christian) mantle Madonnas sheltering needy mankind beneath their outstretched cloaks" (Neumann [1955] 1963, 331).[2]

However, with respect to Our Lady of Guadalupe, Chicana activist-feminist scholar Angie Chabram-Dernersesian would take issue with that positive reading of the cloak's meaning, injecting, instead, her opinion that the mantle constricts and inhibits *la Virgen's* potential to act (Chabram-Dernersesian 1992, 91). In support of her position, she invokes the now-canonic renditions of *la Guadalupana* by such Chicana visual artists as Yolanda López and Ester Hernández. Referring to López's 1978 portrait of Victoria F. Franco, a painting of López's own grandmother, Chabram-Dernersesian characterizes it as "a full length reproduction of an *abuelita* (grandmother), proudly sitting on top of the Guadalupe cloak," adding that the subject exudes "dignity, strength and endurance" (1992, 91). Her characterization of Hernández's memorable etching and aquatint print—entitled *La Virgen de Guadalupe Defendiendo los Derechos de los Xicanos (The Virgin of Guadalupe Defending the Rights of Chicanos,* 1975)—is unequivocal with respect to the cumbersome cloak:

In the portrait by Hernández, which frequently carries the name
"The Militant Guadalupe," a Chicana breaks out of tradition with
a karate kick, shedding the oppressive cloak and motionless stance
of the Catholic Virgin whose hands and legs are bound by the dic-
tates of religious rituals. [1992, 91]

fig 22   Yolanda M. López, *Victoria F. Franco: Our Lady of Guadalupe* (1978),
oil pastel on paper, 32" x 24." Photo: Yolanda M. López.

An interesting and possibly not unexpected source for many earlier misgivings about the Virgin's efficacy as proactive mediator—and one contemporary with *la Morenita*'s apparitions in 1531—is a colloquy by the Dutch scholar, Desiderius Erasmus of Rotterdam. First printed in August 1523 in a Swiss edition, "The Shipwreck" has been criticized for "being irreverent in certain passages dealing with the invocation of saints and the Virgin Mary"[3] (Erasmus 1965, 139).

Not at odds with Chabram-Dernersesian's feminist projections onto *la Morenita*'s clothing, Erasmus, too, philosophizes in some detail regarding vestments in his day. His "The Well-to-do Beggars" colloquy, first printed in Switzerland in 1524, contains many thoughts surrounding the clothing of native peoples in "lands (then) recently discovered" (Erasmus 1965, 203), one of the few allusions in the *Colloquies* to the Americas. One protagonist, an innkeeper, comments that "some boast that their dress was divinely revealed to them in advance by the Virgin Mother" (215).[4] Lastly, Anselm, a protagonist from "The "Exorcism" (or "The Specter") colloquy—first published in Switzerland in 1524—anticipates the tenor of what we shall say below concerning the Native American "Ghost Shirt." Anselm's pronouncement concerns the Franciscan habit: "Long ago—before a Franciscan cowl became so formidable—people used to protect themselves against harmful demons by this armor" (Erasmus 1965, 233).

The relevance of Erasmus's thinking to our work cannot be underestimated, especially acknowledging, as well we must, the considerable extent to which Erasmus influenced Bishop Juan de Zumárraga, the church official to whom Juan Diego brought news of the apparitions, and, ultimately, the miraculous image on his *tilmatli* (Stoetzer 1979, 32).

Not unlike the dichotomous parameters of veiling and unveiling are those of absence and presence. For although the Virgin's visual incarnation is read as her enduring presence, she remains physically intangible and absent. From *la Guadalupana*'s late Amerindian apparitions through popular present-day devotions in her name, our study is informed by an underlying thread of paradox.

III. A Paño's Encoded Revelations: Her Presence in Her Absence (A Handkerchief's Own Lament Unfolds)

The white-tinted surface of an ordinary, mass-produced cotton-and-polyester handkerchief proffers Pepe Baca's resonant "Repentance" (1990), drawn in shades of gray, black, red, and green inks. A work on cloth—an ex-*pinto*'s *paño*[5] from Albuquerque resident Rudy Padilla's collection—foregrounds antithetical notions of presence and absence. Conspicuous in the *paño*'s composition is the depiction of an aura or stylized *mandorla* enveloping a devout, weeping female. Although the Virgin of Guadalupe is iconically absent from the rendering, she is synecdochically present through the radiance/sunburst that traditionally "clothes" her image and in the inclusion in the background of her crucified son. Interestingly, the repentant subject, a remorseful *pinto* signified in the *paño*'s title, is also absent from the drawing, but seemingly not from his *compañera*'s (companion's) memory, as her expressed grief implies. Another plausible interpretation, not at all inconsistent with the first, would contend that the previously cited aura might allude as well to "the disturbances of nature when Our Lord died," dramatized in New Mexico in the ceremony of *las tinieblas* (the Tenebrae), observed during Holy Week ceremonies by *Los Hermanos Penitentes de la Tercera Orden de San Francisco* (The Penitent Brothers of the Third Order of St. Francis) (Rael 1967, 10, 15–16). In this more specific context, the wailing woman herself becomes the present mourner/penitent. A *paño*'s very utility is deduced and reinforced through connotations of a lamentation or allegorical *pietà*.

Artist Pepe Baca's own intentionality doesn't preclude or necessarily supersede other readings of his work such as those suggested above. In fact, he had his own mother and wife in mind—the latter represented grieving—together with *la Guadalupana*. But he didn't consciously strive to elicit *la Virgen*. When told by Rudy Padilla of this interpretation, Baca was pleased to learn that his *paño* was indeed communicating something he had in mind, but about which the *paño* itself was silent. What is *absent* for one viewer is virtually *present* for another. The *presence/absence* dichotomy assumes the function of an overarching trope or Nahua *difrasismo* throughout this paper. It echoes Nuevomexicana playwright Denise Chávez's reflection concerning the "exit" of her birth mother, and the "entry" of her spiritual mother:

> When I *lost* my mother
> I *found* my mother.[6]

IV. A Picture In So Many Words: Nahua *Difrasismo* Renders Guadalupe's Emblematic Presence

The *lost/found* duality and the *presence/absence* couplet are arguably conceived in the tradition of Nahua *difrasismo*. Concerning this stylistic trait of the Nahuatl language, the distinguished scholar of the Aztecs, Miguel León-Portilla, quotes his own teacher, the eminent Nahua studies pioneer, Angel María Garibay K., who writes: "It (*difrasismo*) is a procedure in which a single idea is expressed by two words, either because they are *synonymous* or because they are placed next to each other" (León-Portilla [1963] 1990, 75).

Garibay underscores the contextual and metaphorical character of the *difrasismo*, while León-Portilla suggests that antonymous couplets are not precluded in the envelope of *difrasismo*. Consider that the Nahua *tlamatinime* (sages) "conceived the most profound of all of their *difrasismos*, (in the guise of)

Ometecuhtli-Omecíhuatl, Lord and Lady of duality" (99). That duality itself encapsulates the fundamental duality of opposite genders. No less basic is another pair of opposites: night and day. In that temporal synapse between them, so many "words" render a "picture."

The Nahua *difrasismo* of *presence/absence* or *visibility/invisibility* maps or illuminates that very point in time on Saturday, December 9, 1531, when *la Virgen* first appeared to Juan Diego. This linguistic projection is rooted in the important work of Clodomiro L. Siller-Acuña, a contemporary theologian and anthropologist who combines his academic work in anthropology with extensive pastoral work as a priest among the indigenous peoples of Mexico. In turn, his work informs the feminist scholarship of Ecuadorian theologian, Jeanette Rodríguez, in her book, *Our Lady of Guadalupe: Faith and Empowerment Among Mexican-American Women* (1994). Their joint insights prove instructive for our purposes:

> For the indigenous, *muy de madrugada*[7] (very early in the morning) referred not only to daybreak, but to the beginning of all time. Our Lady of Guadalupe appears early in the morning, just as the *day* is coming out of *darkness* and *night*. This meaningful time defined the Guadalupe event as fundamental, equal in significance to the origin of the world and the cosmos. [Rodríguez 1994, 36, 38]

V. Guadalupe's Emblematic Presence "Sews" Community of the Many Faithful

Might the aforementioned linguistically-defined temporal parameters—night's end and morning's beginning, which render the Virgin of Guadalupe incarnate—also suggest the emergence of an "innocent" or "just" world where racial differences are negligible, where men and women are viewed as brothers and sisters through the "vision" or spiritual guidance of the Virgin? Interestingly, that theological argument finds affirmation in ancient Jewish wisdom:

> It was an ancient rabbi who asked his students how they could tell when night had ended and day was on its way back.
> "Could it be when you see an animal in the distance and can tell whether it is a sheep or a dog?"
> "No," answered the rabbi.
> "Could it be when you look at a tree in the distance and can tell whether it is a fig tree or a peach tree?
> "No."
> "Well, then," the students demanded, "when is it?"

"It is when you look on the face of any man or woman and see that she or he is your brother or sister. Because if you cannot do that, then no matter what time it is, it is still night."[8]

More compelling theological affirmation for this view rests with New Mexico-based theologian, Megan McCinna, who would have Guadalupe bridging differences between Anglos and Hispanics residing in the Southwest:

> In the Southwest, Guadalupe has come to symbolize what happens when the Anglos and the Hispanics come together. Somehow a new people has to be born out of the two cultures, the two races, the two languages, the two ways of perceiving reality, matriarchy and patriarchy. She will be a bridge that pulls them together. She'll be the symbol of what they might become. [Garritano and Sonnenberg 1989]

That the Virgin of Guadalupe is possessed of a unique aura that would galvanize people to put aside their differences and make of themselves kindred spirits is the auspicious possibility that another thinker, Chicano theologian Virgilio Elizondo, foregrounds in his book, *La Morenita: Evangelizer of the Americas* (1980). Envisioning a greater interracial role for *la Guadalupana,* Chicana sociologist Irene I. Blea explains that Chicana/os active in the Catholic church "would like (Our Lady of Guadalupe) to be more fully incorporated into religious services outside the Chicano community" (Blea 1992, 112). And, yet, ironically enough, it would seem that the emergent widespread popularity of the Virgin of Guadalupe—to near cult-like proportions—has taken root in New Mexico outside of ecclesiastical circles. Those circumstances would not, however, surprise religious studies researcher, Alberto L. Pulido, who argues—from the vantage of Texan and New Mexican contexts—that "Mexican American religious symbolism . . . is best described as 'non-official' or 'popular' religiosity that originated from within the laity, separate from the hierarchy of the Roman Catholic Church, and remains outside the structures of institutional Catholicism" (Pulido 1993, 93).

To argue that *la Guadalupana* "sews" community among the many faithful is to posit what she has come to mean *today* versus her meanings *yesterday*—another instance of *difrasismo.* Her contemporary presence might well be somewhat at odds with her past presence. What was highly conspicuous in her makeup of the past might be absent or subtle in her present guise. From the philosophical and theological perspective of two Brazilian proponents of liberation theology:

> The historic figure Mary must enter into dialogue with the time, the space, the culture, the problems, and the actual persons that

relate to that figure.... Each period in history seems to build an
image of Mary and her activity in history both past and present.
[Gebara and Bingemer 1989, xi]

   Virgilio Elizondo's invocation of *la Morenita* is certainly consonant with
Teatro Campesino (Farmworker Theatre) group member Yolanda Parra's singu-
larly uncompromising nationalistic portrayal of her as "an *india* . . . hardcore
stone-ground Mexican Indian . . . because there is a certain amount of ovaries that
go into that part. You're talking the guts of the Universe there" (Broyles 1990, 171).
Yet today's conception of *la Guadalupana* might actually betray a diminished
color consciousness. That is not to mean that the Yolanda Parras among us are
fewer. Rather, in the vein of our presence/absence trope, some choose to see the
presence of color from a hubristic perspective, while others no less reverent find
that color is inconsequential, absent for all intents and purposes from the spiritual experience. Perhaps such instances of ambivalence about the strict ethnic
identity of so important a religious symbol should be no less surprising than the
imminent obsolescence of the sacred *tilmatli* garments threatened to be replaced
among native populations by the *sarape* (Lechuga 1982, 176–177).
   Juan Diego's emblematic *tilmatli* is certainly our tether to the Virgin of

fig 23   *Frank Alderete with '59 Chevy* (1986). From the series "VSJ/Scenes from
an Urban Chicano Experience, Albuquerque, N.M." Selenium-toned
chlorobromide photograph. Photo: Miguel Gandert.

Guadalupe's past, and the ensuing discussion of selected artifacts is our review of contemporary New Mexican perceptions of the Virgin: (a) rendered on clothing and/or clothing accessories; (b) rendered on cloth functioning other than as clothing apparel; (c) inscribed directly on human skin; or (d) rendered in media other than cloth and/or skin, but somehow intrinsically related to our *tilmatli* paradigm. Both men and women of different ethnicities are drawn to depict her. She is a thread that binds in New Mexico.

VI. Threads of Old Still Bind Today: Guadalupe's Emblematic Presence Endures in *Nuevo México*

Tellingly, what is seemingly one of the first documented references to an image of *la Virgen de Guadalupe* in New Mexico elicits an image on cloth as described in testimony given by the Spanish colonist, Don Diego de Vargas, who reconquered the area in the late seventeenth century. Resonating with something approaching Juan Diego's own dramatic presentation of his *tilmatli* to Bishop Juan de Zumárraga, de Vargas recounts his audience with Indian leader Don Luis Picurí on Monday afternoon, September 15, 1692: "He showed me a small silver image of Christ, and a small piece of silk, which had stamped on it the image of Our Lady of Guadalupe, which he was holding in both hands" (de Vargas 1940, 102–103).

(a) Guadalupana Renderings on Clothing and Apparel Accessories: Prologue is Epilogue

Los Matachines, a dance celebrating the birth of Christ, dates to the time of the first Franciscan missionaries in New Mexico. Utilizing costume items adorned with the image of Guadalupe—including the *cupil,* a miter-like headdress—the Pueblo Indians and Hispanos who engage in this annual festivity acknowledge the Virgin's interethnic significance and centrality in the dramatization of her son's life (Champe 1983, 5, 89; Espinosa 1985, 225). Furthermore, the perennial nature of this dance attests to its uninterrupted popularity across centuries.

Contemporary lowriders—known primarily for their low-slung, close-to-the-ground, custom-built and -designed *ranflas* (vehicles)—recognize *la Guadalupana* as their patron saint and talisman. Often, they sport commercially manufactured T-shirts, in black or white cotton, emblazoned with her image. These T-shirt designs differ considerably from the traditional rendition of *la Guadalupana* on Juan Diego's *tilmatli,* however. In one contemporary design, she is not posed in prayer, but carries one of her subjects, apparently lifeless, in her arms. Above and below this *reina* (queen), a caption reads: *Mi vida está/en tus manos* (My life is/in your hands). Her intercession is respectfully petitioned. The *barrio* or neighborhood is implicit in the calligraphic style of the lettering, recalling graffiti or *plaqueasos,* the contemporary and encoded language of the streets (Romotsky and Romotsky 1976).

Understandably, the iconography leads one to conflate lowriders, *pandilleros* (gang members), and the inevitable violence associated with our present-day urban "lived realities." Likened to a *pietà*, the image connotes lamentation and remembrance. Given that many of the barrio's victims are mere children, we are reminded of the work of Ester Hernández and Yolanda López as well as of Gonzalo Carrasco's animated Mexican oil paintings of *La Virgen de Guadalupe (defendiendo) a la niñez mexicana* (The Virgin of Guadalupe (defending) Mexican Youth, ca. 1933). These unusual depictions from the Iglesia de la Compañía (Church of the Company) in the city of Puebla relate a combat between *la Morenita* and a host of anthropomorphic dragons from whose apparent threat six children are rescued. Past and present perceptions of the Virgin emerge congruent; epilogue becomes prologue.

Lynne Wallace was raised a Calvinist in New England. When she and her husband relocated to the Southwest, they chose to live in the north valley of Albuquerque. Today, she resides in Placitas. Over time, she has reflected on her religion and on her identity as a woman. Prior to 1994, she stamped the image of the Virgin of Guadalupe "as a talisman" on the pocket of a favorite shirt (Wallace 1994). Lynne has found her interaction with *la Guadalupana* "a continuing process of getting to know her." She admits to being unfamiliar with the latter designation for the Virgin. Furthermore, Lynne is "confused" by the use of certain words, like Virgin, in her naming. A victim of abuse by her own father, a minister, Lynne finds refuge in "the concept of a new (for her) spirit in religion which reclaims the sacredness of the female."

Lynne was drawn to Albuquerque's Clothesline Project in the summer of 1994. A brochure from the Project (n.d.) explains:

> The Clothesline Project is a group of people from all backgrounds. We stand together committed to challenging our outward and internalized homophobia, racism, and sexism and other oppressions. We make the connections between these violences and the violence we experience as women.

The publication adds:

> The Clothesline Project is a visual display that bears witness to the violence against women. During the public display, a clothesline is hung with shirts. Each shirt is decorated to represent a particular woman's experience, by the survivor herself or by someone who cares about her.

The project, which began as a display of thirty-one shirts in Hyannis, Massachusetts in fall 1990, moved Lynne to fashion another shirt portraying *la*

Guadalupana as her witness, once again stamping her image on a pocket from which the Virgin has a commanding view of much of the garment. A superimposed, silhouetted black cross suggests Guadalupe's own maternal sorrow and pain, or, not implausibly, given the context, her own crucifixion. Choosing a long-sleeved, blue-denim shirt—blue signifying female survivors of incest or child sexual abuse—

fig 24   Guadalupana T-shirt "My Life Is In Your Hands." Guadalupana carries lifeless homeboy. Photo: Miguel Gandert.

fig 25   Gonzalo Carrasco, S. J. One half of a diptych, *La Virgen de Guadalupe (defendiendo) la niñez mexicana* (The Virgin of Guadalupe [defending] Mexican Youth) (ca. 1933). In the accompanying panel, La Virgen keeps a menacing, dragon-like creature at bay. Photo: Ludwig Iven.

Lynne painted somber raindrops ("teardrops") and menacing red lightning bolts ("anger bolts") along the full length of the front of the shirt. At the hemline, she added in red paint the textual inscription: "danger." Between button holes along the length, we read in stark black a searing admonition: "It only hurts when I cry." In sharp contrast, the word "HOPE" appears hand-lettered in upper-case characters along the inside of the collar, where stars also appear, inspired by Guadalupe's own cloak. The arrangement of the sleeves—resembling fetters—raised chest-level and tied tightly together with red fabric, are also a reference to "images of Guadalupe (in which) her hands seem tied." That rendition "seemed an apt metaphor for the emotional knots stemming from abuse" (Wallace 1994). While the vestment liberated Lynne in a symbolic sense, she nonetheless memorializes her painful memories from which there is no escape.

In the instance of Juan Diego's presentation of his *tilmatli* to the Bishop, the image of the Virgin of Guadalupe testifies for herself and to the fact that she did appear to this humble Aztec. In Lynne's artifact, the Virgin also testifies, not for herself, but on behalf of abused women everywhere, a contemporary crisis of staggering proportions. Lynne and the other participants in The Clothesline Project "transform(ed) individual stories into public narratives," the very objective behind artist Peggy Diggs's "(The) Domestic Violence Project," exhibited in 1992 at New York City's Alternative Museum, and her "Sex Bias Shirt Project" of 1993. Through these women's efforts, the private (act) becomes public (knowledge). The public nature of this art is "based not on where it is, but on what it does" (Phillips 1995, 286–289, 307–308).

Religious jewelry and related objects reflecting on *la Morenita* are fashioned by two Albuquerque artists, Chicana Goldie García and Margot Radaelli. Goldie, who grew up on South Broadway in Albuquerque, attended the University of New Mexico and later Harvard. Goldie is not only a jewelry-maker; her business card also identifies her as a "professional comic/speaker." There may indeed be a touch of whimsy in the materials she uses to enthrone Guadalupe: bottle caps and jar tops. As we listen to Goldie and look more closely at her work, however, we come to understand her sobering and controversial thoughts. The bottle tops are Budweiser-made, and, in her view, beer companies and Catholicism have both conspired to "keep people down" (García 1993). And yet consider how the design of the beer bottle cap's recessed interior suggests the Virgin's *esplendor*. The use of glitter has become Goldie's trademark. Here, she generously sprinkles it on cut-outs from chromolithographic sources, defining spectral compositions superimposed on *la Morenita*. The caps and jar tops function as refrigerator magnets, car "medallions," and apparel pins. Pierced earrings in which Guadalupe's icon peers through stars and glitter are signed by the artist on the image's obverse side. Having marched often as a child in feast-day celebrations of Our Lady of Guadalupe, Goldie finds a commercializing tendency at play, and thinks *la Morenita* assumes the status of a "pop icon." Goldie García prices her work reasonably because she wants her community to have access to it (García 1993). That gesture is certainly in keeping with Guadalupe's own charity, bestowed initially on Juan Diego.

(b) *Guadalupana* Renderings on Cloth Grounds other than Vestments: Sewing *Prómesas*

Margot Radaelli recycles fabric from Guatemalan *huipiles,* the loose-fitting blouses with sacred connotations for the Maya (see Note 4) and uses the fabric to wrap fragments of ordinary wooden window louvers. Shaping two of these cloth-covered louvers into a cross, she then affixes religious medallions and pieces of chromolithographic cards depicting *la Morenita,* Juan Diego, and scenes from apparitions of *la Guadalupana.* Radaelli adds brass fittings to the ends of the crossed members, imbuing them with the aspect of "rich Mexican gold" (Radaelli 1993). Radaelli has come to appreciate veneration of Guadalupe as both a process and an event because of *la Virgen's* ability to engage in and promote community solidarity. Currently, Radaelli is doing what she calls "Pueblo crosses," though she appears to be falling prey to what Ramón A. Gutiérrez characterizes as "the confabulation of Pueblo prayer-sticks with the cross" (Gutiérrez 1991, 82–3).

If Margot Radaelli is correct in her assessment that *la Morenita* builds community, it should come as little surprise that her spirit should smite the African

fig 26   Goldie García. Guadalupana bottle caps. Photo: Miguel Gandert.

fig 27   Margot Radaelli. Guadalupana cross. Photo: Miguel Gandert.

American fiber artist, Peggy Randolph. *Hail Mammy* (1993) is Randolph's mixed-media tribute to *la Guadalupana* shaped in fabric, including African textiles, found objects, tin cans, and votive candles. The work's title conflates a "mammy" with the virgin. The former is a term of familiarity, used particularly by children in the southern regions of the United States. A mammy/mammie refers to an African American nurse who cares for white children. The shrine Peggy has built is a kind of synthesis or bricolage of crèche and niche arrangements that she finds nurturing and has often encountered in New Mexico (Randolph 1993). Likewise, she's seen *la Morenita* widely venerated in the area. Along her fabric *esplendor,* Peggy has inscribed her *ofrenda:* "Hail Mammy/Full of Grace/Blessed Art Thou/ Among Women/and the Fruit of Thy Womb/Chil'ren." The Virgin of Guadalupe's angel—that nearly obligatory pendant icon—has ascended and takes on the identity of a black angel, seen hovering over Mammy's head. Mammy's breasts, turned into globes, carry suspended heart *milagros,* offerings made to beget a miracle.

Fabric roses and a cactus pad complete the sculpted environment. Mammy and Guadalupe are one.

A vow or *promesa* (Wroth 1991, 39) to *la Morenita* is an act of faith without bounds. It is a solemn promise made to the Virgin for her divine intervention in human affairs. Just as Gonzalo Carrasco painted children being rescued from monsters by *la Guadalupana,* so a promissory petition can secure a child's rescue from a threatening illness. In return, the mother can quilt *la Morenita* a thank you. Santa Fe fiber artist Vicki Chávez did exactly that. Her son, Andrew, was eleven when diagnosed with a serious illness. Vicki promised the Virgin a quilt upon Andy's recovery (Chávez 1993). *La Promesa* (*The Promise*) is machine sewn with metallic threads, evolved from a simple line drawing, and was completed in December 1992. Measuring 48x42 inches, this striking paean in cloth to Our Lady is largely fashioned of cotton with strips of lamé utilized for the *esplendor.* Additionally, cotton batting is used as a filler. Cloaked in rich blue and lavender, *la Morenita* is levitated by an energetic, upright, and dark-complexioned angel, whose outreach seems to propel her to greater heights, as is more the custom in Nuevomexicano *retablos* (panel paintings) than in Mexican prototypes. Nearly suspended against a densely starred sky, and framed within a flower-studded, niche-like canopy, *la Morenita* and her shrine are themselves enveloped by a border with a *millefleurs*-like design. Enthroned, the Virgin wears a salient orange lamé crown, further linking her quilted image to the New Mexican *santero* tradition. *La reina de mi corazón* (*The Queen of My Heart*) was Vicki's subsequent tribute to *la Morenita.* Executed in 1993, this quilted depiction, measuring 24x30 inches, also originated in a drawing done in white chalk. Vicki wanted "to achieve color and brightness" in this bust-length portrait (Chávez 1993). Between her foregrounded hands held in an attitude of prayer and a nearly "electric" *esplendor*—again shaped in gold lamé with metallic threads—*la Morenita* shows her compassionate face to engage the reverential viewer. Two strips of cloth, one red with a profusion of white dots and a second checkered band in black and white, enclose her portrait. Again, a *millefleurs*-like outermost layer frames the composition.

Vicki explains her method of working as a layering process that begins with the icon's face. In a more recent quilted offering, Vicki has portrayed Juan Diego wearing the emblematic *tilmatli.* A halo surrounds his head, and an *esplendor* echoing the Virgin's own encompasses the whole fabric composition in a visually stunning luminosity rivaling that described in the apparitions. The legendary roses that have just fallen out of the cloak appear in relief at Juan Diego's feet. The artist's palette is nothing short of a rainbow.

We can appreciate the link that a quilt has to clothing. To the extent that people cover themselves with quilts, these unique objects assume the function of virtual clothing. More to the point, however, is an acute observation advanced by Jane Przybysz, a scholar in performance studies: "That many quilts are useful objects made from partial objects, scraps of fabric and scraps of clothing that might be understood metonymically as scraps of skin or scraps of bodies, suggests that quilts are to quilters what charms are to the sorceress" (Przybysz 1993, 170). Virtual clothing aside, Vicki's quilts have certainly been her charm or talisman, answering her prayer.

In Albuquerque, Angela Aragón made her *promesa* to *la Morenita* in 1989,

fig 28 Peggy Randolph. *Hail Mammy* (1993), mixed media.
Photo: Miguel Gandert.

following an accident that left Angela incapacitated (Aragón 1994).[9] In gratitude for restoring her health, Angela offered to make a *colcha* (coverlet/tapestry) embroidery in *homenaje* (homage) to Our Lady. A homemade, embroidered coverlet, often used as a tapestry, this *colcha* was in process from 1989 to 1991. Finished in December 1991, it measures over six feet in height, and is between forty-two and forty-eight inches wide. On an expansive surface of white muslin, the Virgin is the most command-

fig 29   Vicki Chávez. *La promesa* (1992), quilt. Photo: Jerry Chávez.

fig 30   Vicki Chávez. *La reina de mi corazón* (1993), quilt. Photo: Jerry Chávez.

ing image, accompanied by Juan Diego, whose *tilmatli* receives the fabled roses. For Angela, the setting she depicts with cacti and heavenly canopy recalls northern New Mexico's *llano*, the very same terrain in which Antonio Luna Márez—Rudolfo Anaya's protagonist from the now canonic Chicano novel, *Bless Me, Ultima* (1972)— "expected" to encounter Our Lady. Echoing written descriptions of the Mexican *tilmatli*, Angela's *colcha* is both embroidered and painted. Angela added beads and sequins, and hues range from turquoise blue to pinks and reds. Embroidering since her early childhood, the artist has received considerable attention for her accomplished work. The *colcha* has been exhibited on Our Lady's feast days and on the occasion of New Mexico's State Fair.

Gary Valerio from Española, New Mexico, is a thirty-four-year-old *pinto* (inmate) at the New Mexico State Prison, serving a third sentence.[10] He was already behind bars when his infant son was shaken to death by his own grandmother. Grief-stricken over his profound loss and guilt-ridden that he was not free to intervene, Gary dedicated a moving pillow-case *paño* to his son's memory (Valerio 1994). *La Morenita* is the focal image in this mournful cloth *ofrenda.* Compositionally, the black-ink-on-white rendering mirrors elements derived from both the Mexican tradition as well as from local and regional *santero* traditions. Conspicuous decorative roses and highly animated angels are borrowed from both sources. The banderoles with the inscription "In Loving Memory of My Son" would appear to derive more from the Spanish/Mexican iconographic traditions. The injection of an agitated Christ and the calligraphic words *Amor* (Love) and *Hijito* (Son/Sonny) are more in keeping with the vocabularies of contemporary murals, *paños,* and tattoos, while the praying hands are a universal image. A diminutive Juan Diego with open *tilmatli* looks up at *la Morenita;* she appears to gaze back in his direction. Below his figure, a scroll contains a fragment of inspirational text from Psalm 23, "The Divine Shepherd/A Psalm of David."

(c) *Guadalupana* Renderings Inscribed on Skin: Perpetual Talismanic Power Invested in the Body

Pablino Vásquez's back—understood as human/first skin in contrast to the second skin afforded by cloth/fabric—is emblazoned with a full-length *Guadalupana* tattoo, no less impressive than his 31½ x 20½-inch bedsheet rendering of *la Morenita.* Both incorporate the roses associated with Guadalupe's iconographic program as well as textual references alongside the images. *Plaqueaso*-like letters accompany the tattoo, while a not-so-bold script is incorporated into the cloth rendering. *"Viva mi rasa [sic] querida"* (Long Live My Beloved People) and "Chicano Power" are invoked on fabric, and exclaim/proclaim the very sentiments of *orgullo* (pride) that challenge Ronald L. Grimes's mistaken notion that "for Santa Feans, Our Lady of Guadalupe does not have the qualities which would inspire a Chicano militant like César Chávez to carry her banner in protest to a state capital" (Grimes [1976] 1992, 243). César is dead, but his combative spirit and faith live on in Chicanos like Pablino, who describes Guadalupe as "a good saint that I like; (who will) help me with my drawing" (Vásquez 1994). Even Pablino's angel at *la Morenita*'s feet is given a *cholo*'s (hip, urban, Pachuco-like Chicano dude's) hairstyle, his *Virgen* is made-up with a beauty mark, and her *esplendor* is highly stylized—a crossover between cloth and tattoo imagery. Evidently, Pablino enjoyed glamorizing his empowering *Morenita.*

In the person of Pablino Vásquez one might recall a particularly resonant acrylic-on-canvas painting by Texas painter César Augusto Martínez, *Hombre que le gustan las mujeres* (*A Man Who Likes Women*) (1986). Writing about the tattooed man depicted in that work, Chicana artist-writer Amalia Mesa-Bains might well have been describing Pablino, himself: "This is a man who loves women, a man to whom women are so central that he marks his body with them" (Mesa-Bains 1992, 98).

fig 31   Angela Aragón. *Our Lady of Guadalupe* (1991), mixed media.
        Photo: Miguel Gandert.

fig 32   Gary Valerio with pillowcase paño, *In Loving Memory of My Son* (1994).
Photo: Miguel Gandert.

Alberto Ramírez's back is also a "human canvas" for what is surely the most
remarkable tattoo Miguel Gandert and this author documented at the state penitentiary in Santa Fe. Reading like a *plaqueaso* caption, Alberto's surname appears
marquee-like at the foot (his waist) of a dense figurative and representational
"first skin" composition in whose midst, atop a high perch, rules a centrally placed

Guadalupana. A host of other figures, Amerindian and contemporary, are portrayed in her company: a pyramid, palm trees, a lowrider automobile, flowers, and phantom faces. The complex tattoo was done in 1991 in the *pinta* (prison) at Las Cruces, New Mexico by Mexico-born artist Pedro Aragón. Commenting on his tattoo, Ramírez describes the area around his shoulders as "paradise" and underscores the importance for him of his "ancient roots" (Ramírez 1994). He also wanted his tattoo to incorporate imagery he associated with the *veteranos* (older inmates). Some *paño* designs betray a similar kind of compositional density.

Smaller tattoos of *la Morenita* are worn by Rubén Chávez, Deputy Director of Outreach Services for Youth Development, Inc. in Albuquerque, and Gordy Anderson, an employee at the University of New Mexico. Chávez's tattoo, which appears on his right forearm, is a finely delineated portrait in the traditional Mexican idiom. Anderson, while not Latino, was raised a Catholic and has a deep respect for the faith's icons. Tattoo artist Jason Ward, a graduate of the University of New Mexico's Department of Art, did the diminutive *Morenita* on the large toe of Gordy's left foot. Having been injured on the left side of his body, Gordy decided, out of superstition, to be tattooed on the left (Anderson 1993).[11] A sacred-heart tattoo appears on the opposite big toe. The choice of *la Morenita* was based on how frequently Gordy saw others' tattoos of her and because she is

fig 33   Tattooed Pablino Vásquez posing with bedsheet *paños*.
Photo: Miguel Gandert.

part of the heritage of a culture in which he was brought up. Gordy means no disrespect to Our Lady by placing her image on his toe. Rather, as an Anglo, he didn't feel he should flaunt the image to which he relates. She is not his birthright, but he has adopted her as she once adopted Juan Diego. Gordy, who operated a tattoo parlor of his own between 1987 and 1988, is not without a sense of humor when it comes to tattoos. From her vantage on his toe, Gordy argues that *la Morenita* watches over him and his wife, whose image appears on the lower part of his left leg. (Anderson 1993). Recalling Cirlot's interpretation of the *esplendor* or *mandorla* of *la Virgen* as symbolic of the "intersection of the two spheres of heaven and earth" (Cirlot 1962, 194), not to mention the terrestrial connotations of Tonantzín,[12] we would have to regard Anderson's foot tattoo as standing on firm religious ground. Folklorist Alan Govenar, long interested in Chicano tattooing and tattooing in general, notes that "Christian designs are most numerous" in the Chicano context (Govenar 1988a and Govenar 1988b, 209).

(d) Divested of Fabric: Related *Guadalupana* Renderings in Various Media

Sam Vigil is the last of the *pinto* subjects. An inmate of the Santa Fe correctional facility since 1987, he is in his mid-forties. He has developed a repertory of crafted

fig 34   Detail of Alberto Ramírez's tattooed back. Tattoo by Pedro Aragón (1991). Photo: Miguel Gandert.

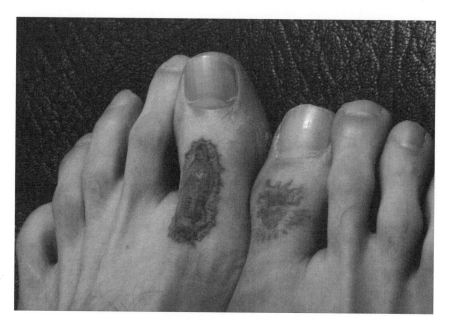

fig 35   Toe tattoo, *Our Lady of Guadalupe* by Jason Ward. Worn by Gordy
Anderson. Photo: Miguel Gandert.

items he makes and sells through the penitentiary's gift shop. Earrings, pins,
crosses, boxes, baby shoes, wishing wells, stage coaches, *ojos de dios* (talismanic
"eyes of God"), and even rocking chairs number among his creations. Using cig-
arette wrapping papers, other papers with Xeroxed patterns, or cut-up cards—
including religious chromolithographs made in Italy with a more or less Mexican
iconography—Sam sews and weaves intricate, dazzling pieces. Crafting his "nee-
dles" out of pieces of rescued plastic and adapting dental floss as "thread," he
creates his sundry forms. One pin, for example, shows a much-truncated chromolithographic portrait of *la Morenita* framed in a woven paper frame of Sam's making, which he fashioned into a wearable pin by attaching a commercial fastener.
Reflecting on his environment and his art, Vigil says that "prison is (his) salvation;
(it's) here (he) learned (his) art" (Vigil 1994).

It would seem that those making *promesas* do so believing that *la Morenita*
will protect them from whatever menace they face. Our Lady and other *santos*
function, in part, as talismans, as has already been demonstrated. *Agua bendita*
(holy water) is yet another magical potion. Clothing, too, can function that way
as we observed above in the context of Erasmus's *Colloquy*, "Exorcism"/"The
Specter," wherein Anselm recalls how a Franciscan cowl could, in the past,
protect one, armor-like, against harmful demons. Santa Fe multi-media artist

Pedro Romero created his own kind of armor in 1991. "New Mexico Ghost Shirt" is a mesmerizing, tableau-like piece realized in tin and fire-glazed clay, and currently owned by the Mongerson/Wunderlich Gallery in Chicago. A recessed box or niche-like environment calls attention to the Ghost Shirt's complex mosaic surface on which an intricate geometry of interlocking *tesserae* (mosaic pieces) distorts balance and perspective. A small ceramic guitar—inscribed with the artist's signature—occupies one corner, and, above it, a window-like opening affords a vista of the New Mexican *llano*. Enclosing this niche is a stamped tin garment, shaped, contoured, or silhouetted like the common T-shirt or poncho, and echoing the concept of the Madonna's protective mantle.

According to the artist, a "flight of fancy" or "whimsical observation" stemming from the guitar and the Nuevomexicano's love of music and dance are what inspired the title, "New Mexico Ghost Shirt" (Romero 1993), and Romero's link to the sacred Native American Ghost Dance and to Native American culture appears almost incidental—that is, until we probe more deeply. The Indian's ghost shirt "was firmly believed to be impenetrable to bullets or weapons of any sort" (Mooney [1896] 1973, 790), and "in some cases the fringe or other portions (of this shirt) were painted with the sacred red paint of the messiah" (790). Other ghost shirts "were fairly covered with representations of sun, moon, (and) stars" (790).

fig 36   Sam Vigil interviewed by Víctor Sorell, February 1994.
Photo: Miguel Gandert.

fig 37   Sam Vigil, Guadalupe pin. Photo: Miguel Gandert.

That a ghost shirt is intrinsically bound up with the ghost dance is a compli-cating factor because the dance is almost non-existent among the Pueblo Indians. Yet the ethnologist James Mooney, whose foregoing observations were made and published through the Smithsonian Institution during the last decade of the nine-teenth century, informs us that the Taos Pueblos did perform the dance as a pastime (Mooney [1896] 1973, 805, 926). A specialist on Native American music and dance, Lynn F. Huenemann adds that Taos Pueblo dances "share certain dance elements of the Plains tribes" (Huenemann 1992, 127). Cultural historian Vincent Scully also observes the intersection of Plains Indian and Pueblo elements—even invoking the ghost dance itself—in his analytical discussion of the Mescalero Mountain Spirit (Gahan) Dancers (Scully 1989, 361–364). Consider the implications for our study—when ghost shirts and Juan Diego's *tilmatli* are conflated—of two lines of lyrics from a Ghost Dance song: "Now the sun's beams are running out,/The sun's yellow rays are running out" (Highwater 1977, 173). Is night merely overtaking day, or is *la*

Morenita's esplendor losing its splendid luminosity as her charted appearance in that synapse between day and night is inexplicably eclipsed?

Mooney adds a very important qualification to his discussion of the ghost shirt: "The author is strongly inclined to the opinion that the idea of an invulnerable sacred garment is not original with the Indians. . . . It may have been suggested by the 'endowment robe' of the Mormons" (Mooney [1896] 1973, 790). Arguably, something akin to this alleged religious syncretism also triggered Romero's conscious or subliminal intention. Perhaps he wanted to introduce a Native American cultural overlay onto a work that is overtly Chicano through the *huelga* (strike) eagle of the United Farm Workers and, more importantly, the *con safo(s)* symbol "C/S," both of which appear stamped on the tin skin of the virtual T-shirt. Romero is given to calling this evocative work "Chicano Ghost Shirt." Given our preceding look at talismans, the concept of *con safo(s)* should resonate loudly. According to the late, witty, and eloquent Chicano writer, José Antonio Burciaga, the phrase translates literally as "with safety" (Burciaga 1993, 6). *Con safo(s)* means, above all, "anything you say against me will bounce back to you" (1993, 6). In one word, deflection.

Against the foregoing backdrop, which cast the Native American ghost shirt in bold relief, another work by Pedro Romero, *Our Lady of Guadalupe* (1993), is intriguing. Romero's Guadalupe appears without her ubiquitous angelic companion. She is clothed in a salmon-hued gown over which she wears a greenish cloak with ochre edging. The moon at her feet is black, and her *esplendor* ranges from off-white to brown. The T-shirt/ghost shirt/*tilmatli* amalgam, on which Our Lady is superimposed, is azure. All of this imagery is conceived in glazed ceramic and has been mounted on tin, which, in turn, is enclosed in a handsomely sculptured wooden frame. Be it T-shirt, ghost shirt, or residual/virtual *tilmatli*, the garment here assumes the almost metaphorical presence of an *hábito*, the habit of a saint sewn for and worn as a *habitito* (small nightshirt) by a child cured through the intercession of that saint.[13] Such tropes are even more plausible, considering Romero's interest in and study of Frida Kahlo's own use of dress imagery in her paintings.

Early on, a snippet of Denise Chávez's writing provided a *difrasismo* woven into the argument. Between 1986 and 1987, an interdisciplinary project spearheaded by Albuquerque-based ceramist, Sandi Roybal Maestas, and Taos-based weaver-painter, Juanita Jaramillo-Lavadie, also involved Denise as a playwright. Additional collaborators included Kika Vargas, an actress, and Patricia Vargas-Trujillo, a tinsmith. The project revolved around a *novena*, the act of reciting prayers on nine consecutive days, usually to seek some special favor and not unlike the practice of making *promesas*.

Denise's play, *Novenas narrativas y ofrendas nuevomexicanas (Novena Narratives and New Mexican OVerings)*, became the hub of the project (Chávez

fig 38   Pedro Romero, *New Mexico Ghost Shirt* (1991), mixed media.
Photo: Courtesy of Mongerson/Wunderlich Gallery, Chicago, Ill.

1988, 84–100). Maestas explains how her ceramic *"Nuestra Señora de Leche y Buen Parto"* (Our Lady of Abundant Milk and Easy Delivery)[14]—which becomes conflated with Our Lady of Guadalupe in the play's script—evolved in a dream: "My Lady came to me in a dream. That is how she came to look as she does— brown skin; singing; pregnant; hands in an open, receiving gesture; *contrapposto* as if she were marching forward with power" (Maestas 1994).

Sandi's *Morenita* "warrior" appears the earthy embodiment of an attitude about pregnancy and ensuing childbirth postulated by feminist anthropologist, Marta Weigle:

fig 39 S. R. Maestas and Patricia Vargas-Trujillo, *Nuestra Señora de leche y buen parto,* showing tin-and-brass *esplendor.* Photo: S. R. Maestas.

> There is need for a way of thinking strongly about birth, whether
> actual, ritual, or imaginative. The mothers, midwives, and gossips
> who think and act strongly about childbirth must be counted among
> the enablers of powerful symbolic processes. [Weigle 1989, 145]

Admittedly, this clay *Morenita* is first and foremost of this earth. Even her
beautiful cloak and startling tin and brass *esplendor* don't suggest her ascension.
She is completely terrestrial, and earth-bound she remains throughout the play's
nine different vignettes. In Maestas's words, she is "the thread that goes to make
the play cohesive and whole" (Maestas 1994). First performed by Kika Vargas on
February 1986 in Taos, the play revolves around nine females ranging in age from
seven to seventy-eight and "was inspired by cultural traditions of *cuentistas* (sto-
rytellers), *santeros* and *ofrendas* . . . as well as by *altares* (altars) and *nichos* (niches)
one finds in (New Mexican) family homes" (Chávez 1988, 85). At the outset of the
play, the set calls for "a tall chest, covered by a lace mantel (tablecloth/altar cloth)
on (which) stands a statue of *la Virgen de Guadalupe*" (87). One actress plays all
nine roles, though no two are really alike. Isabel, Jesusita, and Juana all sew.
Pauline Mendoza sports a tattoo of Our Lady of Guadalupe and, in a make-
believe dialogue, comments about *la Morenita's esplendor,* admitting to being "a
lady and a Chicana and an artist" (98). Corrine, a lesbian, also wears tattoos. María
and Jesús on her knuckles are reminders of time she served as a *pinta*. We, in turn,
are reminded of Ester Hernández's iconic silkscreen, *La ofrenda* (*The Offering*)
(1988–1989), in which a *chola* (hip, urban Chicana) sports a tattoo of *la Morenita*
being offered a rose. In her closing scene, Isabel speaks a line that encapsulates the
spirit of the whole play: "Each of our lives is a song, or a prayer, like a novena"
(Chávez 1988, 100). Juanita Jaramillo-Lavadie wove and embroidered the indigo
manta (coarse cotton cloth) together with the salmon-hued gown that clothed
Maestas's sculpture when it was incorporated into the play. Employing *paño* cloth,
Juanita wanted to exploit the nearly banal nature of cloth—cloth at its most
basic—relating to the essence of survival. "*Paño* as an everyday thing connected
with laughter and tears" (Maestas 1994). For Juanita, this project elicited connections with cloth woven in fulfillment of *promesas* and with *pintos' paños.*

Luis Jiménez, a highly gifted draftsman, painter, printmaker, and sculptor
from Hondo, New Mexico (his work enjoyed a splendid retrospective early in 1994
at The Albuquerque Museum), tried in vain to intervene on behalf of his dear
friend, Luis Carlos Bernal, the distinguished contemporary Chicano photographer from Arizona, when Bernal was ill. Jiménez's printed *ofrenda, Para Luis/For
Luis,* is a small 1992 lithograph that depicts a man with a tattoo of *la Morenita* on
his back, and the inscription *"para Luis Carlos"* (for Luis Carlos) appears within
a banderole. Beneath the banderole, the usual angel is replicated by the Mexican
national symbol of an eagle devouring a serpent atop a cactus pad. Unfortunately,

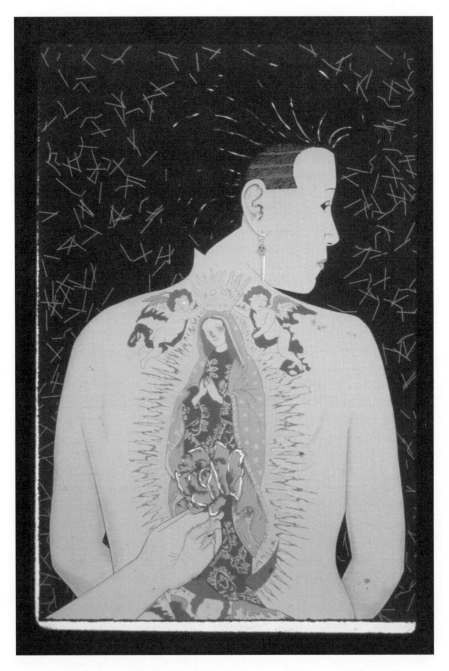

fig 40   Ester Hernández, *La ofrenda* (1988–1989), silkscreen, 33¼" x 23¼". National Chicano Screenprint Taller. Photo: Courtesy CARA Exhibition, Wight Art Gallery, UCLA.

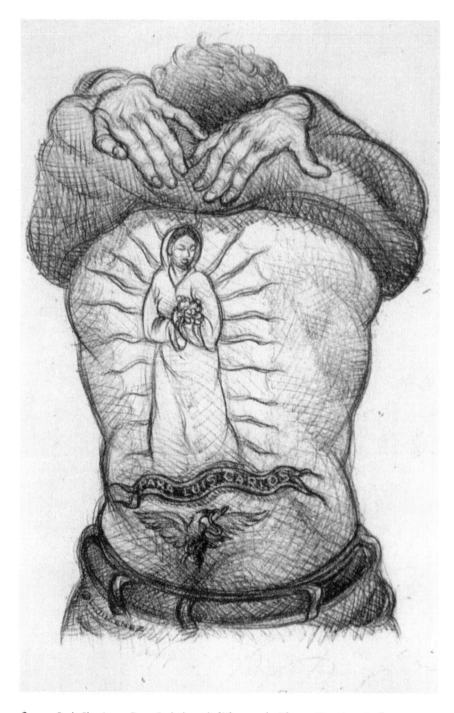

fig 41   Luis Jiménez, *Para Luis* (1992), lithograph. Photo: Damian Andrus.

Bernal did not recover from a long-term coma and was never able to see the *Morenita* offering made by his *tocayo* (namesake).

VII. Conclusion: Guadalupe's Emblematic Presence Endures in New Mexico

This highly selective investigation of the Virgin of Guadalupe's enduring emblematic presence in New Mexico has privileged and discussed in some detail a symbolic link between the Virgin's visual incarnation and the not-incidental context for its manifestation, Juan Diego's *tilmatli*. The emblematic medium of cloth extends to include skin and the human body.

I have also shown, to reiterate jeweler Goldie García's phrase, the extent to which Guadalupe assumes the guise of a "pop icon" in contemporary New Mexico. Furthermore, Guadalupe's recent popularity respects no strict ethnic boundaries and follows no particular gender.

The paper has also shown that perceptions of the Virgin are subject to change over time—both historically and metaphysically. Based on the evidence of artifacts, verbal testimony, and human behavior, however, it is conceivable that a contemporary lowrider could summon the attitude to wear his *Guadalupana* T-shirt with nothing less than the same true faith that Juan Diego invested in his sacred *tilmatli* well over four hundred years ago. The dramatic wonder that animated the miraculous apparitions in the sixteenth century translates into today's turbulent and cynical world as recognition for and belief in talismanic interventions of a higher order. To entrust one's own life to the Virgin's care (*"Mi vida está en tus manos"*) is to have insuperable faith in destiny and the unknown, to possess religious fervor. Such resolute faith in her presence endures in spite of Guadalupe's physical absence.

Notes

1. An *aztequismo,* this word—derivative of *áyatl,* meaning cloak made from *ixtle* or *maguey* fiber (Frances Karttunen, *An Analytical Dictionary of Náhuatl,* Austin, Tex., 1992, p. 16 [reprint of 1983 University of Oklahoma Press edition])—is, in the opinion of one expert, Enrique Graue y Díaz González, the most appropriate term by which to refer to Juan Diego's *tilmatli.* (See Enrique Graue y Díaz González, "La Tilma de Juan Diego," in *Album Conmemorativo del 450 aniversario de las apariciones de Nuestra Señora de Guadalupe,* eds. Fray Fidel de J. Chauvet, Luis Medina Ascensio, Enrique Graue y Díaz González, José Ignacio Conde y Díaz Rubín, María Teresa Cervantes de Conde, Ernesto de la Torre Villar, and Ramiro Navarro de Anda. [México: Ediciones Buena Nueva], 15).
2. An *alabado* from Cerritos, New Mexico, includes a stanza that invokes this mantle of refuge: *"Madre de la soledad, Madre de consolación, cobíjanos con tu manto..."* (Mother of solitude, Mother of consolation, cover us with your mantle) (Rael 1967, 100–101).

3. Of considerable and related interest is a stone monument shaped as a boat with sails and erected on one side of the staircase leading to the old chapel of Guadalupe on Tepeyac hill. According to an inscription, this *"Vela del Marino"* ("Sailor's Sail" or "Candle," if one considers the full narrative context) was placed to commemorate an actual shipwreck during a bad storm. Having invoked Our Lady of Guadalupe's name in view of their plight, the crew promised to bring to her sanctuary remnants of the boat if she saw them to safety. The badly damaged boat did reach safe haven in the port of Veracruz. The crew then carried the salvaged pieces of wood—all that remained of the vessel—and placed their offering inside a stone structure fashioned to protect it from the elements. (Escalada 1995, 723). I thank my friend and colleague, anthropologist John Hobgood, for bringing this narrative to my attention.

4. Weigh the innkeeper's words in relation to present-day Mayan ritual in Tenejapa, near San Cristóbal de Las Casas in the State of Chiapas, México. According to myth, the Virgin appeared in Lake Banabil and asked for a *huipil*—a garment enclosing a woman in a sacred space of its own making—and a skirt so that she could dress as a proper woman. Each year, a weaver is chosen to lead a procession of religious officials to Lake Banabil, where clothing is thrown into the water as an offering (See Walter F. Morris, *Living Maya*, [New York: Harry N. Abrams, Inc.], 137, 143).

5. Unless otherwise noted, this reference—acknowledging an ex-prison inmate's hand-kerchief—and all subsequent references to the dialect of Spanish spoken and written in New Mexico are taken from Rubén Cobos, *A Dictionary of New Mexico and Southern Colorado Spanish* (Santa Fe: Museum of New Mexico Press, 1983).

6. From Denise Chávez's *La Guadalupana: Images and Influences in New Mexico,* fifty-minute videorecording by Jerry Teale from the University of New Mexico of a paper presented at the Río Grande Institute Forum, Abiquiu, New Mexico, 11–12 November 1983.

7. Rodríguez italicizes this phrase taken from *"Nican Mopohua,"* (*Historia de las Apariciones de Nuestra Señora de Guadalupe,* 1552–1560?), a text attributed to Antonio Valeriano, and reproduced in *Testimonios históricos guadalupanos,* compiled with a Prologue, Biographical Notes, and Indices by Ernesto de la Torre Villar and Ramiro Navarro de Anda (México: Fondo de Cultura Económica, 1982).

8. I am grateful to the Reverend Kenneth Fleck, Associate Pastor of St. Barnabas Catholic Parish (in Chicago's southside Beverly community), who delivered this parable in his homily to his congregation on the occasion of Guadalupe's Feast day, December 12, 1997. His source for the "Love of Neighbor" parable is Reverend Paul J. Wharton, *Stories and Parables for Preachers and Teachers* (New York: Paulist Press, 1986), 26.

9. I wish to acknowledge the generosity and expertise of my friend, Jacqueline Dunnington, author of the definitive study of Guadalupe in New Mexico, *Viva Guadalupe! The Virgin in New Mexican Popular Art* (Dunnington 1997). It was through her that I met Aragón.

10. Valerio and eleven other *pintos* were interviewed at the penitentiary in Santa Fe on February 24, 1994. I am grateful to then-Warden John Thomas for his gracious help and am especially thankful for the crucial and unwavering support of Holly Haas, then a member of the education staff at the main facility. She was key in facilitating Miguel Gandert's and my access to the facility.

11. I am grateful to Vangie Samora for referring me to both Gordy and to fiber artist, Peggy Randolph.

12. "The association of the Virgin of Guadalupe with the *Mexican* goddess Tonantzín, though widely accepted, is open to question" (Poole 1995, 5, 9, 12, 215).

13. I am grateful to my wife, Ida Nasarita Guzmán-Sorell, for referring me to both the *hábito* and *habitito* garments and associated *costumbres* (customs) as she remembers them from growing up in the lower Río Grande valley of Texas.

14. Discussing the earliest shrines erected to Our Lady in the New World, author Peter Lappin mentions "a permanent Indian mission . . . established in Saint Augustine (Florida) . . . which included a shrine dedicated to *Nuestra Señora de la Leche* (Our Nursing Mother)" (See *First Lady of the World: A Popular History of Devotion to Mary* [New York: Don Bosco Publications, 1988), 121). He dates the shrine as early as 1620.

Literature Cited

Primary Sources

Anawalt, Patricia Rieff. 1981. *Indian Clothing Before Cortés: Mesoamerican Costumes From the Codices.* Norman: University of Oklahoma Press.

Anaya, Rudolfo A. 1972. *Bless Me, Ultima.* Berkeley, Calif.: Tonatiuh-Quinto Sol International Publishers.

Anderson, Gordy. 1993. Interview by the author and Miguel Gandert. Albuquerque, New Mexico, 27 July.

Aragón, Angela. 1994. Interview by the author and Miguel Gandert. Albuquerque, New Mexico, 24 June.

Barthes, Roland. 1972. *Critical Essays.* Translated by Richard Howard. Evanston, Ill.: Northwestern University Press.

Blea, Irene I. 1992. *La Chicana and the Intersection of Race, Class, and Gender.* Westport, Conn.: Praeger Publishers.

Broyles, Yolanda Julia. 1990. Women in El Teatro Campesino: '*Poco Estaba Molacha la Virgen de Guadalupe*'? In *Chicana Voices: Intersections of Class, Race, and Gender,* eds. Teresa Córdova, Norma Cantú, Gilberto Cárdenas, Juan García, and Christine M. Sierra, 162–187. Austin: University of Texas Center for Mexican American Studies, 1986. Reprint, Colorado Springs, Colo.: The National Association for Chicano Studies.

Burciaga, José Antonio. 1993. *Drink Cultura: Chicanismo.* Santa Barbara, Calif.: Capra Press/Joshua Odell Editions.

Chabram-Dernersesian, Angie. 1992. I Throw Punches for My Race, but I Don't Want to Be a Man: Writing Us—Chica-nos (Girl, US)/Chicanas—Into the Movement Script. In *Cultural Studies,* eds. Lawrence Grossberg, Cary Nelson, and Paula A. Treichler, 81–95. New York: Routledge, Chapman and Hall, Inc.

Champe, Flavia Waters. 1983. *The Matachines Dance of the Upper Río Grande: History, Music, and Choreography.* Lincoln: University of Nebraska Press.

Chávez, Denise. 1988. Novenas narrativas y ofrendas nuevomexicanas. In *Chicana Creativity and Criticism: Charting New Frontiers in American Literature,* eds. María Herrera-Sobek and Helena María Viramontes, 84–100. Houston: Arte Público Press.

Chávez, Vicki. 1993. Interview by author. Santa Fe, New Mexico, 18 November.

Cirlot, J. E. 1962. *A Dictionary of Symbols.* Translated by Jack Sage. New York: Philosophical Library, Inc.

De Vargas, Don Diego. 1940. *First Expedition of Vargas into New Mexico, 1692.* Translated by J. Manuel Espinosa. Coronado Cuarto Centennial Publications, 1540–1940, vol. 10, ed. George P. Hammond. Albuquerque: University of New Mexico Press.

Dunnington, Jacqueline O. 1997. *Viva Guadalupe! The Virgin in New Mexican Popular Art.* Santa Fe: Museum of New Mexico Press.

Eliade, Mircea. 1964. *Shamanism: Archaic Techniques of Ecstasy.* Translated by Willard R. Trask. New York: Pantheon Books.

Elizondo, Virgilio P. 1980. *La Morenita: Evangelizer of the Americas.* San Antonio. Tex.: Mexican American Cultural Center.

Erasmus of Rotterdam, Desiderius. 1965. *The Colloquies—1518–1531.* Translated by Craig R. Thompson. Chicago: The University of Chicago Press.

Escalada, Xavier, S.J., ed. 1995. *Enciclopedia (temática-histórica-onomástica) guadalupana.* 4 vols. México: Editorial a Todo Color, S.A. de C.V.

Espinosa, Aurelio M. 1985. *The Folklore of Spain in the American Southwest: Traditional Spanish Folk Literature in Northern New Mexico and Southern Colorado.* Edited by J. Manuel Espinosa. Norman: University of Oklahoma Press.

Freedberg, David. 1989. *The Power of Images: Studies in the History and Theory of Response.* Chicago: The University of Chicago Press.

García, Goldie. 1993. Interview by the author and Miguel Gandert. Albuquerque, New Mexico, 20 July.

Garritano, Sandy and Dale Sonnenberg, Producers. 1989. *La Fiesta de Guadalupe.* Segment for "Colores!," KNMET-TV Channel 5. Albuquerque, New Mexico, 26 December.

Gebara, Ivone and María Clara Bingemer. 1989. *Mary: Mother of God, Mother of the Poor.* Translated by Phillip Berryman. Maryknoll, N.Y.: Orbis Books.

Govenar, Alan. 1988a. Christian Tattoos. In *Tattootime, No. 2/Tattoo Magic,* ed. D. E. Hardy, 4–11. Honolulu, Hawaii: Hardy Marks Publications.

———. 1988b. The Variable Context of Chicano Tattooing. In *Marks of Civilization: Artistic Transformations of the Human Body,* ed. Arnold Rubin, 209–217. Los Angeles: Museum of Cultural History/UCLA.

Grimes, Ronald L. 1992. *Symbol and Conquest: Public Ritual and Drama in Santa Fe.* Ithaca, N.Y.: Cornell University Press, 1976. Reprint, Albuquerque: University of New Mexico Press.

Gutiérrez, Ramón A. 1991. *When Jesus Came, the Corn Mothers Went Away: Marriage, Sexuality, and Power in New Mexico, 1500–1846.* Stanford: Stanford University Press.

Highwater, Jamake. 1977. *Ritual of The Wind: North American Indian Ceremonies, Music, and Dances.* New York: The Viking Press.

Horn, Marilyn J. and Lois M. Gurel. 1981. *The Second Skin: An Interdisciplinary Study of Clothing.* 3rd ed. Boston: Houghton-Mifflin Co.

Huenemann, L. F. 1992. Northern Plains Dance. In *Native American Dance: Ceremonies and Social Traditions,* ed. Charlotte Heth, 127. Washington, D.C.: National Museum of the American Indian/Smithsonian Institution and Golden, Colo.: Fulcrum Publishing.

Lechuga, Ruth D. 1982. *El traje indígena de México: Su evolución, desde la época prehispánica hasta la actualidad.* México: Panorama Editorial, S.A.

León-Portilla, Miguel. [1963] 1990. *Aztec Thought and Culture: A Study of the Ancient Náhuatl Mind.* Translated by Jack Emory Davis. Norman: University of Oklahoma Press.

Maestas, Sandi Roybal. 1994. Interview by the author and Miguel Gandert. Albuquerque, New Mexico, 2 June.

Mesa-Bains, Amalia. 1992. The Real Multiculturalism: A Struggle for Authority and Power.

In *Different Voices: A Social, Cultural, and Historical Framework for Change in the American Art Museum,* ed. Michaelyn Mitchell, 86–100. New York: Association of Art Museum Directors.

Mooney, James. 1973. *The Ghost Dance Religion and Wounded Knee.* Washington, D.C.: U.S. Government Printing Office, 1896. Facsimile edition, New York: Dover Publications, Inc.

Neumann, Erich. [1955] 1963. *The Great Mother: An Analysis of the Archetype.* Translated by Ralph Manheim. New York: Bollingen Foundation/Pantheon Books.

Phillips, Margaret Mann. 1981. *Erasmus and the Northern Renaissance.* Woodbridge, Suffolk: Boydell Press, 1949. Revised and illustrated edition, Totowa, N.J.: Rowman and Littlefield.

Phillips, Patricia C. 1995. Peggy Diggs: Private Acts and Public Art. In *But Is It Art?: The Spirit of Art as Activism,* ed. Nina Felshin, 283–308. Seattle: Bay Press, Inc.

Poole, Stafford. 1995. *Our Lady of Guadalupe: The Origins and Sources of a Mexican National Symbol, 1531–1797.* Tucson: The University of Arizona Press.

Przybysz, Jane. 1993. Quilts and Women's Bodies: Dis-eased and Desiring. In *Bodylore,* ed. Katharine Young, 165–184. Knoxville: The University of Tennessee.

Pulido, Alberto L. 1993. Mexican American Catholicism in the Southwest: The Transformation of a Popular Religion. *Perspectives in Mexican American Studies* 4:93–108.

Radaelli, Margot. 1993. Interview by the author and Miguel Gandert. Albuquerque, New Mexico, 27 July.

Rael, Juan Bautista. 1967. *The New Mexican Alabado.* With transcription of music by Eleanor Hague. Stanford, Calif.: Stanford University Press, 1951. Reprint, New York: AMS Press, Inc.

Ramírez, Alberto. 1994. Interview by the author and Miguel Gandert. Santa Fe, New Mexico, 24 February.

Randolph, Peggy. 1993. Interview by the author and Miguel Gandert. Albuquerque, New Mexico, 12 July.

Rodríguez, Jeanette. 1994. *Our Lady of Guadalupe: Faith and Empowerment Among Mexican-American Women.* Austin: University of Texas Press.

Romero, Pedro. 1993. Interview by the author. Santa Fe, New Mexico, 17 November.

Romotsky, Jerry and Sally Romotsky. 1976. *Los Angeles Barrio Calligraphy.* Los Angeles: Dawson's Book Shop.

Scully, Vincent. 1989. *Pueblo, Mountain, Village, Dance.* Chicago: The University of Chicago Press.

Stoetzer, O. Carlos. 1979. *The Scholastic Roots of the Spanish American Revolution.* New York: Fordham University Press.

Taylor, William B. 1987. The Virgin of Guadalupe in New Spain: An Inquiry into the Social History of Marian Devotion. *American Ethnologist* 14:9–33.

Valerio, Gary. 1994. Interview by the author and Miguel Gandert. State Penitentiary, Santa Fe, New Mexico, 24 February.

Vásquez, Pablino. 1994. Interview by the author and Miguel Gandert. State Penitentiary, Santa Fe, New Mexico, 24 February.

Velázquez, Gustavo G. 1981. *El Rebozo en el Estado de México.* México: Biblioteca Enciclopédica del Estado de México.

Vigil, Sam. 1994. Interview by the author and Miguel Gandert. State Penitentiary, Santa Fe, New Mexico, 24 February.

Wallace, Lynne. 1994. Personal correspondence with the author, 28 August.

Weigle, Marta. 1989. *Creation and Procreation: Feminist Reflections on Mythologies of Cosmogony and Parturition.* Philadelphia: University of Pennsylvania Press.

Wroth, William. 1991. *Images of Penance, Images of Mercy: Southwestern Santos in the Late Nineteenth Century.* Norman: University of Oklahoma Press.

Secondary Sources

Barthes, Roland. 1990. *The Fashion System.* Translated by Matthew Ward and Richard Howard. New York: Hill & Wang, 1983. Reprint, Berkeley: University of California Press.

Padilla, Rudy. 1991. History of the Handkerchief (Paño). Eight-page unpublished typescript. Paño Arte Project Collection of the Hourglass Prison Art Museum at Youth Development, Inc., Albuquerque, N.Mex.

Peterson, Jeanette Favrot. 1992. The Virgin of Guadalupe: Symbol of Conquest or Liberation? *Art Journal,* 51(4) (winter):39–47.

Wolf, E. R. 1958. The Virgin of Guadalupe: A Mexican National Symbol. *Journal of American Folklore* 71:34–39.

Commerce, Innovation, and Tradition
Three Families of Hispanic Weavers

Helen R. Lucero

Historical Background

𝒪𝓍 FOLLOWING SEVERAL EXPLORATORY expeditions by the Spaniards into New Mexico, Don Juan de Oñate led the first European colonists into the area in 1598. In his expedition were ten Franciscans, 129 soldier/colonists and their families, and some four thousand Churro sheep. The first European settlement was established at San Gabriel, near San Juan Pueblo, on the west bank of the Río Grande. Between 1598 and 1680, the Spaniards explored or settled most of the Southwest, and a trade invoice dated 1638 indicates the use of the upright treadle loom in a weaving workshop in Santa Fe. By the time of the Pueblo Indian Revolt in 1680, when the Spaniards were forced to flee to El Paso del Norte, the Spanish population had grown to thirty-two friars and 2,800 colonists (Fisher 1979).

Following thirteen years of exile, Don Diego de Vargas led the colonists in the reconquest of New Mexico in 1692–1693. Established as a land grant in 1696, Chimayó was one of several communities occupied by the Spaniards following the reconquest. By 1750, Don Gabriel Ortega had introduced Spanish weaving methods and techniques in Chimayó, and weaving became one of the area's major export items. The crowning year for textile exports from New Mexico was 1840 when over twenty thousand textiles were exported south to Mexico (Fisher 1979).

Weaving Types

New Mexican Spanish colonial weavings were greatly inspired by Saltillo sarapes woven by Tlaxcalan Indians in northern Mexico. These magnificent weavings were often used as ponchos and served as status symbols for Mexico's *charros*. A typical weft-faced tapestry design pattern includes either a complex concentric diamond, or lozenge, in the center of the weaving, or a scalloped circle; the latter are believed to have been woven in Oaxaca and other southern Mexican towns. The entire weaving is framed by an elaborately designed border on all four sides. Using hand-spun wool, linen, *ixtle,* and silver and gold threads, these brightly colored textiles had a warp count of fifteen to twenty threads per inch and a weft count of seventy to one hundred threads per inch (Jeter and Juelke 1978).[1]

The New Mexican equivalent of the Saltillo sarape is the Río Grande blanket. Employing poorer tools and lesser skills, the New Mexican weavers produced coarser weavings than those of their Mexican counterparts. The handspun wool in New Mexico produced thread counts of five to seven warp threads per inch and twenty-five to forty weft threads per inch. Saltillo-inspired designs were of necessity larger and less refined. New Mexican weavers were quite ingenious, however, and used design elements and the colors produced by natural dyes to full advantage. Three Río Grande weaving types, based on the Saltillo sarape, evolved: (1) Saltillo central lozenge with smaller tapestry motifs in the background and framed by striped bands on two sides, (2) Saltillo background design covering entire surface, (3) stripes with small Saltillo design elements in alternating bands.

The Spanish colonial settlers also produced other types of weavings: plain or mottled everyday blankets, banded striped blankets, a light-weight fabric called *sabanilla,* and a heavy carpet called *jerga.* The Pueblo and Navajo Indians also influenced the Spaniards' weavings, especially in the use of natural dyes and in the design of banded striped blankets (Fisher 1979).

Between 1865 and 1905, a unique tapestry design was incorporated into the Hispanic weaving repertoire, the eight-pointed French LeMoyne star. Trampas/Vallero blankets, as they are called, contain these stars in each of the four corners and sometimes in the center. The origin of the star design has been a matter of speculation; some believe the star to have been patterned after Eastern American quilts while others equate it with Moorish designs. Trampas/Vallero weavings derive their name from the villages of Las Trampas and El Valle where they are purported to have been woven (Fisher 1979).

The newest type of Hispanic weaving dates from the turn of the century and was developed to meet tourist demand for souvenirs. Chimayó weavings are usually made with commercial wool warp and weft in deeply saturated colors. The external shape of most weavings is rectangular, with the length most often twice the width. Weaving sizes are determined by such considerations as the dimensions of a table or dresser. Rarely is the illusion of three-dimensional space created. Rather, colors, lines, and internal shapes are manipulated to emphasize a two-dimensional plane. Abstract patterning is arranged symmetrically around the vertical and horizontal axes. Typically, there are striped, transverse end bands and a central field. Within the central field are a large central motif and smaller auxiliary designs. The auxiliary designs are found in the space between the transverse end bands and the central motif. These auxiliary designs may be arranged to fill the space densely or leave it relatively simple, as is the case with *jaspes,* a stippling design element. Larger, blanket-size weavings feature secondary and tertiary design elements arranged around the central motif (Lucero and Baizerman 1999).

Contemporary Weavers

In the mid-1980s, 137 Hispanic weavers were identified as living in two northern New Mexico counties (Lucero 1986). This number has grown substantially in the past decade. Although these weavers, and those living in other areas of the state, are carrying on a centuries-old tradition, no two weave exactly alike nor do they have the same experiences to relate regarding their weaving. In an effort to present an introduction to contemporary Hispanic weavers and their lives, three families are documented here: (1) Ortega, (2) Trujillo, and (3) Martínez.[2] These three families have been singled out because they reflect different facets of Hispanic weaving: commerce, innovation, and tradition. In many ways, however, these three families are more similar than different. All live in rural northern New Mexico as large, extended families; can trace their weaving heritage back through several generations; create unique and beautiful weavings inspired by the designs of their ancestors; and deal in trade in textiles, especially to tourists.

The Ortega Family: Commerce

The best-known family of weavers in northern New Mexico is the Ortega family of Chimayó. Billboards along the main highway between Santa Fe and Taos divert visitors through the countryside to this village where the family business is located. Tour buses regularly stop at the Ortega's on their north and southbound routes.

Nicasio and Virginia Ortega originally established their business as a general store in 1918. Since then, it has gone through many remodelings, and visitors today find a large store geared to tourists' needs. Ortega's weavers produce a full range of woven items. The majority come in standardized sizes ranging from 4" x 4" coffee mug mats to the ever-popular 10" x 10" mats, long table runners (*congitas*), and twin or full-size bed blankets (*frazadas*). Rugs and cushions also come in standardized sizes. Various items of clothing such as vests, coats, ponchos, and purses are made from loom-woven fabric and are displayed on many racks and shelves.[3]

More than a place to buy weavings, Ortega's Weaving Shop is a place where visitors can make contact with weavers even when converging tour buses create a frenzied atmosphere. The store also carries a vast array of conventional tourist goods: American Indian jewelry and pottery, postcards, and an extensive selection of books on the Southwest.

David Ortega, the current patriarch of the Ortega family, was born in 1917. After almost fifty years in the business, he retired in 1992 and passed the shop on to one of his four sons, Robert. Another son, Andrew, owns and operates an art gallery next door. David's "making way" for his sons was not unlike his own experience when his father, Nicasio Ortega, founder of the store, turned the business over to him.

Nicasio, one of fourteen children, had entered the business world in 1912, when he accepted a large order for weavings, and then had to recruit his relatives to help him. Nicasio's brother, Reyes, also of Chimayó, developed his own weaving concern, having already been involved with the business side of weaving while working for curio dealer J. S. Candelario of Santa Fe. Another brother, Victor, had a general store in Chimayó where he also sold weavings. By 1922, Nicasio's own business was successful enough to enable him to buy the first car in Chimayó (Ortega 1992).

As Nicasio's four sons, José Ramón, Ricardo, Medardo, and David, grew up, they became accomplished weavers and contributed to the expansion of the family business. Trade in weavings was nothing new to the Ortega family, whose proud weaving heritage dates to the original resettlement of northern New Mexico in the last years of the seventeenth century, when the Ortegas were issued a family land grant. The first documented Ortega weaver, Nicolás Gabriel Ortega, was born in 1729. He and later Ortega descendants undoubtedly participated in the widespread trade in blankets that prevailed during the Spanish colonial and Mexican periods of New Mexico history, a trade that stretched as far as Mexico and California.

fig 42   David Ortega (center) in 1992 with two of his sons, Robert (left) and Andrew, in front of a striped blanket woven by José Ramón Ortega in 1875. Photo: Miguel Gandert.

The Ortegas' longevity in Chimayó and their prominence as weavers have made them a part of northern New Mexico's elite. A main irrigation *acequia* was named after the Ortegas, and the family maintains its own nineteenth-century chapel, the Oratorio de San Buenaventura, in the old Plaza del Cerro. During the past half-century, David Ortega has been active in politics, has promoted the revival of Spanish colonial arts, and has been instrumental in bringing paved roads, a fire department, and a dump site to the village of Chimayó.

The Ortegas' success lies not only in the family's historical connection to the area, however, but also in the way in which they have developed their business acumen, drawing on business practices outside of northern New Mexico. In the 1930s, when Anglo commercial weaving ventures opened in Santa Fe and sought Hispanic weavers to operate looms, David went to work for Burro Weavers. This experience afforded David a window on then-modern Anglo business practices. Later, when two Santa Fe weaving concerns, McCrossen Textiles and Southwest Arts and Crafts, closed their doors, David acquired their weaving equipment.

At his father's request, David returned to Chimayó after service in World War II to save the family business, which had deteriorated because of the shrinking tourist market. David brought with him his wartime bride, Jeanine Williamson. Between 1947 and 1950, the Ortegas remodeled the family store, adding a new front and closing the grocery business in favor of a shop devoted primarily to weaving. David also instituted some important changes at Ortega's Weaving Shop. For example, he added jackets, coats, and vests to his inventory. He also switched to using 100-percent-commercial-wool yarn instead of the cotton warp introduced at the turn of the century.

During the 1940s and 1950s, David and his brother José Ramón began marketing Ortega's weavings beyond Chimayó. They traveled throughout the Southwest, wholesaling Chimayó weavings at national parks and shops. The family has continued to respond to changes in consumer needs. For instance, as tastes changed in the 1950s, highly saturated turquoise blues and reds replaced the muted color harmonies of the post–World War II period. In the 1960s, when tourist interest in Navajo rugs increased demand for woven floor coverings, a line of rugs was added to the inventory. Hand-woven shawls were added in the 1980s (Ortega 1983).

In the mid 1970s, following Nicasio's death in 1964, and José Ramón's in 1972, "new blood" was recruited: David's sons entered the family business. The business further expanded in 1978 when David's brother, Medardo, opened an Ortega's Weaving Shop outlet in Albuquerque's Old Town.

As Santa Fe and Taos gained prominence as art centers, the Ortegas capitalized on their High Road location linking the two cities and expanded their marketing efforts in the arts. In 1983, David's son, Andrew, and his wife, Evita, opened the Galería Plaza del Cerro, now called the Galería Ortega. At the gallery, the couple exhibits and sells the work of Hispanic, Indian, and Anglo artists and artisans of the area. More than any other weaving family in New Mexico, the Ortegas have received widespread newspaper and magazine publicity. On May 9, 1953, *The Saturday Evening Post* published an article by Neil M. Clark, "The Weavers of Chimayo: An Ancient New Mexico Craft Lives On" (later reprinted as a pamphlet [Clark 1953]). Other notable articles have appeared in *The New York Times, National Geographic, Vista Magazine, Countryside, Southwest Profile, Culture and Leisure,* and *New Mexico Magazine.* Many television, film, and video programs also have been devoted to the Ortegas.

The relatively small physical scale of Ortega's Weaving Shop belies the scope of this large enterprise. Behind the scenes are dozens of weavers who weave in their own homes in a cottage industry. According to David, in 1983 the Ortegas had 115 looms and sixty active weavers whom they paid about a quarter of a million dollars in wages. The number of weavers has remained relatively constant. A decade later, Robert's roster of contract weavers still numbered sixty, but many more were working full time, indicating a greater commitment to the weaving profession. The weavers are located within a wide geographic radius. Most live in northern New Mexico, but some are scattered throughout the state; one weaver resided in El Paso, Texas.

An important ingredient in the business's success has been the recruitment and retention of good weavers. The first Ortega weavers were Nicasio's relatives and in-laws. A cousin, Juan Melquíades Ortega, wove for the Ortega family business well into his nineties. Another distant cousin, Georgia Serrano, daughter of Agueda Martínez, has become one of the Ortegas' best weavers. Others, such as the Vigil family of Cundiyó, and the various factions of the Trujillo family of Chimayó, are linked to the Ortegas through ties of marriage and *compadrazgo* (godparenthood).

Non-related community members also have been trained to weave. Today, some of the most prominent Ortega weavers include members of other families: García, Martínez, Manzanares, Rodríguez, Serrano, Trujillo, Valdez, and Vigil.[4] Constant recruitment is necessary, as weavers work seasonally or leave the area to work for themselves or for other dealers or to pursue other endeavors.

David Ortega speaks with pride of the weavers the family has trained, many of whom have worked for the Ortegas for decades. He also points out that many families have stayed off welfare rolls because of their weaving. Ortegas' weavers include young mothers, women whose families have grown and left home, retired people, and college students home on vacation. Most are individuals who prefer to work part-time at home in their own communities.

The Ortegas supply the weavers with yarn, and a loom can be supplied if the weaver does not own one. The loom is warped in the basement of Ortega's shop using a large warping device, ensuring a uniform warp tension critical to the quality and evenness of the finished piece. Yarn is ordered primarily from J. & H.

Clasgen's of Richmond, Ohio, and Crescent Woolen Mills of Two Rivers, Wisconsin. In 1991, David Ortega purchased 10,000 pounds of commercially spun and dyed wool, 88 percent of which was weft yarn. The brightly colored wool is warehoused in a large room behind the store showroom (Ortega 1985).

When completed, weavings are brought to the Ortegas and weighed. Finished pieces are then steam-pressed before being sold in the showroom. Each weaver is assessed the cost of yarn utilized per weaving according to its weight. David generally sells a 54" x 84" blanket for about $350.00, the weaver being paid approximately one-quarter to one-third of the sale price, depending upon the product's complexity. From all accounts, David has made a substantial income from serving as middleman and has, in turn, played a benevolent role in the lives of the weavers and the community.

The Ortegas maintain a high degree of control over their weavings. Regarding the quality of work brought to him by his weavers, David stated:

> If it's good, we pay them immediately. If it's bad, we sort of reprimand them and try to correct it. If it's not saleable, we do something else with it. We don't just sell it as straight goods. We have the facility to turn a piece of weaving into other than a straight line of goods, like a cushion, or a purse, or a coat, or a jacket—something like that. [Ortega 1983]

In addition to the work displayed in the store, the Ortegas fill many special orders. "Send anything, we can weave it," is their motto. They take pride in weaving complex organizational emblems, logos, lettering, and pictorial images, as well as replicas of historic Hispanic or Navajo blankets. For example, the Ortegas do not hesitate to produce blue-, black-, and white-striped blankets, patterned after the old Spanish colonial designs, to satisfy Anglo consumers' demands for copies. They have designed blankets for many dignitaries, including two presidents. Richard Nixon owned an Ortega Chimayó weaving, and Franklin Delano Roosevelt wrote to Nicasio Ortega in 1934 expressing his pleasure with an eagle-motif blanket that Señor Ortega had woven (Ortega 1983).

Despite resounding success in the weaving business, the Ortegas still maintain their agricultural holdings, depending upon local farmers to work their property. It is likely that the farm is worked more out of a sense of continuity with the past and ethnic identity than for its viability as a source of livelihood.

Outside the community, David Ortega has been involved with the support of Hispanic arts and crafts. He has been a member of the board of the Spanish Colonial Arts Society and has served as a judge at Santa Fe's annual Spanish Market. David believes strongly in the role of Hispanic weaving as a vehicle for transmitting information about Hispanic culture. He regales visitors with stories

regarding weaving while inserting his views about cultural values, historical incidents, and political preferences. David has helped fill the notebooks of dozens of
researchers and journalists seeking information about Chimayó and Hispanic
weaving, opening family records and photo archives and proudly displaying family heirloom weavings.

Mr. Ortega has been a successful entrepreneur who has earned the respect of
his community. His sensitivity to his market, his ability to recruit and retain
weavers, his participation in the greater business world, and his alertness to
changing business practices have enabled him to become a leader in the weaving
industry. At the same time, his local roots and the Ortegas' eight-generation weaving heritage have remained of utmost importance to him. Now retired, he can survey what he has accomplished and become his sons' advisor as they carry on a
thriving Ortega family business.

The Trujillo Family: Innovation

No family better exemplifies the conflict between the rural Hispanic community
ruled by old-world family values and the fast-paced, competitive, Anglo-
dominated outside world than the Trujillo family of weavers: Jacobo, Irvin, and
Lisa. Jacobo "Jake" O. Trujillo was born in 1911. He grew up in rural Chimayó, but
spent thirty years of his life in Los Alamos. There he worked for the federal government by day and taught weaving classes by night. His son, Irvin L. Trujillo,
born in 1954, grew up in Los Alamos but, after college and an engineering career,
chose to return to the homestead to establish a weaving business. For many years,
father and son commuted on weekends and during summers between Los
Alamos and Chimayó, maintaining contact with both worlds.

Jake Trujillo was born into a family with a long weaving tradition. In fact,
Jake could lay claim to being a sixth-generation weaver descended from Nicolás
Gabriel Ortega and a third-generation weaver descended from his paternal grand-
father, José Concepción Trujillo.

Jake and his five siblings—Teresita, Fedelina, Mercedes, Antonio, and
Rosinaldo—all learned to weave. The family wove striped blankets made with
handspun yarns and, for blanket dealers, weavings made with commercial yarns.
Jake was taught to weave by his mother in the 1920s when he was fourteen or
fifteen. He then worked as a cottage-industry weaver for his brother-in-law,
Severo Jaramillo, husband of his oldest sister, Teresita, who opened a shop in
Chimayó in 1922. Jake refined his skills while working for his brother-in-law and,
while still in high school, was assigned to fill the more difficult special orders.

In fall 1932, Jake was recruited to serve as a teacher in a new WPA program
set up by the State Vocational Education Department at the San José Training
School in Albuquerque. Soon Jake was teaching teachers from all over New

Mexico how to card, spin, dye wool with natural dyes, warp a loom, and finally, weave blankets. After his tenure at San José, Jake was sent to the El Rito Vocational School (1934–1935) and then transferred to Española (1936–1937). At each place he had to set up a weaving classroom and gather more dye plants. When his WPA employers attempted to move him to yet another site, he quit and returned home to weave. During his years as a teacher, he was liked and respected by the many weavers whom he taught, several of whom are still weaving today (J. Trujillo 1983).

In 1942, Jake was inducted into the Navy, went to gunner school, and expected to be shipped overseas. He was already aboard ship in Norfolk, Virginia, when he received a telegram asking him to report to Treasure Island, near San Francisco, for a special assignment. Reflecting on his military service, Jake reminisced:

> I thought they were going to send me where the fighting was really going on. But the officer had been checking the records and they discovered that I had been an instructor in arts and crafts here in New Mexico and they wanted somebody to be in charge of a rehabilitation center where they could teach the sailors different crafts and keep them occupied in learning some kind of trade. [J. Trujillo 1985]

Jake was delighted with the news and spent the duration of the war supervising an arts-and-crafts program and teaching weaving.

After the war, Jake searched for a job to earn money to start his own weaving shop. Employed as a time keeper with the Atomic Energy Commission, he moved to Los Alamos with his new bride, Isabelle García. Later he worked as a property manager with the National Laboratory, operated by the University of California. He thought he would work in Los Alamos for two or three years "but thirty years went by very fast," and his dream of having his own shop did not materialize until 1982 (J. Trujillo 1985).

Weaving became Jake's major occupation after his retirement in 1975. However, always the workaholic, Jake continued to work long hours tending his gardens and orchards and teaching weaving classes at Los Alamos High School. Together with his wife, Jake also participated in many markets and fairs in those years, including Spanish Market, Feria Artesana, Rancho de las Golondrinas, Los Alamos Fair, and the New Mexico State Fair. At the fairs, and in his weaving shop, the loquacious Jake was able to pursue his other love, educating people: "I get a real satisfaction from telling people the type of work that we do and how we do it . . . because it is very important that people understand and know, be able to tell the difference between good quality work and bad quality" (J. Trujillo 1983).

Jake always had high standards. During the sixty-five years he spent at the loom, he mastered every style associated with the Hispanic weaving tradition:

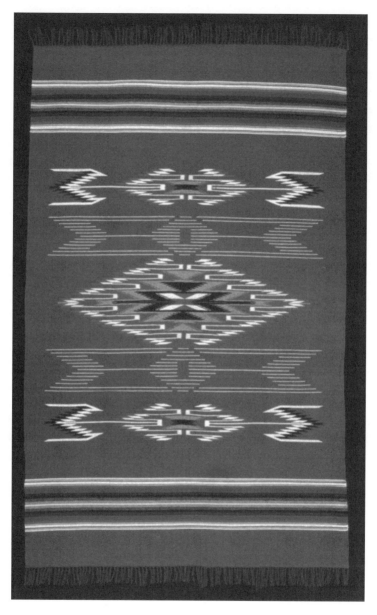

fig 43   Classic Chimayó blanket, 1950s. This blanket exhibits all of the
characteristics associated with classic Chimayó weavings: a central
design element flanked by two smaller designs, receding secondary
designs *(jaspes)*, and two striped transverse end bands framing a
solid (turquoise-blue) background. Collection of Mrs. Norman
Carson. Photo: Petronella Ytsma.

Saltillos, Río Grandes with stripes or tapestry designs, Trampas/Valleros, *jergas,* and Chimayó blankets. His weavings won him numerous ribbons and other prizes.

This country boy, who got swept up in the global events of his day, spent much of his life working in an Anglo culture. However, he always maintained strong ties to his Hispanic community. Through his Hispanic values, Catholic Church affiliation, Spanish language, *compadrazgo,* and congenial personality, he remained a valued citizen of Chimayó. Jake died on April 18, 1990 and was buried 1,000 feet from where he was born.

When Jake's son, Irvin, was ten, his father taught him to weave by placing a little soap box next to his own loom where his young son could watch him create. Irvin proved to be a fast learner. After only two weeks of experimentation, Jake told Irvin that he was ready to weave on his own. Ten-year-old Irvin then spent his entire 1965 summer vacation as an Ortega production weaver working "from 8:00 in the morning until 9:00 at night ... weaving 20" x 20"s; it's very difficult to design a new design every 20" x 20". . . . My record at that time was weaving ten [pieces per day] with a 2½" design [working] about twelve hours" (I. Trujillo 1991).

While Irvin was precocious and hard-working, weaving would not become truly important in his life until he reached his twenties. Until then, Irvin had pursued a career as an engineer and a serious avocation as a musician—a drummer with a preference for rock music. It was only after selling his weavings at Spanish Market in 1977, and seeing wonderful examples of Spanish colonial weaving in Nora Fisher's 1979 publication, *Spanish Textile Tradition of New Mexico and Colorado,* that he reevaluated his ideas about his father's craft and the examples of weaving that had surrounded him all his life. Previously, he had either taken weaving for granted or even denigrated the tradition. Irvin also resented the low wages that weavers were paid by dealers; he wanted a much better salary.

His feelings about Chimayó weaving notwithstanding, Irvin continued to weave throughout high school. Later, he remembers a turning point in his life: "I got a music scholarship to go to Eastern New Mexico University to study ... a full four-year scholarship and I turned it down ... because my parents felt that being a musician ... was a hard life, and it wasn't a very lucrative way of making a living" (I. Trujillo 1991).

Acceding to his parents' wishes that he pursue a different area of study, Irvin earned two Associate Degrees in 1974 from Eastern New Mexico University—in Civil Technology and Machine Design Technology. He then worked as a technician, drafting for Sandia Laboratories in Albuquerque. Irvin was bored by the work so he returned to school, this time at the University of New Mexico, where, in 1979, he earned a Bachelor of Science degree in Civil Engineering. Although he majored in engineering, Irvin never abandoned his love for music and took private lessons whenever possible. He also satisfied his passion for music by playing drums and percussion instruments in different bands.

Irvin met Lisa Rockwood, an eighteen-year-old Jewish Californian, on a Friday night in 1980. She asked for help finding a drummer for a pop band she was forming. In addition to playing the electric guitar with her band, Lisa was pursuing a degree in business administration at the University of New Mexico. They married two years later (I. Trujillo 1991).

Shortly after their marriage, Lisa learned to weave from Irvin and quickly became a highly accomplished weaver in the Hispanic tradition. Soon she was challenging herself to weave increasingly finer and more intricate designs. Lisa and Irvin immersed themselves in learning about natural dyes, spinning, and traditional weaving techniques. Jake was a willing instructor, and the couple read everything they could find on the subject.

In 1980, the Trujillo family met in Chimayó; present were Jake and Isabelle, Irvin and Lisa, and Irvin's sister, Patricia (Pat), and her husband, Marco Oviedo. They discussed their lives' goals and decided to open a business where they not only could produce and sell their creative work but also could strive to be self-sufficient; they gave themselves seven years. Theirs was a fortunate situation because Jake owned good roadside property on which to build a shop and he had extensive knowledge about the weaving business. Moreover, Lisa's last class project at the university—development of a plan for a business—launched their own shop. Centinela Traditional Arts officially opened on the weekend of July 4, 1982. Deriving its name from the historic importance of the site as a sentinel outpost, the shop was located next to the Trujillos' fields and orchard, which provided a lovely ambiance (I. Trujillo 1983).

Centinela Traditional Arts was initially conceived as a single-family business. It soon developed into a multi-faceted family enterprise consisting of four businesses operating out of the same showrooms. Weaving was the family's major product. During the shop's early years, however, Irvin's brother-in-law, Marco, displayed and sold his looms, weaving accessories, carved corbels, *vigas, santos,* and wooden figurines under the banner of "Oviedo's Wood Carving." Pat, his wife, also sold her handpainted *retablos* in the shop and operated a business, Paseo de la Tierra Vieja, which provided guided trail rides on burros and donkeys or in a mule-drawn wagon. Pat and her mother were instrumental in operating yet another subsidiary business, Miel de Chimayó and Centinela Fruit Stand, where their local produce and honey were sold.

Unfortunately, disputes arose over the way in which the business was run. Lisa's desire to use her marketing skills to upgrade the business was pitted against Jake's old-fashioned ways. To resolve their problems, Irvin and Lisa built their own shop next door to Jake's. In 1988, the Oviedos also separated their business from the Trujillos and opened their shop, Oviedo's Carving and Bronze, across the road.

The Centinela Traditional Arts shop initially had three rooms: two for display and one for storage. Over the past few years, Irvin and Lisa have expanded the shop to include three display and two storage rooms. They also have added post-cards, books, and woven clothing to their array of merchandise. Their show-room—with its high ceiling, light walls, and track lighting that spotlights large weavings—was designed as an art gallery.

Although they sometimes weave standard Chimayó-style weavings, Lisa and Irvin have moved their work into the fine-arts sphere. Their work has evolved into large, canvas-like fine-art weavings that reinterpret historic examples and to which they add a contemporary twist. Both Lisa and Irvin not only employ the artistic convention of titling their work but also weave their signatures in, another hallmark of their identification as artists.

For the creation of her increasingly more intricate works, Lisa "depends upon the chromatic complexities derived from natural dyes." She frequently spins yarns as fine as kite string for her Saltillo-inspired weavings. Her interpretation of his-toric Saltillo sarapes has become her specialty. Lisa's weavings bear titles such as *Hyperactive* (1984), *Devotion* (1987), *Spider Soul* (1988), and *Passion in the Web* (1989) (Olson n.d.).

Irvin's pieces are bold, highly individualistic, innovative statements. In his *48 Roses to the Vallero Spirit* (1986), Irvin combined two weaving techniques: tapestry-woven Vallero stars and an ikat-woven dove. Some of Irvin's more impressive weavings include *Chimayó, Topical Paradise* (1987), *Buscando la Malinche* (1989), *Río Grande Fusion* (1990), and *Una Pieza Galáctica* (1991). One particularly striking weaving, *Spider from Mars* (1988), was included in an exhi-bition at the Smithsonian Institution's National Museum of American History. New Mexico was selected by the Smithsonian to convey the story of the world-wide encounters that took place between Native Americans, Africans, Asians, and Europeans in their 1992 "American Encounters" exhibit (Morrison 1992).

Perhaps because of their insider/outsider status in Chimayó, Irvin and Lisa are freer to experiment than are most other weavers in the area. The numerous tourists who stop by the shop, and Irvin's and Lisa's personal interests, make the Anglo world ever-present in their lives. However, they do not have the security that Jake did in being rooted in Chimayó even as he dealt with the outside world. They are pulled by many conflicting forces as they straddle two worlds: Hispanic vs. Anglo, Catholic vs. Jewish, rural vs. urban, production craftsman vs. fine artist, and weaver vs. student.

Irvin's challenge also has always been to integrate many talents and skills. When asked about his profession, Irvin revealed his complex personality by stat-ing: "I am an artist, musician, engineer, and weaver." He said he had left "weaver" for last because "it's what holds everything else up . . . how I make most of my liv-ing. Music is what I really want and weaver is what I've got" (I. Trujillo 1991).

Both Irvin and Lisa have won many awards for their weavings. They con-sciously create pieces with the goal of winning competitions, and their success has

fig 44   Irvin Trujillo, *Río Grande Fusion* (1989). This innovative fine art
weaving merges Saltillo design elements with contemporary color
variegation and design placement. Photo: Richard Wickstrom.

helped establish them in the fine-arts market. Their weavings range in price from $2,000 to $40,000. Those produced by their cottage-industry employees sell for much less.

The Trujillos have been featured in several family exhibitions, and individual examples of Irvin's and Lisa's innovative weavings have been exhibited in national and international venues. Jake's weavings remain on display in a memorial gallery located in the entryway to Centinela Traditional Arts, where Adam and Emily, Irvin's and Lisa's children, greet customers. Jake would have been proud of his grandchildren, the new generation of Trujillos growing up amidst their grandfather's, father's, and mother's weavings, in much the same way that he and his son grew up with weaving as an integral part of their lives.

The Martínez Family: Tradition

Agueda Salazar Martínez, the matriarch of Hispanic weaving, was born on March 13, 1898. Each fall, her tin-roofed adobe home in Medanales is alive with bright red chile *ristras* (braids or strings of dried chile pods) hanging from the walls, piles of orange pumpkins, plots of colorful cosmos, and kittens basking in the sunlight. Although past the century mark, Doña Agueda, as she is respectfully known, continues to weave almost daily.

This feisty *anciana* wove for blanket dealers for half a century. During this time she also raised her family. In 1996, her family numbered ten children, sixty-six grandchildren, 114 great-grandchildren, and fourteen great-great-grandchildren, a grand total of 204. Figuring that she has done more than her share toward insuring that the government's taxes are paid, Doña Agueda wittily remarks, *"Ya me hubiera de dar una pensión el presidente porque tengo tan grande familia y todos trabajan"* (The president should give me a pension because I have such a large family and they all work) (Martínez 1991).

This matriarch of Hispanic weaving is also the head of the largest family of weavers in the state—a clan that, in 1994, numbered sixty-four active weavers spanning five generations (Clark 1994, 32–37). Because it is impossible to do justice to this large family here, what follows is a portrait of Doña Agueda and a brief introduction to some of the Martínez women who have particularly distinguished themselves through their weaving: daughters Epifania (Eppie) Archuleta (b. 1922), Georgia Serrano (b. 1925), and Cordelia Coronado (b. 1933); granddaughter Norma Medina (b. 1941); and great-granddaughter Delores Medina (b. 1967).

Although of Hispanic descent, Agueda Martínez can trace part of her ancestry to a great-grandfather, Enríquez Córdova, a Navajo weaver raised by the Spanish. Doña Agueda is very proud of her Indian heritage but identifies herself as a *mexicana*. Spanish is her native language, although she kiddingly says that she can also speak English because she can say "yes" and "no."

fig 45   Agueda Martínez at her loom surrounded by personal memorabilia,
1992. Photo: Miguel Gandert.

While still a teenager, Doña Agueda was taught to weave rag rugs by an eld-
erly neighbor. It was not until 1921, however, after she married Eusebio Martínez,
a weaver from Chimayó, that her weaving skills were refined under the tutelage of
her *compadre* Lorenzo Trujillo. From nearby Río Chiquito, Trujillo was a prominent weaver of Chimayó blankets and was godfather to Doña Agueda's daughter,
Epifania.

Eusebio Martínez's ancestry and weaving tradition in Chimayó date back to
the seventeenth century. Although the Martínezes are not directly related to the
Ortega and Trujillo weaving families, they, like so many families in northern New
Mexico, are related through *compadrazgo* and marriage. The Martínez family is
related to the Trujillos through the mid-nineteenth-century marriage of Manuel
Trujillo and Antonia (Toñita) Martínez Trujillo.

In 1924, the Martínez family moved to the village of Medanales. Weaving
became an important source of income for Doña Agueda and her husband, especially as their family grew to include ten children. Weaving became the means by
which they could augment their limited income from subsistence farming. As a
young couple, the industrious Martínezes worked their farm—and sometimes
even neighbors' farms—during summer days. At night, they wove by kerosene
lamp into the pre-dawn hours of the morning. One of their children's first memories was the sound of the loom beater in the middle of the night. In winter, weaving became their primary occupation. As their children grew, they helped with
weaving-related tasks such as carding and spinning, gathering dye plants, and
filling bobbins with yarn for the shuttles (the tool used to pass the weft through
the opening in the warp). When tall enough, they joined their parents at the loom.

The family's weavings were marketed through blanket dealers, primarily to
tourists. Doña Agueda continued to weave for blanket dealers for ten years after
the death of her husband in 1962. Then, because of her initiative and creative and
technical mastery, she made the transition from working for others to selling
weavings directly from her home.

One of her three handmade treadle looms occupies Doña Agueda's kitchen.[5]
Adjacent to the kitchen is a room with two large looms. One loom is over one
hundred years old and is used to weave the larger pieces. To weave, Doña Agueda
stands at her loom, shifting her weight from treadle to treadle. From a large repertoire of Saltillo, Río Grande, Navajo, and Chimayó weaving designs, complex concentric diamonds, hourglasses, and chevrons slowly take form as she rhythmically
manipulates the dozens of colored threads across her loom. Doña Agueda's weaving designs are not drawn beforehand, but spring forth from her mind as if from
an endless reservoir of memorized images. Although she can no longer weave the
long hours she once did, she is noted for saying, "There are times that I weave
until 12:00 at night. As they say, from sunrise 'til sundown. . . . Until then you'll
find me dancing on the loom" (*Agueda Martínez* 1977).

fig 46   Rag rug by Agueda Martínez, 1994. Traditionally produced as floor
coverings, these rag rugs with intricate tapestry designs are now sold
as works of art. Courtesy of the National Museum of American Art,
Smithsonian Institution, Washington, D.C.

After producing thousands of blankets in more than eighty years of weaving, Doña Agueda confidently juxtaposes colors and designs in a daring and original manner. Much of her work is recognizable because of the vitality and boldness of the variegated colors in her diamond motifs.

Surrounding Doña Agueda in her weaving room are not only the tools of her trade and piles of colorful skeins of yarn, but also an array of personal memorabilia ranging from a large depiction of the Virgin Mary to a major-league baseball cap. The amazing variety of artifacts and images in this room reflects both Doña Agueda's roots and her continuing awareness of the outside world, despite the isolation of the rural village in which she has spent most of her life. Here is a tough individual, a hardy woman of dry wit and humor, a woman whose lively conversations are punctuated by *dichos* and *cuentos* (sayings and tales) meant to guide and entertain her listeners. Consider her views on widows who remarry: *El que enviuda y se vuelve a casar, algo le debía al diablo, y le debe de pagar* (A person who is widowed and remarries must have owed the devil something and has to pay up) (Martínez 1991).

During the past twenty years, Doña Agueda's artistic talents have attracted much public recognition. In 1975, New Mexico awarded her the prestigious Governor's Award for Excellence in the Arts. Critical to her growing reputation was her role in a documentary about her life that was nominated for an Academy Award. The 1977 documentary, *Agueda Martínez, Our People, Our Country,* catapulted her into national prominence. Suddenly she was in great demand, and everyone wanted her to attend a showing of the film. In typical fashion, she questioned, "Why? They've already seen the face on the film—why do they want to see it in person, too? I don't have the time to go everywhere just so people can look at me. I've got work to do" (Sagel 1991, E-6).

In 1980, she was selected as first honoree of the Feria Artesana, an annual Hispanic arts and crafts fair held in Albuquerque. Doña Agueda's work has been collected and exhibited nationally. Most recently, one of her rag rugs with tapestry design was selected as the official poster image for the 1992 Festival of American Folklife sponsored by the Smithsonian Institution. In 1993, the National Women's Caucus for Art selected Doña Agueda as their first Hispanic honoree for outstanding achievement in the visual arts; her daughter, Eppie, accepted the award on her mother's behalf at the organization's annual conference in Seattle, Washington. The Smithsonian's National Museum of American Art acquired one of her tapestry weave rag *jergas* in 1995; it is included in an exhibition, Arte Latino, that began a national tour in 2000.

The continuity of Doña Agueda's craft is assured by her many descendants who are successful weavers. In her family, it is the women who have distinguished themselves in weaving although, until recently, popular literature continued to portray weaving as a craft that was passed on from father to son (Lucero and

Baizerman 1999, 97). Three of Doña Agueda's daughters have received national recognition for their weaving. Eppie Archuleta was even awarded the highest honor bestowed a folk artist: a 1985 National Heritage Fellowship presented by the National Endowment for the Arts.

Living in southern Colorado, Eppie has taken her family's weaving tradition one step further and established the San Luis Valley Wool Mill, where she prepares much of the yarn used by the rest of her family. In 1991, like her mother before her, Eppie received a Governor's Award for her weaving, this time from the state of Colorado. Also like her mother, this strong and feisty woman loves a challenge. When told that it was impossible to weave a portrait, she promptly wove one of the Archbishop of New Mexico. She has since woven many other "pictorials," and, on her nine-foot-wide loom, has produced some of the largest pieces attempted by any Hispanic weaver (Archuleta 1993).

In 1986, Doña Agueda accompanied Eppie, granddaughter Norma, and great-granddaughter Delores to Washington, D. C. where the four generations demonstrated carding, spinning, dyeing, and weaving at the annual Festival of American Folklife. Doña Agueda also tended the plot of chile peppers growing beside their booth, which had been planted from the seeds she had sent to the Smithsonian.

In 1992, another daughter, Cordelia Coronado, was selected to represent New Mexico's Hispanic weavers at the same festival. Cordelia has distinguished herself as a "weaver, farmer, shop owner, mother, school board candidate, ditch commissioner, carpenter, community activist, and [was the] Medanales postmaster" for over thirty years (Sagel 1987, 8). She sells many of her own and her family's works—especially pieces produced by her daughters Marcela and Teresa—in her weaving shop, La Lanzadera, where, a decade ago, she also had taught weaving classes to over five hundred students. This dynamic woman has a philosophy about teaching that transcends the transmission of weaving skills:

> The most rewarding part in teaching is to share not only the knowledge of weaving, but also the therapeutic values that they pick up. I get a lot of nurses, doctors, lawyers, and therapists, that come for therapy here, and I don't really say, "Well, this is therapy." But you automatically feel very, very serene, very at home, quiet. Weaving doesn't give them time to think about other problems. And they have something to show for it at the end, and they're very happy with it. [Coronado 1991]

Another of Doña Agueda's daughters, Louisa García, has been living with her for several years. During this time, she has started to weave, producing pieces quite similar to her mother's. Yet another daughter, Georgia Serrano, lives next door and has been weaving since the late 1970s, when she and her family returned

fig 47   Coronado family weavings on display at La Lanzadera Weaving Shop,
Medanales, New Mexico, 1992. Photo: Miguel Gandert.

to Medanales after living twenty-four years in Utah. For years, Georgia has woven
almost exclusively for the Ortegas, producing some of their finest Chimayó blankets. Georgia sometimes weaves pieces for family use, and has woven some rag
rugs, not unlike her mother's, with intricate tapestry designs. During the 1980s,
Georgia also worked for a weaving concern in Medanales owned by Janusz and
Nancy Kozikowski. Their European-style tapestry weavings are noted for pictorial designs with variegated shading (Serrano 1983).

Eppie Archuleta's daughter, Norma Medina, and her granddaughter, Delores
Medina, are perhaps the most accomplished weavers in the third and fourth generations of Martínez weavers working today. Although she has mastered all of the
styles of weaving regarded as Hispanic, Norma specializes in a style she calls "contemporary" (Medina 1991). She weaves pictorial tapestries depicting landscapes,
churches, and still lifes. She dyes her own colors and blends them so delicately
that, seen from a distance, many of her weavings appear to be painted canvases.
On the other hand, Delores prefers to work in the most traditional of styles, Río
Grande weavings with alternating bands of stripes and tapestry designs reminiscent of those produced by her great-grandmother, Agueda.

Doña Agueda introduced dozens of women to weaving during the 1960s and
1970s through the Home Education Livelihood Program (HELP), a federally sub-

sidized program. As an instructor and mentor, she played a major role in keeping the weaving tradition alive at a time when few were aware of its significance. In 1983, the ever-pragmatic *anciana* reflected on the teaching of Hispanic weaving to non-Hispanics:

> *Pues, yo soy de opinión que todo el que quiera aprender, tiene uno que ayudarle. Si es americano, mejicano, indio, lo que sea. Todos estamos obligados hacer la vida, según la habilidad de la criatura.* (Well, I am of the opinion that one must help all who wish to learn, whether he/she is American, Mexican, Indian, or whatever. We are all obligated to make a living to the best of our ability.) [Martínez 1983]

Doña Agueda continues to practice a folk art that is intimately connected with the rhythms of the daily and seasonal cycles. Her life has been remarkably prolific—acres and acres of chiles, hundreds of descendants, and thousands of weavings. While she has received national recognition as a premier folk artist, she continues to be nourished as much by her life as a farmer, member of her nearby church, and head of a large family. Doña Agueda's own words best describe the intimate and vital connection her craft has to her life: *"Pues, lo único que yo pienso es que mientras que yo me pueda mover, yo voy a tejer"* (Well, the only thing I can say is that as long as I can move, I will continue to weave) (Martínez 1983).[6]

Conclusion

As exemplified by the Ortega, Trujillo, and Martínez families, many internal and external factors have influenced the development of Hispanic weaving in New Mexico. The need to earn a living, a desire for fame, and ethnic pride had an impact on individual weavers. External forces—such as United States colonization, two world wars, and tourism—have also left their mark on this art form. The interaction among weavers, merchants, and consumers also continues to play a crucial role in the evolution of Chimayó weaving and to enhance the development of this vital, living tradition four hundred years after the Spaniards first settled in New Mexico.

Notes

1. The longitudinal threads of a textile that are arranged on a loom are called the "warp." Openings are formed in the warp into which the weft, the transverse threads, are inserted, forming woven fabric.
2. A version of this essay was published as *Tres Familias: Profiles of Three Contemporary Hispanic Weaving Families,* chapter five (131–160) in *Chimayó Weaving: The*

Transformation of a Tradition, a book co-authored with Dr. Suzanne Baizerman (University of New Mexico Press, 1999). I am indebted to Suzanne Baizerman and to photographer Miguel Gandert for their contributions to this chapter.

3. A price list with weaving sizes may be obtained by writing to Ortega's Weaving Shop, Post Office Box 325, Chimayó, NM 87522 or by calling the shop at 505-351-4215.

4. From a 1992 promotional flyer produced by Ortega's Weaving Shop.

5. The weaver uses treadles to raise or lower one or more of the harnesses, which are the rectangular frames on the loom that hold the parallel cords or wires that separate and guide the warp threads and make a path for the shuttle. On a treadle loom, the weaver "walks" on foot pedals to raise the harnesses.

6. Sadly, Doña Agueda passed away on 6 June 2000 at the age of 102. Four days before her death, Doña Agueda had used up the last of the warp on her loom, creating a small runner with the remaining wool. The piece was displayed on the altar at her funeral in Medanales, which was attended by virtually the entire community as well as by members of her family from across the United States. When Doña Agueda died, she left no unfinished work on her looms.

Literature Cited

Primary Sources

Agueda Martínez: Our People, Our Country. 1977. San Francisco, Calif.: Moctezuma Esparza Productions.

Archuleta, Eppie. 1993. Interview by author. Seattle, Washington, 2 February.

Clark, Neil M. 1953. *The Weavers of Chimayo: An Ancient New Mexico Craft Lives On.* Santa Fe, N.Mex.: Vergara Printing Co.

Clark, William. 1994. Dancing on the Loom. *El Palacio* 99(1/2) (winter):32–37.

Coronado, Cordelia. 1991. Interview by author. Medanales, New Mexico, 7 December.

Fisher, Nora. 1979. *Spanish Textile Tradition of New Mexico and Colorado.* Santa Fe: Museum of New Mexico Press.

Jeter, James and Paula Marie Juelke. 1978. *The Saltillo Sarape.* Santa Barbara, Calif.: New World Arts.

Lucero, Helen R. 1986. *Hispanic Weavers of North Central New Mexico: Social/Historical and Educational Dimensions of a Continuing Artistic Tradition.* Ph.D. diss., University of New Mexico.

Lucero, Helen R. and Suzanne Baizerman. 1999. *Chimayó Weaving: The Transformation of a Tradition.* Albuquerque: University of New Mexico Press.

Martínez, Agueda. 1983. Interview by author. Medanales, New Mexico, 12 May.

———. 1991. Interview by author. Medanales, New Mexico, 17 December.

Medina, Norma. 1991. Interview by author. Medanales, New Mexico, 4 December.

Morrison, Howard. 1992. *American Encounters.* Washington, D.C.: National Museum of American History, Smithsonian Institution.

Olson, Audrey Janet. n.d. "Trujillo Weaving at Centinela Ranch: Old Traditions New Explorations." Exhibit handout from the Roswell Museum and Art Center, March 31–July 29, 1990.

Ortega, David. 1983. Interview by author. Chimayó, New Mexico, 5 July.

———. 1985. Interview by Suzanne Baizerman. Chimayó, New Mexico, 20 June.

———. 1992. Interview by author. Chimayó, New Mexico, 13 March.

Sagel, Jim. 1987. Being a Woman Doesn't Keep an Activist from Being Involved. *Albuquerque Journal North,* 20 February.

———. 1991. *Que Haceres*—Weaver's Way of Life Makes Art of Work. *Albuquerque Journal North,* 5 December.

Serrano, Georgia. 1983. Interview by author. Medanales, New Mexico, 13 May.

Trujillo, Irvin. 1983. Interview by author. Chimayó, New Mexico, 20 September.

———. 1991. Interview by author. Chimayó, New Mexico, 18 December.

Trujillo, Jacobo. 1983. Interview by author. Chimayó, New Mexico, 5 July.

———. 1985. Interview by Suzanne Baizerman. Chimayó, New Mexico, 31 March.

Secondary Sources

Baizerman, Suzanne. 1987. Textiles, Traditions, and Tourist Art: Hispanic Weaving in Northern New Mexico. Ph.D. diss., University of Minnesota.

Hufford, Mary, Marjorie Hunt, and Steven Zeitlin. 1987. *The Grand Generation: Memory, Mastery, Legacy.* Washington, D.C.: Smithsonian Institution Traveling Exhibition Service and the University of Washington Press.

Hunt, Marjorie and Boris Weintraub. 1991. Masters of Traditional Arts. *National Geographic Magazine* (January):74–101.

Kozikowski, Janusz. 1979. Agueda Martínez: Weaver of Many Seasons. *New Mexico Magazine* (August):44–46.

Padilla, Carmella. 1991. Artists Struggle to Balance Old and New. *New Mexico Magazine* (June):50–52.

Pardue, Diana. 1992. *¡Chispas! Cultural Warriors of New Mexico,* Phoenix, Ariz.: The Heard Museum.

Images in *Penitente* Ritual and *Santo* Art
A Philosophical Inquiry Into the Problem of Meaning

Michael Candelaria

IF CULTURAL EXPRESSIONS in ritual and art reveal basic meanings of life, then an interpretation or a reading of those cultural expressions becomes imperative for those who seek cultural understanding. Nuevomexicano New Mexico has produced many religious images called "*santos.*" Of these the most prevalent images are those of Christ and the Virgin Mary.[1] For the purposes of this study, which is restricted to *Penitente* religion and *santo* art, I will focus on the Christ Crucifix, Jesus Nazarene, and the *Angel de Muerte* (Death Angel) or Doña Sebastiana. What can these images show us about Nuevomexicano culture? This question presupposes the assumption that meaning is possible and, hence, that interpretation is not an empty exercise. Thus, alongside the first question, I will also simultaneously raise questions concerning the problem of meaning. Ultimately, for the purposes of this investigation, these questions collapse into the following one: What are the referents of the images of Christ and of Doña Sebastiana in *Penitente* ritual and *santo* art and what do they reveal about Nuevomexicano culture?

Other related questions come to mind. What motivates our desire to know the meanings embedded in Nuevomexicano culture? Is there some hidden meaning, objectively present, waiting to be uncovered or, rather, some arbitrary and subjective meaning in the process of being constructed? Do the *Penitentes* and *santeros,* through ritual and art, preserve, in some way, the spiritual core, the ethos of Nuevomexicano culture? What inward essence is being externalized and made objective in religion and art? What self-knowledge do we hope to discover in the mysterious interplay between inner content and outward form? Dare we find in these cultural expressions a rich resource for an authentic Nuevomexicano philosophy?[2] Who has the competency to interpret them truthfully and the right to speak for Nuevomexicano culture?

Alejandro López raises this latter question and makes it the basis for his critique of Larry Frank's coffee table book on *santo* art, *New Kingdom of the Saints* (Frank 1992). López accuses Frank of the unpardonable sin of selling out the "soul" of Nuevomexicano culture. According to López, Frank makes the Hispanos "incidental" to their own story, appropriates to himself the title of "discoverer" of this tradition, and wrongly declares the tradition dead (López 1993). In fact, López argues that New Mexico Hispanos live under a kind of colonialism that is maintained by denying Nuevomexicano genius. Recognition of our Hispanic genius, López hopes, would result in the end of victimization. Frank, however, does not allow Hispanos to be "interpreters of their own culture" (López 1993).

Perhaps here lies the answer to our question. The motivation behind our cultural inquiry and public expression is that Hispanos want to be interpreters of their own culture so that the world will stand up and notice their real Nuevomexicano genius.

Every culture has its genius. As the German idealist philosopher Georg Wilhelm Friedrich Hegel claims in his *Lectures on Aesthetics*, "[E]ach epoch always finds its appropriate and adequate form" (Friedrich 1953, 334).[3] Though there exist many questions about adequacy, the claim that the ethos of each epoch is expressed in idiosyncratic forms has the force of intuitive clarity. I also agree with Hegel regarding the symbolic form of art. On this matter, Hegel says: "We must pass beyond the sensuous form in order to penetrate its more extended and more profound meaning" (Friedrich 1953, 337).

This study, too, will take as a guide the proposition that behind sensible forms lies intelligible meaning (Friedrich 1953, 338). In short, religious symbols are forms of the imagination by which a people expresses its innermost secret sentiments.

Moreover, what Hegel said of Greek art applies no less to *santero* art: "[T]he divine beings of the Greeks are not yet the absolute free spirit, but spirit in a particular mode, fettered by the limitations of humanity, still dependent as a determinate individuality on external conditions" (Friedrich 1953, 56). Analogously, the images of the Crucifix, Nazarene, and Doña Sebastiana do not convey the idea of freedom. Rather, they represent the idea of human suffering and death. Following Hegel's line of thinking, one could conclude that Nuevomexicano culture does not fully experience human freedom. Hegel would probably say that Nuevomexicano culture is alienated, for it conveys the idea of human alienation. To the extent that the religiously inclined Nuevomexicano postulates a heavenly realm occupied by real holy personages, then the *santos* indicate an alienated culture, and the thesis that Nuevomexicano culture takes "flight from the world" corresponds to Hegel's theory.

Common to religious world views is the bifurcation of the world into two realities. Such ontological dualisms generally lead to ethical dichotomies where the different realms are ranked hierarchically according to some criteria of value. Consequently, in religious models the heavenly realm stands higher, in the ranking of the Good, the True, and the Beautiful, than the earthly realm.

Ludwig Feuerbach transformed Hegel's idealism, making religion the result of psychological projection. According to Feuerbach, "The divine being is nothing else than the human being, or, rather, the human nature purified, freed from the limits of the individual man, made objective—i.e., contemplated and revered as another, a distinct being" (Feuerbach 1957, 14). In other words, the idea of god is none other than the image of an ideal human projected without limitations and defects. According to Feuerbach's view, the idea of God is the idea of human perfection. The images of the suffering Christ, in this respect, are only projections of human suffering. The idea of Christ is the reflection of human suffering: "God as Christ is the sum of all human misery" (Feuerbach 1957, 14).

Albert Schweitzer echoes the views of Hegel and Feuerbach. Speaking of the historical quest for Jesus in the history of Christianity, Schweitzer quipped: "There is no historical task which so reveals someone's true self as the writing of a life of Jesus" (Feuerbach 1957, 14). Following Schweitzer, one is inclined to believe that the portrayals of Jesus in Nuevomexicano culture are not so revealing of Jesus of Nazareth as they are of Nuevomexicano character.

The images of Jesus in the New Testament are imaginative interpretations, not accurate representations. There is no singular image of Jesus in the New Testament. The images of Jesus in the Gospels, and the images of Christ in the Pauline epistles, are all the result of a long process of interpretation. Thus, when Jaroslav Pelikan (1985) asserts that every later picture of Jesus is based on a picture of Jesus in the New Testament, he really means that all images of Christ are pictures of pictures. Cultural images of Christ, like the images of Christ Crucifix and the Jesus Nazarene, ostensibly based on interpretations of Christ drawn from the Gospels, are really interpretations of interpretations. As Jean Baudrillard would say, they are signs of signs—simulacra.[4] So what can the religious images of the *santeros* and Penitents tell us about Nuevomexicano self-understanding?

Santo art features two forms. *Bultos* are carved wooden images in the round and are usually polychromed. *Retablos* are two-dimensional paintings on wood. Both forms function to transmit religious meaning. But the *bultos,* unlike the *retablos,* are used in ritual. For this reason, the preferred form for the depiction of Christ is the *bulto.*

Images of the Christ Crucifix depict Christ hanging on the cross. Invariably, these depictions are sanguinary. Streaks of blood are shown flowing from the wounds and, interestingly, from beneath the loincloth. Usually, these streaks of blood follow a decorative pattern and, consequently, offset the overall morbidity of the subject. At times, the image is depicted with the head hanging down as if to show the dead Christ rather than the dying Christ. The Jesus Nazareno, a popular subject matter with clearly defined *Penitente* associations, also displays the marks of the passion and is usually shown wearing a robe and a wig of human hair. The hands of the figure are often tied. William Wroth compares the Nuevomexicano Nazarene to the European "Man of Sorrows" and indicates a continuity existing between these images. "This representation of Christ as the man of Sorrows shows the remarkable continuity of penitential imagery surviving in New Mexico in the late 19th century" (Wroth 1991, 71).

One of the first things that strikes the observer of the images of the Crucifix and Nazarene is their starkly life-like character. Unlike the *retablos,* in which the depictions of human figures are almost ethereal, the *bultos* exhibit a strong sense of naturalism and realism. Realism is achieved "by careful carving of teeth, the making of wigs of human hair, the use of translucent material and mirrors for eyes, and the loving attention given to sacrificed flesh" (Mills 1967, 55). As George Mills sees it, the naturalism of the *bultos* is for imitating human flesh. For the Penitents, human flesh approximates the death of Christ, so wooden images are carved to approximate human flesh (Mills 1967, 52). The goal of such naturalism, according to Mills, is to personalize art. Personalization puts art in the real world (Mills 1967, 52). E. Boyd, too, in describing the *bulto* images, emphasizes their realism, naturalism, and muscularity (Boyd 1974). Such realism constitutes proof for her that the crucifixes are works of laymen and not of priests.

No image symbolizes, in as gruesome a manner, the personification of death as much as the Doña Sebastiana (Death Angel). The image depicts a rather ghastly and horrific image of an aged female skeletal figure wielding a bow and arrow and riding on a wooden cart. This is a master signifier of death, a reminder of personal death. E. Boyd calls the Death Angel a "peculiarly specialized feature of the *Penitente morada*" (Boyd 1974, 462). Death Angel has been traced by several writers to Petrarch's *Il Triomphi,* a poetic allegory of fame and death.

Two ideas converge in Petrarch's Death Angel. First is the personification of the human skeleton. Second is the cart of triumph of Roman military victory processions. The Death Angel is a synthesis of both ideas. Petrarch's images of Death and Fame, according to Boyd, were carried over into the Tarot cards that were popular in Spain and serve as the link between Doña Sebastiana and Petrarch's Death Angel.

How can interpretation lead us to the real meaning of the *santos?* What do the *santos* really represent? One approach to the theory of meaning is to postulate a relation of representation between a sign and the object it stands for. In the *Tractatus,* Wittgenstein says that the "imagined world must have something in common with the real world" (Wittgenstein 1961, 2.022). What is the meaning of the relation between the imaginary world of the Penitents and the *Santeros*—Doña Sebastiana, images of Christ, Saints, Angels, Virgins, purgatory, heaven, hell—and the real world of living and dying? If pictures are models of reality, then what reality is being modeled by *Penitente* religion and *santo* art?

Thomas J. Steele, in *Santos and Saints* makes strong metaphysical and historical claims about the status of referents (1974, 46). God, Christ, the saints—eternal entities—and events in the historical past are the indisputable referents of the *santos.* For Steele, the "saint in the picture" has for its referent the "saint of reality...."

The connection between the saint in the picture and the saint of reality was a matter of great importance" (Steele 1974, 46). The phrase "saint in reality" is ambiguous. According to Steele, the *santos* are valued in terms of being able to imitate the original. Steele refers to this mind-set as "folk Platonism." But what serves as the original, as the saint in reality? What is most real—the mystical saint in heaven or the historical figure (Steele 1974, 48)? For Steele, the saint in reality, the referent of the *santo,* is the saint in heaven: "The New Mexican *santero* founds his likeness upon what is most real and most holy: the saint in heaven" (Steele 1974, 51). Steele, however, draws a different conclusion for the Christ figures. The referent for these is the earthly Christ narrated in the Gospels. "The validation of these Christ-figures stems not from heavenly being as it does in the case of saints but from a particular set of earthly actions, the Passion" (Steele 1974, 51).

Of course, it is difficult to agree with Steele if he is claiming that the referents of the saints are real holy personages in heaven and that the referent of the images of Christ is the earthly and historical figure of Jesus. Nonetheless, Steele is correct to attribute these beliefs to Nuevomexicano culture.

What meanings are conveyed by the Christ images? Writers commonly suggest that the images exhibit sorrow and tragedy. E. Boyd only notes the obvious when she says that the Crucifixes suggest "spiritual sorrow to convey the sufferings of physical torture." Virgil Barker, too, sees in the images a tragic intensity drawn from an inheritance of intense feeling. He believes, however, that the content of grief and dread mask a hidden joy (Barker 1943). As I see it, and in accordance with my earlier comments, these *bultos* are polysemous and multivalent in reference. Only at one level do these *bultos* refer to the Christ of the Christian tradition. At another level, they are unique works of religious art reflecting the inner character of Nuevomexicano culture in New Mexico. From another angle, the carved *bultos* and the two dimensional *retablos* are self-referential—the images stand for themselves. Signifier and signified, in this case, become one. The wooden image draws the eye to its own sheer awesomeness and to its own particular fascinating form at the moment. At a higher level of abstraction, the images can be interpreted as prototypes of human beings. They represent any man and any woman. Can one who has observed the emotionally charged *Encuentro* ritual, the fourth station of the cross that is performed on Good Friday, fail to see the identification between the Nazarene and every man, and the identification between *Nuestra Señora de Soledad* (Our Lady of Solitude) and every woman? Using Freud's language, we can say that the manifest images of the *santos* reveal the latent meanings of culture.

What is the meaning of the Doña Sebastiana? For Steele it is a "straightforward confrontation with personal death. This entails involuntary death, unprepared death, and encouragement for *buena muerte.*" It also means self-mortification or ascetic discipline "dying to the human self." As mentioned above, the Death Cart symbolizes the "impending death of their very culture" (Steele

1974, 12). Boyd, again noting the obvious, says that the Death Angel was a reminder of mortality. Peppino Mangravite in "Saints and a Death Angel," sees the Death Angel as the product of intense feeling and a dejected mood (Mangravite 1940, 162). In his view the function of the death cart was "to meet fervent emotional needs in a highly emotional and traditionally superstitious people" (Mangravite 1940, 162).

It is clear from a consideration of the image of the Death Angel that there is no historical referent. In this case the referent is an idea, the idea of a peculiar kind of death, an unprepared-for death. Perhaps it may be difficult for the reader to get free of the idea that the images of Christ refer to the historical Jesus, and this is why I chose the image of the Death Angel. With the latter, the problem of a historical referent does not arise; hence, it is easier to demonstrate that religious signs refer to ideal content.

The Crucifix and the Jesus Nazarene are, first of all, mythical portrayals of Christ, creations of faith, projections of Nuevomexicano self-understanding and, only secondarily, if at all, representations of the historical Jesus. It is the Jesus of myth not the Jesus of history that inspires the Penitentes. There exists, after all, an unbridgeable distinction between the historical Jesus and the Christ of Faith. Whoever the historical Jesus might have been, it is faith that establishes Jesus as Savior, Lord, Redeemer. For the Penitentes and *santeros,* Jesus' historical humanity is of little value. That he died on the cross holds symbolic value, not historical significance. Thus, I am led to accept the proposition that images of Jesus are really reflections of human self-understanding (Pelikan 1985, 2).

By peeling back the layers of manifest cultural expression, we discover a latent nucleus of earthly pessimism. But the real question remains, as Mills puts it: "What aspect of culture produced a need to suffer so urgent that it spilled over from a realistic re-enactment of Christ's passion into the most powerful folk art to be found within the border of the U.S.?" (Mills 1967, 1). If E. Boyd is correct when she notes that the image of the crucifixion was the favorite subject of the *santeros* (1951), then one must ask, Why? What encourages the representation of suffering?

By framing the question in this manner, we are no longer inquiring into the meaning of images but seeking explanatory causes. One answer to this question is given by William Wroth in his book, *Images of Penance, Images of Mercy* (1991). In his viewpoint, the Penitente brotherhood has been a preserver of Hispanic Catholic values and cultural identity in the face of a dominant and hostile Anglo culture. After the American Occupation of 1846 it was the Brotherhood, Wroth claims, that resisted domination by an incoming Anglo culture and heroically tried to preserve their Hispanic Catholic heritage. According to this thesis, the Brotherhood in the late nineteenth century constituted the spiritual core of Hispanic society (Wroth 1991, xv). Nuevomexicano religion and culture values were attacked by dogmatic Roman Catholic clergy like Bishops Lamy and

fig 48 Drawing of Penitentes Ceremony at Mora, New Mexico. Courtesy of the
Museum of New Mexico.

Salpointe and by iconoclastic Protestant missionaries like the Presbyterian, self-
styled "apostle to the Mexican," Alexander M. Darley. Economically, of course, the
traditional way of life began to disappear under the unrelenting onslaught of
entrepreneurial capitalism. As Wroth sees it, Anglos and Hispanics constituted
opposed social orders. Whereas Hispanics placed a high value on religion and tradition, Anglo Americans, by contrast, esteemed the material realm and earthly
rewards. Consequently, for the Anglos, Hispanic New Mexico was perceived as a
static society out of touch with modern life (Wroth 1991, xvi). The Brotherhood,
Wroth argues, as the self-appointed preserver of the core religious values, rejected
the cheap commercial images and demanded the traditional *santos* for their ritualistic needs. This, Wroth concludes, accounts for the preponderance of the
images of Jesus Nazarene, Our Lady of Solitude, Christ Crucified and Christ in the
Holy Sepulcher (Wroth 1991, xvi–xvii).

Thomas J. Steele, like Wroth, seeks to provide a similar explanatory account
for the "immediate acceptance and the rapid spread of the *carreta de la muerte*"
(Angel of Death and/or Doña Sebastiana) (Steele 1974, 3). He, too, finds explanatory factors in the sociopolitical situation of New Mexico beginning with the
Anglo occupation in 1846. "Old Spanish Way of life was being threatened by a new
way—accounts for the emergence of the *carreta* in 1860" (Steele 1974, 8). Steele
believes that the *carreta* does something to prevent the stagnation and death of

New Mexico Spanish Catholicism (Steele 1974, 8). A clue, he claims, is to be found in the Spanish attitude toward the Anglo conqueror.

According to Steele, the origin and spread of the Death Cart, which includes the image of the Angel of Death or Doña Sebastiana, indicates that the Spanish were intensifying their culture and religion in the face of incoming Anglo settlement (Steele 1974, 10). Steele goes back at least to the Taos Rebellion of 1847 to find the source of this attitude. He refers to it as "religious sublimation of a frustrated psychic force" (Steele 1974, 10). Steele places Padre Martínez as the personality behind the attempt to revitalize Spanish religious life—"energies released in the death cart and onto the making of *bultos* in the latter one-half of the nineteenth century" (Steele 1974). Resistance to Anglo domination and preservation of Nuevomexicano cultural values, the same forces that Wroth identifies as the causes behind the increased bulto production of the images of Christ in the latter part of the nineteenth century, account for the emergence of the Death Cart.

It appears that the images of Christ and the images of Doña Sebastiana reveal cultural attitudes about death. The images of Christ Crucifix and Jesus Nazarene convey the idea of the *buena muerte* (good death) and provide motivation for preparing for the good death. The images of the Angel of Death, Doña Sebastiana, and the *carreta de muerte* convey the idea of the bad and ignoble death and warn against the unprepared-for death. For George Mills, the attitude toward death separates the Mexican from the New Mexican. No doubt, a social political philosophy of equality is implied in the death symbolism. All are equally destined to die—*rico* and *pobre.* Death is even-handed and erases all social distinctions. This idea of universal equality, implicit in the culture, can be a *punto de partida,* a point of departure, for elaborating an ethics of liberation. But to the extent that this idea is sublimated in religious energies, Nuevomexicano culture, a culture long worn down by alienation and exploitation, will not be able to realize its inherent beliefs about justice, freedom, and equality in new political institutions and social arrangements.

It is worthwhile to examine some *Penitente* terminology (paradigm cases) that share a family resemblance and are historically tied to the larger Christian tradition. The terms selected are "*Señor*" (Lord), "*Christo*" (Christ), and "*Jesús*" and they have been selected from Penitente literature—constitutions, prayers, rituals, and *alabados.* In an apparent citation from the Gospels, a *Penitente* constitution contains the following phrase regimen: "Do penance and believe in the Gospel; says the Lord." Here is an excellent example of the addressor instance. The "Lord" (*Señor*) occupies the position of the addressor. In the addressor instance, the authorial presence of the Lord is stressed. "Lord" is the origin, source, and authority behind the message.

Many phrases contain "Christ" in the referent instance. For example, *Penitentes* are urged to meditate on the "passion and death of Christ." Here,

"Christ" functions as a referent. But what kind of a referent? As stated, the images of Christ, though they may ostensibly refer to the Christ of Gospel narratives, really refer to some ideal content. The ideal content of the signification contains ritual associations, a mythical quality, and is connected with a chain of signifiers. "Christ" must be seen in light of its metonymic relation with other signifiers, tradition, and use by the community. The phrase *"pasión y muerte de Christo,"* an oft-repeated refrain of Penitente cultic formula, is a full signifier, a set of corresponding images. Intertextuality links this signifier with others (apparently narrative events)—the capture in the Garden of Gethsemane; the trials before the Jewish high priests and the Roman provincial governor Pontius Pilate; the cruel scourgings and mockings; the presentation of the buffeted Ecce Homo before the mob; the way to the cross; the encounter with Mary, the Mother of Sorrows; the Crucifixion itself. Of course, some of these signifiers take on the form of dramatic performance—*las estaciones de la cruz, el encuentro, las tinieblas,* etc.

The name "Jesus" always appears as part of the traditional title of the Penitente confraternity: "Nuestro Padre Jesús Nazareno" (Our Father Jesus the Nazarene). "Our Father Jesús the Nazareno" names a lay penitential organization, a pious confraternity, a mutual-aid society. The reference is to an abstract social entity, not to the character of Jesus in the passion narratives of the Gospels, and certainly not to the historical Jewish Jesus from the Galilean town of first-century Nazareth. As such it functions as an organizational title, purely and simply. The term "Nuestro Padre Jesus Nazarene" also occupies a place as an element in a *Penitente* prayer formula: "In the Name of Our Father Jesus the Nazarene." It is a formula used in rituals like the *"Entrada"* or Entrance ritual (Wroth 1991). Initiates are to enter the fraternity "In the name of the Lord." (Lord and *Señor* are used interchangeably as well as *Nuestro Padre Jesús Nazareno.*) In *Penitente* theology, the name "Jesus" often substitutes for other traditional Christian titles for Jesus—"Our Lord," "Our Father," and "Our Redeemer."

Another metonym/metaphor linked with the name of Christ is the multivalent signifier, "blood/*sangre.*" According to Martha Weigle, the *hermandad* (brotherhood) was originally referred to as the *Fraternidad de la Sangre de Christo* (Fraternity of the Blood of Christ) (Weigle 1991, 50). The symbolic use of the term "blood" frequently appears in cultic formulas:

> "Most Precious Blood of Our Lord Jesus." "The blood which Our Redeemer Jesus Christ shed." "I ... venerate your most holy body, the wounds of your most holy side, the water and blood which flowed from it. ..."

The term "blood" in these instances belongs to the Penitent mythological code and signifies a quality of redemption found in many theologies of sacrifice—

Near Eastern, European, and Mesoamerican. It would be a gross misunderstanding to confuse the use of the term in mythical discourse with the use of the same term in medical discourse.

At times the use of the term "Christ" refers to the carved or painted religious image itself. The phrase "statue of Our Father Jesus the Nazarene" in the 1915–1916 Cochití Rule books clearly has a religious art object as its reference. But reference is sometimes made to the *santo* as though it were more than an object of art. For example, the 1915–1916 Cochití Rules contain a statement referring to a particular *bulto* in the *morada* as the "true image and representation" of the "passion and the death of Our Redeemer Jesus Christ" (Steele and Rivera 1985, 77ff). Clearly, this means that a consciousness exists of the symbolic function of the *santo*. Even more curiously, statements are made that virtually identify the religious image with Christ himself as though Christ were the image itself. In the 1915–1916 Cochití Rules, the following phrase seems to make reference to Christ, but in reality it makes reference to the carved wooden *santo*—"the place where the Lord himself is placed." Religious formulas of praise are also addressed to the *santos*, the wooden saints:

> "We adore thee, O Christ."
> "Lord Jesus Christ, I am a poor *Penitente* who comes to perform my exercise and fulfill my devotion."

Note also the synonymous parallelism in the adoration of the cross where the Penitentes say: "We adore the holy cross." and "We adore thee, O Christ."

According to Thomas J. Steele's description of the *Entrada*, the entrance ritual, the initiate is to profess faith in Christ making reference to the crucifix, "this divine Lord," uttering: "The cross will deliver us. . . . I avail myself of the Redeemer." The words "cross" and "Redeemer" are used interchangeably. In *Echoes of the Flute*, Lorin W. Brown, also known as Lorenzo de Córdova, describes a procession on *Semana Santa* (Holy Week) and mentions a cross at the end of the sacred path between the *morada* and *Calvario* (the place of the Cross usually on a hillside close to the *morada*) as "the present cross of Calvary." He adds that it is an object of worship representing "the true Cross" (Brown 1972, 38). Like the religious consciousness in general, the *Penitente* consciousness concerns itself with sacred time and sacred space.

The use of the name of Jesus in Trinitarian formulas obviously reflects a Trinitarian theology. What the reader may not be aware of is the duplication of the Trinity in Penitent thought. For the *Penitente* there are two Trinities: the Holy Trinity of God the Father, the Son, and the Holy Spirit of traditional Catholic theology; however, there is also the Trinity of the Holy Family that reflects the sacredness of the family in Nuevomexicano culture. The prayer formulas for these need closer comparative study. For our purposes, a bit of comparison will suffice. The formulas say, in effect:

> "Long live Jesus, Mary, and Joseph."
>> "Mystery of the Most Holy Trinity, Father, Son, and Holy Spirit."

Therefore, the placement of the name "Jesus" in these two different formulas gives the term certain qualities the other lacks. Because of its linkage with "Mary" and "Joseph," the human qualities of Jesus are stressed. In the formula for the Holy Trinity, on account of the association of "God the Father" and "Holy Spirit," it is the divinity of the "Son" that is emphasized. In the former we have a theology of immanence, in the latter a theology of transcendence. This duality is typical of Nuevomexicano culture. However, one may prefer to see it as a dialectic with each side interpenetrating the other—immanence in transcendence, the divine/human encounter.

Other familial qualities are borne out in formulas that associate (couple may be the better word) Jesus with the Virgin. The following invocation is typical: "In the name of Our Father Jesus the Nazarene and of the ever Virgin Mary." At the end of a *tinieblas* service (Tenebrae ceremony) on *Viernes Santo* in Madera, New Mexico, I heard a beautiful *alabado* sung, lifting the spirits of the congregants, called *"El Alba"* (the Dawn). It begins with the words: *"Viva Jesús, Viva María."* The sacred couple is not Mary and Joseph, nor the Father and the Virgin, but Jesus and Mary, the Son and the Mother. What does this say about Nuevomexicano culture? This is an interesting question that deserves further exploration.

As I've tried to point out, referential function is ambiguous. Names and terms are used in different ways, and use determines reference and meaning.

Conclusion

If *Penitente* faith and *santo* art express the ethos of Nuevomexicano culture, then one must conclude that Nuevomexicano culture is essentially a religious and artistic culture. I do not claim to have found the key to unlock the mystery of this profound culture, yet I feel the images open a window on the Nuevomexicano soul. No one meaning is embedded in these wonderful images. My first objective was to show that images of Christ do not have a historical referent. They are, rather, and even more profoundly, mirrors of self-understanding. A second objective was to demonstrate the referential ambiguity inherent in signs. Signs make reference at several different levels. Reference may be direct, indirect, implicit, explicit, self-referential, historical, nominative, linguistic, or extra-linguistic. The type of reference is partly clarified by use in context. Nevertheless, when dealing with signs, their meanings, and their referents, we are ultimately dealing with ideal content—ideas.

We do not on that account discard the material form of the images. Form serves to convey content. Material form transmits spiritual meaning. A unity exists between spirit and nature. Wooden saints represent the spiritualization of nature and, conversely, the naturalization of spirit. On the natural level, humble materials extracted from nature—pine, cottonwood root—are transformed by human creativity—through bold use of line, expressive color choice, decorative design, and symmetrical composition—into pictorial representations of the saviors and redeemers concocted by the human imagination. On the spiritual side, a religious ethos of suffering, fear of death, hope of eternal reward, discomfort in earthly life—rooted in Medieval Catholic and Islamic Moorish eschatological beliefs about the hope for paradise and the fear of purgatory and Hell—become externalized and objectified in statues of wood and painted wooden panels.

In one sense, the *santos* reveal a liberating ethics. Nuevomexicano culture does not deal with philosophical abstractions, generalizations about theoretical ideas with no practical application. Instead, the Nuevomexicano imagination, due to a corporeality firmly fixed on *terra firma,* through its religious art and artistic religion, unlike the humanly removed religions of the East, humanizes transcendence, personifies divinity, and makes God speak with the warm domestic voice of the hearth. In this way, Nuevomexicano culture is really sacralizing the earthly and elevating the human to divine status. *Penitente* religion and *santo* art summarily make use of human form to objectify the deepest religious convictions of culture bound by faithfulness to tradition, a limited theological canon, and iconography. This culture evinces a liberating ethic based on equality and communal social philosophy driven by a zeal for self-preservation, cultural resistance, and collective ego-identity.

In another sense, it is an alienated culture whose liberating ethic is weighed down by religious and artistic sublimation. It is driven by a sense of emotional urgency and not by intellectual rationality. It is an unhappy soul expressing worldly sorrow.

Notes

1. Boyd states, "The theme of the Crucifixion engaged the attention of the New Mexico santos more than any other . . ." (1951, 235). William Wroth makes this observation regarding late nineteenth-century New Mexico: "One is immediately struck by the preponderance of images associated with the passion and crucifixion of Christ . . ." (1991, xi).
2. See Raul Fornet-Betancourt: *Problemas actuales de la filosofía en Latinoamérica* (Buenos Aires: Ediciones FEPAI, 1985), *Estudios de filosofía latinoamerica: 500 años después* (Mexico: Universidad Nacional Autónoma de México, 1992), and *Filosofía intercultural* (Mexico: Universidad Pontificia de México, 1994).

3. See also Georg Wilhelm Friedrich, *Hegel, The Philosophy of History* (New York: Dover Publications, Inc., 1956).

4. See *Jean Baudrillard: Selected Writings,* Mark Poster, ed. (Stanford: Stanford University Press, 1988). "The process of signification is, at bottom, nothing but a gigantic simulation model of meaning.... Of what is outside the sign, of what is other than the sign, we can say nothing ..." (91). According to Jean Francois Lyotard, signs always refer to other signs: "Signification is always deferred, and meaning is never present in flesh and blood" (see Andrew Benjamin, ed., *The Lyotard Reader* [Oxford: Basil Blackwell, Ltd., 1989], 1–2). Lyotard also speaks of "infinite postponement," "recurrence," and "reiteration" of the signifying function. Derrida's translator, Gayatri Spivak, points out that, for Derrida, one sign leads to another (see Jacques Derrida, *Of Grammatology,* translated by Gayatri Spivak [Baltimore: Johns Hopkins University Press, 1976], xvii). Similarly, Charles S. Peirce says "one sign gives birth to another" (cited in Justus Buchler, ed., *Philosophical Writings of Peirce* [New York: Routledge and Kegan Paul, Ltd., 1955], 99).

Literature Cited

Barker, Virgil. 1943. Los Penitentes. *Overland Monthly and Out West Magazine* 82:151–153.

Boyd, E. 1974. *Popular Arts of Spanish New Mexico.* Santa Fe: Museum of New Mexico Press.

———. 1951. The Source of Certain Elements in Santero Paintings of the Crucifixion. *El Palacio* (August):235.

Brown, Lorin W. [Lorenzo de Cordova]. 1972. *Echoes of the Flute.* Santa Fe, N.Mex.: Ancient City Press.

Feuerbach, Ludwig. 1957. *The Essence of Christianity.* Translated by George Eliot. New York: Harper and Row.

Frank, Larry. 1992. *New Kingdom of the Saints.* Santa Fe: Red Crane Books.

Friedrich, Carl J., ed. 1953. *The Philosophy of Hegel.* New York: The Modern Library.

López, Alejandro. 1993. Whose Kingdom? *The Sun* (February): 7.

Mangravite, Peppino. 1940. Santos and a Death Angel. *Magazine of Art* 33(3):161ff.

Mills, George. 1967. *People of the Saints.* Colorado Springs, Colo.: Taylor Museum.

Pelikan, Jaroslav. 1985. *Jesus Through the Centuries: His Place in Culture.* New Haven, Conn.: Yale University Press.

Steele, Thomas J. 1974. *Santos and Saints: Essays and Handbook.* Albuquerque: Calvin Horn Publishers.

Steele, Thomas J. and Rowena A. Rivera. 1985. *Penitente Self-Government. Brotherhood Councils, 1797–1947.* Santa Fe, N.Mex.: Ancient City Press.

Weigle, Marta. 1991. Penitential Practices in New Mexico: The Brotherhood of the Sangre de Christ. Introduction to *Images of Penance, Images of Mercy; Southwestern Santos in the Late Nineteenth Century* by William Wroth. Norman: University of Oklahoma Press.

Wittgenstein, Ludwig. 1961. *Tractatus Logico Philosophicus.* London: Routledge and Kegan Paul Ltd.

Wroth, William. 1991. *The Images of Penance, Images of Mercy: Southwestern Santos in the Late Nineteenth Century.* Norman: University of Oklahoma Press.

Contributors

Olivia Arrieta received her doctorate in cultural anthropology from the University of Arizona and specializes in *mexicano* and Native American populations of northwestern Mexico and the southwestern United States as well as in social and cultural change. Her research on *mexicano* voluntary associations includes *La Sociedad Nuevo Mexicana de Mutua Protección* in Alameda, New Mexico. She resides in Tucson, Arizona where she has been involved in language-and-culture curriculum development, program evaluation, and social-services programs and is currently participating in a multicultural grassroots community project.

Michael Candelaria is originally from Roswell, New Mexico. He received his Th.D. from Harvard University, and he has taught philosophy and religious studies at California State University-Bakersfield and classics at St. John's College in Santa Fe. He currently teaches in the Honors Program at the University of New Mexico and at Albuquerque's Technical-Vocational Institute. He is the author of *Popular Religion and Liberation* (SUNY Press, 1990), in addition to many articles on Hispanic culture, philosophy, ethics, theology, and history. He lives in Albuquerque, New Mexico with his son Zac. He has two daughters in California, Misha and Candice Candelaria.

Miguel Gandert, a native of Española, New Mexico, is a fine-arts and documentary photographer and Associate Professor of Communication and Journalism at the University of New Mexico. His recent work explores the contrast between the Hispanic life in Spain and Old and New Mexico. His photographs have been shown in galleries and museums throughout the world and are in numerous public collections including the Museum of Fine Arts in Boston, the National Museum of American History at the Smithsonian, the Center for Creative Photography in Tucson, the Beinke Rare Book and Manuscript Collection at Yale, and the Museum of Fine Arts in Santa Fe. His series, *Nuevo México Profundo: Rituals of an Indo-Hispano Homeland,* was the subject of a book (Museum of New Mexico Press, 1999) and a one-person exhibition for the National Hispanic Cultural Center of New Mexico in 2000. His work was also selected for the 1993 Whitney Museum Biennial.

Ramón A. Gutiérrez is Professor of Ethnic Studies and History at the University of California, San Diego, where he was the founding chair of the Ethnic

Studies Department and director of the Center for the Study of Race and Ethnicity. He is the author of numerous articles and books on culture and ethnicity in the Southwest, including *When Jesus Came, the Corn Mothers Went Away: Marriage, Sexuality and Power in New Mexico, 1500–1846* (Stanford University Press, 1991); co-editor of *Contested Eden: California Before the Gold Rush* (University of California Press, 1998); and editor of and a contributor to *Home Altars of Mexico* (University of New Mexico Press, 1997).

Enrique R. Lamadrid is Professor of Spanish at the University of New Mexico. His research interests include ethnopoetics, Southwest Hispanic and Latin American folklore and folk music, Chicano literature, and contemporary Mexican poetry. His research on the Indo-Hispanic traditions of New Mexico charts the influence of indigenous cultures on the Spanish language and imagination. His literary writings explore the borderlands between cultures and between popular traditions and literary expression.

Luis Leal is professor emeritus at the University of Illinois at Urbana-Champaign. Currently a visiting professor at the University of California-Santa Barbara, he has published widely on Latin American, Mexican, and Chicano literatures. His books include *Breve historia de la literatura hispanoamericana* (1971), *Juan Rulfo* (1985), and *No Longer Voiceless* (1995). Among his honors are the Aztec Eagle from Mexico in 1991, the National Humanities Medal in 1997, and an Honorary Doctorate from the University of Illinois in 2000.

Francisco A. Lomelí is professor of Spanish & Portuguese and of Chicano Studies at the University of California at Santa Barbara. He has served as chair of the Chicano Studies Department since 1996. His areas of expertise include Chicano literature (all genres and literary history) and Latin American Studies and Literature (all genres with an emphasis on Mexico, Chile, Argentina, Costa Rica). Among his publications are *La novelística de Carlos Droguett; Aztlán: Essays on the Chicano Homeland* (1989, with Rudolfo Anaya); *Dictionary of Literary Biography* (Vols. 82, 122, and 209, with Carl Shirley); a translation of *Barrio on the Edge* by Alejandro Morales (1998); and *Handbook of U.S. Hispanic Cultures: Literature and Art* (1993).

Helen R. Lucero received her Ph.D. in 1986 from the University of New Mexico and is currently Director of Visual Arts at the National Hispanic Cultural Center of New Mexico. In addition to overseeing the Center's visual arts program, she curated the center's inaugural showing of "Nuevo México Profundo: Rituals of an Indo-Hispano Homeland," an exhibition of photographs by Miguel Gandert. She is the co-author of *Chimayó Weaving: The Transformation of a Tradition* (University of New Mexico Press, 1999) and, in 1997–1999, worked on a major national traveling exhibition, "Arte Latino," at the Smithsonian American Art Museum in Washington, D.C. Lucero's legacy to her Hispanic ancestry in New Mexico continues to be The Hispanic Heritage Wing at the

Museum of International Folk Art in Santa Fe, where she co-directed the exhibition "Familia y Fe."

A. Gabriel Meléndez is a writer-scholar whose research is centered on Hispano-Mexicano culture and society in the Southwest Borderlands. He is the author of *So All Is Not Lost: The Poetics of Print in Nuevomexicano Communities, 1834–1958* (University of New Mexico Press, 1997) as well as a number of scholarly articles that document the literary heritage of Hispano New Mexicans. He is a Research Associate at the Southwest Hispanic Research Institute at the University of New Mexico. He serves on the board of the Recovering the U.S. Hispanic Literary Heritage Project and is a co-editor of UNM Press's "Pasó por Aquí: Nuevomexicano Literary Heritage" series.

Genaro M. Padilla is Associate Professor of English and Vice Chancellor for Undergraduate Affairs at the University of California-Berkeley. He is the author of *My History, Not Yours: The Formation of Mexican American Autobiography* (University of Wisconsin Press, 1994), the editor of *The Short Stories of Fray Angelico Chávez* (University of New Mexico Press, 1987), a co-editor of *Recovery of the Hispanic Literary Heritage,* Vol. 1 (1993), and a contributing editor to *Power, Race, and Gender in Academe: Strangers in the Tower?* (Modern Language Association 2000). He is also an editor of the University of New Mexico Press's "Pasó por Aquí: Nuevomexicano Literary Heritage" series. His literary scholarship was recently recognized with the award of the third annual Premio Crítica. He has written numerous essays on Chicano autobiography, immigrant narrative, multiculturalism, and issues bearing on minority access to higher education in California.

Ana Perches received her Ph.D. in Spanish from the University of New Mexico in 1985. Since 1988, she has been a faculty member at the University of Arizona, where she teaches Chicano literature, Mexican culture, Latin American Theater, and Spanish for Heritage Learners. She was born in Chihuahua, Chihuahua, lived in Juárez for her first seven years, and then emigrated with her family to El Paso, Texas. She considers herself to be a product of the border. Her current interest is writing plays for her students to perform in the university setting. She has one son, Andrés Perches Lemons.

Tey Diana Rebolledo is Regents' Professor of Spanish at the University of New Mexico, where she teaches Chicano and Latin American literature. She is the author of several books and articles on Chicana literature. Born in Las Vegas, New Mexico, she continues to study the contributions of women to the development and history of the Southwest.

José A. Rivera is professor of Public Administration at the University of New Mexico. Formerly, he served as Director of the Southwest Hispanic Research Institute where he was Project Director of the Rockefeller Fellowships in the Humanities. His most recent book is *Acequia Culture: Water, Land, and Community in the Southwest* (University of New Mexico Press, 1998).

Sylvia Rodríguez received her Ph.D. from Stanford University and is now Associate Professor of Anthropology at the University of New Mexico. Her research focuses on interethnic relations in the U.S.-Mexico Borderlands, with emphasis on the Upper Río Grande Valley of New Mexico. Her publications have dealt with ethnic identity and expressive culture and the interactions among ethnicity, cultural politics, and tourism. She won the 1997 Chicago Folklore Prize for her book, *The Matachines Dance: Ritual Symbolism and Interethnic Relations in the Upper Rio Grande Valley* (University of New Mexico Press, 1996). Her current projects include books about the Taos Fiesta and about the custom and practice of the *acequia* (community irrigation) system.

Víctor Alejandro Sorell is Professor of Art History and Associate Dean of the College of Arts & Sciences at Chicago State University and Institutional Director of the CSU-University of Minnesota MacArthur Foundation Undergraduate Honors Program in International Studies. Between 1980 and 1983, he served as Senior Program Officer at the National Endowment for the Humanities. He has published and lectured widely in the United States and internationally on Chicano/a, Latino/a, Afro-American, and Latin American art theory and criticism, and he is active as an exhibition curator and consultant in the production of documentary films, the most recent of which is devoted to the Mexican muralist José Clemente Orozco. He recently co-curated the traveling exhibition, "Carlos Cortéz Koyokuikatl: Soapbox Artist & Poet," and edited the accompanying catalog. He is the co-author of the forthcoming monograph, *Illuminated Handkerchiefs and Prison Scribes: The Rudy Padilla Paño Collection.*

Index